THE CONDUCT OF LOCAL AUTHORITY BUSINESS

REPORT OF THE COMMITTEE OF INQUIRY INTO THE CONDUCT OF LOCAL AUTHORITY BUSINESS

Chairman

Mr David Widdicombe QC

Presented to Parliament by the Secretary of State for the Environment, the Secretary of State for Scotland and the Secretary of State for Wales by Command of Her Majesty June 1986

LONDON
HER MAJESTY'S STATIONERY OFFICE
£12.50 net

Cmnd.9797

The Conduct of Local Authority Business

Report of the Committee of Inquiry

Research Volume I: The Political Organisation of Local Authorities

Research Volume II: The Local Government Councillor

Research Volume III: The Local Government Elector

Research Volume IV: Aspects of Local Democracy

COMMITTEE OF INQUIRY INTO THE CONDUCT OF LOCAL AUTHORITY BUSINESS

MEMBERS OF THE COMMITTEE

Mr David Widdicombe, QC (Chairman)

Sir Lawrence Boyle, DL, JP

Mrs Diana Eccles

Mr Peter Newsam

Mr George Russell, CBE

**COMMITTEE OF INQUIRY INTO THE CONDUCT OF
LOCAL AUTHORITY BUSINESS**

Church House, Great Smith Street, London SW1P 3BW

(Telephone 01-212 3461/3465)

Chairman: David Widdicombe, QC
Secretary: R S Dudding

To

The Rt Hon Kenneth Baker MP
  Secretary of State for the Environment

The Rt Hon Malcolm Rifkind MP
  Secretary of State for Scotland

The Rt Hon Nicholas Edwards MP
  Secretary of State for Wales

Sirs

We submit our Final Report on the Conduct of Local Authority
Business.   It is unanimous.

(Chairman)

ES Dudding

(Secretary)

P. Rucall

(Assistant Secretary)

9 May 1986

REPORT OF THE COMMITTEE

SUMMARY OF CONTENTS

CONTENTS

11

CHAPTER SEVEN: ELECTORAL ARRANGEMENTS AND COUNCIL SIZE

CHAPTER EIGHT: DISCRETIONARY SPENDING

12

LIST OF ANNEXES

FOREWORD BY THE CHAIRMAN

1. Our terms of reference assume the continued existence of democratic local government. This principle, to which we all firmly subscribe, has been the starting point for our work, and our recommendations are all intended as means of strengthening the democratic process at the local level.

2. The desirability of such strengthening has not been disputed by those who have given evidence to us, nor has the need to allow for the increased politicisation of local government which has occured in recent years. Party politics in local government are of course not new. But there has undoubtedly been an increase in the intensity and polarisation of political activity, and the evidence suggests that it is here to stay.

3. The formal framework of local government does not recognise the existence of party politics. In law, decisions are taken by the council as a whole, not by the members of the majority party, and officers serve the council as a whole. The increase in politicisation has placed strains on this statutory framework. There is uncertainty about the proper relationship between majority party councillors and those in minority groups, between councillors and their local party organisation, between councillors and officers, and between the council and the public whom they serve. There is also uncertainty about the proper boundaries of council activity.

4. We have been impressed by the way in which councillors and officers have in most cases coped with these uncertainties. Indeed the solutions adopted by some authorities provide models for wider usage. Wherever possible we have based our recommendations on the best existing practice. There is a solid basis of normality in local government which we have not overlooked.

5. But to enable local government to accommodate the increased political activity changes do need to be made, in our view. The rule of law needs to be re-asserted, particularly in the areas where conventions have broken down.

6. Although most of the problems we have perceived have been ones of uncertain relations, there have been some cases, albeit a few, where power has been abused. Our recommendations are intended to limit the possibilities for abuse, but we are under no illusion that it is possible to close every loophole by means of new rules. In the last analysis the only way to stop those determined to undermine the democratic process is the vigilance of citizens through the ballot box.

7. Our recommendations are closely inter-related. We see them as a whole, a balanced package.

8. Finally, we have sought to ensure that this Report is firmly based on fact. We have considered almost a thousand submissions of evidence and our research programme provides the most complete and detailed review of the conduct of local government carried out for 20 years. Whatever view may be taken of our recommendations, this factual basis should promote a greater knowledge of local government and thereby provide for informed debate hereafter.

CHAPTER 1

INTRODUCTION

APPOINTMENT OF THE COMMITTEE

1.1   We were appointed by the Secretaries of State for the Environment, for Scotland and for Wales, with the following terms of reference:

'To inquire into practices and procedures governing the conduct of local authority business in Great Britain, with particular reference to:

(a)   the rights and responsibilities of elected members;

(b)   the respective roles of elected members and officers;

(c)   the need to clarify the limits and conditions governing discretionary spending by local authorities;

and to make any necessary recommendations for strengthening the democratic process.'

1.2   These terms of reference, together with the appointment of the Chairman of the Committee, were announced in the House of Commons by the Secretary of State for the Environment on 6 February 1985. The appointment of the other members of the Committee was announced on 8 March and 16 April.

1.3   In announcing the terms of reference on 6 February, the Secretary of State listed a number of items to which he invited the Committee to pay particular attention:

'— ensuring proper accountability for decision taking to elected members and to the electorate generally; and examining possible ways of strengthening local democracy within the existing structure of local government;

— clarifying the status and role of party groups in decision taking;

— ensuring the proper participation and the accountability of individual elected members in the decision taking process;

— examining any problems of propriety which may arise from members' conflicts of interest, particularly where officers of one council serve as councillors of another;

— considering the merits of the development of full-time councillors; and the related issues of the use of members' allowances and the remuneration of councillors generally;

— reviewing the system of co-option of non-elected members;

— studying officers' relationships, particularly in view of their legal and professional obligations, with elected members and political groups;

— clarifying the limits and conditions governing discretionary spending, including use of sections 137 and 142 of the Local Government Act 1972 (and sections 83 and 88 of the Local Government (Scotland) Act 1973) for political purposes in local government, or in relation to bodies set up, and largely financed by, local authorities.'

17

1.4 On the other hand he made clear that local government franchise[1], finance and structure were outside our terms of reference.

1.5 The Secretary of State went on to say:

'In view of the growing public concern about the use made by some local authorities of their discretionary powers to engage in overt political campaigning at public expense, I am asking the committee to submit an early Interim Report on this question. As far as the report as a whole is concerned, I am asking the Committee to aim to report within a year.'

THE INTERIM REPORT

1.6 Our Interim Report 'Local Authority Publicity' was submitted on 31 July 1985, and subsequently published by the Government[2]. In the report we reserved the right to return to the subject of publicity with particular reference to its tone and presentation and said that we would discuss the matter with the local authority associations. We also said that we would consider whether further means of challenge should be available to the citizen where a local authority is thought to have exceeded its publicity powers.

1.7 Subsequently the Government introduced legislation on publicity in what is now the Local Government Act 1986, and also initiated consultations with the local authority associations on a draft code of practice under the Act. The Act was the subject of amendments carried against the Government's advice, and the Government have announced that they propose to reverse these amendments by a further Bill in the next session of Parliament. We have decided not to comment on the Act, either as introduced or as amended, except where it is relevant to issues other than publicity. Our views on publicity are already set out fully in our Interim Report.

1.8 As regards the further work we proposed to undertake on the tone and presentation of publicity, we wrote to the local authority associations in January 1986 saying that in view of the initiatives taken by the Government we would not be pursuing discussions with them. In the new circumstances, it seemed more sensible that discussions should take place direct between the Government and the associations. Although our letter left open the possibility that we would comment on tone and presentation in this Report, in the event we decided not to do so.

1.9 Chapter Nine of our Report contains proposals for the public challenge of local authority actions. Although not specifically directed at publicity, these proposals are designed to ensure that the law on all local authority matters—including publicity—is effectively enforced.

METHOD OF WORKING
General

1.10 Our views derive principally from the formal written and oral evidence we received, and the results of the research which we commissioned. This formal

---

[1] Subsequently we were told that the reference to franchise should be read as including the electoral system — see Chapter Seven.
[2] Interim Report of the Committee of Inquiry into the Conduct of Local Authority Business, 1985.

process was supplemented by informal visits and discussions. We met on 40 days including 12 days for the hearing of oral evidence.

Evidence

1.11 We wrote on 21 March 1985 to some 150 representative bodies inviting written evidence. Our letter is at Annex A. We also held a press conference on 2 April 1985 to publicise our willingness to receive evidence from other bodies and individuals. We asked for evidence on the question of local authority publicity to be submitted by 27 April 1985 and for evidence on the wider issues to be submitted by 21 June 1985. Many submissions of evidence were received after these deadlines, but were nevertheless considered. We received evidence from some 682 bodies and indiviuals and they are listed in Annex B. Many respondents wrote more than once and the committee considered in all some 1,000 submissions. We are grateful to all those who responded to the request for evidence.

1.12 We also sought supplementary written evidence on three matters. We wrote to 37 local authorities asking for details of their publicity (those who responded are listed at Annex B to our Interim Report); to the four main political parties about the rules governing party groups on local authorities; and to representatives of employers about time allowed off work for council duties. We are grateful for the full response we received to these three requests.

1.13 The written evidence has been placed on deposit at the Public Record Office, where it is open to public inspection, with the exception of those submissions which were expressly made to the Committee in confidence. Several of the authors of the main submissions have separately published them themselves.

1.14 We also heard oral evidence from the 29 bodies listed at Annex C.

Research

1.15 We considered it most important that our recommendations should be based on a firm foundation of fact. This would not only tell us about the state of local government in 1985–86, but would also show what changes had taken place since the research undertaken in 1964–65 for the Maud Committee[1] and in 1976–77 for the Robinson Committee[2].

1.16 At the outset of our work we appointed Dr Ken Young of the Policy Studies Institute to act as our research adviser. He organised a major programme of research on behalf of the Committee, including four surveys. These were:

(a) a questionnaire survey of all local authorities concerning their political organisation, backed by an interview survey in 100 authorities;

(b) a questionnaire survey of 10% of councillors about their background, council work, and attitudes;

(c) a questionnaire survey of all local authorities about their expenditure on councillors' allowances, and under section 137 of the Local Government Act 1972 (section 83 of the Local Government (Scotland) Act 1973);

---

[1] Report of the Committee on the Management of Local Government, 1967.
[2] Report of the Committee of Inquiry into the System of Remuneration of Members of Local Authorities, 1977. Cmnd 7010.

(d) a public attitude survey, exploring perceptions of local government and voting behaviour in local elections.

1.17   The results of these surveys, together with papers which we commissioned by leading academics on particular issues of interest, appear in the four research volumes associated with this Report. As we refer frequently to the research results in our own Report, we have for convenience set out a brief account of the subject matter of the various projects at Annex D.

1.18   We are grateful to all those in local government who co-operated with the four surveys, as much depended on a high response rate. We are also grateful to the research teams for completing their work in a very limited timescale.

Informal visits and discussions

1.19   We thought it important to get some first hand informal impressions of local government. Accordingly members of the Committee visited the 13 local authorities listed at Annex E: 10 were in England, two in Scotland and one in Wales. We are grateful for the co-operation we received in arranging these visits, which we found of value to our work. We would like to have undertaken more visits, if time had permitted.

1.20   We decided, given the time available, not to make overseas visits to study other systems of local government, but have had regard to a paper[1] we commissioned on such systems.

1.21   We held an informal seminar in April 1985, to which we invited a cross-section of leading councillors and officers, to discuss the issues raised by our terms of reference. During the course of the year we also had informal discussions over lunch with a range of theorists and practitioners in local government.

INTERPRETATION OF TERMS OF REFERENCE

1.22   We were conscious of the limits set by our terms of reference, which excluded finance, the electoral system and the structure of local government, including its functions. At the same time, however, we were conscious of the wide range of what that still left us and the short time of a year in which we were asked to report. Some of the many topics before us could have justified committees of inquiry in their own right—just as, for example, councillors' remuneration was the subject of such an inquiry in 1977[2].

1.23   Given the time limit, we had to set some boundaries on what we could reasonably look at, and we should mention three. First, we have concentrated our attention on 'principal' councils, by which we mean district and county councils and their equivalents, and our general references to 'local government' and 'local authorities' should be construed accordingly. We have not considered the special position of parish and community councils, although some of the principles underlying our recommendations will be applicable to them. Second,

---

[1] Goldsmith and Newton, *Research Volume IV*.
[2] Report of the Committee of Inquiry into the Remuneration of Members of Local Authorities, 1977. Cmnd 7010.

we have made firm recommendations only on matters applying across the range of local government services. Where an issue has arisen which applies in particular to one service, we have said that it should be studied further. Third, on those matters where we have made recommendations, we have sought to cover all the key issues, but not necessarily all points of subsidiary detail. It would be an injustice to the subject matter to suggest that we could deal with all aspects of it in one year.

FORM OF REPORT

1.24　The Report is in two parts. Chapters One to Four set out the background: the way local government is working, arguments about its role, and the general approach we have adopted to our remit. Chapters Five to Nine deal with the individual topics within our remit, and contain our recommendations. These recommendations are then listed together in Chapter Ten.

ACKNOWLEDGEMENTS

1.25　It is very easy for acknowledgements in a Report of this kind to be a matter of form. In the present case that would be quite inappropriate. We could not have dealt with such a range of subject matter in the space of a year without an outstanding Secretary. We pay tribute to Richard Dudding for the quality of his contibution to our work and for his unstinted dedication to an exacting task, and equally to the other members of the Secretariat, Priscilla Russell, Pamela Conlon and Jerry Bishop. All deserve high praise for their work. Together with other staff members, they made a most competent team. We also wish to thank Ken Young for the excellent way he organised the research work.

CHAPTER 2

THE STATE OF LOCAL GOVERNMENT

INTRODUCTION

2.1 When we were first appointed we said that 'we propose to examine the facts and only then to form a judgement on the issues'. We have done this primarily through our programme of research to which we referred in Chapter One. Our research stands in its own right, and should do much to remove myths and generalisations and replace them with facts. Whatever view may be taken of the recommendations we make, the research reports should provide a sound basis for discussion about them.

2.2 We have also been assisted by the evidence which we have received, which has contained information as well as opinions. Lastly, we have gained first hand impressions from our visits, which have added much to our understanding of local government.

2.3 We shall be drawing from all this material, subject by subject, in the forthcoming Chapters of this Report. Some of the main findings are, however, brought together here in this Chapter, which is a snap-shot of local government as we found it in 1985–86. Where appropriate we have compared this snap-shot with the equivalent findings of research carried out in 1964–65 for the Maud Committee[1] and in 1976–77 for the Robinson Committee[2].

2.4 Our findings are summarised under the headings of 'diversity', 'politics', 'law and reality', 'accountability' and 'initiative'—all of which were recurring themes in our deliberations. These are overlapping themes. In particular diversity, as well as being a theme in its own right, underpins the other four themes.

DIVERSITY

2.5 Our research has shown that some of the commonly held assumptions about local government are valid only in a minority of authorities. Moreover, even where a characteristic holds good of the majority of authorities, the exceptions remain important.

2.6 We shall be looking in the next two sections at differences in the politicisation of authorities and in the way that politics have been reflected in procedures. In this section we look at statutorily imposed differences in structure and functions, at a few examples of strikingly different practices which arise from local traditions rather than statute, and at the differing characteristics of councillors.

---

[1] Report of the Committee on the Management of Local Government, 1967. (This Report was published in five volumes, of which volumes two to five were research reports.)
[2] Report of the Committee on the Remuneration of Councillors, 1977. Cmnd 7010. (This Report was published in two volumes, of which volume two was a research report.)

Differences deriving from statute

(i) Structure

2.7   There are 514 principal authorities in Great Britain. They are listed in Annex F, together with their populations. The Annex also contains two maps. 404 authorities are in England, 65 in Scotland and 45 in Wales.

2.8   A similar system of local government obtains throughout the 'shire' areas of England, the whole of Wales and mainland Scotland. In all these areas there are two tiers of multi-purpose local authorities. The upper tier authorities are known as counties in England and Wales and as regions in Scotland. The lower tier authorities are known as districts. There are nine regions in Scotland, eight counties in Wales and 39 counties in the shire areas of England. There are 53 districts in Scotland, 37 in Wales and 296 in the shire areas of England.

2.9   A different system of local government obtains in Greater London and the six metropolitan counties of England. At the time of our appointment these areas also had two tiers of multi-purpose authorities. In London the upper tier was the Greater London Council, with the lower tier consisting of 32 London boroughs and the City of London. In the metropolitan areas the upper tier consisted of six metropolitan county councils, and the lower tier of 36 metropolitan district councils. The position was however changed from 1 April 1986 by the Local Government Act 1985, when the upper tier authorities were abolished[1]. Their functions were transferred in part to the lower tier authorities, in part to new single-purpose joint authorities and in part to the Secretary of State. A new directly elected single-purpose authority has responsibility for education in Inner London, but otherwise there is now only one tier of elected local government in these areas.

2.10   There is also only one tier of local government in the Islands Areas of Scotland. These areas each have an all-purpose Islands Authority.

(ii) Functions

2.11   The functions vested in local government as a whole, and in the different tiers of local government, vary between different parts of the country. For example, water is a responsibility of regional councils in Scotland but is the responsibility of separate water authorities elsewhere. Police and public transport functions are normally the responsibility of the upper tier local authority but are controlled by central government in Greater London and by joint authorities in the metropolitan counties. Social services responsibilities rest with regional councils in Scotland and county councils in shire areas of England and Wales, but with district authorities in metropolitan areas and London boroughs in Greater London. This situation pre-dates abolition. Education is allocated to the same authorities as are social services except that there is an Inner London Education Authority with responsibility for education in the area of the 13 inner London boroughs. Libraries are a function of lower tier authorities in Scotland, London and metropolitan areas of England, but of county council in shire areas of England and in Wales.

---

[1] Our research was carried out before abolition took effect, and hence includes data for these authorities. There are also references to them in this Report.

2.12   As well as the differences between categories of authorities across Great Britain, there are a number of local variations. For example, the Isles of Scilly, which are not included in the figures above, have an all-purpose council the constitution and functions of which are specified by the Secretary of State by order. The City of London retains a number of unique features including a special police force and a legislative power to modify its own constitution.

(iii)   Size and population

2.13   The population of authorities varies considerably. With the abolition of the Greater London Council and the metropolitan counties, Strathclyde Regional Council has become substantially the largest multi-purpose council with a population of some 2.3 million. At the other end of the scale, seven Scottish district councils have populations of less than 20,000. The populations of metropolitan districts are broadly similar in range to those of shire counties. The population of some shire districts (Bristol—397,000; Cardiff—281,000) is as great as that of the smaller counties (Northumberland—301,000; Isle of Wight—121,000; Powys—111,000).

2.14   As a function both of variations in population numbers and in spheres of responsibility, there are wide variations in the annual budgets of local authorities. Strathclyde Regional Council has annual rate and grant borne expenditure of approaching £1,500 million and the equivalent figure for the largest English shire counties is over £500 million. At the other end of the scale, there are a number of district councils with annual rate and grant borne expenditure of less than £1.5 million.

2.15   The numbers of councillors serving on a council vary from ten in four of the Scottish districts to 161 in the City of London. The average number per council is 48. The general pattern is that there are more councillors on upper tier authorities, but this is by no means universally true. Overall, there are some 20,650 district and borough councillors and some 4,100 county, regional and islands councillors. Expressed in national terms, there are some 1,670 councillors in Scotland, 2,060 in Wales and 21,000 councillors in England.

2.16   There is on average in Great Britain one councillor for every 2,200 members of the population. However, councillors are fewer per head of population in Scotland and, since abolition, in Greater London and the metropolitan areas. For every councillor, there is a population of some 3,100 in Scotland, 3,500 in Greater London and 4,500 in metropolitan areas. As between individual authority areas, the differences can be extreme. In Birmingham, for example, there is one councillor for every 8,600 people. In Powys, on the other hand, there is one councillor for every 590 people.

Differences in practices

2.17   In addition to the variations in structure and functions which derive from statute, there are a host of differences in the practices and approach of different councils which derive from different local traditions. Some of these are a survival from the different structural arrangements applying before the reorganisations of local government in 1974 (England and Wales) and 1975 (Scotland), when the total of 1,822 pre-existing local authorities outside London was reduced to 494. Most rural and urban districts were subsumed into larger districts and the formerly powerful county boroughs were reduced in status as districts. Other differences derive simply from different national, regional and local traditions. Some illustrations are given below.

(i) Elections

2.18 The pattern of elections varies between types of authority depending in part on statute and in part on pre-reorganisation traditions. Prior to the reorganisations of 1974 and (in Scotland) 1975, all members of county councils were elected at a single election every three years. Boroughs and county boroughs, on the other hand, had annual elections with a third of all councillors retiring each year. Rural and urban districts operated under the former system unless they opted for the latter. The reorganisation legislation provided that all county and regional councils should be elected on a whole council basis, but every four years, while metropolitan districts—the majority of which were former boroughs and county boroughs—should hold elections by thirds. The new shire districts in England and Wales were given powers to opt for elections by thirds in preference to whole council elections. Of the 333 shire districts in England and Wales, 129 have done so. reflecting the pre-reorganisation tradition, these are concentrated among the larger districts, many of whose areas broadly coincide with those of former boroughs and county boroughs.

(ii) Territorial factors

2.19 The pre-reorganisation structure of local government often has a continuing influence through territorial loyalties which are unique to the authority in question and over-ride national political allegiances. This tends to be particularly true where a former county borough has been incorporated into a shire county. The former county borough is often resentful of its loss of powers, especially over education, while the outlying areas are resentful of the sharper political climate introduced by councillors from the former county borough. This is not just a matter of differences between political parties. Territorial allegiances can create sharp differences within parties. Our research shows that territorial factors can sometimes be as important as party in the allocation of committee places[1].

(iii) Appointments

2.20 There are marked regional differences in the extent to which councillors are involved in the appointment of staff, with a particularly strong tradition of involvement in Wales. Our research shows that councillors are routinely involved in the selection of officers below deputy chief officer level in 95% of all Welsh authorities while the comparable percentage for England is 68% and for Scotland 52%[2]. Within these regions councillor involvement in appointments is greatest in small rural authorities which are not in party political control.

(iv) Allowances

2.21 There are striking regional differences in the claiming of allowances. According to our research, the average attendance allowance paid in Scotland in 1984−85 was £2,112 per annum as compared to £728 in England and £1,075 in

---

[1] Leach et al, *Research Volume I,* Chapter Three.
[2] Leach et al, *Research Volume I,* Table A 87.

Wales. 2% of all councillors claimed no attendance or financial loss allowance in Scotland as compared to 12% in England and Wales. 93% of members of local authorities claimed some travel expenses in Scotland as compared to 79% in England and 86% in Wales. In Scotland, 80% of councils paid special responsibility allowance while the equivalent figure was only 41% in England and 16% in Wales. There are significant variations within these national averages, and there are a variety of factors influencing the differences. But it is clear nonetheless that receipt of allowances and expenses in Scotland is considerably greater than elsewhere even though the statutory arrangements are the same.[1]

(v) Meeting arrangements

2.22 At the regional level, organisational patterns reflect different lifestyles. For example, in response to our questionnaire to councillors, Welsh county councillors reported that only 4% of the meetings they had attended over the last month had started at 5.00 pm or thereafter. In contrast, 85% of the meetings attended by London borough councillors had started after that time. Over the country as a whole about 50% of meetings start after 5.00 pm[2].

Councillors

2.23 The traditional councillor stereotype is a white, middle-aged, white-collar male. The survey of councillors in 1976 undertaken for the Robinson Committee[3] showed that 83% were male, 74% were aged 45 or over and 66% were, or had been, in non-manual occupations. Overlaid on this traditional stereotype, a common perception is that the type of people who are becoming councillors is changing. There are thought to be increasing numbers of younger and female councillors. Councillors are also commonly thought to be drawn increasingly from public sector employment and from the unemployed, and to be devoting increasing amounts of time to council work. Our reseach shows that the traditional stereotype disguises a far more diverse picture in reality, and also that recent changes in the characteristics of councillors have matched popular perceptions in only a few authorities.

2.24 Councillors continue to be predominantly middle-aged or older. As in 1976, only 26% of all councillors are under 45. Only 7% are under 35 compared with 9% in 1976[4]. This reflects a general pattern of alienation among the young, who are less likely to vote[5] in local elections and less well informed about council activities[6] than their elders.

2.25 There are interesting differences in councillors' age between types of council and between parties. In the English metropolitan areas and Greater London, there has been a marked increase over the last 10 years in the numbers of councillors aged under 45, but a decrease in the number of councillors in this age group serving on shire district councils. As many as 50% of councillors serving on London borough councils are now under 45 (compared with the Great Britain

---

[1] IPF, *Research Volume II,* Tables 3.2, 3.3, 3.5 and 3.15.
[2] IPF, *Research Volume II,* Table A3, and SCPR (unpublished data).
[3] Report of Committee on the Remuneration of Councillors, 1977. Cmnd 7010, Volume 2, Tables 2, 3 and 10.
[4] SCPR, *Research Volume II,* Table 2.3.
[5] Miller, *Research Volume III,* Table 3.7.
[6] Young/NOP, *Research Volume III,* Table 2.1.

average of 26%). There is a much higher than average proportion of Liberal councillors in the under-45 age group (49% against an overall average of 26%) and a disproportionate number of Independent councillors who are over 60 (52% against an overall average of 36%)[1].

2.26   There are less marked differences between the parties and between types of authority in the representation of women among councillors. The picture remains a general one of under-representation of women. 81% of all councillors are male. The balance between genders in all of the main political parties is within a few percentage points of this national figure. For classes of authority, women are best represented on Scottish districts, metropolitan districts and London boroughs (24%, 23% and 22% respectively). The most marked divergence from the norm is among the Welsh counties, where only 5% of all councillors are female[2].

2.27   The popular perception of council membership increasingly dominated by the unemployed and by those employed in the public sector is not supported by the evidence at the aggregate national level. Only 4% of councillors are unemployed (6% of those councillors who are not willingly out of work). This is well below the national unemployment rate of 13%. Of those councillors in employment 36% work in the public sector, no more than the proportion in the working population at large (37%). 10% of all councillors (16% of those employment) work for a local authority—the so-called phenomenon of 'twin-tracking', over half of them as teachers or lecturers[3].

2.28   These employment figures conceal variations by region and type of council (although the details which follow should be treated as indicative rather than precise given the small sample base at this level of detailed analysis). Reflecting higher unemployment rates in Scotland, some 9% of Scottish councillors (as against 4% of councillors in Great Britain as a whole) are unemployed. Of those councillors in work,employment in the public sector is commoner in Scotland and Wales than in England, in metropolitan areas than in shire areas, and in authorities which are not education authorities than in those which are. This last factor has a particularly strong influence on the proportion of councillors who are 'twin-trackers' (ie employed by other local authorities). Although this phenomenon might be expected to be concentrated in metropolitan areas, it seems to be slightly more common of councillors in shire districts (not education authorities) than of those in metropolitan districts (education authorities). There are certain to be further marked variations within the regions and classes of authorities described above[4].

2.29   The employment and social characteristics of councillors also vary by political party. Labour councillors are four times more likely to be unemployed than are Conservative councillors. Half of Conservative councillors are from the two highest socio-economic groups as compared with only a quarter of Labour

[1] SCPR, *Research Volume II*, Tables 2.4 and 4.5.
[2] SCPR, *Research Volume II*, Tables 2.2 and 4.5.
[3] SCPR, *Research Volume II*, Tables 3.1, 3.6 and 3.8.
[4] SCPR, *Research Volume II*, Tables 3.7 to 3.9.

councillors. However, even Labour councillors are greatly over-represented in these groups when compared with the population as a whole[1].

2.30   There is no clear evidence to support the commonly held view that councillors are devoting increasing amounts of time to council work. This was certainly the perception of councillors and officers interviewed in the course of our study of the political organisation of authorities[2]. But the view is not supported when information provided by councillors themselves in response to our sample questionnaire survey[3] is compared with that collected for the Robinson Committee. These returns suggest that councillor time commitment to council business has reduced from an average of 79 hours a month in 1976 to 74 hours a month in 1985. Nor do the returns indicate any marked increase in time input by certain categories of councillors who might perhaps be expected unduly to influence public perceptions—such as leaders or those in metropolitan areas.

2.31   There are marked variations between the time spent on council work by different types of councillor. Scottish councillors devote on average 102 hours a month to council business, Welsh councillors devote 80 hours and English councillors 72 hours. The average time commitment among English shire county councillors is 101 hours a month as against 58 hours a month by their district council counterparts. Office holders (for example committee chairmen) devote on average 80 hours a month while the average councillor not holding any office devotes 64 hours. Labour councillors put in an average of 92 hours a month while the average Conservative and Liberal councillor puts in 68 hours.[4] These averages disguise considerable variations. There are some leading councillors who, as has been true in the past, work virtually full-time on council business. Our study of political organisation[5] suggests that there are one or more such councillors in about half of the larger authorities but in rather less than half of all authorities. There is little evidence to suggest that the 'full-time' councillor is a major phenomenon nor that there has been a significant general increase in recent years in such councillors.

Scotland and Wales

2.32   The issues which arise in this Report apply to some extent throughout Great Britain, but we have been conscious of the differing national circumstances of Scotland and Wales. Some of these differences—in organisation, conventions, traditions and social composition—have been brought out in the above review. Our research reports, where sample sizes allow, have given separate results for Scotland and Wales. Scotland has a different structure of local government to that in England and Wales. It also has a more varied pattern of local government containing within its borders the largest and the smallest authorities in Great Britain in terms of population and expenditure. Our research has shown several ways in which Scotland differs markedly in its characteristics, most notably in the role of the councillor: Scottish councillors represent more people, devote more time to council duties, and receive more remuneration. Scotland also has differences in law on several matters to which we shall come later in this

---

[1] SCPR, *Research Volume II,* Tables 3.4 and 4.5.
[2] Leach et al, *Research Volume I,* Table 3.2.
[3] SCPR, *Research Volume II,* Table 5.1.
[4] SCPR, *Research Volume II,* Tables 5.2 and 5.3.
[5] Leach et al, *Research Volume I,* Table 3.4.

Report. Wales has the same legislation and the same structure of local government as in England, but does not have any metropolitan areas. It has more councillors per head of population, a higher percentage of independent councillors and councils, and a tradition of detailed involvement by elected members in staff appointments.

The overseas context

2.33   Although British local government is diverse, it would be wrong to suppose that it is more so than systems of local government abroad. In Britain diversity remains in spite of the greater rationalisation achieved by the 1974 and 1975 reorganisations. Most other countries have not undergone equivalent reorganisations, and generally have a more complex and varied pattern of local government. This is brought out in the paper we commissioned on local government abroad[1]. In the USA for example, some local authorities have only specific competences while others have at least a degree of general competence to undertake what activities they will. Some have executives headed by directly elected mayors, while others have appointed city managers. The position is further complicated by the existence of elected special purpose agencies (for example for education and transportation) acting alongside and in addition to multi-purpose authorities. Similarly in West Germany there are wide variations in structure, functions and management. This is influenced by their federal constitution. The states have their own sovereign powers to determine, within the bounds of the constitution, what activities should be undertaken by the local authorities in their areas. Two local authorities are city states in their own right. The variations are also influenced both by pre-federal traditions and by the local government traditions of the post war occupying powers—especially in differing arrangements for internal management; some authorities vest power in elected mayors, others in appointed mayors, others in commissions, others in city managers. Throughout Europe and the USA, moreover, there is a far greater variety in the size of local authorities than in Great Britain: a range between authorities of 1,000 in population to one million is by no means unusual. By international standards, therefore, British local government may be seen as ordered and homogeneous.

POLITICS: ITS GROWTH AND CHARACTER

2.34   An increasing proportion of local authorities are organised on party political lines. The intensity of politics has also sharpened in those authorities which have been politically organised for some years.

2.35   The distinction we make between political organisation and political intensity is an important one, which was also made in the paper we commissioned on local government abroad[2]. This paper shows that the level of political organisation encountered in British local authorities is by no means unique and is paralleled in countries in Scandinavia and continental Europe. However, the recent sharpening of the intensity of British local politics has no obvious overseas parallel.

---

[1] Goldsmith and Newton, *Research Volume IV*.
[2] Goldsmith and Newton, *Research Volume IV*.

Political organisation

2.36 Political organisation can be measured by the proportion of councillors elected on party labels, the proportion of local authorities where control is held by a political party or alliance of parties, and the extent to which councillors of the same party on an authority organise through political groups.

(i) Councillors and party labels

2.37 When research was conducted for the Maud Committee[1] in 1965, 39% of councillors described themselves as 'independents'. This was primarily a phenomenon of lower tier rural councils. Only 4% of councillors in the county boroughs were 'independents', compared with 71% in rural districts.

2.38 Our own research[2] shows that in 1985 only 15% of councillors described themselves as independents. Many Conservative and Liberal party members in rural areas who previously would have stood as independents now stand under their party label. Of those councillors who are Conservative Party members 85% stood as Conservatives and only 15% as independents. The respective figures for Liberal Party members are 92% and 8%, and for Labour Party members are 98% and 2%. Those councillors who are elected as independents are increasingly a hard core of true independents: 62% of them are members of no political party.

(ii) Councils controlled by political parties

2.39 In 1965 the Maud Committee found that the percentage of councils in party political control ranged from 100% of London boroughs, 75–92% of county boroughs, 20–40% of counties, to 8–28% of rural districts. The ranges for each category reflect definitional difficulties[3]. As a broad statement, 50% of local authorities were controlled by a political party or a coalition of parties.

2.40 Our own research[4] shows that in 1985 the proportion of councils in political control had risen to 84%. This is largely the consequence of reorganisation, which greatly reduced the number of district councils and increased their size. There can be no doubt however that the erosion of independent dominated councils has continued steadily after reorganisation. Indeed it continued during the course of our Inquiry. One of the participants at our seminar at the end of April 1985 was the chairman of Cornwall County Council, 44 of whose 79 councillors were at that time independent. Two weeks later the number of independents on the council was cut to 28 in the elections, with the result that there are now no county councils in England on which independents hold a majority. Two remain in Wales. The remaining independent councils are primarily lower tier authorities in rural areas in Scotland, Wales and—to lesser extent—England.

(iii) Political groups on councils

2.41 It is now almost universal practice for councillors of the same political party on an authority to organise themselves in a political group which meets to pre-determine the line to be taken on matters coming before the council.

---

[1] Report of the Committee on the Management of Local Government, 1967, Volume 2, Table 7.2.
[2] SCPR, *Research Volume II,* Table 4.4.
[3] Report of the Committee on the Management of Local Government, 1967, Volume 5, Page 97.
[4] Leach et al, *Research Volume I,* Table 2.1.

2.42 Our research[1] has given us information about the organisation of the largest single party group on all councils where parties are represented. All such groups meet before council meetings, some before committee meetings as well. In 37% of authorities the group 'always' votes together at council meetings, and in a further 57% of cases 'usually' does so (23% and 68% respectively for Conservative groups, 59% and 40% for Labour groups). Group discipline is more relaxed at committee meetings: in only 11% of authorities does the group 'always' vote together, but it nevertheless 'usually' does so in a further 71% of authorities. Labour groups meet more frequently than Conservative groups.

2.43 Opinion has changed since 1965 when the Maud Committee found that two thirds of councillors considered that council work would be done better without the party system[2]. The existence of party groups, and the fact that all councillors of the same party will normally vote together as a group, is now widely accepted. However, relations between the local party and the party group remain a matter of controversy, not just between the parties but within the parties. The Conservative, Labour and Liberal political parties issue national guidance or rules governing such relations, making clear that there should be close liaison between local party and local group but without the former having voting rights at the meetings of the latter or otherwise determining the line to be taken by them on matters coming before the council. Despite this our research has revealed that party representatives vote at meetings of the majority party group in 36 local authorities. While this might be thought to be mainly a characteristic of Labour groups, 12 of these cases involve Conservative groups and three involve Alliance groups [3].

(iv) Local authority associations

2.44 Political organisation in individual authorities is replicated by political organisation in the national local authority associations. Each association has its political groups, and this is at present particularly evident on the Association of County Councils—on which no party has had overall control since the May 1985 elections. When the Association gave oral evidence to us, separate statements were made by the leaders of the Conservative, Labour, Alliance and Independent Groups. In London a second association—the Association of London Authorities—has recently been formed. This is primarily an association of Labour controlled councils. The longer established London Boroughs Association is now primarily an association of Conservative controlled councils. A full list of the local authority associations is at Annex G.

Political intensity

2.45 The sharpening of political intensity is reflected in relations between the parties on individual authorities, relations between councillors and officers, and relations between authorities and central government.

(i) Relations between parties

2.46 Even where authorities are organised on party lines it is possible for the

---

[1] Leach et al, *Research Volume I,* Tables A20 and A23.
[2] Report of the Committee on the Management of Local Government, 1967, Volume 2, Table 7.11.
[3] Leach et al, *Research Volume I,* Table A62 and unpublished data.

parties to operate on a bi-partisan basis. There has however been a general tendency towards greater polarisation, with the result that (in a two party context) there is often effectively an administration drawn from one party and an opposition drawn from the other.

2.47 This is reflected for example in the allocation of committee chairmanships. Our research shows that in 94% of all authorities organised on party lines the majority party take all committee chairs, in 91% all committee vice-chairs, and in 90% all sub-committee chairs [1]. It can be seen from these figures that the allocation of offices on party lines is a general characteristic, not just confined to those authorities with a long tradition of partisanship between the parties. A small district council now will often operate much as a county borough did 20 years ago.

2.48 An interesting dimension to this is provided by the policy of the Conservative Party towards 'hung' councils (ie councils which are organised on party lines but where no single party holds an overall majority). In their evidence to us they said that where they were not in overall control they preferred to act as an opposition rather than take part in 'power sharing'—where, for instance, committee chairs might be apportioned or rotated between the parties.

2.49 Despite the tendency for one party to form an administration in this way, it is rare for the majority party to take all the seats on a committee—even though they have the legal power to do so. Our research[2] shows that one party committees exist in only about 20% of authorities. In most of these cases there is only one such committee—a purely deliberative committee with no power to take decisions on behalf of the council. It is however not unusual for the majority party to take a greater share of seats on committees than they have on the council as a whole.

2.50 In authorities where power alternates regularly between Conservative and Labour parties we have found that there is often reasonable consensus between those parties on proper procedures for allocating chairmanships and committee places. Complaints about minority party rights tend to come more strongly from parties which have not recently hold political control, and the Alliance, and (in Wales) Plaid Cymru in particular have argued for legal entrenchment of minority party rights rather than reliance on convention. Indeed the strongest source of challenge to existing ways of proceeding has often come from Alliance councillors, and they have brought three successful cases in the High Court in the last two years where they have felt themselves unjustly to be excluded from council business. The increased success of the Alliance in local elections has also increased the number of hung authorities. The elections of May 1985 produced an overall majority in only 20 out of the 47 counties in England and Wales. This has meant that two party conventions based on an administration and an opposition have broken down. New ones have been devised giving greater equality of treatment between the three

---

[1] Leach et al, *Research Volume I,* Tables A13, A14 and A15.
[2] Leach et al, *Research Volume I,* Table A18.

parties, and in some cases these have been committed to paper. The conventions adopted by Cheshire County Council are at Annex H.

2.51   The growing intensity in political relations between the parties has also been reflected in a growing stress on ideology as a determinant of policies and in a growing polarisation between the ideologies of the Conservative and Labour Parties. Our survey of councillors [1] reveals that 63% of councillors agree rather than disagree that 'the first concern of the elected member is to implement the party manifesto', (87% of Labour councillors and 61% of Conservatives). Increased ideological polarisation can be found on issues such as contracting out, privatisation, implementation of the right to buy, assisted school places, and—above all—on the balance between spending on services and the level of the rate.

(ii)   Relations between councillors and officers

2.52   Despite differences between them on policy issues, the political parties find common cause in pressing for a greater assertion of the power of councillors over officers. 59% of councillors agree rather than disagree that 'council officials have too much influence over decision making'. This includes a clear majority of Conservative, Labour and Liberal councillors and of councillors on all types of authority. The view is particularly strongly held by councillors of the party in a minority on the council (77% of such councillors)[2].

2.53   This greater assertiveness has led to a challenging of the established frontiers between councillors and officers and has increasingly drawn councillors into day to day management issues. This has in particular caused frictions between committee chairmen and chief officers. The evidence we received from the Federated Union of Managerial and Professional Officers complained strongly of recent interference in detailed administration citing as an example a chairman who read the chief officer's incoming mail with him. This is not entirely new. Similar interference was complained of 20 years ago as shown by the research carried out for the Maud Committee[3]:

> 'It is easy for a situation to develop in which the chairman becomes involved in the minutest details of administration. During our own limited investigations our attention has been drawn to a number of notorious examples of this tendency..... One officer referred somewhat scathingly to a colleague in his previous authority who had 'had the chairman sitting on the other side of his desk every day'. We heard, too, of a vice chairman who used to find it convenient to spend the hour between spells of duty in examining the post in a local office.'

2.54   What perhaps is new is the combination of administrative intervention and political objectives. This can occur in particular where the majority party

---

[1] SCPR, *Research Volume II,* Table 7.17. This is the first of several instances where we give percentages of people holding certain views. In this Report we have calculated these percentages after the exclusion of 'don't knows' and 'no views'. The Research Reports give a fuller picture, with percentages of 'don't knows', etc also shown where appropriate.
[2] SCPR, *Research Volume II,* Tables 7.2 and 7.4.
[3] Report of the Committee on the Management of Local Government, 1967, Volume 5, Page 183.

has an ideological view on a management issue, such as the role of the direct labour organisation or the decentralisation of services. There can be no doubt that this has caused tensions in many authorities.

2.55   A particular aspect of councillor involvement in management is the appointment of staff. Our own research[1] shows that in as many as 4% of authorities councillors are involved in the appointment of staff at all grades. This seemed to us a very high level of councillor involvement. However, the research for the Maud Committee[2] shows that such involvement was much greater in 1965, when councillors were involved in all staff appointments in about 30% of authorities. On closer examination both of our own research and that for Maud it transpires that councillor involvement in staff appointments is a feature of small authorities dominated by independent councillors. It is not particularly a feature of party politics at all, although it is in party dominated authorities that it has recently attracted most attention. This illustrates the danger of generalisation, and in particular of the need for care in use of the term 'politicisation'. While it is generally true that councillor assertiveness and party politics tend to be found together, there is also a tradition of close councillor involvement in business that is associated with non-party control.

(iii)   Relations between central government and local government

2.56   An added dimension to politics in local government has been provided by a growing political polarisation of central and local government. This is referred to repeatedly in the evidence, and we quote here from the Association of District Councils:

'Another telling factor has been the changed relationship between central and local government. Greater control from the centre, especially in relation to rate support grant, through such devices as grant related expenditure assessments, targets, penalties and culminating in ratecapping, have, undoubtedly intensified politicisation and polarisation. The same could be said of major controversial issues, such as the proposed abolition of the Greater London Council and the metropolitan counties. It could not be expected that the affected authorities would stand aloof.'

2.57   With a Conservative central Government, it is not unnatural that this process of polarisation should be most felt in Labour authorities. This has been marked in Scotland, where the great majority of the population have councils under Labour control. At one stage in 1985 the Convention of Scottish Local Authorities decided only narrowly not to break off all relations with the Scottish Office. It has also been marked in England in those councils (all Labour controlled) that were abolished on 1 April 1986 and those (almost all Labour controlled) that have been ratecapped. Such circumstances, where a Labour majority party is in conflict with a Conservative Government, tend to lead to a sharpening of political relations with the Conservative minority on the council—who will see the Government as their natural ally. Conflict

---

[1] Leach et al, *Research Volume I,* Table 6.1.
[2] Report of the Committee on the Management of Local Government, 1967, Volume 5, data derived from Tables XLI and XLIA.

between local and central government can, therefore, sharpen political conflict within local government.

2.58　However a different situation often arises where Conservatives hold the majority on a council. There has been a marked difference in the evidence between the views of Conservative majority groups on the one hand and those of Conservative minorities and of Conservative national politicians on the other. The Association of District Councils, which we quoted above, is itself Conservative controlled and represents the great majority of Conservative controlled councils in the country. Their preparedness, and that of individual Conservative councils, to criticise centralism when they perceive it to be excessive, tends to lead to a more consensual and bi-partisan approach between the parties on the authorities concerned and takes some of the sting out of politicisation.

LAW AND REALITY

2.59　The formal legal structure of local government is corporate rather than adversarial. Statutory functions are vested in the council as a whole, not the majority party or its leadership. Equally, officers serve the council as a whole. This does not reflect the reality of party politics (as summarised in the preceding paragraphs), nor of modern management needs. Local authorities have, however, devised a range of means for bridging the gap between law and reality. As is characteristic of local government these arrangements are diverse. In the paragraphs below we list the main examples we have encountered. All are arrangements which are normally based on consensus within the authority concerned, and are by no means regarded as abuses.

Officer attendance at party groups

2.60　We have seen that party groups meet in the great majority of councils. Subject to a few exceptions (on which see paragraph 2.62) they do so outside the formal council committee structure. As such there has always been some doubt about whether officers should attend. The research carried out for the Maud Committee[1] in 1965 found that

> 'There is no doubt that in many authorities operating on party lines the party group makes a more significant contribution than any single 'constitutional' committee towards general policy initiation.'

They also found that officers did not, by convention, attend party groups and that this led to concern about the lack of advice before policies were decided. Some officers tried to bridge the gap, short of attendance, through 'methods which are at best ingenious devices to mitigate the worst affects of a basically unsatisfactory situation'.

2.61　The problem encountered by Maud to a large extent remains. It is now more generally accepted that officers may attend party groups without any impropriety, but our research shows that attendance remains the exception rather than the rule. The chief executive 'sometimes' attends the party group in

---

[1] Report of the Committee on the Management of Local Government, 1967, Volume 5, Pages 193 and 109.

about 6% of authorities organised on party lines, 'occasionally' in about 27%, and 'never' in about 66%[1]. Attendance is most frequent in authorities in Labour control. Where officers attend the group, it is normally only to provide factual advice and it is general practice for them to withdraw before the group deliberates.

2.62 A few authorities have instituted arrangements whereby the party groups, of majority and minority parties alike, are formally constituted as sub-committees of the council. This is, in particular, a feature of the metropolitan areas of Yorkshire and has been found to create a forum in which officers find it easier to give advice.

One party policy and resources committees

2.63 Almost all local authorities (94%) have a committee responsible for the overall policy of the council[2]. In most cases all parties are represented on such committees. However, in about 11% of authorities the committee consists solely of members of the majority party—normally the leader, committee chairmen and other leading councillors. Where this is the case the committee is normally purely deliberative with no executive powers. Such committees will be serviced by officers in precisely the same way as other formal committees of the council, and hence provide a forum akin to a 'cabinet' in which the majority can formulate council policy together with officers. Arrangements of this kind are commonest in Scotland. They are normally accepted by the main opposition party.

Informal briefing groups

2.64 What is much more widespread practice is for there to be a less formal arrangement through which an inner circle drawn from the majority party leadership meets to discuss policy. Such arrangements might be entitled for example 'leadership consultative groups' and tend to have an indeterminate status which is neither a formal council committee nor an organ of the party group. Such inner circles exist in about two thirds of authorities which are in party control, and officer attendance is much more frequent than is the case with party groups. The chief executive 'always' attends in 27% of instances, 'sometimes' in 21%, 'rarely' in 11% and 'never' in 41%. Interestingly there are similar, but non-party based, inner circles in a majority of councils dominated by independents[3]. The findings of the Maud Committee research in 1965[4] suggest that such inner circles are a long established feature of local government, and in this they are unlike one party policy and resources committees and officer attendance at party groups—which are relatively recent devices.

Contacts between the leader and the chief executive

2.65 Although the legal duties of officers are to the council as a whole, it is not surprising that their day to day contact should in practice be greater with

---

[1] Leach et al, *Research Volume I,* Table A55.
[2] Leach et al, *Research Volume I,* Table A31.
[3] Leach et al, *Research Volume I,* Tables A12, A70 and A74.
[4] Report of the Committee on the Management of Local Government, 1967, Volume 5, Page 194.

leading members of the majority party. Our research[1] gives some interesting quantification of this. In about 90% of authorities chief executives have contact weekly or more often with the leaders of the majority party. This is, however, true of their contact with the leaders of the minority party in only about 10% of authorities.

Role of committee chairmen

2.66   In law chairmen of committees have no powers in their own right, but in practice they frequently operate in a manner more akin to that of a central government Minister—working closely with their chief officers and taking routine decisions between committee meetings. As a result the reality of local government business is often based more on personal authority than the corporate legal basis would suggest. This, however, is by no means new and much the same was found by the research for Maud in 1965, which said

> 'There is evidence in a few instances of a chairman behaving in some ways like a Minister—developing policy, playing an active role as political head of his department and staking his reputation on its achievements'[2].

Then as now briefing meetings between the committee chairman and his chief officer provide an important forum in which professional advice and political objectives can be dove-tailed. It would seem, however, that the chairman is increasingly taking an active rather than a passive role in such meetings. Chairmen are increasingly initiating policy, or acting as advocates for policies initiated in the party group.

Officers attached to the political groups

2.67   In law officers serve the council as a whole, and by tradition have been politically neutral. In some authorities councillors have sought forms of officer advice that are more closely attuned to their political objectives. This has in a few instances led to pressures for officers carrying out the normal functions of the council to be appointed on the basis of their political sympathy, or to councillors developing direct contact with existing middle-ranking officers who are known to be politically sympathetic. Such practice tends to be covert, and although by its nature it cannot be quantified, appears to be rare. It has been generally condemned in the evidence.

2.68   At the same time, however, some 30-40 local authorities have developed overt arrangements whereby a small number of middle-ranking officers are designated specifically to serve the party groups, or their leaders rather than the council as a whole. In some cases such officers are career local government officers seconded for short periods, and are not selected for their political sympathies. In other cases they are appointed from outside on a political basis. These arrangements are a recent innovation, but appear to be well accepted in the areas where they apply[3].

---

[1] Leach et al, *Research Volume I*, Tables A26 and A27.
[2] Report of the Committee on the Management of Local Government, 1967, Volume 5, Page 171.
[3] Leach et al, *Research Volume I*, Chapter Six.

ACCOUNTABILITY

2.69 Much of the evidence we have received, especially from those within local government, has laid great stress on the electoral accountability of local authorities. For instance, we quote below from the Society of County Secretaries:

'There is no clearer or more defined sanction against actions which are not to the liking of the electorate than the fact that every county councillor must face his or her electorate every four years. Whilst it is fashionable to decry the real value of local elections (but not, strangely, parliamentary elections) on a range of grounds, the facts are that except in a handful of county councils where socio-demographic factors in effect guarantee that one political group or another is likely to be returned to power repeatedly, power now regularly changes hands in a majority of county councils.'

2.70 The point has also been made that local authorities are not only accountable through regular elections, but also through the close contact between councillors and their constituents and through mechanisms for consultation and local participation in decision formulation. In the paragraphs below we make some observations on how this accountability is operating in practice.

Electoral turn-out

2.71 Turn-out in local elections in Great Britain has traditionally been low. This was in the past largely ascribed to an insufficient public sense that local government was important. It was hoped that the reorganisation of local government into larger more coherent councils in 1974 and (in Scotland) 1975 would remedy this. This has not occurred. The spread of party politics has resulted in more seats being contested, but turn-out remains much the same as prior to reorganisation. Average turn-out for contested seats in the new authorities was as follows over the period 1973–78:

Greater London Council	40%
London Boroughs	40%
English Metropolitan Counties	39%
English Metropolitan Districts	36%
English Shire Counties	42%
English Shire Districts	42%
Welsh Shire Counties	53%
Welsh Shire Districts	52%
Scottish Regions	48%
Scottish Districts	50%

While systematic figures have not been kept for more recent elections there is little evidence of any change. Turn-out in the English shire county elections in 1985 was 41%.

2.72 In a paper commissioned for the Committee, Professor Miller[1] has carried out a detailed analysis of electoral behaviour, including levels of turn-out, using a survey undertaken for us by NOP Market Research Ltd. We

---

[1] Miller, *Research Volume III.*

also have the benefit of foreign comparisons given in the paper by Professors Goldsmith and Newton[1].

2.73   It is clear that turn-out in British local elections is lower than in most European local elections (for example France 70%, Italy 85%, Sweden 90%), but compares less badly with English speaking countries (eg USA 25%, New Zealand 53%). What is perhaps more a cause for concern is that, within Great Britain, local election turn-out remains so much lower than that in recent general elections (average 76%).

2.74   The analysis undertaken by Professor Miller suggests that those who vote in local elections are in most respects a fair cross-section of the community and of those who vote in general elections; and that low turn-out therefore produces no serious distortion in the results. Those who are dissatisfied with their local authorities are just as likely to vote as those who are satisfied, rate payers just as much as non-rate payers, Conservative supporters just as much as Labour supporters. The main area of concern relates to young people. Although 32% of the electorate are beneath the age of 35, only 25% of those saying they are certain to vote in a general election are under that age, and fewer still—a mere 19%—of those saying they are certain to vote in a local election. Put another way those over 55 are more than twice as likely to use their vote in a local election as those under 35.

Influences on election results

2.75   The extent to which local elections are determined by local rather than national issues is likely to remain a matter of debate. There is evidence in the literature, and in the interview survey[2] carried out for the Committee in 100 local authorities that local factors—such as rates increases and school closures—can and do influence elections. Certainly local issues must be a factor in those seats where independent councillors are elected. There is, however, little evidence that local issues will be **decisive** except in authorities which are otherwise very marginal. Professor Miller's analysis[3] suggests that the great majority of electors would vote in the same way in a general and local election if they were held at the same time. Those who would vote Labour or Conservative at a general election would sometimes abstain at a local election, or vote for a third party or independent candidate, but they would practically never vote for the other party. National party allegiances and attitudes to national politics play a major part in local election results.

2.76   Nevertheless it should be noted that local election results are much more volatile than those of general elections, especially where the whole council is elected simultaneously. For example, in the metropolitan county council elections of 1977 the Conservatives gained four out of the six counties, and then lost them again in 1981. In 1977 the Conservatives won 82 of the 106 seats in Greater Manchester. In 1981 they won only 19. In both years these results reflected the mid-term unpopularity of central government. While electors might vote largely on the basis of national factors, those national factors are

---

[1] Goldsmith and Newton, *Research Volume IV*.
[2] Leach et al, *Research Volume I,* Chapter Three.
[3] Miller, *Research Volume III*.

more likely to lead them to vote against their normal party in a mid-term local election than in a general election—when there is a closing of ranks.

2.77 There is one factor of local electoral behaviour which we should highlight, which is the relationship between electoral choice and payment of rates. In their Green Paper 'Paying for Local Government'[1] the Government say:

'This poor linkage between those who vote and those who pay has been further weakened by the fact that many of those who are entitled to vote for higher standards of local authority services either do not pay rates at all, or do not pay full rates..... There are over 35 million electors in England. Of these about 18 million are liable to pay rates. Of course, many of those remaining will be spouses of ratepayers; but they are not billed direct, nor do they personally make any payment to their local authority; and other adult members of ratepayers' families may have even less appreciation of the cost of local services. Of the 18 million who are liable to pay rates, only about 12 million actually pay their rates in full. 3 million receive partial assistance with their rates and the remaining 3 million receive full relief from their rates bill. For those who receive only partial help, the rebates damp the effect of increased local authority spending. And under the present arrangements those who receive full relief can vote for higher services without having to pay anything towards them.'

2.78 Our own survey of public attitudes[2] suggests that the linkage between voting and paying rates might not be quite as poor as the figures quoted above would suggest. When asked whether or not their household pays rates 94% of electors said 'yes' and only 4% 'no'. This indicates two things. First, most electors who do not themselves pay rates are members of a household that does. Second, many electors perceive of themselves (or their households) as 'ratepayers' even where their rates are partially or wholly rebated. It was only through a subsequent more detailed question that our survey was able to discover that many of the 94% receive rebates, and even then this was probably under-stated by respondents.

Public perceptions of, and contact with, local government

2.79 Our attitude survey[3] shows that local government is generally held in good regard by the electorate. Over 80% of the electorate expressing a view consider that their county council (or equivalent authority) runs things very or fairly well, while over 75% say so of their district council (or equivalent authority). While this satisfaction rating is much higher than central government normally achieves, it is however less than that found in the research for the Maud Committee[4]. In 1964 95% of the electorate expressing a view thought their county council ran things very or fairly well and a similar percentage thought so of their district or borough council.

---

[1] Paying for Local Government, 1986. Cmnd 9714, Paragraphs 1.36 and 1.37.
[2] Young/NOP, *Research Volume III*, Table 1.2 and unpublished data.
[3] Young/NOP, *Research Volume III*, Table 3.1.
[4] Report of the Committee on the Management of Local Government, 1967, Volume 3, Table 91.

2.80   Although so few vote in local elections there is strong support for the continued elected basis of local government. 78% of people think it would be a bad idea (56% 'very' bad) for those running local government to be appointed by central government, while only 14% think it would be a good idea (4% 'very' good). 61% consider that their local council should try to get the best deal for their area from central government, while only 32% say that this should be left to their MP[1].

2.81   There is a reasonable level of contact between councillors and the public. 30% of the electorate correctly named at least one of their local councillors, and 54% correctly named their party. 26% of electors have made a complaint at some stage about their council. Most were dissatisfied with the response. 44% of electors have contacted their council for reasons other than to complain, and the great majority were satisfied with the outcome. In both cases satisfaction has been higher when the contact has been with a councillor rather than with an official. In all 20% of the electorate have had some contact with their councillor. Two thirds have been satisfied with the outcome (45% 'very' satisfied)[2].

Representative and participatory democracy

2.82   The paragraphs above have looked briefly at the traditional representative role of councillors: they are elected by the community at large and deal with particular constituency issues that may arise. There has however always been an extent to which the community is an aggregate of sectional interests. The research carried out in 1965 for the Maud Committee[3] pointed out that 'there is not, of course, a unitary public but a diversity of publics'. Sectional interests seek to participate actively in local democracy rather than allow themselves passively to be represented. They do so by bringing pressure to bear on councillors but also through direct involvement in council proceedings.

2.83   This aspect of local democracy was explored in some detail in a paper which we commissioned from John Gyford[4]. He argues that the last 20 years has seen a significant transformation of local democracy, especially in the metropolitan areas, from one based mainly on councillor representation of the community as a whole to one based on active participation of sectional interests. This is exemplified by the position of ethnic minorities. Ethnic minorities are under-represented through the electoral process, but in many areas play an active role through other forms of participation. Fourteen local authorities in Greater London now have race relations committees with co-optees from ethnic minorities. The range of sectional interests impinging on local government is however far wider, including for example chambers of commerce, trades unions, voluntary organisations, environmental groups, women's groups and the National Farmers Union.

2.84   Developments of this kind cannot readily be quantified, except in the particular instance of co-option—which has been one of the main subjects of comment in the evidence we have received. There are some 6,000 people

---

[1] Young/NOP, *Research Volume III,* Tables 5.2 to 5.9.
[2] Young/NOP, *Research Volume III,* Tables 2.9, 2.12, 3.9 and 4.1.
[3] Report of the Committee on the Management of Local Government, 1967, Volume 5, Page 26.
[4] Gyford, *Research Volume IV.*

co-opted onto committees of local authorities, or one for every four elected members. The pattern is, however, far from uniform. Co-option is infrequent in Scotland, with one co-opted member for every 11 elected members, while there is one co-opted member for every two elected members in Inner London boroughs[1].

2.85 This level of co-option might seem to be high, and there is some (unquantified) suggestion that there has been a recent increase. Certainly the majority of councillors believe that there is too much rather than too little co-option. Under a third of councillors in our survey favoured wider co-option, with council leaders being particularly opposed to co-option[2]. Co-option was, however, much more widespread at the time of the Maud Committee[3] research in 1965. There were then some 16,000 co-opted members (there were also more elected members, giving a ratio of one co-opted member for every three elected members). Then as now co-option was commonest in London and the main urban areas, and in upper tier authorities.

INITIATIVE

2.86 Local government has a long tradition of responding in new and innovative ways to new pressures and new demands. In our comments on 'law and reality', we have pointed to some of the new procedural mechanisms that have been developed to accommodate the growing importance of party politics in the conduct of local authority business. In this section, we comment briefly on two areas in which local authorities are currently evolving new approaches to deal with current pressures: namely, their growing involvement in the promotion of the local economy and the moves towards decentralising services.

Economic development

2.87 Initiatives to promote the local economy are a growth area of local government activity, and one in which authorities in all parts of the country, at both tiers of local government and of all political persuasions are participating. Although there are certain specific and local Act powers, much of this activity is undertaken under local authorities' general discretionary powers— section 137 of the Local Government Act 1972 and section 83 of the Local Government (Scotland) Act 1973—to incur expenditure which is in their opinion in the interests of the area. Our research on section 137/83 shows that expenditure under these sections on such activities has grown from some £15 million in 1981–82 to some £90 million in 1984–85. After allowing for inflation, this is a four-fold increase[4].

2.88 In previous decades, local authority activities in this sphere were limited largely to the provision of land, industrial sites and premises. Over the last ten years, there has been a marked diversification into a range of new activities. Local authorities are playing a part in the promotion of co-operatives, in training schemes, in business advice centres, in the development of new

---

[1] IPF, *Research Volume II*, Table A1.
[2] SCPR, *Research Volume II*, Tables 7.9 and 7.10.
[3] Report of the Committee on the Management of Local Government, 1967, Volume 5, data derived from Tables XXIV and XXIVA.
[4] IPF, *Research Volume IV;* Table 1.7.

technology and in support for individual firms through rent subsidies, grants and guarantees.

2.89 New organisational structures have been developed to co-ordinate these activities and to respond effectively to the particular market with which they are concerned. Many authorities now have a specialist committee or sub-committee dealing exclusively with economic development issues and a specialist unit, or even a whole department, to support it. A few authorities have gone further and created separate wholly-owned companies to undertake activities on their behalf in this area, the best-known examples of which are the Greater London and West Midlands Enterprise Boards. Inevitably, some of these initiatives are controversial. But they demonstrate the capacity of individual authorities to respond to new pressures creatively and in ways which often become adopted nationally.

Decentralisation

2.90 Some local authorities, primarily in metropolitan areas, have experimented in the decentralisation of services. These experiments are reviewed in the paper which we commissioned from John Gyford[1]. We also received written and oral evidence on the subject from the Association of London Authorities (whose chair is also leader of Islington London Borough Council, which has been a pioneer of decentralisation).

2.91 Recent experiments in decentralisation originated in Walsall Borough Council, where 32 neighbourhood offices were opened between 1980 and 1982. Since then a number of authorities have committed themselves to a similar course, including the London Boroughs of Camden, Greenwich, Hackney, Haringey, Islington, Lambeth, Lewisham and Richmond-upon-Thames, and the Metropolitan Districts of Sheffield, Manchester and Birmingham. The most advanced example is that of Islington. The borough has been divided into 24 areas of about 6,000—8,000 in population. Offices are due to be open in all of them by summer 1986, manned by 1,000 staff. They provide under one roof for personal social services, housing management, improvements, lettings, repairs, rent collection, community development, environmental health and welfare rights. 'Neighbourhood forums' are being established to oversee each of the area offices and decide on spending priorities. An integrated approach towards services tends to cause problems of demarcation between professions and unions. This has slowed progress in other boroughs, which have concentrated more on area-based housing management.

2.92 Decentralisation is not the sole province of any particular party. It has in practice been adopted mainly in Labour controlled councils, but there are many other Labour councils, of both right and left, who are opposed to decentralisation on principle or who do not believe that the extra cost can be justified. It has also been adopted in Liberal controlled authorities. It is not at present a discernible feature of Conservative councils, and cost is undoubtedly a factor in this. The costs of decentralisation do not just arise from the need for local offices and staff to man them. Decentralisation can also lead to higher costs through a higher standard of service delivery; for example more

---

[1] Gyford, *Research Volume IV.*

minor housing repairs might be done because it is easier to notify the need for them.

2.93 Cost is not the only ground on which decentralisation has been criticised. There have been allegations, which we encountered in one metropolitan district which we visited, that area based arrangements too easily become a means by which the controlling party can channel resources into wards on whose electoral support it depends for its continued majority. The dividing line between providing services to win votes, and winning votes because of good services, will always be a fine one. We consider this later in the Report. At this stage we simply note that decentralisation typifies local authorities' search for new means of tackling the problems of their areas.

CHAPTER 3

THE ROLE AND PURPOSE OF LOCAL GOVERNMENT

INTRODUCTION

3.1 Our terms of reference require us to make recommendations concerning the conduct of local government business with a view to 'strengthening the democratic process'. It is a necessary preliminary to this that we must raise some wider questions about what is meant by 'local government', about the form it takes in this country, about its attributes, and about the rationale for its continued existence. We are conscious that the answers to these questions will have implications for matters going beyond our remit—ie for finance, structure, functions, and the electoral system. It will be for others to take those matters forward. But some discussion of these questions is necessary in order to place in a proper context our conclusions on those matters which are within our remit. It might also contribute to a wider debate about matters that are beyond our remit.

THE CHARACTERISTICS OF LOCAL GOVERNMENT

3.2 The character of local government in Great Britain is determined by:

(a) the fact that it is the creation of Parliament; and

(b) the particular legislative form that Parliament has given it.

These are considered in turn below.

The constitutional position of local government

3.3 In Great Britain Parliament is sovereign. Although local government has origins pre-dating the sovereignty of Parliament, all current local authorities are the statutory creations of Parliament and have no independent status or right to exist. The whole system of local government could lawfully be abolished by Act of Parliament. Central government is not itself sovereign, and indeed its powers are—or may be—circumscribed by Parliament just as much as those of local government. In practice however central government is drawn from the political party with a majority in Parliament and its de facto political strength is accordingly much greater than that of local government.

3.4 The place of local government in the political system is not, however, derived solely from its formal constitutional relationship with a sovereign Parliament. Many other countries have a written constitution which legally entrenches the existence of those institutions that are most important to their political system, so they cannot be removed by a simple majority vote of the legislature. Such institutions will typically include the legislature itself, the judiciary, central government and regional and/or local government. The fact that the United Kingdom does not have a written constitution is, however, primarily a matter of political and legal tradition. It does not mean that institutions such as local government are necessarily held in lower esteem than in those countries with written constitutions nor that their summary abolition is constitutionally acceptable. The sovereignty of Parliament is underpinned by a corpus of custom and convention as to the manner in which that sovereignty should be exercised.

3.5   The position of local government in our political system is therefore governed by constitutional convention as well as by the simple fact that it derives its existence and its powers from Parliament. It would, however, be wrong to assume that such constitutional convention amounts to or derives from any natural right for local government to exist. It is a convention based on, and subject to, the contribution which local government can bring to good government.

3.6   It follows that there is no validity in the assertion that local authorities have a 'local mandate' by which they derive authority from their electorate placing them above the law. The electoral basis of local authorities lends added authority to actions they take within the law, and to any proposals they may make for changes to the law, but does not provide a mandate to act outside or above the law. Local authorities may properly lobby for changes in the law, but in their day-to-day conduct of affairs they must act within the law as it stands.

The legislative form of local government

3.7   The principal characteristics of modern local authorities in Great Britain can be traced to the origins of elected local government in the 19th century. There have however been important changes, particularly in the functions they undertake and in their size. The system has never been a static one. Major re-organisations took place in 1974 and, in Scoland 1975, following the reports of the Redcliffe-Maud[1] and Wheatley[2] Commissions. Although a further re-organisation took place in London and the metropolitan counties on 1 April 1986 (to which we briefly refer in paragraph 3.9) the characteristics of the great majority of local authorities were determined by those re-organisations, and can be summarised as follows:

(a)   they are directly elected by popular franchise;

(b)   they are multi-purpose: in most areas responsibilities are divided between two tiers of multi-purpose authorities;

(c)   they cover large areas as measured in population (about 120,000 people on average for lower tier authorities);

(d)   they have substantial responsibilities for the delivery of services. Indeed this is one of the reasons why it has been felt necessary to create such large authorities. The extent of autonomy from central government in the delivery of services varies between services.

(e)   they may only act within the specific powers set by Parliament. It would be possible for Parliament to grant local government a 'general competence' to act for the good of its area. Instead they rely primarily on specific powers granted service by service.

(f)   they may raise their own revenue. About 60% of national local government expenditure is currently financed from locally determined and collected rates and rents, from other charges for services and from borrowing. The balance is financed from central government grant.

---

[1] Report of the Royal Commission on Local Government in England, 1969. Cmnd 4040.
[2] Report of the Royal Commission on Local Government in Scotland, 1969. Cmnd 4150.

(g) they are corporate bodies. The powers of local authorities are vested corporately in their councillors as a whole. They are not vested in the majority party, nor in individual councillors, nor in officers. They rely on full-time professional officers, however, for the day-to-day discharge of their functions.

3.8 These characteristics should not be taken as being necessarily part and parcel of local government. There are many systems of local government which lack some of them. This is shown by our research paper on local government abroad[1]. Local authorities abroad are based less on the optimum size for efficiency of services and more on existing communities. As a consequence they are generally much smaller; for instance lower tier authorities have an average populaton of 30,000 in Sweden, 12,000 in the USA and 1,000 in France, as against 120,000 in Great Britain. There are also examples of single purpose authorities, notably school boards in the USA.

3.9 Differing systems can also be found within Great Britain. In London and the metropolitan counties there has been from 1 April 1986 a general pattern of directly elected lower tier multi-purpose authorities overlaid by an upper tier of single purpose authorities. These are indirectly elected with the exception of the Inner London Education Authority, which is directly elected; as such it is similar to single purpose boards in the USA and to school boards in late 19th century Great Britain.

3.10 The key characteristics of local government in Great Britain can be illustrated by comparison with our parish and community councils. We have said in our introduction that we are limiting our considerations to principal councils—ie district and county councils and their equivalents. Hence the description at paragraph 3.7 applies only to such authorities. It is, however, illuminating to mention parish and community councils at this stage because their characteristics are in many ways the converse of those of district and county councils. They are very small, they do not administer major services, they rarely have any full-time officers, and they have a general power to spend for the good of the area. They tend also to be based on areas with a strong and long-standing community identity.

THE VALUE OF LOCAL GOVERNMENT

3.11 The value of local government stems from its three attributes of:

(a) pluralism, through which it contributes to the national political system;

(b) participation, through which it contributes to local democracy;

(c) responsiveness, through which it contributes to the provision of local needs through the delivery of services.

3.12 Some protagonists of local government would place more stress on one attribute rather than the others. They are however interlocking and complementary rather than mutually contradictory. We discuss each in turn below.

---

[1] Goldsmith and Newton, *Research Volume IV*.

Pluralism

3.13   The case for pluralism is that power should not be concentrated in one organ of state but should be dispersed, thereby providing political checks and balances, and a restraint on arbitrary government and absolutism. This is not an argument for fragmentation of the state, nor for divided sovereignty, but rather for increasing the cohesiveness and stability of the state by making it less brittle and allowing within it some safety valve for the expression of contrary views.

3.14   Pluralism is not concerned with the internal democracy of local authorities, but with the spreading of power within the state. As such the argument for pluralism pre-dates democracy, and was one widely put for example in the 17th century against the centralism of an absolute monarchy. Local institutions, albeit non-elected, were seen as a counterweight.

3.15   The case for pluralism was again influential in the 19th century when modern local government and the popular franchise were introduced. For Lord Salisbury, whose 1886–92 administration created county councils (including the London County Council), these two phenomena were of linked significance. Salisbury's proposals for local government were based on a fear not of centralising monarchs but of the centralising tendencies of a popular franchise. In his view, the enfranchisement of the working class would make welfare politics the central electoral issue, and lead inexorably to the rise of a powerful administrative state. This could be avoided only by the creation of new local authorities whose value as counterweights would be realised 'by diminishing the excessive and exaggerated powers' of central government.

3.16   More recently precisely the same arguments, if less politically stated, are to be found in the Reports of Redcliffe-Maud[1], Wheatley[2] and Layfield. Thus we find, eg, the following statements in the Layfield Report[3] about local government:

> 'By providing a large number of points where decisions are taken by people of different political persuasion . . . it acts as counterweight to the uniformity inherent in government decisions. It spreads political power'.

and

> 'It also provides a safety valve which allows adjustments to be made to accommodate pressure or dissatisfaction before they build up to major proportions'.

3.17   We developed some of these arguments in our Interim Report, and they have informed much of the subsequent debate on the publicity provisions of what is now the Local Government Act 1986.

---

[1] Report of the Royal Commission on Local Government in England, 1969. Cmnd 4040.
[2] Report of the Royal Commission on Local Goverment in Scotland, 1969. Cmnd 4150.
[3] Report of the Committee of Inquiry into Local Government Finance, 1976. Cmnd 6453, page 53.

Participation

3.18 Arguments about participation are less concerned with local government's position in the wider political system and more concerned with the quality of democracy within local government. As such they are relatively modern arguments, originating with the introduction of a popular franchise and remain in a continuing state of development as the nature of democracy itself continues to develop.

3.19 In their earliest, and somewhat paternalistic, form arguments about participation were essentially based on the educational value of local government as a training ground for democracy. Such arguments were developed in 19th century England, particularly by J S Mill, who saw the principal value of local self government as raising the political capacities of the people.

3.20 Local government offers two kinds of participation; participation in the expression of community views and participation in the actual delivery of services. It does so both through the process of electing representatives as councillors and through the opportunity to influence local government more directly through consultation, co-option, and local lobbying. These factors have led to much recent debate as to the quality of local democracy and how it might best be promoted.

3.21 The issue was one addressed by the Redcliffe-Maud[1] and Wheatley[2] Commissions. At the time of their reviews, units of local government both in England and Scotland were relatively small and based mainly on areas with a tradition of community identity. This in many ways maximised the opportunities for the public to participate—both through being councillors and being in regular direct contact with their local authority. The two Reports however argued that participation in local government was an empty exercise if it was not organised in such a way as to be **effective**. Both recommended authorities covering larger areas and with a reduced number of councillors. They argued that the new structure would give participation greater substance, but recognised that it would not necessarily provide a sufficient means of expressing local views. As a counter-weight they recommended an enhanced role for parish councils (England) and the creation of community councils (Scotland).

3.22 Although many of the recommendations of the Redcliffe-Maud Report and (to a lesser extent) the Wheatley Report were not accepted, the basic theme of larger more **effective** authorities was embodied in the subsequent re-organisations of 1974 (England and Wales) and 1975 (Scotland). The number of authorities was reduced from 1,857 to 521 and of councillors from 46,000 to 26,000.

3.23 Whether the re-organisations have achieved the right balance between effective local government and local participation is still widely debated, but the focus of recent debate has shifted more to the machinery by which participation takes place. There has been criticism of the electoral arrangements. Turn-out

---

[1] Report of the Royal Commission on Local Government in England, 1969. Cmnd 4040.
[2] Report of the Royal Commission on Local Government in Scotland, 1969. Cmnd 4150.

remains low (average about 40%), and many sections of the community (especially women, ethnic minorities and council tenants) remain under-represented through the electoral process. The first past the post electoral system is widely criticised, and during the course of our Inquiry the House of Lords passed a private peer's Bill[1] (rejected by the Commons) which would have introduced proportional representation for local government. There has also been criticism of the procedural arrangements within local government: some argue that the quality of participation is threatened by the power of officers, others by the power of majorities, others by party political group discipline, others by the limitations placed on decision taking by economic circumstances and central government.

3.24   Some also argue that the role of the councillor as representative (and hence the elected basis of local government) is being challenged by the more direct impact that some sections of the community are able to make on local government business through co-option, consultation and lobbying.

3.25   There is clearly a lack of consensus as to the form which participation should take and as to whether the current local government arrangements provide the best means of providing for it. There is, however, equally clearly a strong demand for participation in local government.

Responsiveness

3.26   Proponents of local government argue that it is an **effective** means of delivering services because it has the ability, unlike a non-elected system of local administration, to be responsive to local needs. There is an important distinction between efficiency and effectiveness. Efficiency is concerned solely with output, effectiveness is concerned also with the meeting of needs. It is a distinction which applies in industry as much as it does in government. Efficiency in the production of manufactured goods is of little value if there is no market for those goods. A successful private industry needs to be responsive to its customers. Similarly those delivering local services need to be responsive to the local community, and it is argued that local government alone possesses that ability.

3.27   The strength of this argument depends greatly on the service to which it relates, and it is informative to look in this context at the major changes which have taken place in local government responsibility for service delivery over the last 100 years. Services can broadly be categorised as between those which are directed at the community at large and those which are directed at individuals with particular need within the community. The early development of local government in the 19th and early 20th centuries was associated largely with the former category of 'community' service—its priority being what has been called 'the conquest of the material environment[2]'. As late as 1945 well over half of local government gross expenditure was on such services, which included water, gas, electricity, public transport, fire, police, refuse and parks. 'Personal' services, such as hospitals, education and poor relief, played a relatively minor part. Since then there has been a major shift. Local government no longer has

---

[1] The Local Government (Choice of Electoral Systems) Bill 1985, introduced by Lord Blake.
[2] William Robson in A Century of Municipal Progress, 1835–1935. George Allen and Unwin 1935.

responsibility for gas, electricity and (except in Scotland) water. It has also lost two personal services (hospitals and poor relief), but this loss has been more than compensated for by the effect of the post-war welfare state on the expansion of education, housing and social services. Real expenditure on education has increased five-fold since the war, and now accounts for a third of local government gross expenditure (about one half of net rate fund current expenditure). Personal services now account for two-thirds of total local government gross expenditure.

3.28   This shift of emphasis is important. The allocation of services remains haphazard, especially insofar as schools are a local government responsibility but not hospitals, but there can be no doubt that local government now concentrates more on those services where responsiveness to the public is most important (eg social services) and less on those where the main requirement is simple efficiency of output (eg public utilities).

3.29   It is necessary to examine a little more closely the assertion that local government is responsive in the delivery of its services. This responsiveness may be considered to have three aspects: sensitivity, initiative and co-ordination.

(i) Sensitivity

3.30   There is inevitably a tension between sensitivity of service delivery and efficiency. At some point along the scale will be an optimum point at which effectiveness of service delivery will be maximised, but it is not yet clear whether this point has been found. As with the arguments about participation, much depends on the size of the unit of local government. The Redcliffe-Maud[1] and Wheatley[2] Reports considered that education and social services should be administered by authorities with a population of at least 200,000 and this is reflected in the current local government structure. This has been considered by some authorities as putting efficiency too far ahead of sensitivity, and they have experimented in systems of decentralisation—accepting that extra costs are involved.

(ii) Initiative

3.31   The changes in the services provided by local government have not simply been externally imposed. To the extent that local government has taken on new tasks this has often been through their own initiative. This was most certainly true for example in Joseph Chamberlain's Birmingham of the 1870s. That council pioneered a range of municipal initiatives, including gas undertakings, which subsequently became the norm for local government. More recently this role of innovation and enterprise remains to the fore despite public expenditure constraints, and we saw it still at work in Birmingham when we visited the West Midlands Enterprise Board. Other notable examples of local authority intiative include the pioneering of local clean air legislation in post war Manchester. In all such cases authorities were responding entrepreneurially to the changing needs of their area.

---

[1] Report of the Royal Commission on Local Government in England, 1969. Cmnd 4040.
[2] Report of the Royal Commission on Local Government in Scotland, 1969. Cmnd 4150.

(iii) Co-ordination

3.32 Lastly local authorities can respond corporately to multi-dimensional local issues, such as inner city problems, in a way which national services are less able to do. This is an advantage of multi-purpose units of government which is not easily replicated in a system of local administration. Thus while the health service might maximise efficiency in its vertical integration of a single service between district health authority and Whitehall, local government will tend to have the advantage in horizontal integration of a range of services at local level.

3.33 Despite these arguments there are those who criticise current local government arrangements for **a lack of** responsiveness. To an extent these criticisms are allied to those which we discussed earlier about participation, but there are also criticisms based on the current system of local government finance. The Government argue in their Green Paper 'Paying for Local Government'[1] that the decisions of local authorities have often become divorced from the wishes and views of their electors because

> 'accountability is blurred and weakened by the complexities of the national grant system and by the fact that differences arise among those who vote for, those who pay for, and those who receive local government services . . . in almost every respect the existing local government finance system makes it almost impossible for local electors to relate what they pay to the services provided'.

There are also arguments, which we shall look at more closely in the next section, that the political process is sometimes acting as a barrier between the views of the electorate and the policies of the council rather than a means of harmonising the two, and that as a result the public is not getting the services to which it is entitled.

THE CONTINUED VIABILITY OF LOCAL GOVERNMENT

3.34 There will always be a need for the local delivery of services. There are, however, means other than local government through which local services may be provided and it needs to be considered what distinguishes local government from other public sector local institutions—such as health authorities, water authorities, electricity boards, or indeed local offices of Government Departments.

3.35 Local government is government **by** local communities rather than **of** local communities. It is a means by which local communities may take decisions affecting the delivery of public services in their area. It is not a necessary element of local government that it should itself deliver services. In practice it normally does, but there are examples of local authorities abroad where all services are delivered by some other body under the direction of those authorities. Nor is it necessary that it should have the sole power of decision over those services, because unfettered powers of decision are rare in modern government. But it is necessary that local government should allow a local view to be expressed through the taking of decisions. For this reason the mere delivery of services is not of itself sufficient to consititue local government. Health authorities deliver local services, but they are not a means by which local people may take decisions

---

[1] Paying for Local Government 1976. Cmnd 9714, page vii.

about those services. They are not therefore local government, but local administration.

3.36 Clearly the three attributes of local government—pluralism, participation and responsiveness—provide a strong case for its continued existence as the principal means of local service delivery. There are, however, pressures on, and within, local government which have led some people to question its continued viability. These pressures are of two kinds:

(a) centralising pressures, which may have the effect of eroding or negating the attributes of local government to such an extent that it has no obvious advantage over a system of local administration;

(b) internal weaknesses, relating to the legislative form and conduct of local government, which may raise doubts about whether local government should continue to be a major provider of services.

To an extent, and this is the main danger, the pressures are mutually reinforcing.

Centralising pressures

3.37 The Layfield Report[1] of 1976 based its analysis on two opposing models of local government: centralist and localist. These models can be summarised as follows:

Centralist: a system in which local authorities act virtually as agents for the central government, the primary justification for their existence being that as custodian of local interests and repositories of the detailed knowledge of local circumstances, they mitigate the dangers of remoteness and bureaucratic administration which are likely to emerge if government is wholly centralised;

Localist: a system in which real political authority and power are decentralised to local authorities in respect of those functions which can appropriately be performed at the local level.

3.38 It is not however clear that this dichotomy is a helpful one because it describes on the one hand an ideal (localism) and on the other hand a fact of life (centralism). Few would suggest that centralism is a preferable model of government to localism. In practice, however, the modern political and economic environment creates a number of pressures towards the centre. The question therefore is not so much whether localism is a better form of government, but whether it remains a practicable one.

3.39 Local government employs almost 3 million people and accounts for 28% of public expenditure. This sheer scale determines that it cannot be insulated from the macro-economic policies of central government. Where central government is pursuing a policy of economic expansion, it can achieve such expansion by loosening the reins on local government and enabling it to spend at its discretion. Since the IMF crisis of 1976, however, the climate has been one of public expenditure retrenchment. As has often been quoted, the then Secretary

---

[1] Report of the Committee of Enquiry into Local Government Finance, 1976. Cmnd 6453.

of State for the Environment said to local government 'The party is over'. Retrenchment in any organisation can usually only be achieved by a drawing in of power to the centre. That is an inevitiable fact of life. If it is well managed it will be achieved without major pain and possibly with consent. It is however idle to believe that it can be achieved in the context of local authorities without some diminution of their discretion to meet what they perceive to be the needs of their areas.

3.40   Similar considerations apply to political pressures towards centralism. The more local authorities provide services that are central to people's lives, and seen to be so, the less realistic it becomes that they can be autonomous in the provision of those services. The political parties come to regard those services as the proper province of national politics, and make pledges in general elections for them to be organised according to their particular philosphy. There are two good examples of this: first, the legislation introduced by the 1945 Labour Government to develop a national system of social security to replace local government poor relief; second, and more recently, the present Conservative Government's introduction of a national right for council tenants to buy their homes at a discount. In introducing national policies of this kind, the political parties are to a large extent reacting to the wish of the citizen that there should be a reasonably consistent, although not necessarily uniform, right to services throughout the country.

3.41   It is pointless to debate whether or not such centralising forces should exist, in much the same way as it is pointless to debate whether politics should exist. They do exist and will continue to do so, and the more realism about this the better. What does, however, need to be considered is whether the cumulative affect of centralism is eroding local government to such an extent that it no longer possesses the attributes on which its case depends. The Redcliffe-Maude Report[1], in a statement which we endorsed in our Interim Report said that

> 'Local government is more than the sum of the particular services provided. It is an essential part of English democratic government.'

That, however, is a statement of the ideal. It might be argued that the reality is now that local government has become, or is in danger of becoming, **less** than the sum of its parts—ie that it lacks sufficient financial and political discretion to reflect local choice even in the basic statutory services which it delivers.

3.42   If that is indeed the case then there is an onus on central government to consider whether this consequence is acceptable, and whether there are workable alternatives. These need not necessarily involve full blooded localism. There might also be middle ground. One possibility, which has its critics as well as its advocates, is one of partnership under which local government would continue to deliver services, would accept that those services will increasingly be determined by national decisions, and would have a greater and more formalised say in those national decisions. If there are perceived to be solutions which are more acceptable than a continued drift towards centralism, then central government needs to impose on itself the same restraint in dealing with local government that

---

[1] Report of the Royal Commission on Local Government in England, 1969. Cmnd 4040, page 146.

a written constitution would provide. The price of that restraint may often be short term political inconvenience, but that price must be accepted.

3.43   There is an extent to which the present government have recognised these considerations, in the context of finance, in their Green Paper 'Paying for Local Government'[1]. They say

'Local government finance is at a crossroads . . . There are three main possibilities for reform:

— changing the structure of local government;

— imposing much greater central control over local authorities;

— financial reform designed to improve local accountability.'

They reject the first option on the grounds of the upheaval it would cause, and the second because the administration of a centralist regime would make unacceptable demands on central government manpower. Their preference is for the third option because:

'It guarantees the continued existence of a healthy, democratic system of local government. It should reduce the tension between central government and local authorities. In the longer term it should help to ensure that services are provided more efficiently.'[2]

Internal weaknesses

3.44   While we do not propose to get drawn into debate about the merits of the finance proposals in the Government's Green Paper, we think they are right to see the strengthening of the democratic process within local government as a means of avoiding excessive centralism. It is not enough to say that local democracy is being eroded by centralising forces if the reason for such forces is, in part, a weakness in local democracy. Such a weakness might arise from the particular legislative form of local government, of from the way it is operated locally, or from a combination of both.

3.45   As we have said, local government has no independent right to exist. Its continued existence is based on the contribution it can make to good government. It needs to be able to demonstrate that it is a more effective means of government than local administration; and this effectiveness depends on the good health of all three of its attributes of pluralism, participation and responsiveness.

3.46   The viability of local government is threatened not only if these attributes are neglected but if there ceases to be a proper balance between them. We give three illustrations.

3.47   First, a situation may arise where local government concentrates excessively on national policy issues (ie on its contribution to pluralism), but at the expense of its responsiveness to the local community. If this happens its

---

[1] Paying for Local Government, 1976. Cmnd 9714, pages 7—8.
[2] Paying for Local Government, 1976. Cmnd 9714, page 9.

pronouncements on national policy may prove a nuisance to central government but it may lose touch with the views of its electors or may fail to provide the services they are looking for. This makes it very vulnerable. Second, a situation may arise where a local authority opens itself up to the maximum degree of participation by the community in decision taking, but by doing so becomes paralysed by indecision through lack of a structured basis for carrying out its functions. As a result it is unable to be responsive to its community's needs. Third, a local authority might concentrate on responsiveness to its community but through a benevolent paternalism that lacks the vigour of participatory democracy. This might occur for instance where decisions are taken in practice by strong and able officers with passive elected members. The question then arises as to why there is a need for local elections rather than a simple scheme of local adminstration.

3.48   If therefore local government is strong on the delivery of services but weak in the extent to which it provides for local democratic self expression, it ceases to be sufficiently distinct from local administration. If on the other hand it is strong on democratic self-expression, but weak on service delivery the danger is that it will in the long term become **only** a means of democratic expression, and that services will be administered by other means. These are the Scylla and Charybdis between which local government must steer if it is to continue to be viable.

SUMMARY AND CONCLUSIONS

3.49   Local government enables local communities to take decisions about the delivery of public services in their area, and in this respect is distinct from local administration. It is, however, a creation of statute and has no right to exist independent of statute. The fact that it is elected may lend political authority to its actions within the law, and to proposals it might make to change the but does not provide a mandate to act outside or above the law. Its continued statutory existence is underpinned by constitutional convention, but depends on the contribution it can make to good government.

3.50   Being more than a system of local administration, that contribution is not simply one of **efficiency** but of **effectiveness**. This effectiveness depends on its three attributes of pluralism, participation and responsiveness. These attributes, and hence the viability of local government, can be eroded by centralising pressures, which may cumulatively leave so little power to take decisions that it has no obvious advantage over a system of local administration. Alternatively, the viability of local government may be threatened through internal weaknesses as a result of which it can no longer demonstrate its value as a means of delivering services. Without such services it becomes simply a talking shop, and while this would still remain a form of local government it is doubtful whether it would be a worthwile one. If local government is to retain major service responsibilities, there is an onus on it to act responsibly in the exercise of those responsibilities.

3.51   The future viability of local government therefore depends both on its external constitutional place within the wider political system, and on its internal conduct. The former consideration lies largely outside our terms of reference. Our Interim Report touched on the subject in dealing with local authorities' publicity on national proposals affecting them, but there is very little of direct relevance in our Final Report. We can do no more than draw attention to the issues, the prime one in our view being that care is needed before taking decisions which, singly or cumulatively, might alter local governemnt's status in the political system. This need is increased rather than diminished by the lack of a written constitution.

3.52 Our recommendations are concerned principally with the internal conduct of local government: with the statutory framework and the manner in which it operates within that framework. Here again major considerations are outside our terms of reference: structure, the electoral system and finance. In our discussion of the attributes of local government, we have shown how those of participation and responsiveness are to a large extent determined by these considerations. We do not however underestimate the importance of matters which are within our terms of reference. We make a number of recommendations concerning the political process within local authorities that should clarify and strengthen local government's role of enabling participation. Equally our recommendations should have an impact on responsiveness, and we see it as a fundamental aspect of our remit that local authorities should deliver the services that the public want.

3.53 Whether our recommendations taken alone will ensure the future viability of local government, in the absence of action on other fronts, we do not and cannot judge. Our terms of reference, however assume that there will continue to be local government. We see it as our task to maximise its potential to be viable even if we cannot ourselves ensure it.

3.54 The terms of reference require us to suggest ways to 'strengthen the democratic process'. From our discussion in this Chapter it can be seen that this must be done at two levels. First, there is the need to make sure that the internal procedures of local government are such that the full range of local viewpoints can be expressed and are properly reflected in decisions reached. Second, there is the wider need to create conditions in which local government can be an effective means of delivering local services—thereby ensuring that they continue to be delivered by locally elected bodies. Our overall objective, insofar as our terms of reference allow, is to marry these considerations and can be expressed as follows: to make recommendations for the conduct of local authority business which will assist in the development of a way of operating that is stable, locally responsive, widely accepted and attuned both to political reality and the effective delivery of services; and thereby to help maximise the potential of local government to provide major services, and meet other local needs, within a local democratic framework.

CHAPTER 4

THE POLITICAL FRAMEWORK

INTRODUCTION

4.1   The main theme underlying the evidence we have received, and our research, has been the impact of politics on local government in recent years. Equally our own recommendations in the remaining Chapters of this Report are concerned largely with the need to reflect these political developments in the way local authorities conduct their business.

4.2   The purpose of the Chapter is therefore twofold. In the first place we analyse the various manifestations of politics. Second, against this background, we set out the main themes of our recommendations in the later Chapters.

4.3   In doing so we are conscious that there have also been important developments in local government that have not been political (except on a very wide definition), and that some of our recommendations are equally not directly related to the political process. We do not propose to neglect such matters. But we do believe that the underlying theme of politics is sufficiently pronounced for most of what follows in this Report to be encompassed by the analysis in this Chapter.

4.4   We are also conscious that there are still some authorities which claim that they remain apolitical and many more which are political but which do not perceive the existence of politics as posing a problem for them. We recognise both these points. We do however see a clear and continuing trend towards politicisation, and we must base our recommendations on the future as much as on the present needs of local government. We do not see that politicisation need pose a problem. It has however done so in some instances, and is much more likely to do so if we do not make recommendations to ensure that the local government system fully reflects its existence.

POLITICS AND ITS MANIFESTATIONS

4.5   Politics has existed for as long as local government, the very genesis of which was political (see for instance our reference in Chapter Three to Lord Salisbury's motivation in creating the London County Council and other county councils). There is nothing novel in local elections being contested on party lines, in local government being used as a stage for national political issues, in councillors taking an active part in the management of local authorities, nor in service delivery being governed by party philosophies. All of these things can be found in London in the 19th century towards the end of the life of the Metropolitan Board of Works and the beginning of the London County Council. They can be found in the Victorian cities such as Birmingham, Glasgow and Manchester. They can also be found although less sharply, in rural areas in vestries and school boards. Indeed some commentators argue that local government has traditionally been political, and that the main break with tradition has been the growth in the influence of professional officers in the quarter century after the Second War. On this argument elected members are merely re-asserting the traditional basis of local government.

58

4.6   The early development of politics in local government is reviewed by Dr Young[1]in the research paper which we commissioned. Its current manifestations are reviewed in the research report on the Political Organisation of Local Government[2], and the main threads are brought together in Chapter Two of this Report.

4.7   We need here to distinguish between the existence of party politics, its intensity, and some of the particular ways in which it manifests itself.

4.8   Our research shows that the great majority of councillors and councils are now elected and organised on party lines. Only 15% of councillors in 1985 had stood for election as independents[3] and only 16% of councils (mainly district councils in rural areas) were controlled by independents[4]. It has also been clear throughout our work that politics have taken on a new intensity in those authorities which have anyway been elected and organised on party lines. This new intensity is well illustrated in the evidence of the National Local Government Advisory Committee of the Conservative Party, from which we quote:

'It would be unwise to underestimate the tidal force of the changes which are taking place. They are by no means confined to the left-wing in politics, though to some extent they began there.......there has developed an area of political commitment in local government which used not to exist. There is commitment on the left, to make local government an alternative political base from which to challenge a right-wing central government, claiming an equal validity from the support of the ballot box. There is also a commitment from Conservative councils, seeking to emulate the radical approach of the Government to received administrative orthodoxy, of which the most obvious manifestation is the commitment to privatisation and generally contracting out. Both of these commitments are foreign to the traditions of the professional officers. The wise ones have accepted the new regime and led it. The weak ones have allowed it to happen and have seen their ill-informed members failing to secure an attainable degree of efficiency. Too many officers, being neither wise nor weak, have tried to obstruct the new practices of determined political leaders and have created tensions within their authorities which could have been avoided. They have failed to recognise that the demand for exercising power by the elected leaders has to be accommodated if it exists, and that in those circumstances the practices and conventions of local government need to be adapted to ensure that the power is exercised wisely and that the political management is efficient.'

4.9   This quotation encapsulates much of the flavour of recent politicisation, and indeed of the issues it raises. It shows that the growing intensity of politics is not a single party phenomenon. It has sometimes been more marked in recent years in Labour councils because of the added dimension of conflict with a central government which has itself adopted a highly political approach in its relations with local government, but in many ways it has been a feature equally of both the main parties. Councillors from both Labour and Conservative parties,

---

[1] Young, *Research Volume IV*.
[2] Leach et al, *Research Volume I*.
[3] SCPR, *Research Volume II*, Table 4.4.
[4] Leach et al, *Research Volume I*, Table 2.1.

when they have had majority control on a council, have encountered tension with senior officers.

At the same time there are many authorities in which minority parties have been increasingly assertive in challenging what they see—conversely—as too close a relationship between majority party and senior officers. This has been a particular feature of Alliance politics.

4.10   Although there has been a general growth in the geographical spread of politics, and in its intensity, it is important to distinguish between the differing ways in which this has manifested itself. From the research, and our own observations, we would highlight the following manifestations, all of which are separable and do not necessarily flow from each other:

a)   elections being contested on party lines;

b)   formal council offices (membership of committees, chairmanship, etc) being allocated on party lines;

c)   party groups determining an agreed policy line in advance of meetings of the council or its committees;

d)   services being delivered according to party political policies (privatisation, direct labour organisations, etc);

e)   party political policies being set out in election manifestos and subsequently regarded as committing the majority party;

f)   councillors playing a fuller role vis a vis officers in decision taking;

g)   councillors taking a fuller role vis a vis officers in day to day management;

h)   appointment of officers as a means of political patronage;

i)   use of council services and funds as a resource for political patronage;

j)   use of local government as a platform for national political issues and ambitions.

THE DESIRABILITY AND INEVITABILITY OF POLITICS

4.11   The list above is by no means definitive. We believe it important however to distinguish between the items in it because different views can be taken on them. The blanket term 'politicisation' is misleading in discussing both its desirability and its inevitability.

4.12   At its best politics is the essential currency of representative democracy. It provides an organisational basis through which citizens can achieve the type of government and the type of services they want without themselves needing to partake directly in the process of government. If the political party for whom they vote fails to deliver, that party can be held accountable through the ballot box at the next election. As such politics is by no means incompatible with efficiency in service delivery, especially where efficiency is measured in qualitative as well as quantitative terms. The Controller of Audit for England and Wales told us he could find no direct connection between the politicisation of a council and the degree of efficiency in the delivery of services.

4.13 Moreover local government has to an extent become more 'political' independently of the impact of councillors. Over the last decade the climate of financial retrenchment has increasingly required decisions as to priorities between and within services. At the same time local communities have become less prepared to accept professional approaches to service delivery, notably in relation to housing, planning, and—most recently—social services, and have sought direct participation through consultation. Lastly local government's internal management has become more corporate and less based on the old service professions. All these factors have contributed to a greater stress on 'political' approaches to decision taking. The organisation of councillors on party lines creates an appropriate framework of accountability in which such increasingly political decisions can be taken.

4.14 At its worst, politics can be a malign influence. It can operate as a means of distributing spoils rather than serving the community, as indeed characterised the early development of politics in the 18th and early 19th century. Spoils can be distributed in local government through for example the appointment of political allies to officer posts, misuse of planning and development powers, and decisions to fund outside bodies that are supportive of the policies of the majority party. Similarly there is a danger of services being channelled towards particular sectional groups or areas simply in order to win votes rather than on a balanced assessment of the merits. It would be unrealistic to expect all sections of the community to benefit equally from any form of government, whether or not party political. The dividing line between the acceptable and the unacceptable will not always be clear, but we have seen trends in some areas towards the use of patronage and towards a highly sectional view of community interests which we believe are unlikely to be in the public interest.

4.15 The political process can also become an end where it should be a means, and as a result the public can suffer. We have been particularly concerned where politicians (whether central or local) have placed local services at risk by brinkmanship over resource decisions. Local government has sometimes become part of an ulterior conflict with the result that decisions have had little to do with the interests of the public which local government is there to serve. This not only damages the good name of local government, but also that of party politics, and we believe that this is recognised by the national political parties. It is interesting in this respect that our Attitude Survey[1] showed that most electors would prefer local government **not** to be organised on party political lines.

4.16 In common with the great majority of those who commented in the evidence, we regard the continued presence of political organisation in local government as inevitable for the foreseeable future. Indeed we would expect to see a continuing trend towards political organisation in those authorities which at present are relatively apolitical. We do not regard this in itself either as desirable or undesirable. There are, however, particular aspects of politics—those summarised in paragraphs 4.14 and 4.15—which we regard neither as inevitable or desirable.

---

[1] Young/NOP, *Research Volume III*, Table 6.5.

THE NEED TO ACCOMMODATE POLITICS IN LOCAL GOVERNMENT

4.17   Politics is now the main determining factor in the decisions of most local authorities. It is however not recognised in the statutory arrangements and is often regarded as an alien presence. As a result insufficient distinction has been made between the fact of the existence of politics, which is a reality which any system of government must recognise and accommodate, and particular manifestations of politics that should not be sanctioned. This is something which we shall seek to remedy in our recommendations. Our ability to do so is limited. By analogy with free market economics, politics is a service industry designed to ensure that the consumers (the electorate) receive the goods (the public services) that they want. On this analogy the most effective form of regulation is the market place, and the market place for politics is the electoral process. If the electoral system works well it should ensure that the balance of political advantage reflects local opinion and that politicians are held fully accountable for their actions.

4.18   The electoral system is outside our terms of reference. Nevertheless, the issues do lie in considerable part within our remit, as do the solutions. Although politics in local government are by no means new, the formal statutory local government system has never explicitly recognised politics in the way that is, for example, the case at central government. The statutory institutions of local government are corporate rather than adversarial in nature. In law, power is vested in the council as a whole with no distinction between majority and minority parties, and the loyalty of officers is equally to the council as a whole. These arrangements fail to provide a focus within the formal statutory system for political organisation. As a result political organisation has tended to develop outside and alongside the statutory framework, without the regulation and checks that would apply if it was inside. The successful bridging between the formal statutory arrangements and the informal political arrangements has relied much on improvisation and local convention. It has also relied on the good will and good sense of councillors, both of the majority and minority parties, and of officers.

4.19   In our visits and in our dealings with the local government world we have seen that good will and good sense do both remain abundant, even in cases where newspaper headlines suggest otherwise. But there are definite strains and stresses. Among councillors there has been a growing impatience with established ways of running things, (see for instance the evidence quoted at paragraph 4.8). This impatience has resulted not only in a desire to see things changed, but to be actively involved in the management of change. The contribution which officers can make has not always been fully recognised with consequent implications for morale and turn-over. On the other hand, although officers have often shown political sensitivity and the abiltity to accommodate change, they have sometimes reacted as if political influences on council business were alien and improper. This has exacerbated tensions and heightened pressures for political appointments.

4.20   At the same time strains have developed between majority and minority parties. Their relationships depend on a balance whereby the majority party is able to pursue the policies for which it was elected, but within a corporate framework where decisions are formally taken by the council as a whole (either directly or through delegation). This relationship can break down where the majority party, or their leaders, operate as if they hold executive power in their own right—in the manner of central government Ministers. It can also break down if minority parties do not recognise political realities, and fail to accept that their most effective role will often be one of scrutiny and constructive criticism rather than a direct impact on the formulation of decisions. Strains have also developed within majority parties, most notably over differing views as to their proper relationship with the local party organisation.

4.21   In summary local government institutions are in many respects poorly attuned to the modern political environment. This weakness has always existed but has been masked by the successful operation of conventions in a period of growth and relative consensus. More recently the extent and pace of political change has exposed this weakness. The political process, instead of fitting into a regulated framework within the local government system, is tending to operate outside and at odds with the system. At best this is causing uncertainty and instability. At worst power is being abused. The means to remove uncertainties and check abuses are not there because the local government system does not formally recognise the existence of politics.

4.22   The potential losers are the public, and it is from their viewpoint that we must assess the need for change, because it is for them that local government exists. This applies equally whether local government is viewed primarily as a means of providing statutory services to the public or as a means of reflecting more general local needs.

4.23   The circumstances we describe above should not be exaggerated. In the great majority of authorities, the circumstances would not be recognised at all, and our Attitude Survey[1] shows that over 70% of electors are satisfied with the services provided by their local authority. We do however believe that a need for some action has arisen—for three reasons.

4.24   First, in a very small number of authorities, real problems have occured and power has been abused.

4.25   Second, there is a rather larger number of authorities where considerable instability and uncertainty in relationships has arisen because of the pace of political change. This applies particularly in the main urban areas, but also in some shire county councils. Particular difficulties have also arisen in hung councils, where conventions have previously relied on there being a party with a clear majority. These authorities need a more stable way of working which reflects the modern political environment.

4.26   Third, the weaknesses which have caused problems in the first category of authorities, and instability in the second, potentially exist in all authorities. The Committee's remit is not just to deal with present problems, but to provide a framework to strengthen democracy in future years. Given the clear trend towards politicisation, we must ensure that there is a framework able to cope with it as and when it arrives.

---

[1] Young/NOP, *Research Volume III*, Table 3.1.

THE MAIN THEMES UNDERLYING OUR RECOMMENDATIONS

Evolutionary development rather than institutional change

4.27 Our approach has been to develop existing institutions, to make them more closely attuned to the modern political environment, rather than to suggest sweeping them away. As shown in the analysis above the existing statutory framework has weaknesses. There are various possibilities for radical institutional change, discussed more fully in the next Chapter, which would in theory remove or reduce some of these weaknesses. These include the adoption of a Ministerial model of government, such as that applying in central government. Radical options of this kind however received very little support in the evidence, and would undoubtedly create problems of their own. They would moreover of themselves be disruptive, and we do not believe the disruption of major institutional change can be justified unless there is a much clearer benefit than we have been able to identify. We have found that the existing model of local government, although possessing weaknesses, has great strengths. It provides for participation and openness in decision taking. It also has the adaptability to accommodate a wide diversity of political arrangements. It should be retained.

National and local solutions

4.28 Within the framework of current institutions we have then found ourselves at several points with a choice between:

a) national statutory rules;

b) national codes of conduct;

c) local arrangements devised by individual authorities.

4.29 One of the main strengths of local governement is its diversity, and we do not wish to prescribe national uniformity. We have recommended nationally applicable rules only where there has been some major point of principle which has been clearly applicable to all local authorities. Where this has been the case the issues have generally been of sufficient importance to justify enforceable rights and obligations. We have accordingly recommended statutory rules wherever the issue has been one amenable to legal definition. Where it has not, we have recommended a code of conduct that is enforceable through the local ombudsman. We see no point in recommending national rules unless there is some means of effective enforcement.

4.30 On lesser matters, we believe that the need is not for national uniformity but for local clarity and certainty. We have therefore recommended that local authorities should prepare, and make public, their own explicit local conventions governing the conduct of their business. This should do much to reduce frictions and tensions in individual authorities, without impairing diversity or introducing excessive central regulation.

4.31 Our recommendations, whether they are for statutory or non-statutory action, are whenever possible based on the best practice currently being adopted by individual local authorities. Almost all our recommendations for the way local authorities should conduct themselves are already proving themselves successfully in practice in some parts of Great Britain.

The content of our recommendations

4.32 Our recommendations are set out and justified in detail in the ensuing five Chapters. In view of the breadth of the subject matter we cover, we believe it is useful to set out here the main unifying themes of these recommendations. These themes, which are not co-terminous with our Chapter headings, are as follows:

(i) The Rule of Law

4.33 Local government is a creation of statute, and in this Report as in our Interim Report we place emphasis on the need for councils and individual councillors to act within the law. Accordingly in our recommendations we have sought to clarify the law where it is currently in doubt, to ensure that councillors act within the law, and to provide that they are advised where they propose to take action that is unlawful. Where the law is breached we have recommended improved means of enforcement including a new procedure by which members of the public may bring the matter before the courts. We have also recommended a strengthening of the role of the ombudsman in relation to maladministration.

(ii) Law and reality

4.34 In this Chapter we have drawn particular atention to the gap between the statutory local authority framework and political reality. Decisions are **taken** within the statutory framework but policies are often **formulated** outside it. Our approach to this dilemma has been threefold.

4.35 First, we have sought to ensure that the procedures for **decision taking** are clear and open to the public, and provide for a proper contribution by all councillors of all parties. To this end we have proposed certain statutory requirements to be contained in standing orders, the most important of which is provision for pro rata membership of political parties on all committees with powers to take decisions on behalf of the council.

4.36 Second, we have sought to make the formal council system more accommodating to the political process of **policy formulation**, so that this process is not driven underground. Accordingly we have made recommendations to enable committees drawn only from the majority party to meet in privacy within the council system, with full officer participation, provided they have no powers to take decisions on behalf of the council.

4.37 Third, we recognise that, despite this, council policies will often continue to be formulated outside the formal council system in party groups. We see nothing improper in this, but have recommended that the national political parties apply certain rules to the conduct of such groups.

(iii) The councillor's obligations

4.38 The current law vests executive authority collectively in councillors. This places them in a position distinct from Members of Parliament. Councillors are not just constituency representatives, but major employers and responsible for budgets often well in excess of £100 million per annum. The direct participation of councillors in executive decisions has democratic strengths. We believe, however, that the councillor's executive power carries with it essential duties. Councillors should not act as the delegate of some sectional interest within the community, nor should they serve their own private interest. They should serve the whole community according to the council's legal obligations. The distinction is not always easy, but we see a need for fresh clarification and make recommendations to that end.

(iv) Councillors and officers

4.39   Local government has derived strength over the years from a complementary relationship between part-time councillors drawn from and representative of the general public, and full-time officers with professional expertise. We accept that this cannot be a rigid or static model. Some councillors will need to devote considerable time to council business, and there has sometimes been too great a stress on officer professionalism. Councillors moreover have the right to ensure that their decisions, for which they are statutorily responsible and accountable, are implemented by officers. Nevertheless a merging of roles is not desirable. Councillors should leave the day to day implementation of council policies, including staff management, as far as possible to officers, and officers should demonstrate that they are sensitive to the political aspirations underlying those policies. We recommend a clarification of relationships, and in particular an enhanced role for chief executives in relation to local authorities' staff.

4.40   Although councillors should not become full-time administrators, the current system of remunerating them does little to reflect their responsibilities, and we recommend that the system should be re-structured and made more equitable.

(v) Officer neutrality

4.41   Under our proposed arrangements officers would continue to serve the council as a whole, not just the majority party or its leaders. Our recommendations re-inforce this position by placing on chief executives an enhanced role as arbiter of the internal conduct of council proceedings. As such they must ensure a proper balance between majority and minority parties. Consistent with this, and also with the traditions of public service in this country, we believe that there should continue to be a permanent corps of politically impartial officers. Accordingly we have made recommendations to debar senior officers from political activity, to ensure that appointment is based on merit not on patronage, and to guard against precipitate dismissal.

4.42   At the same time we wish to ensure that councillors, especially those of the majority party, are able to rely on advice that is sensitive to their political aspirations. We have recommended regularisation of officer attendance at party groups, and of arrangements for the attachment of a limited number of officers specifically to the groups or their leaders.

(vi) The council and the community

4.43   As stated in our last Chapter local government needs to provide for participation by the community and needs to be responsive to the community. There is however a need for the means by which it does so to be clarified, especially given the increasingly sectional nature of community interests.

4.44 Councils should adopt an open attitude to the community, with the maximum opportunity for consultation, lobbying, and advice. The participation of the community in the formal process of decision taking, as opposed to policy formulation, should be solely through their elected councillors, and we make recommendations to ensure this. Any other arrangement blurs accountability, and weakens the electoral basis of local government—and hence its rationale.

4.45 Councils should respond creatively to the needs of their area, over and above the statutory services they must provide. We recommend a revised basis for the financial limit on discretionary spending, which should be more rational and more equitable to authorities in metropolitan areas. We also recommend rules for clearer accountability and for the avoidance of party political gain in such spending. Although the internal machinery of local authorities needs to recognise that councillors are organsied on party political lines, the decisions of local authorities must nevertheless be based on the legal obligations of the council to the community as a whole.

CHAPTER 5

THE DECISION TAKING PROCESS

INTRODUCTION

5.1 Before considering our detailed recommendations, we needed to decide whether we would recommend some radically new framework for the taking of decisions by local authorities, or whether we would work within the broad parameters of the current framework. In order to stimulate debate on the issue, our request for evidence raised the idea that local authorities might adopt a ministerial system of decision taking similar to that on which central government is based. In this Chapter we review, and reject, the case for radical structural change of this kind and then go on to outline changes which we propose should be made within the framework of the current decision taking model.

THE CURRENT DECISION TAKING MODEL

Statutory provisions

5.2 The main distinguishing feature of the current local government model is that decisions are taken corporately by, or on behalf of, the whole council. There is no source of executive authority other than the council itself. As such it is a quite different model to that of central government where executive decisions are taken not by Parliament but by Ministers. Ministers are drawn from Parliament and accountable to Parliament, but do not act on behalf of Parliament. They derive their authority separately from the Crown.

5.3 The Local Government Act 1972 and the Local Government (Scotland) Act 1973 provide that local authorities are corporate bodies, and vest all functions in the council of each authority. Councils are expressly empowered (section 101 of the 1972 Act and section 56 of the Scottish Act) to arrange for their functions to be discharged by committees, who may in turn arrange for them to be discharged by sub-committees. The council, committees and sub-committees may also arrange for functions to be discharged by individual officers. All such arrangements are generally referred to as 'delegation'—and we use the term in this Report. Where a function is delegated it is not relinquished. If the council delegates a function to a committee, they may recall it and indeed have the responsibility to do so if they consider that it is being discharged wrongly. Ultimate responsibility for decisions always rests in the council itself.

5.4 A council has no power to delegate functions to individual councillors. It has been widespread practice for the leader and chairmen of committees to take action between meetings of the council and committees—especially where there is urgency. However, there is no statutory basis for this (see paragraph 5.72).

5.5 Section 112 of the of the 1972 Act (section 64 of the Scottish Act) enables authorities to appoint officers for the discharge of their functions. Appointments are made by the council as a whole, and officers are servants of the council as a whole. Although the policies of a council may in practice be determined by the majority party, the law recognises no special allegiance to the majority party. Nor does the law enable any individual councillor or group of councillors to instruct an officer to discharge a function.

Criticisms of the current system

5.6   Although this statutory framework has undergone changes of detail it is basically the model that has existed since the creation of elected local authorities in the 19th century. Reflecting the 19th century origins of local government it is a system analogous to that of a board of trustees. Some have however questioned whether it is a system that is appropriate to the managerial and political environment of the late 20th century. The main criticisms of the current system fall under the following three headings.

(i) Lack of political realism

5.7   The corporate nature of the current system does not recognise the existence of adversarial party politics. This creates particular difficulties in those authorities which are effectively controlled by the majority party, with the minority party acting as an opposition rather than contributing to the formulation of decisions. In such authorities the political parties have created arrangements of their own, outside and alongside the formal statutory framework, whereby they can develop their policies in a one party setting. Often policies will be developed in meetings of the full party group, although in other authorities informal meetings of the leader and committee chairmen will be more influential. Ultimately decisions must still be taken formally within the council structure, but this formal process can become a hollow ritual devoid of substance if the issue has been pre-determined elsewhere. This is undesirable for four reasons. First, the formal system is brought into disrepute if it is seen to lack substance. Second, the public cannot see where, or by whom, or on what grounds decisions are formulated. Third, it is wasteful of time and resources to have two systems operating in parallel. Fourth, officers are placed in an ambiguous position: the law requires them to serve the council as a whole through its formal machinery, but political reality—and the need to ensure that decisions take account of their advice—requires them to work closely with the majority party through the informal machinery.

(ii) Lack of accountability

5.8   Most forms of democratic government provide for the concentration of executive power in a small group of political leaders who are accountable to a larger elected assembly. This, for instance, is the basis of central government in the United Kingdom. Ministers take executive decisions and Parliament calls them to account for those decisions through debate, questions and inquiries by select committees. The proposition has been put forward that this form of government strengthens accountability in two ways. First, it provides machinery through which the executive is open to constant scrutiny, not just at election time. Second, it makes the executive visible and assists the public in forming a judgement about their performance. British local government, however, is differently based. Executive power is in law held corporately by the whole elected council. Even though in reality the decisions of the council are often those of the majority party or its leadership, the corporate nature of the legal framework is not well suited to the creation of machinery within the council—equivalent to a select committee—to scrutinise those decisions. The minority party will often see it as its prime role to criticise the decisions of the majority, but such a role does not fit easily in a corporate framework. It is only by recognising that the majority hold power that it is possible to create the machinery by which the exercise of that power can be held effectively to account.

69

(iii) Lack of efficiency

5.9   Local authorities in Great Britain are on average larger than those in any other country, both in terms of population and budgets[1]. For instance the largest shire counties have budgets over £500 million per annum and populations of over one million. The average number of councillors per council is also large by international standards—48 over Great Britain as a whole and typically 75–100 for the largest councils. This combination of large scale activities and large numbers of councillors creates management problems, which the Audit Commission drew attention to in their written evidence. In other major spending institutions such problems can be solved by concentrating decision taking powers in a small executive. The Cabinet of the UK has only 22 members, the boards of major private companies normally have fewer than 20. Local government systems abroad also often provide for a small executive—whether an elected mayor, a city manager or a commission—to carry out day-to-day decisions. The current model of local government in Great Britain does not allow this because power is vested corporately in all councillors. The dispatch of business requires complex hierarchies of committees and sub-committees, which can be time consuming and cumbersome.

Strengths of the current system

5.10   Against that there can be no doubt that the currrent local government model has considerable strengths, which can again be summarised under three headings.

(i) Adaptability

5.11   There are some 500 local authorities in Great Britain varying greatly both in size and political organisation. At paragraph 5.7 we have highlighted weaknesses of the current local government model in authorities with adversarial party politics where one party effectively forms a *de facto* administration and the other acts as an opposition. This is only one of many circumstances, however, which the system needs to be able to cater for. Our research[2] shows that in mid 1985 there remained about 80 authorities—mainly district councils in rural areas—controlled or dominated by independents. In such authorities the corporate basis of decision taking has substance and is not just a means of legally ratifying decisions effectively made elsewhere. This is also so to a considerable extent in many of the authorities organised on party lines; there remain a range of issues, especially in committee work, which are not pre-determined by the parties. The position of 'hung' authorities also needs consideration. Where there is no overall majority, and—as is often the case—no firm coalition of parties with a majority, then a corporate basis of decision taking becomes a positive necessity as the only means of conducting business. The current model of govenment is one which has proved itself sufficiently adaptable to accommodate all these various circumstances.

(ii) Open-ness

5.12   Local government is open to the public view. The legislation in this respect was strengthened during the course of our Inquiry by the Local Government

---

[1] Goldsmith and Newton, *Research Volume IV*.
[2] Leach et al, *Research Volume I*, Tables A1 and A2.

(Access to Information) Act 1985. Except in certain specified exceptions, meetings of the council, its committees and sub-committees are open to the public and the public are entitled to see copies of agenda and minutes of the meetings and of reports which form the basis for discussion (see paragraph 5.61). This provides a guarantee of open-ness in the formal taking of decisions. In this country such open-ness is unique to local government with no parallel among other public sector institutions. It is particularly important given the immediacy of local government decisions to people's lives. It may be argued that the process of debate at the formal decision taking stage will often be very limited because it is known that the majority party have pre-determined their position and cannot be outvoted. Although this might sometimes be true of debate, it is not so of the documentation on which decisions are based. Local authorities need, as a matter of law, to show that in taking decisions they have taken into account all relevant considerations. They will therefore have before them the advice of officers, given on the open record; this not only enables the public to see the basis on which decisions are taken but ensures that the council as a whole—not just the majority—has the benefit of the assessment of officers.

(iii) Participation

5.13   The corporate nature of decision taking maximises councillor participation in the decision taking process. Our research[1] shows that over 75% of councillors in Great Britain sit on at least three main committees (ie other than sub-committees). In the great majority of cases these will be committees with delegated executive powers to take decisions on behalf of the council. This gives councillors as a whole, including those from minority parties and independents, a direct involvement in the process of government which they would not have if executive power was concentrated in fewer hands. It might be argued that a Member of Parliament does not participate in executive decisions, but nevertheless plays a significant role in the democratic process. Parliament however has a legislative role, for which there is no analogy in local government. If therefore backbench councillors were cut off from the decision taking process this would be a significant diminution in their role.

ALTERNATIVE DECISION TAKING MODELS

5.14   We have looked at a number of alternative models, which for the purposes of discussion we categorise as follows:

   (a) Maud Management Board

   (b) Ministerial

   (c) Separation of powers

In the paragraphs below we describe how each would operate, and indicate their strengths and weaknesses.

Maud Management Board

5.15   This is the model recommended in 1967 by the Committee of Inquiry chaired by Sir John Maud[2]. The Maud Committee recommended that each local

[1] SCPR, *Research Volume II*, Table 5.6.
[2] Report of the Committee of Inquiry into the Management of Local Government, 1967, pages 22 to 63.

authority should appoint a Management Board of five to nine leading councillors. This Board would be the sole committee to have delegated powers to take decisions on behalf of the council. All other committees, including those dealing with particular services, would be purely advisory. Detailed decisions would be delegated by the Board to officers. The Maud Committeee saw the Management Board proposal not only as a means of improving management efficiency but also of sharpening accountability and reflecting reality. For instance paragraph 390 of the Report states:

'Our proposals will, if acted on, clearly identify where power lies in the council. We see it as a means whereby party political responsibility in a council is made apparent in an organ which is clearly part of the authority rather than resting remotely in a party group which is outside the scrutiny of the council and without the benefit of advice from senior officers of the authority'.

5.16   The recommendation for a Management Board was not accepted by the Government, and was strongly opposed by local authorities themselves. The majority of opinion shared the view put by Sir Andrew Wheatley in a Note of Dissent to the Report that:

'these proposals will vest far too much power in the small number of members who will be members of the management board, and will deprive the great majority of the members of the council of the opportunity of participating effectively in the formulation of policy and the development of services which are the responsibility of local government. Local government is fundamentally a means of associating representatives elected by the people with government, and so, far from detracting from it, everything should be done to encourage it.'

5.17   The compostion of the Management Boards would have been for each local authority to determine. The Maud Report itself recommended, on the balance of argument, that authorities should normally include minority party members. In the sharper political climate of today, however, it would be expected that a large number of authorities would limit membership to the majority party. This would have important implications for officers. Under Maud's proposals officers' main day-to-day line of management accountability would have been through the chief executive to the Board, not to the full council or the advisory service committees. This would have placed officers in an even more ambiguous position than at present, and it is difficult to see how their accountability to a one party Management Board could be readily squared with their legal obligation to serve the council as a whole.

5.18   Before leaving this proposal, it is useful to outline changes that did take place following the Maud Report. The Local Government Act 1972 and the Local Government (Scotland) Act 1973, while not providing for Management Boards, did give local authorities increased discretion to determine their own internal organisation. With certain limited exceptions (most particularly the requirement to appoint committees for education, social sevices, fire and police) authorities were enabled to appoint, and delegate functions to, such committees as they wished. They were also enabled to delegate functions to officers. In principle therefore it would have been possible for authorities to follow some of the

72

Maud principles by concentrating delegated powers in a central decision taking committee, which would delegate more detailed matters to officers. Most local authorities, influenced by the Bains[1] and Paterson[2] Reports of 1972 and 1973, have indeed appointed an influential central committee—most commonly a policy and resources committee. However, far from decision taking powers being concentrated in this central committee, it is quite common for it to have no such powers at all, and for its role to be primarily one of policy co-ordination. Nor have decision taking powers been delegated on a significant scale to officers. Decisions are most commonly taken, as they always have been, by service-related committees and sub-committees. This is a rejection of Maud's approach to decision taking.

Ministerial

5.19   We use this term to describe a system of decision taking similar to that of central government. It has similarities with the Maud system, but differs in two respects.

(a) Under a ministerial system power is held by separate authority, whereas the Maud Management Board would hold power only by virtue of delegation from the full council.

(b) Under a ministerial system power is legally held by individual persons (even though they may in practice meet collectively). In contrast the Maud Management Board would exercise power corporately, not through individual board members.

5.20   The institutions of central government could not be transplanted in full to local government because it would not be possible to devise at local level an analogy for the sovereignty of Parliament nor for the position of the Crown as the source of ministerial authority. It would however be possible to transplant the main elements of the system as follows. There would continue to be a council of elected members, but the executive powers currently vested statutorily in the council as a whole would instead be vested statutorily in 'executive members' appointed by the council from among their number. These executive members would be the political heads of the various service departments and would have responsibility for taking—or delegating to officers—all decisions relating to that department. They would be accountable to the council as a whole for the proper exercise of their functions, and the council could make this accountability a reality by the ability to refuse to vote supply and the ability to terminate the appointment of the executive members. The executive members would meet together as a 'cabinet'. In politicised authorities it is to be presumed that they would all be drawn from the majority party. Officers would serve the executive members heading their departments, not the council.

5.21   There can be little doubt that such a system would provide an answer to the two criticisms of the current local government system set out at paragraphs 5.8 and 5.9: it would provide for much sharper accountability, with power being visibly concentrated in the executive members; and it would allow for speedier and more efficient decision taking, with no need for everything to be processed

[1] The New Local Authorities, Management and Structure, 1972.
[2] The New Scottish Local Authorities, Organisation and Management Structures, 1973.

through committees. In some authorities it would also reflect current realities. There are a number of authorities, including some of the larger counties, where committee chairmen have adopted a ministerial style in relation to service departments and meet together on a regular basis in a 'cabinet' chaired by the leader.

5.22 There are, however, also many authorities where this 'ministerial tendency' is not pronounced. Even among many of the more politicised authorities there is often a feeling that power should be spread democratically across the whole majority group not just vested in its leadership. A ministerial system is not therefore a ready made solution for politicisation. In short the current system's strength of 'adaptability' would be lost. So also would participation and openness, and the objections here are much the same as apply to the Maud Management Board. It should be noted however that the position of officers would not be the same as under the Maud proposal. The problem of ambiguity in their role would be removed because they would unambiguously be serving the executive members and not the council as a whole. This need not affect officers' political neutrality. It would, however, inevitably have a significant impact on minority parties—who would lose their current rights to officer advice.

5.23 It would be possible to reduce, although not eliminate, some of the objections to a ministerial system by developing a hybrid arrangement incorporating some elements of ministerialism but within a framework whereby power is held corporately by the council. This was essentially the form of government proposed for Wales in the Wales Act 1978, but never implemented. Under such a scheme all functions would be statutorily vested in the council, which would be required to delegate such functions to committees. The committees would, however, be able to delegate all their functions to their chairmen, who would sit together collectively as an executive committee. Where powers were delegated in this way, the committees would remain in existence but their role would be to be consulted prior to decisions and to scrutinise decisions already taken. They would not themselves take decisions.

5.24 This proposal is half way between Maud and full ministerialism. As in a ministerial system power would be held individually rather than corporately, but, as under Maud, it would be held by virtue of delegation from the full council not by separate authority. The proposal would have the advantage of greater adaptability than a full ministerial system in that councils could if they preferred continue to take decisons corporately through the full council and committees without any delegation to executive members. Officers would in law serve the whole council, as at present. But in those authorities which decided to delegate substantial powers to executive members, officers would clearly have problems in practice of dual loyalties—as under the Maud Management Board proposal.

Separation of powers

5.25 Under the Maud and ministerial models there would be an executive that was distinct from the council but drawn from it. It would be possible to devise instead an arrangement where the executive was quite separate from the council with no overlap of membership. The council would be responsible for the main policy and budgetary framework, but the day-to-day administration of the local authority would be the separate responsibility of the executive. Provided that the relative responsibilities of council and executive were clearly drawn, this could sharpen accountability. It could also make for greater management efficiency, avoiding the need for day-to-day decisions to be taken through a committee structure. There would tend to be a corresponding diminution in open-ness and participation. There are two main variants of such a system: one where the executive is directly elected, and one where it is appointed.

(i) An elected executive

5.26   There are arrangements in the USA, Canada and West Germany[1] where executive power is vested in a directly elected commission or, more commonly, 'strong' mayor. The term strong mayor is used to differentiate such mayors from ones with a figurehead role. The best known example of a strong mayor is the mayor of New York. The system has the advantage that the mayor is a visible figure. This heightens public interest in, and comprehensive of, local government and assists in clear accountability. Election of an executive enhances democracy and side-steps the problems, which we shall see below, arising from appointment. Indeed this is one of the reasons why the USA has adopted direct election of a wide range of officials, from dog catchers to judges and mayors. The main problem with an elected mayoral system is that it runs counter to British traditions in two respects. First it personalises politics in a way which is accepted in countries with a presidential system at central government, but generally disliked in Great Britain. Second it results in two rival sources of directly elected authority—the council and the mayor. Depending on the timing of elections they may be of different political persuasions. This is regarded as unexceptionable in other countries. In Britain, however, it is difficult to believe that there would not be considerable frictions, especially as the mayor's powers would be created at the expense of the existing powers of the council.

(ii) An appointed executive

5.27   The problem arising from election would be avoided if the council itself appointed the executive. This is the system that obtains in Ireland and those parts of the USA which have a city or county manager. There are no such arrangements on a general basis in Great Britain, but an analogy is provided in the particular instance of public transport in the main conurbations, where each authority appoints a passenger transport executive. All such arrangements have in common that the appointed executive, whether a person or a board, has its own sphere of responsibility in which the council may not legally intervene except in very limited circumstances. The council's role is confined to setting the basic budgetary and policy parameters for the executive.

5.28   This approach could be developed in Great Britain by requiring each local authority to appoint a chief executive, in whom would be statutorily vested all matters of detailed administration and management. Chief executives would be solely responsible for most executive decisions—eg planning permissions, council house allocations, improvement grants, care orders—within the budget and broad policy set by the council. They would be responsible for all other staff appointments, and all staff would report to the council through them.

---

[1] Discussed more fully in Goldsmith and Newton, *Research Volume IV*.

5.29　A division of responsibility of this kind would mean a substantial change in the role of elected members. Under the Maud and ministerial proposals, **backbench** councillors and minority parties would be excluded from the detailed decision taking process. With a separate appointed executive **all** elected members, including leading councillors, would be excluded. Moreover, it could not be argued—as with an elected executive—that power was merely being transferred from one elected organ to another. There would be a substantial change in the character of local government, greatly reducing the position of its political leadership and enhancing the role of its adminstrative leadership. It should be noted in this respect that in the USA such arrangements are most common in smaller and less politicised authorities. Whether or not this change might be considered desirable, it would certainly be a reversal of recent trends towards the politicisation of local government and would not reflect current political realities. As a consequence the system would be subject to considerable strain. An initial source of strain would arise over the appointment of chief executives. Their role would be such a powerful one that there would be great pressure to appoint people who were prepared to follow the wishes of the majority on the council even on those issues where the council held no responsibility. It would therefore probably be necessary, as is the case in Ireland, to have some provision for an independent staff commission to approve or nominate the appointee. This, however, would further diminish the power of councillors and probably make for bad relations between the council and the chief executive.

CONCLUSION ON DECISION TAKING MODELS

5.30　Discussion of these alternative models is instructive. All have significant weaknesses, but each helps to highlight those respects in which the current local government model is itself weak, and thereby helps to suggest means of improvement. We do not however believe that any of the alternatives is acceptable for general application to local government in Great Britain. In saying that, we recognise that the alternatives might work well in other contexts and even in **some** local authorities in Great Britain. The following four factors weighed particularly in our considerations.

5.31　First, we believe that the decision taking model must be one that is sufficiently adaptable and robust to be applicable to all local authorities in Great Britain, regardless of size and political development. The current system has shown it has these characteristics.

5.32　Second, insofar as the current system has weaknesses, particularly in relation to highly politicised authorities, they do not give rise to widespread problems and we believe that these are largely, although not entirely, capable of resolution by adaptation without radical institutional change. We shall make a number of recommendations to this end.

5.33　Third, we believe that the onus of proof should always be on those who propose insititutional change, especially where this is of a major structural character. Great Britain has a strong tradition of evolutionary change and improvisation in its institutional arrangements and a healthy suspicion of solutions that are theoretically logical or transplanted from elsewhere. Unless there is a clear case to the contrary it is preferable to build on what is already there.

5.34 Fourth, the great majority of those submitting evidence on the subject have defended the retention of the current local government decision taking model. They have in particular strongly opposed any suggestion that it should be replaced by a ministerial model. This has been true of all the political parties and of councillors and officers alike. While some have perhaps not fully addressed the criticisms which we have listed at paragraphs 5.7 to 5.9, there can be little doubt that these criticisms are considered by most to carry less weight than the strengths of the current system listed at paragraphs 5.11 to 5.13. In particular, echoing the reaction to the Maud Committee proposals, great stress has been placed in the evidence on the need to retain an open decision taking process in which councilors as a whole—not just leading councillors of the majority party—are involved.

5.35 Our approach therefore is to base our proposals on the existing model, which we define as one where:

(a) the council is a corporate body;

(b) decisions are taken openly by, or on behalf of, the whole council—without any separate source of executive authority;

(c) officers serve the council as a whole.

Indeed our recommendations are designed to ensure that these three fundamental points are reinforced and clarified. At the same time we seek—within this framework—to bring the formal machinery of local government more into line with political reality and thereby to lend it greater substance. Doing this should also sharpen accountability and promote management efficiency.

5.36 We therefore recommend that:

the system of decision taking in local government should continue to be one in which:

(i) the council is a corporate body;

(ii) decisions are taken openly by, or on behalf of, the whole council, without any separate source of executive authority;

(iii) officers serve the council as a whole.

(Paragraphs 5.30 to 5.35)

DECISION TAKING AND POLICY FORMULATION

5.37 In the recommendations which follow in this Chapter we make a fundamental distinction between the formal legal process through which a decision is taken, and the less formal process through which the policy contained in the eventual decision is formulated. We call the former decision taking and the latter policy formulation.

5.38 By decision taking we mean for example the formal decision of the council to set a rate, or the formal decision of the planning committee to grant a planning permission.

5.39   By policy formulation we mean for example the process through which the majority party might agree its policy in a meeting of the party group, or through which a committee chairman and a chief officer might discuss a report before it is considered by a committee. We also use the term to describe discussion in committees which are within the formal council system but which do not have delegated powers to take decisions.

5.40   It is in the realm of **decision taking** that we believe that the current corporate framework of local government should be re-inforced. The decision taking process should so far as possible be open to public view, reflect the overall balance of political control on the council, and should be confined to councillors. Such rules for decision taking, which we shall elaborate on below, are not only desirable but are enforceable. They are enforceable because no decision of a local authority would be valid in law unless they were followed.

5.41   It is not however possible to enforce laws relating to the less formal process by which policies are formulated prior to the taking of a decision. This process will be determined by political reality. If the statutory local government framework does not reflect political reality then policies will be formulated outside it. We do not believe this is desirable, for reasons which we outlined in paragraph 5.7. We therefore make recommendations which are designed to encourage policies to be formulated, as well as decisions taken, within the statutory local government framework.

5.42   Throughout we use the term 'decision taking committees' to describe those committees which have formal delegated powers to take decisions on behalf of the council, and 'deliberative committees' for those which do not.

MEMBERSHIP OF COMMITTEES

The current position

5.43   The Local Government Act 1972 (and the Local Government (Scotland) Act 1973) provide that decisions to set a rate and to promote local or private legislation must always be taken in full council. All other decisions may, however, be delegated to standing committees and sub-committees. Where a decision is taken on a vote in full council, the outcome (leaving aside absences) will precisely reflect the political balance of the authority. Where a decision is taken in a committee or sub-committee this will not necessarily be so. There are no statutory rules governing the composition of such committees (other than in regard to co-option of non-councillors – on which see paragraphs 5.79 to 5.107) and the party with a majority on the full council may, if they so wish, provide that committees and sub-committees should be consituted exclusively of councillors from their own party.

5.44   In practice one party committees are the exception rather than the rule. Our research[1] shows that one party committees exist in about 20% of authorities. In most of these authorities there is only one such committee—normally a policy and resources committee with no delegated powers to take decisions on behalf of the council. One party sub-committees exist in about

---

[1] Leach et al, *Research Volume I*, Chapter Two and Tables A18 and A19.

30% of authorities, and cover a broader range of functions. Twenty four authorities, for example, have a one party personnel sub-committee. At the extreme there are two authorities with eight or more one party committees and 14 authorities with eight or more one party sub-committees.

5.45 While one party committees are exceptional, it is relatively common for committees to depart in some lesser respect from the composition of the council as a whole. In some cases, especially where a minority party has very few members on the council as a whole, the majority will give it more than its *pro rata* share of committee places. In others minority parties are under-represented. It is quite common for the majority party to give itself a safer working majority on committees than it has on the council as a whole, reducing the risk of defeat through absences and individual members failing to follow the group line. Sometimes this is accepted by the largest minority party as a convention it would itself wish to follow if in power. Particular difficulties can, however, occur for third parties and it is noticeable in this respect that the Liberal party and Plaid Cymru both argued in their evidence for *pro rata* representation of the parties on committees. There are not only difficulties of under-representation but also of finding a seconder for motions where they have only one member on a committee.

Decision taking committees

5.46 Committee composition is one of the issues where we believe that the statutory rules should depend on whether or not the committee in question has powers to take decisions on behalf of the council. Where the committee does have such powers, we believe that representation of the parties on that committee should as far as practicable be in proportion to their representation on the council as a whole. Where local authorities decide whether powers should be delegated to committees, this should be purely on management grounds: the effect of delegation on political balance should be neutral.

5.47 Provisions for party balance on committees are well precedented. They exist in the standing orders, or written conventions, of some councils—especially those that are hung. They were contained in legislation for regional government in the Northern Ireland Consitution Act 1973 and the Scotland and Wales Acts of 1978. Most recently, statutory provision has been made for party balance on the joint authorities in metropolitan areas which took over some of the responsibilities from the metropolitan county councils on 1 April 1986. Section 33 of the Local Government Act 1985 provides that:

'Each constituent council shall, so far as practicable, exercise its power to make or terminate appointments to a joint authority so as to ensure that the balance of parties for the time being prevailing in that council is reflected in the persons who are for the time being members of the authority and for whose appointment the council is responsible.'

5.48 We recognise that this provision has caused some difficulty in practice, for two reasons:

(a) in the case of joint police authorities, the requirement to co-opt magistrates can result, and has resulted, in the party with a majority of the elected members on the committee losing overall control of the committee;

(b) it has sometimes been difficult to nominate appointees in a proportion sufficiently close to the party balance on the council.

Additionally, although less of a problem in metropolitan areas, we need to consider a third area of potential difficulty

(c) representation of independent councillors, who do not adhere to a party group.

5.49 The first of these difficulties would not arise under our recommendations for co-option (see paragraph 5.107).

5.50 The second difficulty largely arises from the fact that each metropolitan district council nominates only a very small number of councillors. It is difficult for a council with say 40 Labour members, 20 Conservative and 15 Alliance to retain proportionality in making only three appointments. This problem would be much less where a council is making appointments to its own committees rather than to joint authorities. If, on the example above, the council had to make appointments to say a planning committee of 15 members, proportionality could be easily maintained (eight Labour, four Conservative, three Alliance). We would expect that local authorities, in fixing the overall number of councillors on a committee, would have regard to whether this number was readily divisible according to whatever formula was required to achieve proportionality. In some cases this might mean avoidance of very small sub-committees, although we would certainly hope that committees would not become unwieldy simply to ensure precise proportionality. It must be accepted that some difficulties would occur, especially in relation to small parties. In most cases such difficulties would be capable of resolution by negotiation between the party whips (as they commonly are in authorities at present). Slight under-representation on one committee could be traded against slightly over-representation on another. However, we believe it unsatisfactory to rely solely on negotiation and believe that a neutral arbiter is required. We believe that this role should be given to the chief executive of the local authority, who often informally performs such a role at present. The implications of this for the post of chief executive are separately considered in Chapter Six. The task of chief executives would be to prepare a proposal for comittee membership on which they would then consult the political groups. Following consultation their decision would be final.

5.51 The position of independents is not as difficult as may at first sight appear. Independents on a council do not, by their nature, organise on the same basis as do councillors from the political parties. Where, however, there are a significant number of them we believe—as is already the practice in some authorities—that they would be prepared to form a group for the purposes of allocating committee places. Where they prefer not to do so, then any difficulties should be capable of resolution by the chief executive.

5.52 In order to maintain an important element of flexibility, parties and individual members should be permitted to waive their rights to committee places. This would enable those majorities who currently allow over-representation of small minorities to continue to do so. We would certainly not wish to discourage this, and indeed would also wish to encourage authorities to devise arrangements whereby very small parties are able to move motions even where there is only one representative on a committee. We would equally not wish to discourage conventional arrangements whereby a minority party accepts that the majority party should have slight over-representation on committes in order to conduct business effectively and efficiently. A minority should not be required to take up its full right to seats where it preferred to operate a convention giving it lesser rights. Minority parties should however only be able to waive their own rights, not those of other minority parties or independent councillors.

5.53   It remains to consider the means of implementing our proposal. We believe it is the kind of basic rule where statutory provision is essential. We propose that the statute should require local authorities to incorporate provision for *pro rata* membership in their own standing orders. (This technique is discussed more fully at paragraphs 5.112 to 5.127).

5.54   In summary we recommend that:

local authorities should be statutorily required to include provisions in their standing orders governing the composition of committees and sub-committees with delegated powers to take decisions on behalf of the council. These provisions should provide:

(i) for the composition of such committees and sub-committees to reflect, as far as practicable, the composition of the council as a whole, except in so far as individual parties or councillors might waive their rights;

(ii) for the chief executive to be responsible for the detailed application of this rule.

(Paragraphs 5.46 to 5.53)

Deliberative committees

5.55   We do **not** propose that the requirement for party balance on committees should apply to committees which are purely deliberative and have no powers to take decisions[1]. Indeed we can see circumstances where it is proper for such committees to be drawn solely from the majority party.

5.56   Although the same considerations arise to some extent in respect of all deliberative committees, we are particularly concerned about the position of committees such as 'policy and resources' committees which have a strategic policy co-ordinating role. Our research[2] shows that some 94% of local authorities have a central policy committee of some kind. In most cases this is an all party committee, an arrangement consistent with the Bains Report[3] of 1972, which 'on balance' favoured minority party representation on such committees. There is however a significant number of authorities (some 11%) which have a one party policy and resources committee. Where this occurs

---

[1] We are aware that there are sometimes committees which, while normally deliberative, exceptionally take executive decisions. Where this is the case they would need to conform to the *pro rata* membership rule whenever executive decisions were taken.
[2] Leach et al, *Research Volume I*, Table A31.
[3] The New Local Authorities, Management and Structure, 1972, paragraph 4.27.

the committee is normally purely deliberative, and in most cases the practice is accepted by the main opposition party.

5.57 What is striking from our research is that while only 11% of authorities have a one party policy and resources committee, some 64% have an informal 'inner circle' of the majority leadership which meets regularly[1]. Such arrangements are commonest in upper tier authorities and in metropolitan areas, but also occur in the majority of shire districts. The meetings are normally attended by senior officers. We ourselves visited one authority which had had a tradition under both Conservative and Labour majorities of having a one party policy and resources committee. Recently the Liberals had pressed for, and been given, the right to attend. The result was that meetings of the committee were now preceded by a meeting of an informal inner circle drawn solely from the majority party leadership.

5.58 It is wrong that authorities should have to resort to informal devices of indeterminate status. If the political reality is that the general policy of the council is formulated by the majority party, we see no reason why this should not be recognised by the creation of a single party policy and resources committee within the formal structure of the council and with full access to officer advice.

5.59 We should also mention the practice, in a relatively small number of authorities (about 30), of party groups being constituted as committees or sub-commitees of the council[2]. This arrangement is distinct from the one party policy and resources committee in that it involves the whole group (not just its leadership) and normally applies equally to all parties (not just that of the majority). The committees (or sub-committees) have no executive powers but provide a forum for the groups to meet within the council system with full access to officer advice. We shall be discussing party groups more generally later in Chapter Six of the Report. Suffice it to say here that it is an arrangement to which we see no objection. It provides a further reason for not applying the *pro rata* rule to committees that are purely deliberative.

5.60 We recognise that there will also be many cases where deliberative committees will benefit from all party membership, particularly where they are developing policy in functional areas that are not partisan. We certainly would not wish to discourage cross party membership in such cases. We believe however that this is an area best left to the discretion of individual authorities.

ACCESS TO COMMITTEE MEETINGS AND DOCUMENTS

Members of the public and the press

5.61 The legislation governing public (and press) access to committee meetings and documents was significantly altered subsequent to our appointment by the Local Government (Access to Information) Act 1985. This measure was introduced by a private member (Robin Squire MP) and in its final form had the support of all the local authority associations as well as

---

[1] Leach et al, *Research Volume I*, Tables A70 to A77.
[2] Leach et al, *Research Volume I*, Table A71.

both sides of the House. This Act amended the Local Government Act 1972 and the Local Government (Scotland) Act 1973, which now provide as follows:

(a) subject to certain specified exceptions (see (b) below)

(i) meetings of the council, committees and sub-committees are open to the press and public;

(ii) the press and public may inspect the agenda and reports for the meeting in advance of the meeting together with any background papers for the reports;

(iii) after the meeting the press and public may additionally inspect the minutes.

(b) these rules do not apply to information given in confidence by the Government to the council nor to 'exempt information'. The latter includes for example personnel matters, details of child care cases, and tenders for council contracts.

(i) Decision taking committees

5.62 In our earlier comments we have cited the open-ness of decision taking as one of the strengths of local government, and insofar as the new Act reinforces this we very much welcome it. Clearly a balance must be struck in all matters of open government between the reasonable rights of the public to information and any burdens of time and cost that might be imposed on local authorities. We are conscious however that these considerations were discussed in some detail between Mr Squire, the Government and the local authority associations during the passage of the legislation and we do not propose to suggest any amendments in that respect. The amendments made by the Act only came into force on 1 April 1986 and, insofar as they relate to decision **taking**, should be given time to prove themselves in practice.

(ii) Deliberative committees

5.63 What concerns us about the 1985 Act is that it applies equally to committees that have no decision taking powers but are purely deliberative. We think that this is misconceived, and that the same distinction between decision taking and deliberative committees should be made with regard to access to information as with regard to committee membership. It is a simple reality, which no legislation can alter, that politicians will develop policy options in confidence before presenting their final choice for public decision. We do not think this unreasonable. If the law prevents them from conducting such discussions in private in formal committees, then they will conduct them less formally elsewhere. We have heard that some local authorities have been creating new informal mechanisms expressly to avoid the effects of the 1985 Act. It is unsatisfactory to force policy deliberation out of the formal committee system into groupings of indeterminate status. It is also unnecessary. No decision can be taken by a local authority without it eventually being referred to a decision taking committee or the council, where there will be full public access to the meeting and the documentation. Given this basic safeguard, we can see no benefit in applying the Act also to deliberative committees. We would not in any way wish to discourage individual local authorities from opening deliberative committees to the public and press if that is appropriate to their particular circumstances, but do not believe that they should be required by law to do so.

5.64 We therefore recommend that:

the legislation should be amended so that the rights of members of the public and the press to attend meetings and inspect documents do not apply to meetings of committees and sub-committees which are purely deliberative with no powers to take decisions on behalf of the council.

(Paragraph 5.63)

Councillors

5.65 The legal rights of councillors in relation to council proceedings are greater than those of the public at large. Under common law it is long established that they have a right to inspect documents wherever this is necessary for the performance of their duties. The position is set out in the case of *R v Barnes BC ex parte Conlan (1938) 3 AER 226*, where it was held:

'As to the right of a councillor to inspect all documents in the possession of the council there was no dispute... that such a right exists so far as his access to the documents is reasonably necessary to enable the councillor properly to perform his duties as a member of the council. The common law right of a councillor to inspect documents in the possession of the council arises from his common law duty to keep himself informed of all matters necessary to enable him properly to discharge his duty as a councillor... There must be some limit to this duty.'

This passage was cited and followed by the House of Lords in the leading case of *R v Birmingham City Council, ex parte O (1983) 1 AER 497*.

5.66 Additionally amendments introduced by the 1985 Act give to councillors the statutory right to inspect all documents relating to council, committee and sub-committee meetings except where they contain certain classes of exempt information. In some cases this right will go further than the common law right, in other cases it will go less far. The two rights are additional to each other.

5.67 Prior to 1984 it was thought that no councillor had a right to attend the meeting of any committee or sub-committee of which he was not a member—except insofar as he might attend in the public gallery as an ordinary member of the public. This position has been changed as a result of three court cases brought by Alliance councillors who had been excluded from committees. In the case of *R v Hackney London Borough Council ex parte Gamper (1985) 1WLR 1229* it was held that a councillor had precisely the same right to attend meetings as he had under common law to inspect documents— ie the test was whether attendance was necessary in order to perform his duties properly as a member of the council. This judgement was confirmed in the subsequent cases of *R v Sheffield City Council ex parte Chadwick The Times 19 December 1985* and *R v Hyndburn Borough Council ex parte Strak 17 December 1985 (unreported)*.

5.68 Consistent with our views on committee composition and on public rights of access, we do not believe that the provision described above should apply to committees that are purely deliberative. There will be cases where individual councils will find it appropriate to extend such rights to such committees, but they should not be required to do so. It is not right that a member of one party should be legally entitled to attend, or inspect the documents of, a committee in which another party are formulating their policy on matters coming before the council. Again this will merely drive discussion underground. The important safeguard, which we propose should be maintained, is that all councillors should have the right to attend, and inspect the documents of, the council and of committees that take decisions.

5.69 There are two relatively minor respects in which we also propose amendment of the law. First, there needs to be a simple neutral procedure for deciding whether councillors have a need to inspect a document or attend a meeting in order to carry out their duties. At present this is governed by common law rather than statute, and it is for the council itself to determine whether such a need arises. This effecively places the decision with the majority party. By contrast the provisions introduced by the Local Government (Access to Information) Act 1985 place similar responsibilities in respect of public rights of access on the proper officer. We shall be proposing in Chapter Six that proper officer functions of this kind should be vested in the chief executive. We consider that the chief executive should also be given the function of deciding whether a councillor has a need to inspect a document or attend a meeting. In order to achieve this it would be necessary to place the current common law provisions on a statutory footing. This would have the incidental advantage of simplifying the law on councillors' access, which is at present part in common law and part in statute.

5.70 Second, an anomaly has been created by the Local Government (Access to Information) Act 1985, whereby councillors are entitled to inspect documents containing certain categories of exempt information (ie information not open to the public) even though they may have a pecuniary interest in the matter. The effect is that, for example, councillors may inspect the tenders of firms for council contracts even where they are proposing to tender in a private capacity. This is clearly wrong. Councillors should never be entitled to inspect documents in which they have a pecuniary interest, unless they are open to the public.

5.71 **We therefore recommend that:**

the law in respect of councillors' rights to inspect documents and attend meetings should be amended so that:

(i) these rights are all contained in statute, with no reliance on common law;

(ii) these rights do not apply to committees and sub-committees which are purely deliberative with no powers to take decisions on behalf of the council;

(iii) the chief executive is responsible for deciding whether councillors have a need to inspect a document or attend a meeting in order to carry out their duties;

(iv) councillors do not have a right to inspect documents in which they have a pecuniary interest if those doucments are not open to public inspection.

(Paragraphs 5.68 to 5.70)

DELEGATION TO CHAIRMEN OF COMMITTEES

5.72   As noted in paragraph 5.4, the current legislation does not allow committees or sub-committees to delegate functions to their chairmen, or to other individual councillors. Any doubt as to this was recently removed by the case of *R v Secretary of State for the Environment ex parte London Borough of Hillingdon (1986) 1 AER 810.* Any decision which a committee chairman purports to take is therefore illegal. It is sometimes argued that this illegality can be 'cured' by subsequent ratification by the committee cr sub-committee concerned, but there are conflicting views. Certainly it is not a satisfactory basis for decision taking.

5.73   Delegation to chairmen is another area where law and practice diverge. Some form of delegation to chairmen is widespread, most commonly in respect of urgent matters and matters too routine to warrant delay until the next meeting. In several authorities the position is set out in standing orders, sometimes with accompanying safeguards (such as a requirement to report the decision at the next meeting of the committee). The inclusion of procedures in standing orders, however, does not of itself make them lawful.

5.74   There is nothing new in arrangements for delegation to chairmen. They were found to be widespread by the Maud Report[1] of 1967. Five years later the Bains Report[2] commented:

'it would be unrealistic not to recognise that despite this [ie the legal position] many day-to-day decisions have been and will continue to be effectively taken by chairmen'.

Nevertheless the position is unsatisfactory. We have highlighted the cumbersomeness of the committee system as one of the weaknesses of the current local government model (paragraph 5.9). There are, in most authorities, intervals of six or eight weeks between meetings, and it is essential that there is an effective and acceptable means of decision taking in the interim. It is also essential that clear statutory authority is given to the procedure. This would not only end current uncertainty but provide a framework into which safeguards can be built.

5.75   The problem in devising a solution is that of creating a procedure which is consistent with the corporate framework of local government and at the same time is consistent with sensible administrative practice. If an open-ended power to delegate to chairmen was created this would undermine our earlier recommendation that decisions of local authorities should only be taken in full council or by a committee or sub-committee whose political composition

---

[1] Report of the Committee on the Management of Local Government, 1967, Volume 5, pages 161 to 168.
[2] The New Local Authorities, Management and Structure, 1972, paragraph 4.52.

reflects that of the full council. It is however not practicable for **all** matters to be decided in committees and sub-committtees regardless of any urgency. We considered three possible options for urgent decisions:

(a) delegation to a small urgency sub-committee;

(b) delegation to officers;

(c) delegation to chairmen subject to strict safeguards.

5.76 We would not wish to discourage either of the first two options in circumstances where they are appropriate, but do not consider them a sufficient solution. The difficulty with the first option is basically that which we highlighted at paragraph 5.50: that of keeping *pro rata* representation on a very small sub-committee of, say, three members. If however the sub-committee was enlarged, it would become cumbersome and unsuitable for dealing with urgent matters. The second option certainly makes good sense over a wide range of issues, and we would wish to encourage councillors to delegate as many routine matters as possible to officers. However, where a committee have decided to reserve certain classes of decision to councillors, but such a decision needs to be taken urgently between meetings, we do not think it right that the mere fact of urgency should effectively exclude councillors from the decision. It is possible to retain councillor involvement by an arrangement (which some authorities have adopted) whereby urgent decisions are delegated to an officer, who must first consult the committee chairman. The reality behind such arrangements, however, tends to be that the decision is that of the chairman not the officer and we do not think it right to rely on a device which obscures this reality.

5.77 We believe therefore that the law should allow the possibility of delegation of decisions to chairmen themselves, (ie the third option). Such delegation should not be at large: it should not become a device for avoiding decision taking by committees, not a means of chairmen adopting a ministerial style of administration. The legislation should set clear limits on the scope of delegation to chairmen. It should be permissible only where a decision is required because of urgency. In other circumstances the legislation should state that any decision of the chairman is unlawful, irrespective of whether the council or committee purport to ratify it retrospectively. This should remove the legal doubt about ratification referred to in paragraph 5.72. The chief executive either directly or by delegation to one of his chief officers, should be required to agree in each case that the matter is urgent before any decision can be taken. This is one of several matters on which we propose that the chief executive should have a role in ensuring propriety in the conduct of his authority's business and we shall be discussing the wider implications in Chapter Six. We propose furthermore that the decision taken under delegated powers should be reported to the next meeting of the committee or sub-committee in question, that the provisions introduced by the Local Government (Access to Information) Act 1985 should apply to the report and other documents on which the decision is based, and that the chairman should not be able to take a decision where he or she has a pecuniary interest in the matter. Individual authorities may wish also to supplement these basic safeguards with their own arrangements. Some authorities for example currently have provisions whereby the committee chairman must consult a member of the minority party before taking a decision and others go further by allowing the minority party to 'requisition' that the decision is referred to the responsible committee or sub-committee. We see no reason why such arrangements should not continue on a local basis but doubt whether they are appropriate for national statutory provision.

5.78 **We therefore recommend that:**

the legislation should be amended to allow committees and sub-committees to delegate urgent decisions between meetings to their chairmen, subject to:

(i) the chief executive's agreement in each case that the matter is urgent;

(ii) the decision being reported to the next meeting of the committee or sub-committee;

(iii) the relevant documents being subject to the provisions introduced by the Local Government (Access to Information) Act 1985;

(iv) the chairman not having a pecuniary interest in the matter.

(Paragraph 5.77)

CO-OPTION

The current legal position

5.79 The council of a local authority and its finance committee must consist solely of councillors. Local authorities may, however, co-opt non-councillors onto other committees and sub-committees and in some instances are statutorily required to do so. The legislation is complex and is summarised below.

(i) Education committees

5.80 All local education authorities are statutorily required to appoint an education committee. Schedule 1 to the Education Act 1944 (which applies in England and Wales) provides that a majority of the committee shall be councillors but that the committee shall include:

(a) persons of experience in education;

(b) persons acquainted with the educational conditions prevailing in the area.

The arrangements must be approved by the Secretary of State, and it is normal practice for authorities to co-opt teachers and representatives of the churches. It should however be noted that neither teachers nor the churches are specified in the statute. Indeed the statute does not explicitly require co-option at all, and one authority (London Borough of Croydon) has taken the view that they can meet the requirements at (a) and (b) above from among their own councillors[1].

5.81 The position in Scotland is different. Section 124 of the Local Government (Scotland) Act 1973 provides that at least half of the education committee shall be councillors, but that the committee shall include:

(a) at least three representatives of the churches;

(b) at least two teachers.

(ii) Police committees

5.82 In England and Wales the police authority for an area (other than Greater London) is the police committee. Section 2 of the Police Act 1964 (which applies in England and Wales) requires that such committees be composed of two thirds councillors and one third magistrates. The latter must be appointed from their own number in accordance with a scheme made by the magistrates' courts committee and approved by the Secretary of State. There is no requirement for the co-option of magistrates in Scotland.

(iii) Social services

5.83 All social services authorities are statutorily required to appoint a social services committee. Section 5 of the Local Authority Social Services Act 1970 (which applies in England and Wales) provides that the committee may include co-opted members provided that a majority are councillors. There is no limit on the number of co-opted members on sub-committees. The position in Scotland is covered by section 2 of the Social Work (Scotland) Act 1968; co-opted members must not constitute more than a third of the committee and at least half of any sub-committee must be councillors.

(iv) Other committees

5.84 The statutory position of other committees and sub-committees depends on whether they 'discharge functions' or are 'advisory'. This statutory distinction is basically the same as we have drawn in this Report between 'decision taking' committees and 'deliberative' committees.

5.85 The position for committees discharging functions is governed by section 102(3) of the Local Government Act 1972 and section 57(4) of the Local Government (Scotland) Act 1973. Local authorities may co-opt non-councillors provided that they do not number more than one third of the committee. There is no limit on the numbers authorities may co-opt onto sub-committees (provided that there is at least one councillor).

5.86 The position for advisory committees is governed by section 102(4) of the 1972 Act and section 57(4) of the 1973 Act. There is no limit on the number of co-opted members, either on committees or on sub-committees, and there is indeed no requirement to include any councillors at all.

---

[1] Croydon's arrangements for their education committee have been accepted by the Secretary of State. They are however, at the time of our Report, being challenged in the High Court by the National Union of Teachers.

(v) Status of co-opted members

5.87   Co-opted members must not be persons who are disqualified from being councillors, except that teachers may be co-opted onto education and libraries committees notwithstanding that they would be disqualified from council membership by virtue of being employees of the authority.

5.88   Where there is a statutory requirement to co-opt, co-opted members are full members of the committee with voting rights. Where co-option is discretionary it is for the local authority to decide whether those concerned should have full membership with voting rights or should have some lesser status.

Current practice

5.89   Research carried out in 1965 for the Maud Committee[1] showed that co-option was widespread with about 16,000 co-opted members—about one co-opted member for every three elected members. Our own research[2] shows a marked decline in co-option, with one co-opted member for every four elected members—about 6,000 co-optees in all. (The number of elected members has also fallen considerably over the same period).

5.90   Our research[3] shows that the extent of co-option varies greatly between authorities. Only 26% of shire districts in England have any co-option at all on to committees, and only 6% have co-option on to four or more committees. By contrast 83% of London boroughs have co-option on to at least one committee, while 41% have co-option on at least four committees.

5.91   The incidence of co-option also varies between types of committee. Co-option is general on education committees and, in England and Wales, on police committees; in both these cases there is a statutory requirement. Of other committees co-option is commonest on social services committees (in about half such cases), followed by leisure and recreation, personnel and housing committees (especially in London). Co-option is also common on committees dealing with new initiatives—such as race relations, sex equality and police monitoring—and this is particularly a feature of London and the metropolitan districts. In many cases co-option is on a non-voting basis or is to committees which are purely deliberative. This applies particularly to committees dealing with new initiatives.

Issues raised by co-option

5.92   Co-option is a means by which local authorities can make use of outside expertise and experience which might not be available among elected members and officers. It is also a means of involving the community in local authority proceedings, especially those sections of the community (eg women, ethnic minorities, council tenants) that are under-represented among elected members; for instance only 19% of councillors are women and only 10% are

---

[1] Report of the Committee on the Management of Local Government, 1967, Volume 5, data derived from Tables XXIV and XXIVA.
[2] IPF, *Research Volume II*, Table A1.
[3] Leach et al, *Research Volume I*, Table A84.

council tenants[1]. These are both aims to which we fully subscribe, although co-option is not the only means of achieving them.

5.93 The majority of those commenting in the evidence have expressed reservations about co-option, and many have said that all co-option should be abolished. The main concern which has been expressed is that co-option blurs the accountability of elected members, and hence undermines the elected basis of local government. This concern is one which we share. While we wish to encourage local authorities to take advantage of outside experience and advice in as many ways as possible, this should not be in a way which confuses the roles of those who are and who are not councillors.

5.94 Again there is a crucial distinction between committees that take decisions and those that do not. We see no difficulty in local authorities appointing advisory committees consisting partly or wholly of non-councillors. However, we believe that it is wrong in principle that non-councillors should be voting members of committees with powers to take decisions. While we would hold this view anyway it becomes of particular importance under our recommendation (paragraph 5.54) that the political composition of decision taking committees should reflect the composition of the council as a whole. Co-option can undermine this recommendation by distorting the political balance of committees.

5.95 A statutory requirement to co-opt (as applies with education and police committees) can result in the party with a majority on the council not having a majority on the committee concerned. At present the majority party often guard against this risk by ensuring that their strength on committees is sufficient to out vote the minority party and the co-optees. This, however, would not be possible under our recommendation for *pro rata* representation. Co-opted members often act with restraint where they hold the political balance. It is however clear that problems can arise, as is evident from current experience with the joint police authorities in the metropolitan counties. A third of the members of police committees (in England and Wales) must be co-opted magistrates. In the metropolitan counties there is already a requirement that the councillors on police committees should be nominated *pro rata* to party strength on the council (see paragraph 5.47). The result is that magistrates will hold the balance of power unless one party holds 75% of the seats on the councils concerned. In two out of the six joint police authorities the magistrates have reportedly voted with the minority party to take control from the majority party.

5.96 Police committees (in England and Wales) are unusual in that they are themselves the authority; they do not act under delegated powers from the council(s) appointing them. In other instances the full council (on which there are no co-opted members) may always overturn the decisions of those committees and sub-committees which include co-opted members. It seems, however, to defeat the purpose of delegation to committees if the inclusion of

---

[1] SCPR, *Research Volume II*, Tables 2.2 and 2.6.

non-councillors on those committees makes it necesary to overturn their decisions.

5.97 The problem described above arises from a statutory requirement to co-opt. It would not be a sufficient answer to make co-option discretionary. This would still leave the contrary risk of the majority party on a council giving itself disproportionate strength on committees by co-option of political allies. This might not matter where there was anyway a clear majority on the full council. But it would have a significant effect where there was only a narrow majority on the full council. The co-option of political allies on to service committees, coupled with full delegation to such committees, would enable the majority party to carry its business much more securely than in the full council.

5.98 It would be possible to avoid any distortion of party balance by providing that the political parties should each nominate co-opted members *pro rata* to their strength on the council. We do not believe that this is desirable because it would tend to politicise the process of co-option: the aims of involving outside expertise and involving the community would become submerged by considerations of political patronage. It would mean moreover that community groups would not be able to make their own nominations for co-option.

5.99 We consider, therefore, that the membership of decision taking committees should be limited to councillors, and believe that this would clarify accountability. It should be noted that we do not believe it sufficient simply to withdraw voting rights from co-opted members. In practice many committee decisions are not taken by a vote. It needs to be clear, whether or not there is a vote, that the decision of a committee is a decision of councillors alone and this can only be achieved by limiting membership of decision taking committees to councillors.

5.100 In making this proposal we do not in any way wish to diminish the importance of local authorities involving the community in their proceedings and taking outside advice. This is something we applaud. There remain, however, many avenues through which this would remain possible. Local authorities may consult outside groups and hold public meetings to explain their policies and seek views. They may also appoint advisory committees of the council consisting partly or wholly of non-councillors. It would be possible, for example, to appoint a women's advisory committee, whose role was to ensure that service committees took full account of issues of sex equality before reaching decisions; or an advisory committee of local businessmen to ensure that service committees took account of local commercial considerations.

5.101 In some cases advisory committees might not be the most effective means of taking advice from non-councillors. They will tend to be cumbersome where the need is simply to involve one or two outside experts. Also they might sometimes be too distant from the decision taking process, not allowing a direct dialogue with the councillors on the decision taking committees. Accordingly we consider that councils should, if they wish, be able to invite advisers to attend meetings of decision taking committees. It would be for each council to decide the terms of such attendance (for instance whether there should be standing invitation to attend meetings on a regular basis or whether invitations should be for particular meetings), but such attendance would not constitute committee membership and would not involve the right to vote. Given this purely advisory role we do not propose a statutory limit on numbers of advisers. We would hope however that they are kept within reasonable limits. Local authorities should make the names of advisers publicly available together with the terms of their attendance. The minutes of meetings should record their presence. The attendance of advisers at meetings would be additional to, and not a substitute for, the attendance of officers. Officers would remain the primary source of advice for councillors.

5.102   The status of advisers attending committees should be distinct not only from that of councillors, but also from the public at large. We are concerned that some committees currently have what are known as 'observers' who sit at the same table as the committee but do not have rights to speak or vote. The reason why observer status is created appears to be that it enables people who are disqualified from being councillors, and therefore cannot be formally co-opted, to attend committee meetings. Trade union representatives who are disqualified from council membership by virtue of being council employees are such an instance. We believe that this blurs roles and is wrong. We propose that advisers attending meetings should not be persons who are themselves disqualified from council membership (subject to the possible need to exempt teachers, which is raised at paragraph 5.106). Those disqualified are listed in section 80 of the Local Government Act 1972 and section 31 of the Local Government (Scotland) Act 1973, and include bankrupts, those who have been surcharged, and—most important numerically—employees of the council[1]. We also propose that no one other than councillors, advisers and officers should be allowed to sit at the committee table; all others should sit in a separate area set aside for the press and public unless invited to address the committee on a particular agenda item.

5.103   Our proposals on co-option are based on general principles of accountability. They therefore apply to all committees alike, including education and police committees. The question arises, however, as to whether those groups who now have statutory rights to, or a tradition of, co-option on such committees (ie the churches, teachers and, except in Scotland, magistrates) should instead have rights to some other form of involvement that is compatible with our proposals. The current statutory arrangements could, for example, be replaced by new ones requiring co-option on to advisory committees, or appointment as advisers on to the main decision taking committees. Alternatively special consultative arrangements could be introduced. In the case of teachers, there is a subsidiary question of whether they should continue to be exempt from the general rule that employees of local authorities may not be co-opted on to their committee.

5.104   Although most of the evidence we have received has been opposed to co-option, or has expressed reservations about it, the evidence from the

---

[1] It should be noted that the legislation deals separately with qualification and disqualification. It is for instance necessary to live or work in the area to be qualified for council membership. We are not proposing that advisers should be qualified for membership, only that they should not be disqualified.

churches and the teaching associations has supported co-option. These groups have argued that they can make, and have made, a significant contribution to the education service by virtue of their special experience and expertise. The Magistrates Association decided not to submit evidence about their co-option rights but the Association of Chief Police Officers has said that magistrates make a valuable contribution to police committees.

5.105 We find these special claims very difficult to assess. For example, we can appreciate arguments for the special involvement of teachers and churches in the education service, but see no obvious reason why they should have rights to co-option which parents do not. Our perspective is a local authority wide one, and we have not examined the working of the individual services in sufficient detail to come to a recommendation. We therefore believe that the Government should review the position of education and police committees in the light of the individual services to determine whether a special deliberative or consultative role should be given to teachers, the churches and magistrates. The review should consider the two services separately on their own merits. It should be an aim of the reviews, if special arrangements are to continue, to simplify them and gives them greater consistency and coherence than the present arrangements. It is difficult to see why magistrates should have co-option rights in England and Wales, but not in Scotland. Equally there seems no obvious reason why teachers and churches should be specified in the Scottish legislation, but not in England and Wales.

5.106 In the case of teachers the review should also consider whether they should be exempted from our proposed rule that persons disqualified from council membership should not attend meetings of committees as advisers. In principle we are opposed to exceptions being made, which would undermine the strength of the general rule. We consider, however, that further study is warranted in view of the long-standing arrangements for teacher involvement in the work of education committees. We stress that, whatever is decided on this point, it is not being suggested that local authorities should not seek the advice of teachers. It is only the proper arrangements for such advice that are in question.

5.107 In summary we recommend that:

(a) the legislation should be amended so that:

(i) decision taking committees and sub-committees may consist only of councillors, and in particular only councillors may vote on such committees;

(ii) local authorities may invite advisers to attend meetings of decision taking committees on such terms as they may determine but without the right to vote;

(iii) the names of advisers should be made publicly known, together with the terms of their attendance at meetings;

(iv) anyone else attending meetings of committees should sit in an area separately set aside for the press and public, unless specifically asked to address the committee on a particular agenda item;

(v) advisers attending meetings may not be persons disqualified from council membership (subject to (b)(ii) below).

(Paragraphs 5.92 to 5.102)

(b) in view of the current arrangements for magistrates in relation to police committees and for the churches and teachers in relation to education committees, the Government should review whether these groups should continue to have some special rights in relation to the police and education services. This review should be on the basis that:

(i) any continued role should be purely deliberative or consultative, and should not involve voting rights on decision taking committees, nor should it conflict in any other way with the rules at a(i) to (iv) above;

(ii) in principle the rule at a(v) above should also apply; however, in view of the special circumstances of teachers the review should consider whether they should be able to attend meetings as advisers even though they would be disqualified from council membership by virtue of being employees of the council.

(Paragraph 5.103 to 5.107)

STANDING ORDERS AND LOCAL CONVENTIONS

Current practice

5.108   The procedures of local authorities are governed primarily by their own standing orders. These cover matters such as the calling of meetings, rights to propose motions, the closure of debate, declaration of interests, delegation to committees and the appointment of officers. Some of these matters are the subject of legislation, in which case the standing orders must be consistent with such legislation. On other matters local authorities may devise such standing orders as they wish. Model Standing Orders have been issued by the Government, but they have no force and indeed have not been revised since 1963. Local authorities' standing orders have the force of law. The courts require a local authority to comply with its own standing orders, and decisions taken in breach of them may be declared invalid.

5.109   Many procedural matters in individual local authorities are not the subject of standing orders, but nevertheless are the subject of conventions. These conventions typically impinge on the relationships between the party groups, and between the party groups and senior officers. They may for example deal with the question of party balance on committees, of minority party relations with senior officers, of relationsips between committee chairmen and chief officers and of the level of seniority at which officer/member contact should take place. Our research shows that conventions of some kind exist in about 30% of authorities[1].

5.110   Generally conventions are implicit rather than explicit, and have not been committed to paper because the need to do so has not arisen. Recently, however, such implicit conventions have come under challenge as a consequence of the changing political climate. In some cases it has been the result of a sudden influx of new councillors with a different view of their role, and in others the result of a sharpening of relations between the Conservative and

---

[1] Leach et al, *Research Volume I*, Table A32.

Labour parties. We would however not wish to underestimate the role of the Alliance parties. Our survey of councillors shows that Alliance councillors are significantly younger than those of the other parties and hold distinct views on a number of issues[1]. They have increasingly challenged consensus arrangements between the main parties. This is well illustrated by the recent case of *R v Hyndburn Borough Council ex parte Strak 17 December 1985 unreported* where an Alliance councillor challenged an arrangement under which the Conservative and Labour party leaders held joint informal briefing meetings with senior officers. The increased electoral success of the Alliance has also resulted in an increased number of hung councils where the old conventions, which were based on a party having an overall majority, have no longer been applicable. In some of these hung authorities, Cheshire County Council being a pioneering example, new conventions have not only been developed but have been committed to paper. We attach the current version of Cheshire's conventions at Annex H as an example.

The need for clear rules

5.111 We attach considerable importance both to standing orders and to written local conventions. It is apparent that the 'rules of the game' have broken down in many authorities and need, in some agreed form, to be re-established. Most of the evidence we have received has argued for a strengthening of the rights of minority parties through the introduction of clear safeguards. We are not saying here that rules have necessarily been abused, although there are some instances where this may be so. Nor are we saying that it is wrong that existing conventions have been challenged. We do however believe that there is a need for greater clarity and certainty, and the Society of Local Authority Chief Executives (SOLACE), especially their London branch, put this point to us particularly strongly in their written and oral evidence. In most cases this can be achieved by local authorities themselves reviewing their procedures, ensuring that their standing orders are clear and fair, and supplementing them by written conventions on matters not appropriate for standing orders. We believe that there are also a few issues where there should be national statutory safeguards based on current best practice. This twin approach is developed below.

Statutory standing orders

5.112 We have looked at a selection of the standing orders of individual authorities, and have generally been struck by their fairness and thoroughness. Most have followed the broad format of the Model Standing Orders. Insofar as they have departed from them it has generally been to give enhanced rights to minority parties. On some key issues we have been sufficiently struck by the provisions adopted by individual authorities to believe that these should be adopted by all local authorities. We propose therefore that there should be a basic core of statutory standing orders.

5.113 This approach is not new. Schedule 12 to the Local Government Act 1972 and Schedule 7 to the Local Government (Scotland) Act 1973 already lay down a number of basic statutory rules for the conduct of meetings. We envisage an extension of these rules. The precise legislative technique will need

[1] SCPR, *Research Volume II*, Tables 4.5, 7.2, 7.9, 7.12, 7.15, 7.17 and 7.23.

to be considered further. It might be excessively rigid to list the rules in primary legislation and preferable to introduce a power for the Secretary of State to prescribe rules by statutory instrument. This would facilitate periodic alteration to the rules in the light of changing circumstances. It also needs to be considered whether the precise working of the standing orders should be prescribed, or simply the purpose which local authorities should achieve in standing orders of their own devising. This would depend largely on the extent to which the standing order in question is self-contained. Whichever technique is followed the requirement should be clearly stated, and any decision taken by a local authority in breach of the requirement should be illegal.

5.114   Clearly such an approach must be limited to a few key rules which are sufficiently fundamental to justify legislative action and which by their nature are nationally applicable. We believe that two of the matters on which we have already made recommendations are suited to this treatment, and they are listed at paragraphs 5.115 and 5.116. Paragraphs 5.117 to 5.126 go on to list five further matters which we propose should be the subject of statutory standing orders.

(i) Composition of decision taking committees

5.115   We have already recommended (paragraph 5.54) that local authorities' standing orders should provide for *pro rata* membership of committees and sub-committees with decision taking powers.

(ii) Chairman's action

5.116   We have already recommended (paragraph 5.78) that committees should be able to delegate functions to their chairmen subject to certain statutory safeguards. We believe that these safeguards should be incorporated in local authorities' standing orders.

(iii) Question time

5.117   We attach importance to question time as a means by which minority parties and 'backbench' councillors can not only obtain information but also call the majority party to account. It is a tradition which stems from a ministerial style of government, but one which is also well established within the framework of the current local government system. The Model Standing Orders make basic provision for councillors to address questions to the leader and committee chairmen at the beginning of council meetings. Some individual local authorities have taken this further in their own standing orders with a fixed time set aside for questions (typically between 30 and 60 minutes), and the right to ask supplementary questions. The former Greater London Council's standing order (B19) was a good example:

QUESTIONS

'B19—By notice given to the director-general and clerk to the Council in writing by 1pm on the penultimate working day before a meeting, any member may put questions (not more than two in total) to the Leader of the Council or chairmen of committees about matters for which committees are responsible. No question without such notice shall be asked except a question of urgent importance, of which the Chairman

97

shall be arbiter. Questions must be accompanied by a copy of any document to which they refer. If questions are unsuitable in form, frivolous or derogatory to the dignity of the Council they shall be disallowed. Not more than two supplemental questions arising directly out of the reply shall be allowed by the Chairman, and for the first of these the original questioner shall have priority. Question time shall be restricted to one hour.'

5.118 We propose that it should be a requirement for all authorities to provide in their standing orders for question time at council meetings. The precise form of the requirement would need further consideration, but it should be limited to questions from councillors as opposed to questions from the public gallery. The arrangements should provide for:

(a) a reasonable time limit (at least 30 minutes);

(b) questions to be handed to the chief executive and addressed to the leader or the chairman of the responsible committee;

(c) a reply to be given unless there is good reason to the contrary (eg confidentiality);

(d) a right to at least one supplementary question, with the questioner having priority.

(iv) Minority party business

5.119 Some local authorities have procedures to ensure that minority parties are able to get issues of their choice debated at committee and council meetings. In some cases this is by a right of 'requisition' whereby a given number of councillors can require that a matter for decision by a sub-committee should be referred for debate to its parent committee, or should similarly be referred from a committee to the council. There is a risk that a statutory right of requisition might result in decisions being delayed in some authorities. A determined minority might be able to bring council business to an effective halt. We prefer the approach adopted by Westminster City Council. They have the following standing order, which enables a matter to be selected by the minority party for debate without delaying any decisions.

'6. MINORITY PARTY BUSINESS AT COUNCIL MEETINGS

(1) At each ordinary meeting of the Council, the largest minority party shall after the completion of the report of the Policy and Resources Committee, be entitled to use up to forty minutes excluding any time taken by a chairman or his nominee in reply to the debate for discussion on one topic of their choice being an item on the agenda for that Council meeting other than a motion of which written notice has been given in accordance with S.O.11(5).

(2) The Leader of the Opposition shall notify the Chief Executive at least seven days (excluding Saturdays and Sundays) prior to the date of the relevant meeting of the Council of the choice of item.

(3) Debate on any item brought forward in accordance with this Standing Order shall not exceed 40 minutes excluding any time taken by a chairman or his nominee in reply to the debate.

(4) Not later than the expiration of 40 minutes from the commencement of minority party business the person presiding shall call upon the appropriate chairman or his nominee to exercise his right of reply. If at the expiration of 40 minutes a person other than the chairman or his nominee is speaking he shall resume his seat immediately.

(5) For the avoidance of doubt the rules as to conduct of debate shall apply during minority party business, subject to the modifications required by this Standing Order.'

5.120 We propose that all local authorities should be required to include in their standing orders provision whereby minority parties have a right to select an item for inclusion on the agenda and debate at council meetings, with a minimum allotment of time (say 30 minutes). Where there are several minority parties the right should not be limited to the largest but should rotate between them *pro rata* to their strength on the council.

(v) Disorderly conduct

5.121 The Model Standing Orders provide that the chairman must clear the public gallery in the event of disturbance, and this provision has been widely followed in the standing orders of individual authorities. For example Sheffield City Council's standing order 23 reads as follows:

'DISTURBANCE BY MEMBERS OF THE PUBLIC

23. If a member of the public interrupts proceedings the Lord Mayor shall warn him. If he continues the interruption or repeatedly interrupts, the Lord Mayor shall order his removal from the Council Chamber. In case of general disturbance in any part of the Chamber open to the public the Lord Mayor shall order that part to be cleared.'

5.122 We have been concerned to hear of disturbances at meetings of councils, especially in some London boroughs, and in some cases this appears to have amounted to intimidation. It is important that there should be no suspicion of connivance by the chair in such disturbances, and accordingly that there should be a duty on the chairman to bring them to a halt. We propose that there should be a requirement for all standing orders to include provision to that end.

(vi) Appointment of staff

5.123 Some local authorities currently provide in their standing orders for the appointment of staff, making clear the procedures to be followed and the person or committee to be responsible for the decisions. The example below is from the standing orders of Northamptonshire County Council:

'APPOINTMENT, ETC, OF OFFICERS

55. On a vacancy occurring in any post, other than that of chief officer or deputy chief officer, which is included in the approved establishment of a department and the salary for which:

(a) is in accordance with one or more of the scales of salaries recommended from time to time by the National Joint Council for

Local Authorities' Administrative, Professional, Technical and Clerical Services, or

(b) is in accordance with one or more grades of any other national or local scale of salaries which has been approved and adopted by the Council, or

(c) has been otherwise fixed by the Council,

such vacancy shall be filled, subject to the approval of the Chief Executive, by the chief officer provided that all appointments at assistant chief officer level shall be reported for the information of the Personnel and Management Services Sub-Committee of the Policy and Resources Committee.

56. A vacancy occurring in the post of chief officer or deputy chief officer shall be filled by the Council provided, however, that the Council may empower the Policy and Resources Committee to fill the vacancy.

57. Whenever a vacancy in any office shall occur the Policy and Resources Committee may temporarily appoint some person to carry on the duties of the office until a successor be duly appointed, and may fix the remuneration to be paid to such person.

58. When there are more than two candidates for appointment by a committee and the first voting does not produce a majority of votes in favour of any candidate, the candidate having the least number of votes shall be struck off the list and a fresh voting shall take place; and so on until a majority of the members present and voting shall be obtained in favour of one candidate. The voting shall be by show of hands or, if demanded by at least five members, by ballot. Thereupon the election of such candidate shall be proposed by resolution.'

5.124 It seems to us desirable that there are clear procedures on staff appointments, and that all authorities should be required to include their procedures in their standing orders. We shall discuss the content of these procedures later in Chapter Six.

(vii) Suspension of standing orders

5.125 Where a local authority is statutorily required to include matters in their standing orders it is not open to the authority to suspend the standing orders concerned. Local authorities may however suspend other standing orders, and it is normal for the standing orders to include some safeguard against abuse. The Model Standing Orders require that at least half of the council members must be present if a motion is to be moved without notice to suspend standing orders. Some local authorities apply no special test so that standing orders can be suspended summarily on a simple majority of those present. Others require that there should be a two-thirds majority of those present and voting as in the example below from Strathclyde Regional Council:

'SUSPENSION OF STANDING ORDERS

39. Any of the Standing Orders, upon motion made at any time during a meeting, may be suspended so far as regards any business at such meeting

provided that two thirds of the members of the Council present and voting shall so decide.'

5.126   We think it undesirable that procedural rules should be capable of change in mid meeting by suspension of standing orders. Some safeguard is required. We are not convinced that either the Model Standing Orders or the Strathclyde example are of themselves sufficient, and propose that standing orders should not be capable of suspension or amendment without advance notice of motion except on the vote of two-thirds of the membership of the council. All standing orders should be statutorily required to include such a limitation.

5.127 We therefore recommend that:

local authorities should be statutorily required to include in their standing orders provisons:

(i) to ensure that the composition of decision taking committees reflects the membership of the whole council;

(ii) to include the procedures recommended at paragraph 5.78(i) to (iv) for the taking of decisions by chairmen of committees between meetings;

(iii) to set aside a period at council meetings for question time;

(iv) to set aside a period at council meetings for business chosen by the minority parties;

(v) to require clearance of the public gallery in the event of disturbances;

(vi) to set out responsibility for the appointment of staff;

(vii) to safeguard against summary suspension of standing orders.

(Paragraphs 5.112 to 5.126)

Local conventions

5.128   We have been impressed by the evidence we have heard from the Association of County Councils and SOLACE about local conventions. We see an important role for local conventions in dealing with those matters where the need is for clear rules but which are not sufficiently susceptible to legal definition to lend themselves to standing orders, and on which there is too great a variety of local circumstances for national codes of conduct to be appropriate. The matters that are suitable for such conventions will vary between authorities, but we would suggest the following:

(a) the detailed basis on which committee places are apportioned among councillors;

(b) channels for councillor contact with officers;

(c) the relationship between committee chairmen and chief officers;

(d) responsibility for agenda;

(e) the rights of councillors to obtain information and advice from officers;

(f) any arrangements for informal working groups or regular briefing meetings with officers which are not formally constituted as committees of the council;

(g) attendance of officers at party groups;

(h) the allocation of support services to councillors;

(i) the status of any staff attached to the political groups or individual councillors.

In so far as these conventions relate to councillor/officer relations we discuss them further in Chapter Six, and make more specific recommendations about their content.

5.129 We are in no doubt about the desirability of local authorities drawing up such conventions, and of their being made publicly available. It is however for consideration whether they should be statutorily required to do so, and if so whether a requirement should also be introduced to have regard to those conventions in the conduct of business. It would be possible to provide further that failure to have regard to the conventions, while not of itself an offence, should be taken into consideration in any proceedings that might arise before a court or a tribunal.

5.130 On balance we believe that the conventions should be on a non-statutory basis. The danger of giving them a statutory status would be that the conventions would be over cautious and avoid some of the more problematic relationships. Even without statutory status, the local ombudsman would generally take such conventions into account in deciding whether maladministration had occured. The extent to which local authorities develop conventions, and their content, could usefully be monitored to see whether greater formalisation of their status appears desirable.

5.131 We recommend therefore that:

each local authority should draw up, and make publicly available, conventions setting out the working relationships between the political parties and between councillors and officers in so far as such issues are not covered by standing orders .

(Paragraphs 5.129 and 5.130)

CHAPTER 6

COUNCILLORS AND OFFICERS: ROLES AND RELATIONSHIPS

INTRODUCTION

6.1 The last Chapter focussed on the statutory arrangements for decision taking, and as such was concerned primarily with relationships between councillors—in particular between majority and minority parties. This reflects the fact that the current legal framework, which we propose should be retained, vests functions in councillors and not (with very limited exceptions) in officers. This is in contrast to the arrangements in other countries (discussed in paragraphs 5.27 to 5.29) whereby city and county managers have formal powers in their own right to take all day-to-day administrative decisions. Whatever the formal legal position in Great Britain, however, the operation of our local government system depends in practice—just as much as it does elsewhere—on a successful complementary relationship between councillors and officers.

6.2 In this Chapter we change our perspective, looking less at the decision taking process and more at ways in which this complementary relationship between councillors and officers can be achieved. In doing so we look first at councillors and then at officers, more particularly senior officers, but the discussion of one is relevant to the other. Our aim is to recommend arrangements which will help clarify their roles and hence provide for more stable relationships. Such clarity and stability should be of mutual benefit to both, and we do not see their interests as being in any way incompatible. We are however conscious of three constraints.

6.3 First, we must devise our solutions within a corporate statutory framework for decision taking. This framework gives rise to a number of ambiguities. These ambiguities, which we shall develop later, stem from three things;

(a) the councillor, unlike an MP, has a dual role: he is simultaneously a representative of the local community and responsible in law for the delivery of services;

(b) while the senior officer has little or no formal legal responsibility for delivering services, in practice he has been traditionally regarded as responsible for the day-to-day management of those services;

(c) the senior officer in law serves the council as a whole, but must propose, advise on, and carry out, decisions that are often effectively determined by the majority party alone.

We must accept that the current local government model, for all its strength, is not one which lends itself to total clarity in roles and relationships. We can ease the problems that might arise from these ambiguities, but cannot totally remove them.

6.4 Second, we are in a period where there is no single accepted norm of local democracy. Traditionally the councillor represents and serves the community as a whole—an approach which pre-supposes some homogeneity in the community. Increasingly however there are signs of the community manifesting itself as an aggregate of sectional interests, and this calls the representative role of the councillor into question.

6.5   Third, as has been remarked on earlier, traditional relationships and conventions are being challenged and new ones devised. In particular the role of the professional chief officer is being questioned by councillors who wish to intervene more in day-to-day management, often seeing the style of implementation of a policy as part of the policy itself rather than a separate process; this can be seen in proposals for decentralisation of services and for hiving off to outside contractors. In such a period of flux there will always be some instability.

6.6   Nevertheless, despite these constraints we believe that a number of measures can and should be taken to clarify roles and stabilise relationships, and these are developed in this Chapter.

COUNCILLORS, REPRESENTATIVE DEMOCRACY AND PUBLIC DUTY

6.7   The traditional role of a councillor as representative of, and servant of, the local community is set out in the National Code of Local Government Conduct of 1975. This Code, which is quoted in full at Annex I, is based on a draft recommended by the Redcliffe-Maud Committee of Local Government Conduct[1] and was agreed by central government and the local authority associations. Paragraph 2 of the Code reads as follows:

'2.   PUBLIC DUTY AND PRIVATE INTEREST

(i)   Your over-riding duty as a councillor is to the whole local community.

(ii)   You have a special duty to your own constituents, including those who did not vote for you.

(iii)   Whenever you have a private or personal interest in any question which councillors have to decide, you must not do anything to let that interest influence the decision.

(iv)   Do nothing as a Councillor which you could not justify to the public.

(v)   The reputation of your council, and of your party if you belong to one, depends on your conduct and what the public believes about your conduct.

(vi)   It is not enough to avoid actual impropriety; you should at all times avoid any occasion for suspicion or the appearance of improper conduct.'

6.8   The councillor's duty as set out in the Code presupposes that the local community is reasonably homogeneous. In practice the community is not a single entity but an aggregate of interlocking interests. Nevertheless it has been the assumption of 20th century local democracy that the community has sufficient unifying factors for it to form an identifiable entity which a councillor can represent. As is described in the paper prepared for us by John Gyford[2], this assumption is now less certain. Society is becoming increasingly sectionalised,

---

[1] Report of the Committee on Conduct in Local Government, 1974. Cmnd 5636.
[2] Gyford, *Research Volume IV*.

and this poses problems for the councillors' representative role. Sectional interests may take many different forms—trade unions, environmental groups, ratepayers' associations, chambers of commerce, tenants' associations, racial and sexual minorities, farmers groups, etc. In some cases sectional interests now have a direct input into local government, by-passing the councillor (eg through co-option and consultation). In others sectional interests are bringing pressure to bear through councillors, who thereby find it more difficult to adopt a balanced relationship with the local community. The position becomes even more complex where such groups exercise influence through the local political parties, especially where there are close relationships between the local party organisation and the party group on the council. A chain of loyalties can build up whereby a sectional group influences the local party, who influence the councillors of that party, whose vote is decisive in a decision of the council. In its extreme form the position of the councillor is reduced to that of a delegate.

6.9   Such relationships are part of the process of democracy and exist also at national level. The position in local government is, however, crucially different in that councillors are not only the representatives of the local community but they also are directly responsible for taking decisions on services which affect the community. If the links in chains of loyalties become too rigid a situation can arise where the decisions of the council are being determined by outside sectional interests. Opposing sectional interests may feel shut out of the system, or feel the need to compete through similar mechanisms.

6.10   The 1975 National Code does not deal adequately with such issues. It was issued in the wake of scandals where councillors had been motivated by personal gain. As such it is concerned with conflicts between 'public duty' and 'private interest'. This dichotomy does not recognise the potential conflict between public duty and loyalties to sectional interests that are not motivated by private gain. There is nothing inherently improper in loyalties of this kind. They may of themselves be altruistic (eg loyalty to a voluntary body), and they may in practice coincide with the wider community interest. The problem arises where outside sectional loyalties are allowed to dictate council policy as if they were coterminous with the community interest.

6.11   Councillors should not only be representatives of the community, but should be representative of it. We certainly do not, therefore, believe that the solution to this problem lies in disqualifying those with sectional interests from becoming councillors. The dangers to democracy of excluding people from being councillors are hardly less than those of including them. Nor, with very limited exceptions, do we believe that further disabilities should be placed on those who are councillors simply because they have other loyalties. We do however believe that more needs to be done to ensure that outside loyalties should not determine council decisions and we shall make proposals below.

COUNCILLORS AND THE NATIONAL CODE OF LOCAL GOVERNMENT CONDUCT
Introduction
6.12   We believe that the 1975 National Code of Local Government Conduct serves a valuable purpose in encouraging proper conduct by councillors and

should be retained. However, there are two important respects in which the content should be amended to set out more clearly and precisely what the duties of councillors are. Its status also needs to be enhanced so that it is more effective. We deal with these matters in turn below.

The content of the Code

6.13   Later in this Chapter, we shall be commenting on some detailed aspects of the content of the Code. We limit ourselves here to two major issues of principle arising from the first two paragraphs of the Code (the current version of which is at Annex I).

(i) The councillor and the law

6.14   We attach fundamental importance to the need for councillors to act within the law. In our Interim Report[1] we stated five general principles one of which was:

> '*Local government should act within the law*
>
> Local authorities derive their powers from statute and do not exist independently of it. This means that, although they may properly lobby for changes in the law, in their day-to-day conduct of affairs they must act within the law as it stands'.

While this statement is expressed in terms of local authorities collectively we believe that it applies equally to individual councillors and groups of councillors. What concerns us is not only the actual breach of the law by local authorities, but the making of election promises which are only capable of achievement through breach of the law. It may be argued that no citizen can in conscience undertake to obey the law regardless of circumstance. The position of councillors is, however, distinct from that of other citizens. They hold office only by virtue of the law and should abide by the law for as long as they continue to hold that office. If circumstances arise where they cannot abide by the law they can, and should, resign.

6.15   Accordingly the first paragraph of the 1975 Code should be replaced by a much stronger statement of the councillor's duty to act within the law. It should make clear that councillors owe their position to the law, that they may lobby for changes in the law, but that they should act within the law as it stands. They should abide by national legislation and common law, and the council's own standing orders. If in doubt as to the law they should consult the council's officers.

(ii) Public duty and conflicting interests

6.16   In paragraph 6.7 we quoted paragraph 2 of the 1975 Code, which is based on a dichotomy between public duty and private interest. We went on to point out that it does not deal with sectional loyalties that are not motivated by personal gain but that many nevertheless conflict with a councillor's public duty. In

---

[1] 'Local Authority Publicity', 1975, paragraph 34.

order to deal with this point we propose that the opening of paragraph 2 of the Code should be amended so as to read (the amended words are in italics):

'2. PUBLIC DUTY AND *CONFLICTING INTERESTS*

(i)   Your over-riding duty as a councillor is to the whole local community.

(ii)   You have a special duty to your own constituents including those who did not vote for you.

(iii)   Whenever you have *any other interest or loyalty* in any question which councillors have to decide, you must not do anything to let that interest *or loyalty* influence the decision.'

The opening of paragraph 3 would need consequential amendment, and should make clear that the existence of conflicts of interest is a matter of fact and degree. While the pursuit of interests arising from private pecuniary gain will always be wrong, the pursuit of sectional loyalties will generally not raise such clear cut issues. Certainly, we would not wish to suggest for example that simple loyalty to a political party of itself raises improprieties. The need is for councillors to be aware of the wide range of interests and loyalties that **may** create conflicts, and to be open about them. We shall return at paragraph 6.52 to the question of disabilities arising from such interests.

The status of the Code

(i) Current position

6.17   The 1975 Code of Conduct has no force of law, but the local ombudsmen[1] have made it clear in their reports that they normally regard breach of the code as maladministration in so far as the Code relates to matters within their ambit. Recent research[2] suggests that the Code has been formally adopted by 82% of authorities and is made use of, without formal adoption, in a further 12%. There is some evidence that the adoption of the Code is taken into account by the ombudsman. Of those authorities who have adopted the Code, 86% bring it to the attention of councillors after election. Forty eight per cent include it in their councillor's handbook or similar publication. Only 17% of authorities **regularly** bring it to their councillors' attention, and our own impression has been that councillors are not as conscious of the Code as should be the case.

(ii) Statutory prescription of the Code

6.18   Clearly the rules set out in the Code cannot and should not be given the force of law, for its purpose is to deal with those matters which by their nature are not sufficiently clear-cut to be given statutory force. We do, however, believe that the Code should be given greater prominence. There are various precedents for codes having statutory status without having the force of law. In particular section 4 of the Local Government Act 1986 provides for the Secretary of State to prescribe a 'code of recommended practice' on publicity. It must be drawn up in consultation with the local authority associations and approved by Parliament. Under the Bill as originally introduced local authorities would have been

---

[1] A definition of the powers of the local ombudsman, and proposals to strengthen them, is contained in Chapter Nine.
[2] 'The Administration of Standards of Conduct in Local Government', by Alan Parker, Aidan Rose and John Taylor, 1986 (to be published by Charles Knight). This research only applies to England and Wales.

required 'to have regard' to the code. This requirement was deleted, against the Government's advice, in the House of Lords. The Government have announced their intention to restore it by amending legislation. The peers who argued successfully in debate for deletion of the requirement did so on the grounds that it was unenforceable.

6.19   We have ourselves said in Chapter Four that there is no point in introducing rules that are not capable of enforcement. The 1975 Code, unlike the publicity code, is enforceable by the local ombudsman—who generally regards its breach as constituting maladministration. Accordingly, without passing any comment on the status of the publicity code, we think it correct that councils should be statutorily required to have regard to the 1975 Code. The Code should be prescribed by the Secretary of State following consultation with the local authority associations and should be subject to Parliamentary approval. Individual councillors as well as local authorities collectively should be statutorily required to have regard to it. Moreover, to put the question of enforcement beyond doubt the statute should state explicitly that breach of the Code would constitute prima facie maladministration in so far as the Code comes within the ombudsman's ambit.

(iii) The declaration on accepting office

6.20   The status of the Code could be further enhanced by a requirement that all councillors should subscribe to it in writing when first elected. A proposal to this effect was made by the Labour Party in their written evidence and also by the Federated Union of Managerial and Professional Officers (FUMPO). The proposal needs to be considered in the broader context of the declaration which a councillor must currently make on acceptance of office. At present all councillors in England and Wales are statutorily required on election to sign the following declaration:

> 'I . . ., having been elected to the office of . . . hereby declare that I take the said office upon myself, and will duly and faithfully fulfill the duties thereof according to the best of my judgement and ability'.[1]

6.21   We believe that there is much value in a declaration of this kind, because it is an outward demonstration of the fact that election to the council involves assumption of an executive office carrying with it a public duty. We consider that it should also apply in Scotland and that the declaration should be made in solemn form, ie on oath or by affirmation. It should have similar status to the oath sworn (or affirmation made) by juries. The present wording of the declaration is general, and arguably platitudinous, and it needs to be considered whether it should be more specific as to what the public duty of being a councillor entails. There is, however, a danger that if this were taken too far it might tend to debar people of genuine conscience who may be unable to commit themselves to the precise formulation of the wording.

6.22   Because of this last consideration we do not believe that the declaration could reasonably be framed so as to require councillors to abide by the Code of Conduct. We must bear in mind that the rules of the Code do not have the force of

---

[1] Schedule 3 to the Local Elections (Principal Areas) Rules 1973.

law, and by its nature the Code deals with matters not thought appropriate for legal sanctions. Nor do we believe that there could be an open-ended declaration relating to possible further amendments of the Code. But we see no reason why the declaration should not require councillors to 'have regard to' the Code 'currently prescribed'. The necessary words should be added at the end of the current declaration.

Recommendations

6.23 We therefore recommend that:

(a) the National Code of Local Government conduct should be amended to make clear that:

(i)   the councillors hold office by virtue of the law and must act within the law;

(ii)   sectional loyalties as well as private gain may create conflicts with councillors' public duty.

(Paragraphs 6.15 and 6.16)

(b)   the Code should be statutorily prescribed by the Secretary of State following consultation with the local authority associations;

(Paragraph 6.19)

(c)   it should be made statutorily explicit that breach of the Code constitutes prima facie maladministration;

(Paragraph 6.19)

(d)   all local authorities and councillors should statutorily be required to have regard to the Code;

(Paragraph 6.19)

(e)   individual councillors should also undertake to have regard to the Code as part of their statutory declaration on accepting office;

(Paragraph 6.22)

(f)   the declaration on accepting office should:

(i)   be extended to Scotland;

(ii)   be made in solemn form.

(Paragraph 6.21)

THE DISQUALIFICATION RULES FOR COUNCIL MEMBERSHIP

The present position

6.24   Section 80(1) of the Local Government Act 1972 provides that a person is disqualified from being a member of a local authority if he or she holds any paid office of employment, appointments to which may be made or confirmed by that authority. This means for example that a teacher employed by a shire county council may not be elected to that council (but may be elected to a district council or a neighbouring county council).

6.25 Section 80(1) of the 1972 Act further provides that if a person works for a joint committee or board (ie one appointed by more than one authority) he or she is disqualified from standing for election to any of the authorities making nominations to that committee or board. This last principle has now been applied (by section 35 of the Local Government Act 1985) to the joint authorities which have taken over responsibilities, as from 1 April 1986, from the former metropolitan county councils. These joint authorities are appointed by the district councils concerned. In consequence for example a firefighter employed by a new joint fire authority may not become (or continue to be) a district councillor anywhere in the area covered by the authority. Although the position is not statutorily explicit, the Department of the Environment have said that this prohibition does not apply to employees of county wide passenger transport executives because they are employed by the executive not the authority, and hence a step further removed from councillors.

6.26 The legislation in Scotland is slightly different. Section 31(1) of the Local Government (Scotland) Act 1973 provides that a person shall be disqualified from being a member of a local authority if he or she, or a business partner, holds any paid office or employment (other than the office of chairman) or other place of profit in the gift or disposal of

(a)   the authority itself; or

(b)   any joint committee or joint board the expenses of which are defrayed in part by the authority.

6.27 These rules (as they applied then) were reviewed by the Redcliffe-Maud Committee.[1] They considered that they should not be relaxed, and in particular pointed out the difficulties of selective relaxation in areas where there appeared to be anomalies. They also considered a possible widening of the rules so as to disqualify from membership anyone who was an employee of **any** local authority (eg one of a different tier). They did not recommend such an exclusion, but said:

'Any officer, whether senior or junior, whose work is in any way connected with the decision-making process of his authority and who contemplates seeking election to membership of the authority of the other tier should consider very carefully whether such membership would prejudice his ability to serve, and be recognised as serving, his own authority loyally and impartially as an employee'.

6.28 The Committee have been asked to look particularly at the phenomenon of an employee of one authority being a councillor in another (whether or not of the same tier). We call it for convenience 'twin-tracking'. We also however need to look at the disqualification rules in the round, and are aware that some have argued in their evidence that the rules should be made less rather than more restrictive.

---

[1] Report of the Committee on Conduct in Local Government, 1974. Cmnd 5636, paragraph 113.

'Twin-tracking'

6.29   Our survey of councillors suggests that about 16% of those councillors who are in employment, and about 10% of all councillors, are employees of other local authorities, the majority of these being teachers.[1] There are in all some 3 million local authority employees (full and part-time), 14% of the workforce, including some 500,000 teachers. Local authority employees therefore are not significantly over-represented among councillors, although their numbers might be considered high bearing in mind that they can not stand for their employing authority. The national average however conceals considerable variations between authorities. There will be many authorities where significantly more than 10% of councillors are twin-trackers, and many where significantly less are.

6.30.   Three sources of concern have been expressed in the evidence about the practice of twin-tracking. It has been argued that:

   (a)   councillors might not properly be able to serve the interests of the council on which they sit if they have a separate loyalty as employee of another authority;

   (b)   that employing authorities are giving excessive paid leave to employees who are councillors on other authorities;

   (c)   the fact that officers are councillors of another authority might detract from their ability to serve their employing authority with political impartiality.

6.31.   We do not attach weight to the first argument. Indeed the argument, insofar as it is valid, would apply more strongly to those who are councillors in more than one authority; our survey of councillors shows that this is a more common phenomenon than twin-tracking with 13% of all councillors being councillors of two (or more) authorities.[2] We do not believe that the external loyalty created by being an employee of another authority is any more a cause for prima facie concern than many other external loyalties created by employment that are not the subject of disqualification. For example it would seem quite unjust to disqualify a refuse collector employed by a district council from standing for the county council when a private sector refuse collector working for the district council under contract can stand not only for the county council, but for the district council as well.

6.32.   The second argument does cause us concern, but this concern is not one which gives rise to the need for disqualification. Rather it relates to levels of remuneration, and rules for time-off, which we shall deal with separately later (paragraphs 6.80 to 6.124, and—in particular—paragraph 6.120).

6.33.   The third argument does not relate to the propriety of being a **councillor**, but rather to that of being an **officer**. We believe that senior officers should not be politically active, and as a consequence should not be councillors. Accordingly we shall be recommending that **senior** officers should be statutorily disqualified from being councillors, but that is part of a wider debate about the role of officers which we shall return to later (paragraphs 6.205 to 6.217). It is a con-

---

[1] SCPR, *Research Volume II*, Table 3.8.
[2] SCPR, *Research Volume II*, Table 4.2.

sideration which applies only to about 70,000 local authority employees—less than 3% of the total.

6.34. A more general ban on twin-tracking would deprive 3 million people of the right to be a councillor. This would not only reduce their rights as individual citizens, but would reduce the representativeness of council membership. Few have argued in the evidence for a general ban of this kind, and we do not consider that the arguments described above merit such a ban.

Employees of grant-aided bodies

6.35. The question has also been raised as to whether employees of bodies receiving grants from local authorities should be disqualified from being councillors. This proposition tends to be raised in the context of voluntary organisations receiving funds under section 137 of the Local Government Act 1972 (or section 83 of the Local Government (Scotland) Act 1973). Any disqualification would however need to be framed more broadly if it was to have a logical basis. It would need to apply to voluntary organisations funded under other statutory provisions. It would need also to apply to other bodies, including profit making companies, receiving local authority funding. Lastly it would need to apply to contractual arrangements as well as grants not related to a specific task. It should be noted in this respect that some 40% of local authority funding of voluntary organisations is under contractual arrangements. It can be seen that any logically defensible criterion for disqualification would be very wide-ranging. In order to prevent an unacceptable number of people being caught in the net, it would be necessary to set some rule whereby disqualification only arose if the body concerned received more than a fixed percentage of its income from the local authority. While this would lessen the problem it would lead to invidious positions. A company, in deciding whether to take an increased grant, or a larger contract, from a local authority would have to consider whether this would result in any of its employees being disqualified from being councillors. It would even be possible positively to engineer a disqualification. We do not believe that this is desirable. We do accept that being an employee of a body in receipt of a grant from, or in a contractual relation with, a local authority creates a conflict of interest for a councillor when the grant or contract comes before the council for decision. We do not, however, believe that a general disqualification is warranted. The situation is already covered by the statutory provisions on pecuniary interests (see paragraph 6.40), and the person concerned would therefore not be able to speak or vote in any meeting dealing with the grant or contract. We believe this is sufficient.

Joint authorities

6.36. While we would not wish to see the disqualification rules generally extended, nor do we consider there should be any general widening of council membership. The existing ban on local authority employees being members of their employing council is soundly based. No person in the public sector should be his or her own employer.

6.37 The ban on employees of joint authorities, however, deserves special consideration. We are conscious that this has caused particular concern among all political parties in the context of the new joint authorities in the metropolitan areas. The Association of Metropolitan Authorities have informed us that at least eight district councillors had to resign on 1 April 1986, when the new joint authorities took over from the metropolitan county councils as their employer. The issue, however, arises more generally: there are for example joint police authorities for the three counties of Glamorgan, the two counties of Sussex, and the Highlands and Islands of Scotland.

6.38.   In all the cases mentioned above the joint body in question is a corporate body with a power to precept on the rates. It acts in its own right, not by virtue of delegated powers from the authorities nominating their members. This is also true of joint boards. Their position is quite distinct from joint committees, which are not corporate bodies and act by virtue of powers delegated to them from the authorities nominating their members. We believe that this distinction is crucial. The prohibition on employees of joint committees being members of the nominating authority is soundly based because those employees would be in a position to influence the decisions of the joint committee. There should however be no such prohibition on the employees of joint boards and authorities. Provided that the employees are not themselves nominated to the board or authority, they cannot have any significant influence on the decisions of those bodies simply by being a councillor of a nominating authority. It might be argued that councillors on a nominating council might, through their party group, have some influence on the votes of their colleagues nominated on to the joint authority, and hence on the decisions of that authority. This, however, is too distant a relationship to justify removal of the right to be a councillor. There are many in private sector employment (for example employees of council contractors) who are not debarred from council membership despite a much closer relationship. Where the possibility of a conflict of interest is so distant, it is better dealt with through the rules on declaration of interest (see paragraph 6.40) rather than disqualification. It should be noted that the Scottish legislation already comes close to embodying the distinction we make because it does not disqualify employees of joint committees or boards if they are themselves precepting authorities.

6.39.   We therefore recommend that:

(a)   employees of local authorities should continue to be able to become councillors in other authorities, provided that they are not employed at the rank of principal officer or above;

(Paragraphs 6.30 to 6.34)

(b)   the legislation should be amended to allow employees of joint boards and joint authorities to become councillors on the authorities nominating the members of such boards and authorities provided that they are not themselves nominated to membership.

(Paragraph 6.38)

THE PECUNIARY AND NON-PECUNIARY INTERESTS OF COUNCILLORS

The current position

6.40.   The current legislation distinguishes between pecuniary and non-pecuniary interests. Section 94(1) of the Local Government Act 1972 (section

113

38(1) of the Local Government (Scotland) Act 1973) provides that if a councillor has a pecuniary interest in a contract, proposed contract of other matter being discussed at a local authority meeting at which he or she is present, he or she shall:

(a) declare the interest (unless he or she has given a prior written notice of the interest);

(b) not take part in discussion on the matter;

(c) not vote on the matter.

Breach of these provisions is a criminal offence. The legislation does not require a councillor with a pecuniary interest to withdraw from the meeting, but section 94(4) of the 1972 Act (section 38(3) of the Scottish Act) enables individual local authorities to require withdrawal under their own standing orders.

6.41. No such disabilities apply to non-pecuniary interests, but the 1975 National Code of Local Government Conduct enjoins councillors to treat their non-pecuniary interests as if the statute applied to them.

General principles

6.42. Our approach so far in this Chapter has not been to take a restrictive attitude as to who should be allowed to become a councillor. Clearly if member-ship is to be broad-based it is that much more important for there to be rules ensuring that councillors do not conduct themselves in a manner whereby their outside interests might influence them or be suspected of doing so. At the same time the rules need to take account of the nature of councillors' interests. We drew attention earlier in this Chapter to the growing significance of sectional interests. In some cases such interests will be pecuniary, but in many cases they will not be. For example unpaid membership of the governing body of a volun-tary body or amenity society would not involve any pecuniary interest. The treat-ment of pecuniary interests is generally straightforward. They raise clear-cut issues of impropriety and are amenable to statutory definition. We believe that the current statutory rules described at paragraph 6.40 are broadly correct, although we propose some detailed adjustment of them. Non-pecuniary inter-ests raise more difficult issues. There are cases where such interests will conflict with a councillor's duty just as strongly as pecuniary interests. Insofar as such circumstances can be defined, and we deal with one such instance at paragraph 6.50, we consider that they should be subject to the statutory rules applying to pecuniary interests. The generality of non-pecuniary interests are not, however, amenable to statutory definition, and it would be very difficult to impose statu-tory disabilities on councillors in those instances where they are justified without at the same time preventing people from voting on a wide range of issues where the risk of impropriety is too distant to warrant such disabilities. We think it right therefore that disabilities arising from most non-pecuniary interests should continue to be dealt with by the 1975 Code rather than statute.

6.43. While, however, the broad approach of legislation to pecuniary interests and of the 1975 Code to non-pecuniary interests is correct, we believe that neither place sufficient emphasis on open-ness about interests. As the potential range of conflicting interests becomes wider, and as it becomes more difficult to define where such conflicts arise, it becomes increasingly important that councillors are

114

open about their interests. Other councillors, and the public, can then judge any improper motivation in the way councillors carry out their duties.

Registers of interests

6.44.   The most effective means of achieving open-ness is through registers of interests. The Redcliffe-Maud Committee[1] and Salmon Commission[2] both recommended that there should be a statutory requirement for local authorities to maintain registers of councillors' pecuniary interests. This has not been implemented by the Government. Many councils have however introduced their own registers of interests on a non-statutory basis. Recent research[3] shows that about 50% of local authorities in England and Wales have introduced some form of register of interests. Over 80% of such registers require entry of interests under the following categories:

(a)   land and property owned in the area of the authority;

(b)   companies in which the councillor has an interest greater than a specified minimum;

(c)   all paid employments.

A minority of registers (about 25%) also require entry of non-pecuniary interests.

6.45.   In some cases local authorities have introduced registers in questionnaire form, asking all councillors to state whether or not they have certain specified interests. These cover not only financial matters, but membership of trade unions and voluntary bodies, and also membership of specified societies (eg Freemasons, Rotary Clubs, Royal British Legion). Where this type of register is adopted completion of the register is normally made a pre-condition of membership of committees, a practice which was found to be lawful in the case of *R v Newham London Borough Council, Ex parte Haggerty, 9 April 1985 (unreported).*

6.46.   We are pleased to note that so many local authorities have themselves taken the initiative in introducing registers. Like the Redcliffe-Maud Committee and Salmon Commission, however, we consider that registers should be placed on a statutory basis. This would not only lead to the introduction of registers in authorities which do not have them, but also would provide an upper limit on what registers could require—preventing excessive invasions of privacy.

6.47   We propose therefore that there should be a new statutory requirement for local authorities to maintain a register of interests. Councillors should be required to register any interest **which could reasonably be regarded as likely to affect his or her conduct as a councillor or influence his or her actions, speeches**

---

[1] Report of the Committee on Conduct in Local Government, 1974. Cmnd 5636, paragraphs 55 to 64.
[2] Report of the Royal Commission on Standards of Conduct in Public Life, 1976. Cmnd 6524, paragraphs 163 to 181.
[3] 'The Administration of Standards of Conduct in Local Government', by Alan Parker, Aidan Rose and John Taylor, 1986 (to be published by Charles Knight).

or vote.[1] This should cover pecuniary and non-pecuniary interests. In the case of pecuniary interests the register should specifically require councillors to state any interests in land and property in the area of their authority, all paid employments, and all interests in companies above a specified minimum percentage stake. However, the register should not otherwise be specific as to what 'could reasonably be regarded as likely to affect' a councillor's conduct. This should be left to the individual's judgement, and to such case law as may over time develop. The register should not take the form of a detailed questionnaire of the type described in paragraph 6.45. Registers of interest by their nature involve some loss of privacy, which is part of the price of public life, but we believe that the detailed questionnaires we have seen go much too far in invading privacy without it being clear that the questions asked are sufficiently related to a councillor's duties.

6.48   Councillors who believe that they have no interest meeting the criteria for entry in the register should be required to state this. Failure to complete the register, or the making of an incorrect entry, should be a criminal offence—just as failure to declare an interest orally is at present a criminal offence. Local authorities should, however, not themselves be permitted to impose any disability—such as exclusion from committee membership—for failure to complete the statutory register or any register going beyond the statutory requirement. Legislation should be introduced to reverse the effect of the Newham judgement referred to in paragraph 6.45.

6.49   The statutory responsibility for the upkeep of the register should be placed on the chief executive. The wider implications of this for the post of chief executive are discussed in paragraphs 6.154 to 6.158. The chief executive would be expected to advise councillors on their duty to complete the register, but each councillor would be responsible for his or her own entry. The register should be open to public inspection. Completion of the register would not alter the statutory requirement for councillors to declare interests orally at meetings where they arise, and in this respect would differ from the general written notice arrangements under section 96 of the Local Government Act 1972 (section 40 of the Scottish Act).

Pecuniary interests

(i) The definition of pecuniary interests

6.50   There is one particular set of circumstances likely to give rise to impropriety which we believe can be defined but which is currently not included in the statutory definition of pecuniary interests. The current statutory definition includes those who themselves have a pecuniary interest, including an interest by virtue of employment or through a contractual relationship. It does not, however, appear to include those who, while not having a direct pecuniary interest themselves, are engaged in the promotion of the interests of those who do. This can be illustrated by two examples, one in employment the other in development. An employee of a local authority is at present prohibited from being an elected member of that authority. There is however no such prohibition on someone

---

[1] These words are based on those contained, in analogous circumstances, in section 97(5) of the Local Government Act 1972 (section 41(5) of the Scottish Act), and in the House of Commons Register of Members' Interests.

employed as a full-time officer of a trade union which represents the employees of the local authority. Someone in this position would moreover appear not to be caught by the definition of pecuniary interests because he or she would not stand to gain financially through benefits won for the union's members. Hence he or she would appear to be free in law to vote on issues relating to the pay and condition of the union's members. The other example relates to someone who is acting as a consultant to a developer seeking planning permission. There is nothing at present to stop either the consultant or the developer being councillors, but the developer would certainly be caught by the definition of pecuniary interests and therefore would not be able to vote on any decision on the planning permission. It is less clear that the consultant would be caught as he would not necessarily gain financially from the decision. We believe that the statutory definition of pecuniary interest should be widened so that it clearly includes those who are employed or contracted to promote the pecuniary interests of others.

(ii) Withdrawal from meetings

6.51   At present there is no statutory requirement for someone who has declared an interest at a meeting to withdraw from the room (see paragraph 6.40). We believe that this is wrong. By staying in the room, even though he or she may not speak or vote, a councillor might still influence the decision or might gather information which would help in the furtherance of his or her interest. The Redcliffe-Maud[1] and Salmon[2] Reports both recommended that the councillor should be statutorily required to withdraw, but this was not implemented by the Government. Recent research[3] shows that about 50% of local authorities in England and Wales require withdrawal under their own standing orders, and a further 20% require withdrawal unless the councillor is specifically invited to stay. We propose that there should be a statutory requirement for councillors in all such instances to withdraw. Withdrawal should be from the room, not just to the space set aside for the public. There should be no option to invite councillors to stay, which could place their colleagues in an invidious position.

Non-pecuniary interests

6.52   The 1975 Code (paragraph 3) currently requires councillors to treat non-pecuniary interests precisely as if they were pecuniary ones: that is to say that the councillor should not only declare such interests but also abstain from voting and speaking (and, under our recommendation, withdraw from the room). We do not think this is right. Non-pecuniary interests will sometimes be substantial and clearly justify such disabilities. In other cases they will be much more distant. This can be illustrated by reference to kinship and friendship, which the 1975 Code give as examples of interest which might influence a councillor's judgement. Clearly much would depend in these instances on the closeness of relationship. There might well be an impropriety in voting on a matter affecting one's brother or co-habitee which would not necessarily arise in the case of a

---

[1] Report of the Committee on Conduct in Local Government, 1974. Cmnd 5636, paragraphs 51 to 53.
[2] Report of the Royal Commission on Standards of Conduct in Public Life, 1976. Cmnd 6524, paragraph 156.
[3] 'The Administration of Standards of Conduct in Local Government', by Alan Parker, Aidan Rose and John Taylor, 1986 (to be published by Charles Knight).

more distant relationship. Nevertheless in the latter case it might still be appropriate to declare the interest, so that it is treated openly. The danger is that fewer non-pecuniary interests will be declared if abstention from voting is automatically required following their declaration, and that the 1975 Code will not therefore achieve its desired effect. We propose therefore that paragraph 3 of the Code should differentiate between declaration of interests and disabilities arising from declaration. Non-pecuniary interests should always be declared, even if of a distant nature. The councillor should however only be required to abstain from voting and speaking and, under our recommendation, to withdraw from the room, if the interest is a clear and substantial one. Breach of the 1975 Code constitutes maladministration, and we would expect it soon to become established through the local ombudsman's reports what interests are of such a nature to justify abstention from voting and speaking.

Chairmen of committees and council leaders

6.53   The National Code of Local Government Conduct makes clear that councillors should not chair committees in the subject matter of which they are likely to have a recurring outside interest, whether pecuniary or non-pecuniary. It says:

> 'You should not seek or accept the chairmanship of a committee or sub-committee whose business is closely related to a substantial interest or range of interests of yourself or of any body with which you are associated.'

Breach of the Code would constitute maladministration.

6.54   We have considered whether this should be the subject of a statutory prohibition, but do not consider that the nature of interests that might be relevant—especially those of a non-pecuniary nature—could be sufficiently defined. It is therefore right that the matter should be dealt with in the Code of Conduct.

6.55   We consider, however, that the Code should additionally draw attention to the similar potential problems where the leader of a council has some substantial outside pecuniary or non-pecuniary interest in the area.

Recommendations

6.56   In summary we recommend that:

(a)   local authorities should be required to keep a public register of the pecuniary and non-pecuniary interests of councillors on the following basis:

(i)   the register should include any interest which could reasonably be regarded as likely to affect councillors' conduct or influence their actions, speeches or vote;

(ii)   the register should specifically require entry of land and property owned by councillors in the authority's area, paid employments, and interests in companies above a specified minimum; but otherwise it should be for individual councillors to decide what interests fall within the criteria at (i) above;

(iii)   councillors with no relevant interests should be required to state this;

118

(iv)   the chief executive should be the registrar, with a statutory duty to maintain the register;

(v)   completion of the register should not alter the requirement to declare interests orally at meetings as and when they arise;

(Paragraphs 6.46 to 6.49)

(b)   failure to complete the proposed statutory register should be an offence, but local authorities should be statutorily prohibited from imposing other disabilities for non-completion of registers;

(Paragraph 6.48)

(c)   the statutory definition of pecuniary interests should be widened to include those who are involved, by employment or contract, in the promotion of the pecuniary interests of others on matters coming before the council;

(Paragraph 6.50)

(d)   where councillors declare a pecuniary interest in a meeting they should be statutorily required to withdraw from the room;

(Paragraph 6.51)

(e)   the National Code of Local Government Conduct should be amended so that it distinguishes between the declaration by councillors of their non-pecuniary interest and abstention from voting and speaking where such interests arise: non-pecuniary interests should always be declared, but disabilities on voting and speaking should only apply where the interest is clear and substantial;

(Paragraph 6.52)

(f)   the National Code of Local Government Conduct should be amended to draw attention to the problems of councillors becoming leaders of their council where they have a substantial recurring interest, whether pecuniary or non-pecuniary, in the affairs of the area.

(Paragraph 6.55)

PARTY GROUPS

General considerations

6.57   Our survey of councillors[1] shows that the great majority of councillors (85%) are elected in the name of a political party. There used to be a tradition in some rural areas that Labour supporters were elected under their party label while Conservative and Liberal supporters were elected as 'Independents'. This is no longer the case. Interestingly, 85% of Conservative party members who are councillors now sit as 'Conservatives' rather than as 'Independents', with 90% of Liberal party members sitting as 'Liberals'. The equivalent figure for the Labour Party is over 95%.

[1] SCPR, *Research Volume II,* Table 4.4.

6.58 Councillors of the same political party on an authority invariably organise through a party group, normally with their own standing orders. The Conservative, Labour and Liberal party national organisations all issue model standing orders for party groups. These cover matters such as links between the group and the local party (including attendance of party representatives at group meetings), election of officers (such as chairman, secretary and whip) procedure at meetings, and group discipline. The models are more marked for their similarities of content than their differences. They do however differ in status. The Conservative and Liberal models are for guidance and have no binding force. Labour groups must however either follow the model standing orders or have their own standing orders ratified by the party's national executive committee; their own standing orders must not conflict with the model.

6.59 In authorities where there are party groups, our political organisation study shows that it is almost universal practice for the group to meet before meetings of full council, and for decisions of the group to be binding on members at full council meetings. There is rather more variation of practice in relation to committee meetings; groups do not always meet in advance, and even where they do, voting discipline is often more relaxed. Overall 4% of groups meet weekly, 38% every two to four weeks, and 58% less often. Labour groups meet significantly more frequently than Conservative groups.[1]

6.60 It is clear from this brief review that councillors' relationships with their party groups are crucial to an understanding of their role. They are not free-standing individuals. The party group, however, is not recognised in legislation and often not even in the standing orders of individual local authorities. In this section we look at the implications of the party group for the conduct of council business. In doing so we are assisted not only by our research but also by the evidence of the national organisations of the Conservative, Labour, Liberal and Social Democratic Parties, all of whom sent us a full account of their current arrangements for party groups and their views on possible changes.

6.61 It is clear that party politics are a fact of life in local government. The question which we must answer is how best to accommodate it. In our previous Chapter we have made a number of recommendations which we hope will make it easier for the political parties, especially the majority party, to develop policy proposals in privacy within the formal local government system and with full access to officers. At the margin this should reduce the significance of party groups meeting outside the formal system, but we do not believe the impact would be substantial. It would undoubtedly remain normal practice for party groups to meet regularly, and for many issues of policy to be determined there before they reach the formal system.

6.62 We do not regard this of itself as a matter of concern, but:

(a) there needs to be greater open-ness about groups and their proceedings so that unnecessary suspicions are avoided. Party groups should not meet in a hole-and-corner atmosphere;

---

[1] Leach et al, *Research Volume I*, Chapter Four and Table A53. It should be noted that the data for political groups relate only to the group of the largest party on the council.

(b)   the formulation of decisions in party groups outside the formal local government system should not be allowed to undermine the statutory safeguards that apply within the system;

(c)   there should be adequate access to the advice of officers so that the policy of the majority group does not become pre-determined without full knowledge of the facts and law.

6.63   In the paragraphs that follow we make a number of recommendations designed to achieve the first two of these three ends, and we shall deal with the third when we discuss officers later in the Chapter (paragraphs 6.173 to 6.177). We do not, however, make any recommendations for statutory regulation of the political parties—which in this country would be a major constitutional innovation. While there are respects in which we believe that the arrangements for party groups could and should be improved, we believe that implementation must be left to the political parties themselves.

Open-ness
6.64   The recommendation which we have made for pro rata representation on committees (paragraph 5.54) would necessitate statutory recognition of the existence of political groups on local authorities. We believe this would of itself be a positive step, as it would help remove any sense that such groups are somehow improper or alien to local government. This is a point which several have made in written evidence.

6.65   We believe the political parties should also do more themselves to remove any sense of mystery surrounding party groups. We would certainly not wish to suggest that party groups should meet in public (although our research[1] show that a very few sometimes do) nor that their minutes should be open to public inspection. Where, however, they are discussing issues which will come before the council or its committees for decision, we believe that they should be prepared to make public a list of all those attending including non-councillors. The list should be deposited with the chief executive of the authority. Although the point does not strictly relate to party groups, we also believe that the local party organisations should publish the names of those on their executive committee.

Relations with the local party organisation
6.66   The party group consists of councillors alone, but it is normal for representatives of the local party organisation to have the right to attend meetings of the group on a non-voting basis. The Labour Party model standing orders provide that representatives of the party may attend subject to them not numbering more than a third of those on the group. The Conservative model entitles the local constituency party chairman and agent to attend. The Liberal model entitles at least one member of the local Liberal association to attend. In all cases the models provide for attendance to be on a non-voting basis.

6.67   Links with the local party are not limited to attendance at group meetings. The model standing orders of all three parties make clear that it is for the group, not the local party, to make decisions on issues coming before the council. All

---

[1] Leach et al, *Research Volume I*, Table A52.

parties, however, stress the need for close liaison between group and local party. The preamble to the Labour model standing orders says that 'group members are part of the local party and not separate from it'. The Conservative model standing orders say that one of the objects of the groups is 'to maintain a close liaison with the Conservative area office and the local constituency Conservative associations regarding local government matters'. The commentary to the Liberal model standing orders says 'the local party should be acting as an independent check on the group ... and pushing them into adopting a definite Liberal approach'.

6.68 While the Social Democratic Party do not have model standing orders, their policy on attendance of party representatives and general links with the party is very similar to that of the other three parties. In their evidence they say 'that only councillors should vote in party group meetings, but that other party members, limited to 25% or 33% of councillors, can play a useful advisory role at such meetings and help councillors fulfil their responsibilities'.

6.69 We have spelt out these rules at some length because they raise important issues. We have stressed in this Chapter that councillors, as part of the corporate decision taking process of a local authority, have a role distinct from that of MPs. They hold a public office which carries with it legal obligations. Members of the party who are not councillors are not in such a position. Clearly it is reasonable and realistic that the local party should have considerable influence on the local group. Indeed this is often a mutual process with councillors in turn influencing the local party. Equally clearly councillors who flout the policies of the local party must bear the risk that they will not be re-selected (a point made strongly in the Liberal Party's evidence). It is, however, essential that the ultimate decisions of councillors on matters coming before the council should be theirs alone and should not be dictated to them from outside.

6.70 The constitutional arrangements promulgated by the national political parties, as set out in paragraphs 6.66 to 6.68, are satisfactory in this respect. We note with approval that they place limits on the number of non-councillors attending group meetings; that they do not allow them voting rights; and that they do not give the party any rights to mandate the local group or in any way to decide council policy. However, our political organisation study suggests that these arrangements are not always reflected at local level.

6.71 The research[1] shows that non-councillors attend the meetings of 72% of party groups (55% of Conservative groups, 96% of Labour groups). In as many as 14% of these cases (36 authorities) non-councillors are reported as having voting rights. The research report also says that:

'A variety of arrangements for enhancing 'co-option and consultation' have been developed between Labour groups and their local parties, and it is clear

---

[1] Leach et al, *Research Volume I*, Chapter 4 and Tables A59 and A62. Because of the way in which the research questionnaire was constructed, the figures quoted all relate to the group of the largest party on the council. There will almost certainly be other authorities, not revealed in these figures, where non-councillors attend and/or vote at meetings of the minority party group. Unpublished analysis of the 36 majority party groups where non-councillors have voting rights shows that 20 were Labour, 12 Conservative, three Alliance and one not known.

that in a few cases these arrangements do in practice place certain powers of decision in the hands of the local party.'

This last reference suggests that relations between party and group in some authorities are so close as to amount to mandating. In a very few cases party groups have reportedly thrown their meetings open to all party members with no limit on their numbers.

6.72   The Social Democratic Party have suggested in their evidence that mandating should be made illegal. The Liberals by contrast have pointed out the practical difficulties of this, saying that 'any legal disbarment of mandating would cause problems for a ward party anxious to drop a councillor who disagreed with their policies on a regular basis or on a crucial matter'. We do not believe that a legal ban would be practicable. Where councillors follow the policy of their local party it is not possible to divine whether they do so because they agree with that policy, because they place party loyalty above their own views, whether they fear de-selection or whether they are acting under instruction from their local party. As Elizabeth I reportedly said: 'One cannot open a window into men's souls'.

6.73   We do believe however that the parties should take greater steps to ensure that their model standing orders are observed at local level, stressing to their local parties that:

(a)   councillors have legal obligations which non-councillors do not, and therefore;

(b)   the number of non-councillors attending party group meetings should be kept within strict limits;

(c)   only councillors should vote at party group meetings;

(d)   no attempt should be made by the local party organisation to instruct the party group on matters coming before the council for decision.

Attendance at party groups of party representatives disqualified from being councillors

6.74   In some local authorities it is the practice for party group meetings to be attended by party representatives who themselves would be statutorily disqualified from being councillors—especially people who are council employees. Our research show this to occur in about 40 authorities (almost all Labour).[1] This tends to undermine the statutory rules applying to the council itself. It can also cause some awkwardness for senior officers where they attend party groups as they can find themselves addressing their own junior staff (this is discussed more fully at paragraph 6.177). These problems would be reduced if (as we recommend) the parties were more strictly to enforce their rule that non-councillors should not be allowed to vote at party group meetings. They would not however, be eliminated. In principle we consider that the parties should not allow the attendance of people disqualified from council membership. In practice, we accept—albeit with some disquiet—that the strict application of this principle to

---

[1] Leach et al, *Research Volume I*, Table A63.

those disqualified by virtue of being council employees, who number some 3 million nationally, may be too great a restriction on their ability to play a full part in local politics. We do, however, consider that the principle should be strictly applied in those cases where a person has been disqualified from being a councillor following surcharge proceedings by the auditor. It is wrong that someone who has been guilty of wilful misconduct or unlawful expenditure as a councillor should be allowed by his or her party to have a continuing role in relation to local government.

Conflicts of interest

6.75   It is important that the statutory provisions relating to councillors' conflicts of interest should not be undermined by decisions taken in the party group. A situation might arise for instance where a councillor wishes to develop a site and requires planning permission from the council. He or she will be statutorily debarred from voting or speaking in meetings of the council or its committees dealing with the matter. This however will be of no avail if the councillor is able, at a prior group meeting, to persuade party colleagues to vote in his or her favour as a matter of party discipline.

6.76   Such problems were addressed in the Redcliffe-Maud Report[1], which recommended that:

> 'the political parties at both national and local level should ensure that rules of conduct in local authority group meetings are no less strict than in those of the authority itself'.

This recommendation, which was subsequently endorsed by Salmon Commission[2], is embodied in the 1975 National Code of Local Government Conduct, paragraph 3(ii) of which says:

> 'The principles about disclosure of interest should be borne in mind in your unofficial relations with other councillors—at party group meetings, or other informal occasions no less scrupulously than at formal meetings of the council, its committees and sub-committees.'

6.77   We find, however, that observance of this rule has been poor. The national parties have taken no steps to include provision relating to conflicts of interest in their model standing orders, except that the Liberals have provision for a register of interests. In 1975 the national executive committee of the Labour Party published a report recommending that councillors treat pecuniary interests at group meetings in the same way as at council meetings, but this has not been embodied in their model standing orders. The Labour Party told us that these recommendations reflect 'current practice' and indeed the Conservative and Liberal Parties also assured us that the 1975 Code is followed locally. This is, however, not borne out by our political organisation study[3], which suggests that just over half of Conservative party groups and almost half of Labour party groups have no requirement at all in relating to declarations of interest.

---

[1] Report of the Committee on Conduct in Local Government, 1974. Cmnd 5636, page xii.
[2] Report of the Royal Commission on Standards of Conduct in Public Life, 1976. Cmnd 6524, paragraph 246.
[3] Leach et al, *Research Volume I*, Table A51.

6.78　This position is not satisfactory. We believe that further steps are required by the political parties to ensure that:

(a)　where a councillor has an interest in a matter of council business being discussed in a meeting of their party group, he or she treats it precisely as the law, or 1975 Code, would required if it were a meeting of the council;

(b)　rules for group voting discipline at council meetings are consistent with the requirements in law and in the 1975 Code for councillors to abstain where they have an interest in the matter concerned;

(c)　(a) and (b) above are reflected by amendment to model standing orders and by circular advice to all party groups to amend their existing standing orders.

Recommendations

6.79　Our recommendations on party groups are aimed primarily at the national organisations of the political parties. We believe that there should be an onus on them to ensure that proper procedures are followed locally by the local party organisations and party groups. However, we do recognise that the national party organisations do not in all cases have the power to enforce procedures locally. To the extent that that is so, our recommendations are also addressed directly at local parties and local groups. **Subject to that preliminary point we recommend that:**

the national political parties should take steps:

(i)　to ensure that party groups keep a publicly available list of those attending their meetings;

(ii)　to ensure observance of their model standing orders insofar as they limit the numbers of non-councillors attending meetings of party groups, preclude non-councillors from voting at such meetings and prevent non-councillors from determining the policy to be followed by the party group on matters before the council for decision;

(iii)　to debar from attendance at party group meetings persons disqualified from council membership following surcharge proceedings by the auditor;

(iv)　to ensure that the National Code of Local Government Conduct is implemented in respect of conflicts of interests arising at meetings of party groups, and to amend their model standing orders accordingly.

(Paragraphs 6.65, 6.73, 6.74 and 7.78)

THE TIME COMMITMENT OF COUNCILLORS AND THEIR REMUNERATION

Time required for council duties

6.80　At the beginning of this Chapter we highlighted the dual role of councillors. On the one hand they are representatives of their area, with constituency responsibilities similar to that of a Member of Parliament. On the other hand, they are responsible for the delivery of the council's services. The former role is straightforward and well understood. The latter is more problematic and has caused considerable problems of demarcation between councillors and officers,

125

especially between chairmen of committees and chief officers. The problem is often associated with the suggestion that there is a significant and increasing number of full-time councillors.

6.81   It has long been a feature of local government that some leading councillors have devoted significantly more time to council business than their colleagues, and that in a few cases they have worked full-time, or practically so, on council business. The impression of most in local government, as reflected in the written evidence and the interview survey carried out in the course of the Committee's study of political organisation, is that this is a growing practice. This however should not be exaggerated. The same interview survey showed that only about 50% of authorities had any councillors who might be considered full-time.[1] This survey was concentrated in the larger authorities where full-time councillors are most likely to occur, suggesting that the figure is under 50% nationally. Moreover, our survey of councillors[2] showed that the average councillor in 1985 spent 74 hours a month on council business—considerably more than in 1964 (52 hours) but no more than in 1976 (79 hours). As might be expected office holders spent more time (about 80 hours) than backbenchers (about 64 hours), but even for them these averages are well short of a full-time commitment.

6.82   Although the trend towards full-time councillors has probably been overstated, there can be little doubt that there is concern over the inter-face between chief officers and committee chairmen. Concern has been expressed by chief officers that some committee chairmen are increasingly becoming involved in the managerial minutiae of service departments, exercising more influence (or even full control) over committee agendas, the content of reports, staff appointments, the letting of contracts, relations with the workforce, etc. This was put to us particularly forcibly by the Federated Union of Managerial and Professional Officers, but also to a considerable extent by other bodies representing senior officers. It has become clear through the evidence that it is not an issue which divides left from right, but which divides officers from councillors. Councillors in Conservative authorities have been just as quick to defend their right to intervene in management as have those in Labour authorities. This is reflected in a speech given by the Secretary of State for the Environment on 30 October 1985 when he said:

> 'Since 1974 we have seen a surge in the number of councillors who insist upon participating in management and involving themselves in ensuring that their policies are fully implemented. Quite right too! That is precisely what Ministers have been doing in their Whitehall Departments—and none too soon. The professional officers in local government will have to adjust positively to changes of this kind. It is not possible for them to stand in attitudes of frozen hostility or professional resentment'.

In our survey of councillors a clear majority from all the parties agreed rather than disagreed with the statement that officers have too much influence over decision taking.[3]

---

[1] Leach et al, *Research Volume I*, Table 3.4.
[2] SCPR, *Research Volume II*, Tables 5.1 and 5.3.
[3] SCPR, *Research Volume II*, Table 7.2.

6.83 We do not believe that it is practicable or desirable to exclude councillors from management issues. It might well be the policy of a political party that services should be decentralised to area offices, or that they should be hived off to private sector consultants, or that bureaucratic waste should be eliminated. Such policies involve taking a view on management practice, and it is reasonable that councillors should be able to ensure that they are implemented. Nevertheless we draw a distinction between the direction of general management policy and day-to-day management intervention. It might be that occasional day-to-day intervention, or at least maintenance of the possibility of such intervention, is necessary for the successful direction of policy. We do not however think that councillors should regard it as part of their normal role to intervene in this way. To do so can only duplicate the role of chief officers. This creates a twofold danger. First, there is a danger that chief officers will see their management responsibilities undermined, that they will become demoralised and that this will be reflected in rapid staff turn-over (of which there is some evidence). Second, there is a danger that it will alter the character of councillors so that they become full-time administrators rather than people who are representative of the local community which they serve. We do not believe this is desirable. Councillors, while retaining overall legal responsibility for the delivery of services, should seek to leave the day-to-day management of those services as far as possible to officers.

6.84 In saying this we are not suggesting that it is necessarily improper for councillors to devote their full time to council business. There are some authorities where the political dimension of the work of the leader and committee chairmen is so great that they can easily work full-time without intervening unnecessarily in day-to-day management. We do not however think that it should be regarded as the norm that councillors, even leading councillors, should work full-time nor that such practice should in any way be formalised or encouraged. This has implications for our discussion of remuneration below.

Remuneration: current legislation

6.85 The current legislation provides for a threefold system of remuneration for councillors, as follows.[1]

(i) Attendance allowance

6.86 Under section 173 of the Local Government Act 1972 (section 45 of the Local Government (Scotland) Act 1973) councillors are entitled to receive an attendance allowance for the performance of an approved duty. This allowance is subject to a daily maximum prescribed by the Secretary of State—and was £16.00 per day in 1985-6. Within this maximum, individual local authorities may vary the amounts payable according to the time of day and length of day. They also have considerable discretion in deciding what is an approved duty. Attendance allowance is taxable, and is normally paid net of tax.

(ii) Financial loss allowance

6.87 Under section 173A of the 1972 Act (section 45A of the Scottish Act)[2] councillors may opt to receive financial loss allowance **instead of** attendance

---

[1] The legislation also makes provision for travel and subsistence allowances, but these are not considered in this Report.

[2] These provisions were inserted, respectively, by the Local Government Planning and Land Act 1980 and the Local Government and Planning (Scotland) Act 1982.

allowance. The recipient must demonstrate that he or she has suffered actual financial loss. It is subject to a daily maximum—£24.00 in 1985–86—prescribed by the Secretary of State. It is not taxable.

6.88   Co-opted members are entitled to financial loss allowance (but not attendance allowance).

(iii) Special responsibility allowance

6.89   Under section 177A of the 1972 Act (section 49A of the Scottish Act)[1] local authorities may at their discretion pay an **additional** allowance to councillors with special responsibilities. The maximum which an authority may pay (both in total and to an individual councillor) is prescribed by the Secretary of State. The maxima vary according to the type and size (in population) of authority. In the largest authority[2] the 1985–86 maxima were £23,985 for the whole authority and £4,570 for an individual councillor. In the smallest they were £1,140 and £460 respectively. Individual authorities may decide to pay lesser amounts or none at all.

Remuneration: current practice

6.90   Our research has given us a detailed picture of practice in 1984–85 in relation to allowance.

6.91   Eighty-seven per cent of councillors claimed attendance allowance, and only 1% claimed financial loss allowance. Average receipt of attendance allowance was £852 per annum, but this disguises considerable variations. As might be expected average receipt was much higher in larger authorities than smaller ones: for instance £1,853 in the metropolitan counties and the GLC as compared with £513 in English shire districts. It was also much higher in Scotland (£2,112) than in England (£728) and Wales (£1,057). There were also considerable variations among councillors on the same authority, with the highest payment to an individual councillor being typically more than twice the average for that authority. Average receipt of financial loss allowance was £847 per annum.[3]

6.92   Only 43% of councils made special responsibility allowance payments— mainly larger authorities. The average payment was £518 per annum (£1,402 for leaders, £572 for opposition leaders and £501 for committee chairmen).[4]

6.93   The cost of allowances, adjusted to 1985–86 levels and excluding authorities now abolished, is approximately as follows:

attendance allowance	£18 million
financial loss allowance	£ 0.4 million
special responsibility allowance	£ 1 million
Total	£19.4 million

---

[1] These provisions were both inserted by the Local Government Planning and Land Act 1980.
[2] Leaving aside the Greater London Council, which is now abolished.
[3] IPF, *Research Volume II*, Tables 3.2 and 3.3.
[4] IPF, *Research Volume II*, Tables 3.8 and 3.11.

The total expenditure represents under 0.1% of local authority rate and grant borne expenditure.

Remuneration: the issues

6.94 On no other issue has the evidence been so emphatic as on the current remuneration arrangements. Almost all who have commented have said that the arrangements are unsatisfactory both in terms of the basis of payment and the level of payment. The evidence, however, has been much less clear in coming to a view as to what the basis should be nor indeed as to what the level should be (other than that it should be higher).

6.95 The difficulty of devising a system on which there is agreement lies largely in the lack of a ready analogy for the position of the councillor. It might be argued on the one hand that councillors are representatives of the community carrying out a public duty in very much the same way as someone say on jury service; as such they should be compensated for any loss incurred as a result of carrying out their duties, but should not be remunerated for those duties—that is to say no monetary value should be placed on the councillor's work. On this line of argument a councillor should be entitled to financial loss allowance, but no other form of remuneration. This was in essence the position prior to the Local Government Act 1972 and the Local Government (Scotland) Act 1973.

6.96 On the other hand it might be argued that in the modern political and managerial environment councillors, especially leaders and chairmen of committees, are carrying out major statutory responsibilities which in other public sector contexts would carry substantial remuneration. For example the chairman of a major water authority is paid some £35,000 per annum for a four day week, a vice chairman some £7,000 per annum for a seven day month and other members some £3,000 per annum—£5,000 per annum for a three to five day month. The annual revenue expenditure for the largest water authority is about £450 million—comparable to that of a large shire county. It would however be unusual for the leader of a large shire county to receive more than about £6,000 per annum, including special responsibility allowance, for what is often a full-time commitment.

6.97 The current arrangements fall uneasily between these two approaches in a way which seems to please no-one. The last attempt at a thorough review of the system aimed at putting it on a more rational basis was made in the 1977 Report of the Robinson Committee.[1] They recommended a three element system, consisting of:

(a) A basic annual payment of £1,000 (equivalent to about £2,500 in 1985−86) to all councillors. This was designed to remunerate them for their constituency role which was argued to be similar for all councillors. It would have been payable regardless of financial loss.

(b) Financial loss allowance. This would have been payable in addition to the basic payment but only on a restricted national definition of approved duties. It would have enabled those who spent more time on council business

---

[1] Report of the Committee on the Remuneration of Councillors, 1977. Cmnd 7010.

to receive a higher rate of remuneration than their colleagues, but only if they could prove financial loss;

(c) Special responsibility allowance. This would have been payable in addition to the other allowances to those in key posts. It would have been payable regardless of financial loss.

6.98 The Committee's recommendation for a basic annual payment, which would have replaced attendance allowances, was not accepted. Financial loss allowance was introduced, but simply as an alternative to attendance allowance. No restriction was placed on approved duties. Special responsibility allowance was introduced but in a slightly different form and at a lower rate than recommended. For instance a large council such as Kent County Council would have been entitled to spend a total of £30,000 under Robinson's recommendations—equivalent to about £70,000 in 1985–86—while under the present scheme they were entitled only to a total of £17,130 in that year.

Remuneration: criteria for a new system

6.99 Against the background of the debate described above it would be idle to suggest that there is a ready-made neat solution to the problem of allowances. However we believe that there are a number of guiding principles, on which the allowances system should be based.

6.100 First, the system should be simple to operate and understand, and not susceptible to faulty claims. We do not believe that either attendance allowance or financial loss allowance meet these criteria. Both require detailed form filling and record keeping by councillors and checking by their council. Both raise the possibility of false claims, especially financial loss allowance. Also both systems depend on a definition of approved duty, which vary between authorities for reasons which are not readily apparent.[1] For example some authorities pay allowance for attendance at party groups and for constituency surgeries, while others do not. Lastly the existence of two alternative systems in parallel is of itself complex.

6.101 Second, the system should not encourage the proliferation of meetings or councillors spending more time on council business than is necessary. Attendance allowance has been criticised in the evidence for artificially inflating council duties and does not meet this criterion.

6.102 Third, the system should not be based solely on compensation for financial loss. It is invidious that a wage-earner and someone looking after a home should put in similar hours but that only the former should be remunerated. Moreover the financial loss principle is difficult to apply in practice. In particular it has not proved a satisfactory means of compensating the self-employed, for whom it is often difficult to prove actual loss.

---

[1] IPF, *Research Volume II*, Table 3.19.

6.103   Fourth, the levels of remuneration should not purport to equate to those paid to officers or otherwise suggest that councillors have a role that is interchangeable with that of officers. On this score, at least, the current system can hardly be criticised.

6.104   Fifth, the system should recognise that some councillors have considerably greater calls on their time than others depending on their responsibilities. The system of special responsibility allowances in principle meets this criterion.

6.105   Sixth, allowances should be available as of right to all councillors meeting the statutory criteria for payment. The current special responsibility allowance system does not meet this criterion because authorities can and do opt out of the scheme regardless of the wishes of individual councillors who would be entitled to it.

6.106   Seventh, once fixed the levels of allowance should be regularly and objectively reviewed. We are not saying here that allowances should be linked rigidly to inflation as if no other factors were relevant. But we cannot condone the manner in which attendance allowance has been allowed arbitrarily to fall in real value since its introduction. The original maximum daily allowance was £10. Had it kept in line with average earnings it would have been about £40 in 1985–86. In fact it was £16.

Remuneration: proposed new system

6.107   Building from these criteria we propose a simple system of remuneration based on two elements.

(i) Basic flat rate allowance

6.108   Councillors should no longer be entitled to attendance allowance or financial loss allowance. Instead every councillor should be entitled to a basic flat rate allowance paid as an annual sum. Unlike the Robinson proposal for a basic annual payment, the allowance should vary according to the size (in population) and type of council. We do not believe that it would be possible to devise a single rate of allowance which would be generally regarded as acceptable in smaller councils while providing adequate remuneration in larger ones. Our research[1] has shown considerable variations in the time commitment of councillors by council size and type, and we believe this should be reflected in the basic allowance. Authorities should be banded for the purposes of their rate of allowance according to the bands that are currently used for special responsibility allowance, except that the lowest band (currently all district councils of less than 100,000 population) should be split into two.

(ii) Special responsibility allowance

6.109   Special responsibility allowance should continue to be available for 'key' councillors, but local authorities should not have the discretion to opt out of the arrangements. Each local authority should be statutorily required to draw up a scheme for the disbursement of special responsibility allowance. The scheme should be based on utilisation of the maximum amount to which the authority is entitled. It should specify the posts eligible and the amounts for each

---

[1] SCPR, *Research Volume II*, Table 5.2.

post. The Secretary of State should issue guidelines for schemes. All councillors holding posts specified in the scheme should be entitled to claim the amount specified.

(iii) Subsidiary issues

6.110   Some 13% of councillors are members of more than one authority[1]. The extent to which councillors are able to carry out their duties effectively on two councils will depend largely on two things. First, it will depend on whether they have some additional non-council call on their time. It might well be, for example, that it is easier for an unemployed person to be an effective councillor in two authorities than for someone running a busy company to be an effective councillor in only one. Second, it will depend on the level of responsibility held in the councils. We are aware that some people believe that it is intrinsically undesirable to be a councillor on more than one authority, but believe that is a matter for the political parties and selection panels rather than legislation. We do not see that the time demands of being a councillor are of themselves such that it is not feasible to carry out both sets of duties effectively. Accordingly we see no reason why two basic flat rate allowances should not be received by the same person. Different considerations begin to arise, however, where a councillor holds a post with special responsibility on one or both of the councils. We think that individual councillors, and party groups who elect their colleagues to leading posts, should consider very carefully whether this combination of duties is practicable. Much will depend on the individual circumstances. We consider however that the holding of two posts with special responsibilty is likely in most cases to be too great a combination of duties to be carried out satisfactorily. Accordingly we propose that no councillor should receive more than one special responsibility allowance.

6.111   In the evidence our attention has been drawn to a number of anomalies in the current payment of allowances which stem from wider taxation and social security factors. Some difficulty has been encountered over the deduction of taxation and national insurance from attendance allowance. Companies which have a policy of granting employees paid leave for council duties, but recovering any attendance allowance received, can only reclaim the net sums. Many councillors have been critical of the fact that receipt of allowance adversely affects their entitlement to social security benefits, especially unemployment benefit. These difficulties would continue to arise under our proposed new arrangements. We have not proposed changes because the issues relate more generally to taxation and social security, and extend beyond our remit. We hope, however, that they will be pursued by others.

Remuneration: proposed levels

6.112   The current levels of allowance are substantially below what they should be. They present a disincentive to standing for election and are an inadequate reflection of the responsibilities of, and time spent on, council duties. The current average annual receipt of attendance allowance of £850 per annum equates almost exactly to £1 for every hour spent on council business. While we do not suggest that councillors should be paid a competitive salary we do believe that this is unacceptable.

---

[1] SCPR, *Research Volume II*, Table 4.2.

(i) Basic flat rate allowance

6.113   It is clear, therefore, that the basic flat rate allowance must be substantially higher than £850 per annum. If attendance allowance had kept pace with earnings since its introduction, average receipt would now stand at about £2,250 per annum. The basic annual payment of £1,000 recommended by the Robinson Committee would stand at about the same level—£2,500—when updated for inflation. This is, for comparison, much the same sum as would be earned by a non-manual worker at the average male wage if he worked one day per week. We believe these figures provide a useful benchmark, and would consider an allowance of about £2,500 appropriate in a middle sized authority—eg a district council of about 150,000—200,000 population (such as Luton or Stockton-on-Tees). We need however also to provide a range of rates which at one extreme would be appropriate for an upper tier authority of over 2 million population (Strathclyde Regional Council) and at the other for district councils of under 50,000 (such as Rutland or Radnor District Councils). In devising the range we need to have regard to differences in payment of allowance at present, differing calls on a councillor's time and what might be considered to be fair and appropriate by people living in such areas. We propose that the top end of the range should be £4,000 and the bottom end should be £1,500. Our proposals for authorities of intermediate size are given in detail in the Tables at Annex J, which also show how the proposed rates of flat rate allowance would compare with current receipt of attendance allowance (or financial loss allowance). The examples below illustrate the proposed level of flat rate allowance for some individual authorities.

Authority	Population	Proposed allowance £
Upper Tier:		
Strathclyde Regional Council	2,376,400	4,000
Kent County Council	1,491,700	3,250
Humberside County Council	851,600	3,000
Gwynedd County Council	232,700	2,800
Lower Tier:		
Edinburgh City Council	439,700	3,250
Newcastle-upon-Tyne City Council	281,100	2,900
Westminster City Council	182,000	2,600
Luton Borough Council	165,400	2,500
Lancaster City Council	127,600	2,250
Lincoln City Council	77,200	2,000
Roxburgh District Council	35,200	2,000
Rutland District Council	34,100	1,500

6.114   We have a number of observations on the proposed rates of allowance. First, the proposed rates for Scottish authorities are, in all cases, £500 higher than for authorities of equivalent functions and population in England and Wales. This is designed to reflect the fact that Scottish councillors represent significantly more people (on average 50% more) than their counterparts in

England and Wales, which has implications for the time spent on council business. Second, because of this, and because the largest authority (Strathclyde) is in Scotland, the range of allowance within England and Wales (£3,250 to £1,500) is narrower than the range for Great Britain as a whole (£4,000 to £1,500). Third, although it is not the basis of our calculation, the percentage differential between the highest and lowest allowance in England and Wales (about 215%) is very much the same as that between chief executives' pay in the largest and smallest authorities under the nationally agreed scales (210%). Fourth, the average receipt of allowance over Great Britain would be about £2,400. Fifth, we estimate that fewer than 5% of councillors would be worse off under the proposed rates of allowance compared with what they currently receive. Despite the proposed £500 supplement in Scotland a smaller proportion of councillors would gain in Scotland than in England and Wales. Overall we believe that the proposal should achieve greater simplicity and equity overall with a minimum of loss in individual cases.

(ii) Special responsibility allowance

6.115 We believe that the current rates of special responsibility allowance need increasing for two reasons. First, they have always been too low to reflect the considerable extra burden on leading councillors. Second it was in the past possible for leading councillors to compensate for this through higher than average receipt of attendance allowance (reflecting their greater time commitment); this would not be possible under basic flat rate allowance. We propose that the current maxima, both for authorities and individuals, should be doubled. In round figures, this would enable the largest authority to disburse £50,000 in all with a maximum of £10,000 to any individual; the respective figures for the smallest authority would be £2,300 and £900. These levels should be regularly reviewed.

(iii) Costs

6.116 The public expenditure cost of these proposals can be estimated with some precision. The current cost of attendance allowance and financial loss allowance is about £18.5 million per annum over Great Britain. Assuming that levels of take up do not change, the cost of the proposed basic flat rate allowance would be about £53 million, an increase in public expenditure of £34.5 million. The current cost of special responsibility allowance is about £1 million. The effect of the proposed change in entitlement to this allowance is more difficult to assess. If all councillors entitled to do so were to claim, the cost would double to about £2 million. In practice this seems unlikely, and we have assumed an increase of about £0.5 million, giving a cost of about £1.5 million. The proposed doubling of the maxima would then bring the total cost of the scheme to about £3 million, an overall increase of about £2 million. The total cost of the new arrangements would therefore, be about £56 million, an increase of about £36.5 million. No recommendation involving an increase in public expenditure is welcome. Even, however, after the increase the total cost of allowances would represent under 0.2% of local authority rate and grant borne expenditure. We believe this is a remarkably low price for a system of democratic representation.

Summary of recommendations

6.117. In summary we recommend that:

(a)   attendance allowance and financial loss allowance should be replaced by a basic flat rate allowance payable to all councillors as an annual sum;

(Paragraph 6.108)

(b)   the levels of basic flat rate allowance should be banded according to the type of council and its population;

(Paragraph 6.113)

(c)   the initial rates of basic flat rate allowance should be £4,000 per annum in the largest authority and £1,500 in the smallest, and should be regularly reviewed;

(Paragraph 6.113)

(d)   the special responsibility allowance arrangements should continue, but each local authority should be statutorily required to draw up a scheme for disbursing the allowance on the following basis:

(i)   the scheme should specify amounts payable for particular posts in such a way that the total payable equates to the maximum prescribed for the authority by the Secretary of State;

(ii)   all councillors in posts specified by the scheme shall be entitled to the amounts specified;

(Paragraph 6.109)

(e)   no councillor should be entitled to more than one special responsibility allowance;

(Paragraph 6.110)

(f)   the special responsibility allowance maxima currently prescribed for classes of authority and for individual councillors within each class should be doubled and subsequently kept under regular review.

(Paragraph 6.115)

TIME-OFF WORK FOR COUNCIL DUTIES

The legislation

6.118.   Section 29 of the Employment Protection (Consolidation) Act 1978 requires employers to permit employees to take 'reasonable' time-off work for the purposes of performing duties as a councillor. This applies to private sector and public sector employers alike. There is no requirement to pay employees where time-off work is allowed. There is at present no provision for a statutory code of practice setting out what is 'reasonable', although there is such a code governing the equivalent provisions for time-off for trade union activities.

Private sector employers

6.119. Anecdotal evidence to the Committee suggested that public sector employers were considerably more generous than those in the private sector in giving time-off and that this had led to a preponderance of public sector councillors. We have found this to be misleading. Our survey of councillors[1] shows

---
[1] SCPR, *Research Volume II*, Table 3.6.

that 36% of councillors in employment are from the public sector, almost precisely the same as the percentage (37%) for the workforce as a whole. We have generally been encouraged by the attitude of private sector employers, especially the larger firms, towards time-off work for council duties. We wrote to employers' organisations asking for information about current practice, and the Confederation of British Industry—who carried out a survey among their members—said:

'... the response from our members has indicated a widely held view that it is beneficial for companies to support individuals wishing to undertake public duties to improve councils' understanding of the private sectors needs. Company policies reflect this positive approach.'

Many private sector employees exceed their legal obligations by granting paid as well as unpaid leave. It seems reasonably common practice for large firms to grant about 18 days paid leave, which is the amount also normally granted by the main public sector employer—the civil service. Our survey of councillors suggests that councillors who are private sector employees are less likely than those who are civil servants to suffer loss of earnings, but more likely than those who are local authority employees[1]. Overall the private sector compares well with the public sector. Nevertheless we are aware of wide differences in practice among firms. Our research shows that a significant number of councillors, especially manual workers, do suffer loss of earnings, and we have received evidence of some councillors finding it difficult to remain in their current jobs. We urge **all** private sector employers to take a positive and flexible approach in granting paid and unpaid leave to employees who are councillors.

Public sector employers

6.120.   Some local authorities have been giving excessive paid time-off to employees who are councillors on other authorities. This is certainly not general practice, and one authority for example which we visited imposed a maximum of 18 days per annum paid leave. Other authorities however grant higher levels of paid leave, with virtually full-time paid leave of absence being given in some cases. This has sometimes been influenced by the unsatisfactory level of remuneration for councillors. We do not believe, that it is a proper use of public funds to provide an indirect subsidy for councillors in this way. While leave of absence should continue to be a matter for individual local authorities to determine, we propose that it should in future be subject to a statutory upper limit of 26 days paid leave a year. It would remain possible to grant longer periods of unpaid leave. The 26 day limit, while providing a proper safeguard for public funds, is more than what some local authorities currently grant. It should not be regarded as the norm.

6.121.   We see no reason why the 26 day limit on paid leave should not also be given more general application. It could reasonably be applied statutorily to all public sector employers, as the same principles apply. In the private sector there is not the same need to safeguard public funds, and a statutory limit would not be appropriate. Nevertheless, where private sector employers believe they are under

---

[1] SCPR, *Research Volume II*, Table 6.5.

pressure to grant excessive paid leave we would see no reason why they should not themselves impose a similar limit.

6.122. A further point arises with regard to the safeguarding of public funds. Where public sector employers grant paid time-off, then it is wrong in principle that employees should retain allowances received in respect of the same period— as they would be being paid twice by the public purse. This principle would be more difficult to apply under the proposed system of flat rate allowance, which would be paid on an annual rather than daily basis. Nevertheless we believe that public sector employers should seek to introduce arrangements to recover allowances from their employees where a significant part of the employee's time on council business is attributable to paid time-off work. Again it would be reasonable for private sector employers to do likewise (and many already do so), but that is a matter for their discretion.

Pension rights

6.123. We are concerned by the disincentive to becoming a councillor which might be created by loss of pension rights in respect of leave of absence. This was a point which also caused concern to the Robinson Committee[1]. They found that some employers made up pension rights by devices such as notional payments, but that others did not. We believe that all employers should ensure that employees do not lose pension rights as a result of council service.

Recommendations

6.124. In summary we recommend as follows:

(a) private sector employers should take a positive and flexible attitude to granting paid and unpaid leave to employees for council duties;

(Paragraph 6.119)

(b) there should be a statutory upper limit of 26 days per year on the paid leave which public sector employers may grant to employees for council duties;

(Paragraphs 6.120 and 6.121)

(c) where public sector employers grant paid leave to employees for council duties they should, as far as is practicable, recover from those employees any allowance received by them for the period concerned;

(Paragraph 6.122)

(d) employers should ensure that employees' pension rights are not adversely affected as a result of leave required for council duties.

(Paragraph 6.123)

---

[1] Committee on the Remuneration of Councillors, 1977. Cmnd 7010, paragraph 210.

THE DUTIES AND ROLES OF OFFICERS

Statutory arrangements and other constraints

6.125. Under the Local Government Act 1933 local authorities in England and Wales were required to appoint persons to a number of specified offices, including those of clerk, treasurer, medical officer and surveyor. These officers held a statutory office from which in some cases—eg that of county clerk and medical officer—they could not be removed except with the consent of the Minister. Similar provision was contained in the Local Government (Scotland) Act 1947, except that there was no requirement for Ministerial consent for dismissal. Instead there was the protection that specified officers (including the clerk) could not be dismissed except by a resolution of the council passed by not less than two-thirds of the members present at the meeting; such a resolution could not be passed without prior notice of the motion being given.

6.126. These provisions were replaced by section 112 of the Local Government Act 1972 and section 64 of the Local Government (Scotland) Act 1973. They provide instead that a local authority shall appoint such officers as they think necessary for the proper discharge of their functions. There remain however certain exceptions to this general discretion. In particular a police authority must appoint a chief constable (the Secretary of State's consent for the appointment is required), an education authority must appoint a chief education officer, and a social services authority must appoint a director of social services (the Secretary of State must approve the shortlist from which the appointments are made). There is no statutory requirement to appoint a chief executive.

6.127. Chief constables are in a different position to other officers in two major respects. First they are officers of police authorities, which (except in Scotland) are corporate bodies in their own right and statutorily independent from the local authorities who appoint their members. Second chief constables hold executive authority in their own statutory right, and do not derive their executive authority from councillors. The recommendations in this Chapter do not apply to them.

6.128. Officers other than chief constables, whether or not they are statutory appointments, may only carry out such executive actions as are delegated to them by the council or its committees. The statute does however confer on officers certain duties designed to ensure that the council carries out its functions with propriety. For example section 151 of the Local Government Act 1972 (section 95 of the Local Government (Scotland) Act 1973) requires local authorities to make arrangements for the proper administration of their financial affairs and to secure that one of their officers has responsibility for the administration of those affairs. Section 100D of the Local Government Act 1972 (section 50D of the Scottish Act 1973)[1] provides for the 'proper officer' to decide what documents of the council should not be open to public inspection. Additionally the standing orders of individual authorities often place on the chief executive, or other officer, certain duties which require him or her to act as the arbiter of the conduct of business.

6.129. Officers may be appointed on such reasonable terms and conditions as the authority thinks fit. In practice local authorities, as employers, collectively

---

[1] These provisions were inserted by the Local Government (Access to Information) Act 1985.

agree conditions of service through the Local Authorities' Conditions of Service Advisory Board (LACSAB). LACSAB's terms and conditions, which are arrived at following negotiation with the unions, are not binding on individual authorities, but in practice have been almost universally adopted. In most cases they have been incorporated in the authorities' contracts with their employees. This means that they are enforceable before, for instance, an industrial tribunal.

6.130.   Additionally the 1975 National Code of Local Government Conduct (paragraph 5) has the following to say about officers and their relations with councillors:

'COUNCILLORS AND OFFICERS

(i)   Both councillors and officers are servants of the public, and they are indispensable to one another. But their responsibilities are distinct. Councillors are responsible to the electorate and serve only so long as their term of office lasts. Officers are responsible to the council and are permanently appointed. An officer's job is to give advice to councillors and the council, and to carry out the council's work under the direction and control of the council and its committees.

(ii)   Mutual respect between councillors and officers is essential to good local government. Close personal familiarity between individual councillor and officer can damage this relationship and prove embarrassing to other councillors and officers.

(iii)   If you are called upon to take part in appointing an officer, the only question you should consider is which candidate would best serve the whole council. You should not let your personal or political preferences influence your judgement. You should not canvass the support of colleagues for any candidate and you should resist any attempt by others to canvass yours.'

While breach of the Code in other respects is normally regarded by the local ombudsman as maladministration this is not true of staff matters—which are at present outside the ombudsman's jurisdiction. The ombudsman would not therefore be able to investigate a complaint by a prospective officer that his or her application for a job had not been properly considered.

Potential conflicts of role

6.131.   As we indicated at the beginning of this Chapter the current local government model does not lend itself to a totally clear role for officers, especially senior officers. By way of preface we define what we mean by 'senior officers' and set out their various roles and the reasons why they might conflict.

6.132.   We use the expression senior officers to include all those whose work will normally involve them in giving advice to councillors. This will certainly include chief executives, chief officers and deputy chief officers. It will normally also include officers in principal officer grades. In some authorities, especially smaller ones, it might also include those in senior officer grades but this is less likely. There are some 500 chief executives. They gave written and oral evidence to the Committee through the Society of Local Authority Chief Executives (SOLACE). There are about 6,000 chief officers and deputy chief officers. They gave written evidence to the Committee through their professional associations,

139

and both written and oral evidence was also given through the Federated Union of Managerial and Professional Officers (FUMPO). There are some 60,000 principal officers. They along with more junior non-manual grades are represented by the National and Local Government Officers Association, who gave both written and oral evidence. We do not use the expression 'senior officers' to cover teachers, of whom there are some 500,000; their relationship with councillors, even in the case of headmasters, is very different and much less direct. We have not considered the position of specialist grades.

6.133. The various roles of senior officers may be categorised under three headings, which are set out below (not in order of priority).

6.134. First, they are the *professional managers* of the service departments of local authorities—eg of the education service, the direct labour organisation or the highways department. As such they may have day-to-day responsibility for major budgets and a large workforce. This professional managerial role tends in particular to characterise chief officers.

6.135. Second, they are *advisers*. They are responsible for ensuring that the council and its committees are informed of the facts, the law, and all other relevant considerations, before they make decisions. They are also responsible for proposing, and advising on, policy options. They will normally give advice to individual councillors and parties as well as the council as a whole.

6.136. Third, they are *arbitrators*. As officers they stand outside the political conflicts between councillors and ensure that council business is conducted fairly and with propriety. As has been mentioned, this role is to some extent enshrined in statute and standing orders but to an extent relies also on convention. The role applies in particular to the chief executive.

6.137. In carrying out all these roles the law requires officers to serve the council as a whole. In practice officers will perforce have different relationships as between majority and minority parties, and as between leaders, committee chairmen and backbenchers. This is illustrated by the Committee's study of political organisation[1], which asked about the frequency with which chief executives had contact with majority and minority party leaders. In 90% of authorities there was contact at least once a week with majority party leaders, but in only 10% of authorities was there contact at least once a week with minority party leaders. There are differences not only in the frequency of contact, but the manner of contact. In some authorities officers will 'advise' the majority party leaders, but only 'inform' other councillors.

6.138. Sensitive and skilled senior officers will normally be able to carry out all three roles in a way which is compatible both with their legal duties to the council as a whole and with the political reality of their relationship with the majority party. For others, difficulties arise and this tends to result in a concentration on one or two of the roles at the expense of the other(s). For instance officers who place a very strong stress on professional judgement and on their legal duty to

---

[1] Leach et al, *Research Volume I*, Tables A26 and A27.

serve the whole council might fail to satisfy the need of the majority party leadership for advice, with the result that pressure arises for the appointment of officers who are sympathetic to their political views. Conversely, officers who are seen to spend much time with the majority party leadership, and to be sensitive to their views, might neglect their duties as professional managers and fail to retain the confidence of the minority parties as arbitrators on the propriety of business.

6.139.   We were struck by the assessment of these role conflicts in the evidence of SOLACE (on behalf of chief executives) and of FUMPO (on behalf of chief officers). SOLACE recognised the potential difficulties but stressed the need 'to learn to work with the new realities' and for 'each local authority to determine its own way of working'. They opposed statutory protection for themselves or for chief officers as it 'may well produce situations where an authority is forced to work with its most senior officer unwillingly'. FUMPO on the other hand expressed much greater concern about their working relationships with the majority party and sought new safeguards—through an enforceable code of conduct—for their duty to report to the council as a whole and for their role as professional managers. The differing emphasis between these sets of evidence shows not only a difference of viewpoint, but a differing attitude to the political process. Generally we have found that chief executives are closer to the process, and more at ease with it, than their chief officers. Indeed it is often part of their role to mediate between councillors and chief officers, and resolve tensions between political and professional objectives. Chief executives have found it easier—although not necessarily easy—to reconcile the three roles we have set out: in short to be at the same time a facilitator for the policies of the majority party and an arbitrator between the parties.

6.140.   These considerations show that there are structural ambiguities in the role of officers which are inherent in the current legislative framework for local government. It might be thought these ambiguities can be resolved only through good working relationships rather than any concrete action that a Committee of Inquiry can recommend. We do not, however, believe this is entirely so. We have found a much greater degree of agreement in the evidence about the general principles underlying the role of officers than might perhaps have been anticipated on the basis of the frictions arising in individual authorities. We believe that the clearer application of these general principles will do much to resolve such frictions.

6.141.   The overwhelming view in the evidence we have received has been that officers (subject to very limited and closely defined exceptions) should continue to serve the council as a whole. This has not been a source of difference between officers and members, between majorities and minorities, or between right and left. There has equally been wide agreement that the public service tradition of a permanent corps of politically impartial officers should be retained. That is to say that the majority party should not use their voting strength to appoint officers on the basis of political sympathy with their position. There has also been wide agreement that within this broad framework there is room for, or (depending on the viewpoint) a positive need for:

141

(a) greater political sensitivity and flexibility among senior officers;

(b) the appointment of a limited number of relatively junior officers who are assigned to the political groups or their leaders.

6.142. The proposals which we make below are designed to build on this encouragingly broad basis of agreement.

THE CHIEF EXECUTIVE

Background

6.143. It has been almost universal practice since local government re-organisation for local authorities to appoint a chief executive as their most senior officer. The great majority are solicitors or (to a lesser extent) finance officers by background, but it is unusual for the chief executive to continue to have any departmental role.

6.144. The introduction of the post of chief executive was not based on any statutory requirement but on the recommendations of the Reports of the Maud[1], Bains[2] and Paterson[3]Committees. The underlying theme of these Reports was the need to weld local authorities into a corporate whole rather than a loose federation of service departments. The chief executive would chair the management team of senior officers and the post was seen as embodying corporatism at officer level in much the same way as the policy and resources committee (an innovation of similar vintage) was seen as embodying it at councillor level. The extent to which the chief executive has or should have authority over chief officers, especially on matters relating to the management of their departments, has however never been totally clear. The Bains Committee skirted round the question, recognising the potential sensitivity of relationships between chief officers and chief executives. The two crucial paragraphs of their report read as follows:

'5.11 Local Government has been engaged over a considerable period in the provision of a number of separate services, each controlled by a separate department, with its own independent head of profession. This situation has developed strong professional motivation and loyalty to departments, but has resulted in certain basic weaknesses which are now being tackled by a number of authorities. In this traditional situation the 'primus inter pares' situation of the Clerk of the Council represents tacit acceptance of the fact that in such an organisation somebody has to exercise a co-ordinating role. What those same Chief Officers are now being asked to accept is, however, somebody who is not merely primus inter pares, but is definitively their superior and the fact that in many cases it is the same man as hitherto makes the pill more difficult to swallow. Attitudes cannot be changed overnight and the newly appointed Chief Executive has a critical human relations problem to solve if he is to become effective.

---

[1] Report of the Committee on the Management of Local Government, 1967, paragraphs 170 to 180.
[2] 'The New Local Authorities: Management and Struture' 1972, paragraphs 5.9 to 5.15.
[3] 'The New Scottish Local Authorities: organisation and management structures' 1973, paragraphs 4.29 to 4.32.

5.12   His first task is to gain the respect and esteem of his colleagues, because his true powers will come more from his own qualities and character than from anything written into his, or the Chief Officers' terms of appointment. We do not suggest that there should be no formal definition of his position vis á vis the Chief Officers, but it is, we believe, important to recognise both the difficulties and the limitations of spelling it out, particularly in any detail. There is much to be said for allowing the man himself to develop his own interpretation of the job within a fairly broad framework.'

Reflecting the tentative approach of the Bains Committee, there is considerable variety in the roles adopted by chief executives. Some chief executives have clear management authority over all staff. Others act more as a *primus inter pares*, their role being not dissimilar to that of the former town and county clerks.

6.145.   The need for a more corporate approach to the officer structure has strengthened rather than weakened since the Bains Report. The ensuing period has been one of reduced economic growth and of public expenditure constraints. In such a climate decisions need increasingly to be taken on the basis of a balance between services and expediency rather than simply on professionally judged merits. At the same time there has been greater public participation in local authority decision formulation, accompanied by growing questioning of the judgement of professional officers—characterised in particular by rejection of planning and housing solutions of the 1950s and 1960s. These developments would have called for a more centralised and political (small 'p') approach to decisions even were it not for the parallel development of greater assertiveness and polarisation among councillors. Indeed politicisation among councillors has tended to mask other important changes which would anyway have required a fresh appraisal of local government management. The fact that the pressures on the traditional role of chief officers do not stem merely from politicisation but from wider developments is an important one, and is recognised by FUMPO in their evidence. They say:

'Similarly, the pressure on resources has led to a more intense search for value for money and a greater need to centralise and prioritise the allocation of resources in a way which draws leading members and the chief executive into the traditional areas of individual chief officers.'

The need to enhance the role of the chief executive

6.146.   We consider that, after some 15 years of experience of the post of chief executive, there is now a need for it to be clarified and formalised. This is for three reasons.

6.147.   First, the developments outlined above show that there is a stronger need than ever before to ensure that local authorities are organised corporately (rather than on the basis of service departments), and this would be assisted by vesting clearer responsibility in the chief executive for the overall performance of a local authority's staff.

6.148.   Second, the increasing frictions between councillors and officers will tend to be exacerbated where there is no clear management authority within the officer hierarchy. The chief executive has an important pivotal role in ensuring that officers understand, and are sensitive to, the political aspirations of councillors; and in ensuring that councillors recognise, and do not encroach on, the day-to-day management responsibilities of officers. We have been concerned by suggestions that where there is no chief executive, or a weak one, this has been accompanied by poor relations between councillors and senior officers and a tendency for their roles to merge.

6.149.   Third, management problems tend to arise where formal legal responsibilities are vested in an officer who is not the chief executive. Officers (other than chief constables, who are not covered by the discussion in this Chapter) do not have statutory responsibilities to carry out executive functions which impinge on councils dealings with the outside world. They do, however, have certain statutory responsibilities, and legal responsibilities under standing orders, to ensure that the internal affairs of the council are conducted with propriety (see paragraph 6.128). At present individual local authorities (ie councillors) may decide which officer to nominate to carry out such functions, and this may be a chief officer rather that the chief executive. This is poor management practice. All officer responsibilities should ultimately be the responsibility of the most senior officer.

6.150.   Under the city manager arrangements in the USA and Ireland the city manager is the clear head of other officers, and is personally accountable for the day-to-day administration of the authority. He or she is also the channel of communications with elected members. We have rejected such arrangements insofar as they involve any significant transfer of responsibility from councillors to officers. We are however attracted by them insofar as they provide for clear management responsibility and accountability **within** the officer hierarchy.

6.151.   We propose that all local authorities should be statutorily required to appoint one of their officers as the chief executive. This would not necessarily require an additional post. In small authorities the post could be combined with another leading post such as solicitor or director of finance. The chief executive should be head of the authority's paid staff with clear authority over other officers, and should have ultimate managerial responsibility for the way in which officers discharge the functions of the council. This will largely be a matter of internal management practice, and individual local authorities will need to consider what changes might be required in reporting arrangements and in the staffing of the chief executive's own office. However, where **statutory** functions relating to the propriety of council business are currently vested in officers the law should be amended so that they are vested specifically in the chief executive. Similarly all new statutory functions proposed in this Report should be vested in the chief executive. A list of existing and proposed statutory functions, all of which we propose should be vested in the chief executive, is at Annex K. It would be the chief executive's task either to discharge these functions personally or to ensure that they are discharged. It is recognised that the chief executive will not necessarily have professional qualifications relevant to the function in question—eg ensuring financial propriety or advising on the law. Nevertheless, a distinction can be drawn—as it is in other management structures—between professional and managerial responsibility. The chief officer heading a department should continue to have the same responsibility as at present for the maintenance of professional standards, but the chief executive should have ultimate managerial responsibility for ensuring that officers discharge their functions required of them. Chief executives should also have clearer responsibility for relations between councillors and officers. They should not be the sole channel of communication between councillors and officers, which would clearly be quite impractical and would devalue the role of chief officers. They should however exercise greater control over the channels of communication, and by doing so provide for more orderly relations.

6.152. We therefore recommend that:

(a) local authorities should be statutorily required to appoint a chief executive, who should be head of the authority's paid staff with overall managerial responsibility for the discharge of functions by officers;

(Paragraph 6.151)

(b) all statutory functions relating to the propriety of council business, whether currently existing or recommended in this Report, should be vested in the chief executive rather than any other officer.

(Paragraph 6.151)

RECONCILING THE ROLES OF OFFICERS

6.153. We have identified three roles of senior officers—those of professional manager, adviser and arbitrator—and suggested that they can sometimes be difficult to reconcile. Under our proposed enhancement of the position of chief executives, this difficulty of role reconciliation would focus particularly on their post but also apply more generally. We need to look at each of the roles and consider how they can be clarified, and how potential conflicts between them can be eased. We start with the third role, not because it is the most important, but because our proposals in respect of the officer's role as arbitrator set the tone for our overall approach.

The officer as arbiter

6.154. Our starting point is the consensus in the evidence that officers should continue to serve the council as a whole. This aspect of an officer's duty must not be left open to any doubt, and we believe that it would be strengthened by enhancing his statutory obligations as the arbiter of the propriety of council business. We have proposed in this Report four new procedural matters on which some arbiter of propriety is required, and have proposed that the role should be given to the chief executive. These are:

(a) deciding on the detailed application of the rule for party balance on committees (paragraph 5.50);

(b) deciding whether a councillor has a need to inspect a document or attend a meeting (paragraph 5.69);

(c) agreeing that a matter is urgent before a committee chairman may take a decision on it (paragraph 5.77);

(d) acting as registrar responsible for upkeep of the register of interests (paragraph 6.49).

In all these cases involvement of the chief executive as arbiter ensures that the matter is resolved internally within the local authority. At the same time it also

145

places the chief executive in a position where he has clear statutory duties to the council as a whole, and thereby insulates him or her from pressures to act simply as a facilitator for the majority party.

6.155.   The chief executive should additionally be given a formal statutory role in relation to the legality of council decisions. Where councillors propose to take any action which would be illegal, or alternatively risk breaking the law by failure to take an action, they should be advised by officers before the illegality occurs. We consider it important that chief executives should consider that it is part of their duties to ensure that such advice is given, however unpopular the advice may be. Generally we are satisfied that such advice is already being given. We note, for instance, that officers advised on several occasions of the possibility of illegality during the rate-fixing crisis in Liverpool in 1985[1]. We have considered nevertheless whether there should be a statutory duty placed on chief executives to ensure that councillors are advised in advance of any action or lack of action that might be illegal. There is, however, a danger that the imposition of a statutory duty in this form might encourage councillors to believe that everything was lawful unless they were advised to the contrary, and thereby transfer the responsibility for the council to act lawfully away from councillors and on to chief executives. We believe it would be better to create a new right for any councillors to call on chief executives to provide advice on the legality of any proposed action or inaction by the council. This would place chief executives in a reactive role, and remove any suggestion that a failure to advise that a matter was illegal thereby exonerated councillors. It is of course recognised that chief executives will often not themselves be solicitors, but the duty placed on them would be one of ensuring that advice was provided rather than providing it themselves.

6.156.   In their Green Paper 'Paying for Local Government'[2], the Government make proposals in respect of the financial propriety of council business. Having drawn attention to what they regard as improper accounting practices and rejected the need for some form of external control they go on to say:

> 'The Government would therefore much prefer a 'self-policing' solution which drew upon the professional probity of local government financial management to ensure that sound budgeting practice is maintained in all authorities, ... This could be achieved by establishing a specific statutory role for the treasurer or chief finance officer in relation to the legality and propriety of the expenditure by his local authority.'

The Green Paper then sets out a number of specific items which such a duty might encompass, including certification of the adequacy of a local authority's rate to meet expenditure. It also suggests a requirement that the chief finance officer should be a properly qualified accountant. A similar proposal was made in evidence to the Committee by the Chartered Institute of Public Finance and Accountancy.

6.157.   The rationale underlying this proposal is much the same as that underlying the proposals we have ourselves made for officers to ensure propriety in the conduct of council business. It differs, however, in two respects. First it envisages officers being given very detailed and specific statutory duties. Second it

---

[1] Parkinson, *Research Volume IV.*
[2] Paying for Local Government 1986. Cmnd 9714, paragraphs 7.15 to 7.25.

envisages the statutory duties being placed on the chief finance officer rather than the chief executive. Local authorities are already under a duty to designate an officer as having responsibility for the proper administration of their financial affairs (section 151 of the Local Government Act 1972 and section 95 of the Scottish Act). Under our recommendation at paragraph 6.152 this responsibility would statutorily fall on the chief executive. We are not ourselves clear that there is any need to impose duties on officers in relation to finance going beyond the general duties under sections 151 and 95, but we would not wish to prejudice the outcome of consultations on the Green Paper. If, however, there is found to be such a need then any new duties should be placed on chief executives not chief finance officers. It would be for chief executives, if they were not qualified accountants, to ensure that the duties were delegated to someone who was, but ultimate responsibility would remain with chief executives.

6.158.   In summary we recommend that:

chief executives should be given the following new statutory functions in relation to the propriety of council business:

(i)   to decide on the detailed application of the rules for party balance on committees;

(ii)   to decide whether a councillor has a need to inspect a document or attend a meeting;

(iii)   to agree that a matter is urgent before the chairman of a committee may take a decision on it;

(iv)   to act as the registrar responsible for the upkeep of the register of councillors' interests;

(v)   without prejudice to their general duty to advise the council, to provide advice at the request of any councillor as to the legality of any proposed action or inaction by the council.

(Paragraphs 6.154 and 6.155)

The officer as professional manager

6.159.   The main elements of the officer's role as professional manager have already been discussed in earlier discussion in the Report. We have said:

(a)   Great Britain should not adopt the system in USA and Ireland whereby city and county managers have legal powers to take day-to-day executive decisions in their own right rather than by virtue of delegation by councillors; (paragraphs 5.27 to 5.30);

(b)   councillors cannot be excluded from management issues, especially where their political party has a declared policy on such issues, as with for example decentralisation or privatisation (paragraph 6.83);

(c)   councillors should nevertheless not intervene as a matter of routine in day-to-day management, but should rather seek to direct the general management policy of the council (paragraph 6.83).

6.160.   There is however one specific matter where we believe that a departure from the general rule at (a) above is warranted—and this is the management of staff. At present statutory responsibility for the appointment, dismissal and discipline of staff lies solely with councillors. In practice councillors will normally leave the great majority of appointments and other staff matters to officers. In some cases this will be done formally through standing orders or a scheme of delegation—and we have already quoted an example at paragraph 5.123. In others it will simply be a matter of custom and practice. In the case of the discipline and dismissal of manual staff, responsibility has been placed on chief officers through the nationally agreed terms and conditions of service.

6.161.   Nevertheless our research shows that councillor involvement in staff appointments remains very considerable. In 67% of authorities councillors are 'routinely' involved in appointments below deputy chief officer level, and in 4% of authorities in all appointments. Additionally in about 50% of authorities councillors 'occasionally' are involved in appointments at a lower level than is 'routine'. Councillor involvement in appointments is not exclusively a feature of the big cities nor of councils dominated by political parties. It is equally pronounced in councils controlled or dominated by independent councillors. It is particularly prevalent in Wales. The research also shows, however, that it is growing, and that the growth is most pronounced in Labour controlled urban areas.[1]

6.162.   We can understand why councillors should be involved in the appointment of those officers who regularly give them advice. We note from our survey of councillors[2] that over 80% of councillors expressing a view believe they should be **more** involved than at present in the selection and recruitment of senior officers. We would not take issue with this, and will return later to the appointment of senior officers. We can also see reasons why councillors should have some say in the policy underlying more junior appointments—for example the need to ensure that the council follows equal opportunity policies and to ensure that the right council image is projected by those staff who have regular contact with the public. We cannot see however that this justifies councillors being directly involved in the recruitment of individual staff members to the extent that occurs in some authorities. We believe that this makes for poor management practice. If senior officers are to be effective in carrying out the policies of the council they need to have confidence in the character and abilities of those staff working for them. Line management responsibilities can be disrupted if appointments of junior staff are made by councillors rather than senior officers. Councillor involvement in appointments at a lower level than is operationally necessary also creates a risk of the exercise of patronage—that is to say of appointments being made for reasons other than the merits of the applicant. We do not necessarily mean patronage on the basis of political affiliation, and indeed we note that there is no relationship between the extent of party politics and the extent of councillor involvement in appointments. Patronage can however be based on a much wider range of ties, especially in small district councils where job applicants are more likely to be known to councillors. The dangers are particularly great with current levels of unemployment. The power to make an appointment is often the power to take one person rather than another out of the dole queue. We are not saying that patronage is necessarily being exercised

---

[1] Leach et al, *Research Volume I*, Tables 6.1 and A87 to A89.
[2] SCPR, *Research Volume II*, Table 7.26.

simply because councillors make junior appointments, although there are some individual authorities which do give cause for concern. The possibility is however ever present and it is wrong to create suspicion, especially given the scale of local authority employment. Frequently the council will be the biggest single employer in the area.

6.163. We propose, therefore, that local authorities should be required to provide through their standing orders that the chief executive should be formally responsible for the appointment of manual staff and of non-manual staff below principal officer level. This cut-off point is chosen because it is the level below which staff will not normally be involved in giving advice to elected members. Inevitably any cut-off is slightly arbitrary, but we believe that it is better expressed as a grade rather than as a tier in the hierarchy. The main point on which the cut-off might be unsatisfactory is the appointment of officers designated to serve the political groups or their leaders. In such instances (see paragraphs 6.170 to 6.172) it is reasonable that appointments should be made on a political basis. They tend however to be below principal officer grade, and we propose therefore that standing orders should be framed in such a way as to leave such appointments with councillors. Consideration might also need to be given to the precise position of certain specialist grades. Individual local authorities, reflecting their current practice, may wish to extend the chief executive's formal responsibility to appointments at principal officer level or even deputy chief officer. There is no reason why this should not be done through their own standing orders.

6.164. We propose that formal responsibility for appointments should be placed on chief executives rather than chief officers, as part of our more general theme of enhancing their management responsibility. We would expect chief executives to ensure consistency and fairness in appointments over the whole authority and to ensure that council policies on matters such as equal opportunities were implemented. We would not however expect them, any more than we would expect councillors, to be involved directly in individual appointments at ground level. That would be for them to delegate through proper line management. Authorities would need to review the reporting arrangements for the chief personnel officer to ensure that they were consistent with our proposal.

6.165. We need also to consider the discipline and dismissal of staff. We have been told in the evidence of instances where senior officers have considered that their management authority has been undermined by councillors interfering in individual disciplinary cases—especially where the majority party has close ties with the trade unions. This causes us concern. We propose that where chief executives are to be statutorily responsible for appointments (ie all manual staff and non-manual staff below principal officer) they should also be statutorily responsible for discipline and dismissal. The precise arrangements for discipline and dismissal are the subject of the terms and conditions of service drawn up by LACSAB. They should continue to be so, but LACSAB should initiate their amendment to ensure that they reflect the new statutory position which we recommend. They should be so framed that the final level of internal confirmation or appeal (ie other than an industrial tribunal) is no higher than the chief executive, with no involvement by councillors. The initiation of action would need to be at a lower management level. For more senior grades, where councillors would continue to have the statutory responsibility for appointments, they should continue to have final statutory responsibility for discipline and dismissal. The statute should however provide that such action may only be initiated by, or on the authority of, the chief executive. The terms and conditions of service should therefore limit the involvement of councillors to one of confirmation and appeal. Councillors should remain able to initiate action for the discipline or dismissal of chief executives, subject to the procedure for dismissal proposed at paragraph 6.203.

6.166. We therefore recommend that:

(a)   the chief executive should be statutorily responsible for the appointment, discipline and dismissal of staff below the rank of principal officer, except where staff are appointed to serve the political groups or their leaders;

(Paragraphs 6.163 to 6.165)

(b)   the chief executive should be statutorily responsible for initiating action for the discipline or dismissal of staff at or above the rank of principal officer;

(Paragraph 6.165)

(c)   the Local Authorities' Conditions of Service Advisory Board should take steps to amend the terms and conditions of service of officers so that they reflect the statutory arrangements for discipline and dismissal proposed above.

(Paragraph 6.165)

The officer as adviser

6.167.   It remains to be considered whether officers, in the light of the strengthening of their relationship with the council as a whole, may still adequately perform their role as adviser. In particular it needs to be considered whether their relationship with the council as a whole makes it impracticable for them to give the kind of advice that will be sought by the majority party.

6.168.   In principle we do not see why not. We do not believe from the evidence we have received from them that councillors are looking for advice which **reflects** their political point of view, but rather advice which is factual and honest and which **shows** an **understanding** of their political aspirations and constraints. There is no reason in principle why an officer should not be able to give advice of such a kind to all political parties represented on the council. Nor, to the extent that officers might in practice give advice on a fuller and more regular basis to the majority party, is there any reason why they should not continue to do so just as effectively when there is a change of political control.

6.169.   We recognise at the same time, however, that some senior officers, especially chief officers, have encountered difficulty in striking a balance between their statutory responsibility to the council as a whole and the need to give full advice to the majority party. We believe that the position can be assisted in four ways:

(a)   through special advisers attached to the political groups or their leaders;

(b)   through clearer rules governing attendance at party groups;

(c)   through the development of local conventions defining councillor/officer relationships;

(d)   through training.

We deal with the first three of these in turn below. We consider training later at paragraphs 6.218 to 6.221, as it is an issue which relates to councillors and officers alike.

(i)   Advisers attached to party groups or their leaders

6.170.   In some authorities it might be considered that the political groups' need for advice cannot be fully met by the chief executive and by those staff reporting to him or her through the normal officer hierarchy. This might occur where the chief executive is by natural disposition more a manager and less a political operator. It might occur where a council is hung with three parties all holding the balance of power, or it might happen simply because the political temperature is that much higher. Our research[1] suggests that some 40 local authorities have devised arrangements whereby the party groups or their leaders have officers specifically attached to them, and this number is growing. Their job is overtly to provide back-up for the person or group concerned (eg by research, policy analysis, paper writing) not to serve the council as a whole. The precise role will vary and there will indeed be a continuum from authorities who simply provide secretarial and clerical assistance to groups and their leaders, to those who provide a well-developed source of alternative advice. Generally the officers concerned are at a relatively junior level (typically at the grade of senior officer) and do not purport to replicate the role of chief officers. In some authorities the officers are seconded for limited periods from the mainstream staff anyway working for that authority. In others they are specifically appointed to the post from outside. In the latter instance the appointee might be personally identified with the political party, but in the former there would be no such presumption.

6.171.   In the evidence a sharp distinction has been made between overt arrangements of this kind and covert arrangements whereby officers beneath chief officer level in the main officer hierarchy have become singled out by the political parties as being sympathetic sources of advice. This latter practice is highly damaging to chief officers' management authority and blurs roles insidiously. We believe it is quite wrong and should be stopped, and this view is widely reflected in the evidence. On the other hand there has been widespread acceptance in the evidence of limited overt appointments as set out at paragraph 6.170. They are regarded as providing some flexibility within the system and thereby taking some political pressure off the main officer hierarchy without challenging their authority. The arrangements are supported in the evidence of both the Labour Party and Conservative Party and are also accepted in principle by SOLACE and FUMPO. They are precedented at central government where, since the 1970s there have been arrangements for special advisers to be appointed to serve Ministers on an overtly political basis and also for back-up to the opposition party groups and leaders in the House of Commons—in both cases paid for out of public funds.

---

[1] Leach et al, *Research Volume I*, Table A49.

6.172. Such arrangements are limited to only a few local authorities (of all political colours) at present, and we would not wish to suggest that they would be appropriate on a general basis. We do believe however that they provide a useful means of broadening the basis for advice to councillors in a way which should positively promote rather than damage the role of the main officer hierarchy of serving the whole council. If the law is at present considered insufficiently clear on the matter, then it should be amended to make clear that such appointments are permissible. We do believe however that certain rules should be followed by all authorities making such appointments. These are:

(a)   officers attached to the party groups or their leaders should be clearly differentiated from those serving the council as a whole: they should not exercise executive functions, and should report direct to councillors not through the chief executive;

(b)   they should be very limited in number and in seniority, so that they do not purport to become an alternative administration. For most authorities up to five officers at senior officer grade would be more than adequate;

(c)   the facility should be made available to the minority parties. How this is done would of course depend on the precise political balance and hard and fast rules would be difficult;

(d)   if the appointment is being made from outside the authority on the basis of the political affiliation or sympathy of the applicant this should be stated so there is a clear distinction between such appointments and those seconded from mainstream local authority staff.

(ii)   Attendance at party groups

6.173.   The ability of senior officers to act as effective adviser to councillors will in some authorities depend on whether or not they attend, or are prepared to attend, meetings of the party groups. Our research[1] shows that attendance at present is the exception rather than the rule. The chief executive 'always' attends in 1% of authorities, 'sometimes' in 5%, 'occasionally' in 27% and 'never' in the remaining 66%.

6.174.   Specific provision governing officer atendance at party groups is made in their terms and conditions of service, which state:

'The officer should not be called upon to advise any political group of the employing authority either as to the work of the group or as to the work of the authority, neither shall he or she be required to attend any meeting of any political group. *This shall be without prejudice to any arrangements to the contrary which may be made in agreement with the officer and which includes adequate safeguards to preserve the political neutrality of the officer in relation to the affairs of the council.*'

The words in italics have been added in the case of chief executives, chief officers and deputy chief officers, but not in the case of grades beneath these levels.

---

[1] Leach et al, *Research Volume I*, Table A55.

6.175. We consider that this makes unnecessarily heavy weather of the subject. The safeguarding of the political impartiality of officers is crucial, and we shall return to this in paragraphs 6.180 to 6.217, but the issue of impartiality does not turn on whether or not officers attend party group meetings. There is nothing indeed intrinsically different between attending a one party committee of the council and attending a party group meeting. There can be positive advantage in attendance in those authorities where the party group is the main forum for policy formulation. We recognise that regular attendance at party groups may create workload problems for senior officers, and unreasonable demands should not be placed on them, but such problems are part of more general pressures and do not justify any special restrictions relating specifically to party groups. We believe therefore that the special inhibitions relating to party groups should be removed from the terms and conditions of service. There should, however, be two basic safeguards for attendance.

6.176. First, a party group should not be able to specify which officer should attend, as this creates the danger of individual officers becoming identified with the party concerned. Rather the group should approach the chief executive, who should then attend in person or decide which of his or her officers should attend. Second, where officers attend the party group of one party the chief executive should notify the group(s) of the other party or parties and offer them a similar facility.

6.177. The question arises of whether a further safeguard should be added— that officers should not attend meetings of the party group where non-councillors are present. This is a point which has caused concern to a number of officers, and this is reflected in the evidence from SOLACE and FUMPO. Concern has arisen particularly where the non-councillors are junior council employees. Our research[1] shows that non-councillors attend party groups in about 72% of cases, with employees attending in about 11% (almost all Labour). In 5% of cases the chief executive has attended meetings of the party group where employees of the authority have also been present. This does not suggest that the issue is a widespread one. We do not moreover see that it raises major issues of principle. It is for instance everyday practice for officers to attend meetings of the education committee of the council where non-councillors including employees of the council (teachers) are not only present but actually vote (which is not normally the case in party groups). While we do recognise and understand the sensitivity of some officers on this issue, we believe that there are dangers of over-sensitivity. The presence of non-councillors should not be seen as an inhibition on attendance at party groups.

(iii) Local conventions

6.178. Some of the difficulties that have arisen over officer advice to councillors appear to have arisen through a lack of any clear rules or conventions. We have already referred in Chapter Five (paragraphs 5.128 to 5.131) to the need for each local authority to develop explicit conventions for the conduct of business, and we would expect that these should include clear rules on the extent to which the various parties might be entitled to officer advice. We propose that such conventions should include the safeguards which we have listed at paragraph

---

[1] Leach et al, *Research Volume I*, Tables A59, A63 and A69.

6.172 in relation to special advisers and at paragraph 6.175 in relation to attendance at party groups, as well as such other matters as might be locally appropriate (eg rights to briefing by chief officers prior to committee meetings).

6.179.   In summary we recommend that:

(a)   local authorities should be able, if they wish, to attach staff to the party groups or their leaders;

(Paragraph 6.172)

(b)   such arrangements should be subject to the following safeguards:

(i)   the officers should be clearly differentiated from officers serving the council as a whole: they should not carry out or be involved in executive functions and should report direct to councillors, not through the chief executive;

(ii)   they should be strictly limited in number and seniority;

(iii)   the facility should be made available to minority parties;

(iv)   it should be made clear whether or not the appointment is being made on political criteria;

(Paragraph 6.172)

(c)   the Local Authorities' Conditions of Service Advisory Board should take steps to amend officers' terms and conditions of service so that no special inhibition is placed on attendance at party groups;

(Paragraph 6.175)

(d)   the attendance of officers at party groups should be subject to the following safeguards:

(i)   all requests for attendance should be addressed to the chief executive, who should decide which officers should attend;

(ii)   the chief executive should notify the other parties, and offer a similar facility;

(Paragraph 6.176)

(e)   the safeguards listed at (b) and (d) should be included in the conventions which we have recommended that all local authorities should prepare, as should such other rules governing officer advice as might be locally appropriate.

(Paragraph 6.178)

PATRONAGE AND POLITICAL NEUTRALITY

Introduction

6.180.   Public service in the United Kingdom is founded on a tradition of a permanent corps of politically neutral officers serving with equal commitment whatever party may be in political control. This has not always been the case. In the 18th and early 19th century, public service jobs were regarded as a means of

154

rewarding friends and political allies. This led to reforms in the civil service to ensure:

(a)   selection on merit;

(b)   fair and open competition.

It is the task of the Civil Service Commission, which is independent of Ministers, to certify (with certain limited exceptions) that appointments to Government Departments are based on these two criteria.

6.181.   In some other countries public service is not based on such traditions. Instead there is a spoils system, under which a political party attaining office will appoint its own supporters to key posts. This does not necessarily work badly, and there is an extent to which it is accepted in this country for a very limited number of posts (special advisers attached to Ministers).

6.182.   Local government in the United Kingdom has traditionally been based on the same public service tradition as central government, but this has been a matter of convention and practice. There is no equivalent of the Civil Service Commission. Local authorities make their own appointments and there is nothing in law to prevent them from appointing political supporters of the majority party.

6.183.   There have been allegations in the evidence that precisely that has been happening. The Government in their written evidence have suggested that some posts have been advertised in a loaded way designed to appeal to members of one political party. It is true that some posts have been advertised in 'Labour Weekly' and we have seen copies of job applications where applicants have included their political affiliations under their leisure activities. It is similarly alleged in the evidence that some Conservative councils vet applicants through Conservative Central Office, and this is also referred to in our research[1]. The Government have said in their evidence that we should consider some new mechanism for preventing the exercise of political patronage and that one of the options to be examined is a Local Government Staff Commission: this proposal had been previously considered, and rejected, by the Mallaby Committee[2].

6.184.   Despite allegations about practice in particular instances practically no one in the evidence submitted to us has supported the concept that the generality of local government officers should be appointed on political criteria. The nearest thing we can find to such a view is the evidence of the Association of London Authorities, who state that their members are divided between those who would welcome a move towards a 'spoils' system and those who would not. Our survey of councillors[3] asked whether 'council officials should only be appointed if they are broadly sympathetic with the aims of the majority party'. Of those who stated a clear view only 6% agreed with this proposition.

6.185.   Whatever the wider merits of a spoils system of appointments it must clearly be unworkable in the framework of British local government, where

---

[1]   Leach et al, *Research Volume I*, Chapter Six.
[2]   Report of the Committee on Staffing of Local Government, 1967, paragraph 419.
[3]   SCPR, *Research Volume II*, Table 7.29.

officers are legally obliged to serve the whole council. No minority party could be expected to have trust in officers who had been appointed on the basis of their allegiance to the majority party.

6.186.   The issue of principle is therefore straightforward. There must continue to be a system of permanent and politically neutral officers appointed on the basis of merit. The issue which we need to consider is whether new machinery or rules are required to ensure this, and if so on what basis.

6.187.   We start by making an important distinction between:

   (a)   appointment being based on merit; and

   (b)   officers themselves being politically neutral.

The two issues might in practice overlap, but in principle are distinct. It is for instance quite possible to conceive of a situation where a local authority appoints someone because they are a member of party X rather than because of their abilities, but for that person to carry out their duties in a professional way without their political views being in any way visible. On the other hand another authority might appoint someone because of their undoubted abilities, but that person might at the same time be an active local politician. We shall look first at appointment (and the related issue of dismissal) and then go on to consider political activity.

Appointment of senior officers

6.188.   We have earlier recommended (paragraph 6.163) that the responsibility for appointment of officers below principal officer grade should lie with the chief executive rather than councillors. This should remove any significant risk of political patronage in such appointments, and our main focus in these paragraphs will be on senior officers—ie those at principal officer and above.

6.189.   Whatever else may be decided, we are convinced that all such appointments must continue to be made by the local authorities themselves, not by any outside agency. Local authorities differ greatly in their culture, traditions and service priorities. The kind of senior officer needed for example in a large shire county, with a major budget and workforce but a relatively stable social and political environment, will tend to be very different to that needed in an inner London borough with a smaller budget but a high level of social deprivation and vigorous community politics. Other local factors, such as personalities and working conventions, may also be important and the imposition of appointments from outside would tend only to make for bad relations between councillors and the officer concerned. We therefore rule out any staff commission (such as that discussed by the Mallaby Report and the commission currently existing in Ireland) which would itself make appointments to local authorities and/or have some wider responsibility for career management.

6.190.   It is, however, for consideration whether there should be some regulation of the way in which local authorities **themselves** appoint senior officers. In our view there should be, for two reasons.

6.191.   First, it is clear from the evidence that in some authorities an unhealthy atmosphere of suspicion has developed, with some officers being labelled as 'political appointees'. Insofar as the suspicions are justified some form of regulation would clearly have a desirable effect. We are, however, equally concerned about cases where an appointment is not politically motivated but where it was carried out in a manner which suggested it might have been. This is unfair on the officer concerned. The dangers are particularly great where there are legitimate reasons why a local authority should be looking for a certain type of officer (eg as in our inner London example). Unless procedures are clearly above board this can be made to look like a political test.

6.192.   Second, and the point applies particularly to chief executives, we are conscious that some of our earlier recommendations would positively increase the pressures for political appointments. If for example councillors on a local authority were determined to involve themselves in junior staff appointments, but were prevented from doing so directly by such appointments becoming the responsibility of the chief executive, then the logical course would be to appoint a compliant chief executive. The dangers are not only of appointment of politically sympathetic chief executives. There might be an equal danger in the appointment of someone who is weak, or whose appointment involves a very substantial promotion and who therefore feels strong ties of patronage to those who appointed him or her.

6.193.   What we need to ensure, to allay such fears, is that local authority appointments are based on the two principles followed since the 19th century for the civil service of:

(a)   merit;

(b)   fair and open competition.

The kind of thing which we wish to prevent is appoinments being advertsied in a way which conveys the impression that only supporters of the majority party should apply, or which gives a misleading picture of the job that is deliberately designed to deter applicants other than the candidate who the authority have anyway in mind to appoint. Equally we want to ensure that where several people are interviewed the final decision is taken purely on the basis of who is best fitted for the job.

6.194.   This is precisely the kind of task undertaken for the civil service by the Civil Service Commission. Unlike the kind of staff comission mentioned at paragraph 6.189, they do not themselves make appointments or even nominate people to posts. They simply certify that those who Departments wish to appoint have been selected on merit following fair and open competition. We do not however believe that there should be an equivalent local government staff commission, even on this more limited basis. Our whole approach has been to avoid the creation of new bureaucratic machinery, and we certainly do not believe that the scale of the problem justifies such machinery in this case. It needs to be borne in mind that such a commission would be responsible for appointments to about 70,000 posts covering a wide range of professions in over 500 local authorities. This would require a substantial establishment, probably including regional offices. Moreover, local authorities in reacting to the Mallaby concept of a staff commission and also the more recent suggestion in the Government's evidence, have shown strong opposition to any such body. While some of their arguments would not apply to the more limited role envisaged in paragraph 6.190, we do not

157

judge that local government would accept the need for a new national body regulating the making of appointments and they might well fear that once established its role would be widened.

6.195.   A less radical solution with similar purpose has been proposed to us by the Audit Commission. This is that local authority appointments panels should include an independent outside assessor. Some authorities already do this, and it is something which we would commend—especially in relation to chief executives (see paragraph 6.198). However, if this was to be made a national requirement for all appointments at principal officer and above, it would tend to create a new industry. It would in particular be necessary to establish substantial machinery for approving the assessors to ensure their independence.

6.196.   What we propose instead is that there should be a new national code of practice on appointments. This would be prescribed by the Secretary of State following consultation with the local authority associations. The foundations are already laid by the fact that the 1975 National Code of Local Government Conduct deals to some extent with appointments (the relevant passage is quoted in paragraph 6.130) and by our recommendation that the Code should be given statutory status with a requirement for all local authorities to have regard to it (paragraph 6.19). We propose that these foundations should be built on as follows.

6.197.   First, the existing passage on appointments should be taken out of the 1975 Code (which is directed essentially at individual councillors) and the matter dealt with by a separate code on appointments which would have the same statutory status as we propose should be given to the 1975 Code.

6.198.   Second, the new code should state that all appointments should be based on the two criteria of merit and of fair and open competition. It should then go on to set out basic procedures designed to achieve these criteria. These should cover job descriptions, advertising, drawing up of short lists, composition of selection committees (including minority party representation) and the basis of the final selection. It should distinguish between different grades, and in particular should set more stringent standards for chief executives. In the case of chief executives provision should be made for outside assessors to be included on selection committees; if the assessor is not satisfied with the procedures followed or with the final nomination made by the committee his or her report should be made available to the council before a final decision is taken. We do not consider that this more limited usage of assessors would give rise to the objections stated at paragraph 6.195. The Local Government Training Board (LGTB) are already involved in acting as, and proposing, assessors for chief executive appointments. We suggest that they should draw up a standing panel of assessors. Whenever a local authority makes a chief executive appointment the LGTB should be asked to nominate an assessor from this panel.

6.199.   Third, it should be made statutorily explicit that breach of the code constitutes prima facie maladministration, so that an unsuccessful applicant may complain to the local ombudsman if he or she has suffered injustice through failure to abide by the procedures in the code. At present staff appointments fall outside the local ombudsman's remit, but we propose that this should be changed as part of a more general re-assessment of the ombudsman's powers (discussed more fully in Chapter Nine).

6.200. Although the issues we have been addressing in this Chapter have related primarily to senior staff, the code should apply to all appointments including those made by the chief executive. It would be wrong for prospective junior staff to be excluded from remedies available to their seniors. The code would however need to make special provision for advisers to the party groups or their leaders in cases where they are appointed from outside the authority. Appointment on a political basis is acceptable here just as it is in central government, where analogous posts are not subject to certification by the Civil Service Commission.

Dismissal of senior officers

6.201. The question of dismissals needs to be considered not only from the point of view of injustice to the officer concerned, but from the wider public interest. The two do not necessarily coincide. A local authority cannot summarily dismiss their chief executive or senior officer without compensation any more than can a private sector company. If they do the officer can bring a claim of unfair dismissal before an industrial tribunal. The tribunal can order compensation or reinstatement. In fact summary dismissals in local government seem to be rare. More often there is mutual agreement to leave following the negotiation of compensation. We have moreover received very little evidence of dismissals, even with compensation being paid, purely on the grounds of political incompatibility. Often there is a wider background of poor performance of duties, and it might be that some officers have positively gained through the authority being prepared to compensate for a totally justified dismissal rather than run the risk of being accused of acting on political motives.

6.202. SOLACE have suggested a national basis for compensation, and there might be merit in this. We do not however see compensation as a panacea. It might make removal of senior officer dismissals all too easy because the officer will not resist or appeal—and it is paid at public expense. For the same reason we have reservations about too widespread a move towards fixed term contracts whereby authorities would simply have the option of not renewing a contract if they wished to get rid of an officer. Officers working on such a basis are normally able to negotiate an enhanced salary (reflecting the risk factor) and again the public must pay. Our research[1] shows that fixed term contracts have been introduced in some 14 authorities for chief executives or chief officers. This number seems likely to increase.

6.203. Local authorities must ultimately have the ability to get rid of senior staff where serious issues of incompatibility or incompetence arise, but we see dangers in both the compensation and fixed term contract routes because they make the process too easy and thereby begin to threaten the tradition of a permanent corps of local government officers. In the case of officers beneath the level of chief executive, we believe that sufficient safeguard would be provided by our recommendation (at paragraph 6.165) that any action for dismissal or discipline must be initiated by the chief executive. We believe, however, that an

---

[1] Leach et al, *Research Volume I*, Table A90.

additional safeguard is required for the chief executive's own position. We are particularly conscious of the recommendations we have made to place new responsibilities on chief executives. In some cases the exercise of these responsibilities would require them to be unpopular with the majority party. These recommendations would be undermined if the majority party could get rid of chief executives, and no less so simply because the chief executive leaves by mutual agreement. Accordingly we propose that a chief executive may only be dismissed on the vote of two-thirds of the members of the council. The two-thirds test is precedented by the requirement in the Local Government (Scotland) Act 1947 (see paragraph 6.125), but we have deliberately phrased it more stringently so that it applies to the whole council not just those voting.

Recommendations on appointments and dismissals

6.204.   In summary we recommend that:

(a)   a Code of Practice should be introduced setting out procedures designed to ensure that appointments made by local authorities are based on merit and fair and open competition;

(Paragraphs 6.196 to 6.198)

(b)   in the case of chief executives, these procedures should include provision for an independent assessor on selection committees;

(Paragraph 6.198)

(c)   the Code should be statutorily prescribed by the Secretary of State following consultation with the local authority associations: local authorities should be required to have regard to it, with breach of its provisions constituting prima facie maladministration and subject to the local ombudsman;

(Paragraphs 6.197 to 6.199)

(d)   the legislation should be amended to prevent a local authority dismissing a chief executive except on the vote of two thirds of the membership of the council.

(Paragraph 6.203)

Political neutrality and activity

6.205.   In their evidence to the Committee the Local Authorities' Conditions of Service Advisory Board said:

'the underlying assumption behind all the national agreements is that senior local government officers should be politically neutral.'

This assumption is however not explicitly reflected in the wording of the agreements except in the limited area of attendance at political groups (see paragraph 6.174). We have recommended earlier that the provisions relating to political groups should be deleted. It is for consideration whether there should be a more general provision making clear that officers are to act impartially in all their official activities; that is to say they should not be influenced by preference for one political party rather another, nor indeed by any other sectional allegiance not directly related to party politics.

160

6.206.   Such a provision would help underpin an officer's impartiality, and in some instances might help the officer to resist any pressures that he or she might consider important. It would not, however, deal with the important issue of officers' extramural activities and in particular with the situation where an officer is overtly involved in political activity.

6.207.   In the civil service there are rules limiting the political activity of officers. Civil servants are either 'politically free', 'intermediate' or 'politically restricted' according to grade. Staff in the first group may engage in political activity. Those in the second group may participate in politics only with the permission of their Department. Those in the third group may participate in local political activity with the permission of their Department, but in no circumstances may participate in national political activity. The definition of politial activity covers four main areas:

(a)   candidature for public elected office (councillor[1]MP, MEP);

(b)   holding office in a political party;

(c)   speaking and writing in public on matters of political controversy;

(d)   canvassing at elections.

6.208.   These provisions are all contained in the Civil Service Pay and Conditions Code. There is, however, no similar provision in local authorities' terms and conditions of service. As a result local government officers are free to undertake spare time political activity and in particular may be councillors in other authorities. The question arises as to whether something akin to the Civil Service Code should be applied to local authorities.

6.209.   We have made clear earlier (paragraph 6.31) that there is nothing improper, as far as the duties of a **councillor** are concerned, in a councillor being a local government employee. What we need to consider here is the converse. Does being a councillor, or otherwise being engaged in political activity, conflict with an officer's duties?

6.210.   In our view the answer depends essentially on what the duties of the officer are. Certainly there can be no conflict in the case of manual workers. Nor do we see any significant problem for junior non-manual grades. There might perhaps be some difficulty where junior staff have considerable contact with the public, but we do not see this as a major area of concern. Nor do we see any problem for teachers. We do not see that political activity conflicts with the professional requirements of teaching, and it would indeed rewrite the political map of the country if teachers were not to be allowed to engage in politics. In all these cases we see the only need being to ensure that they are not given excessive paid time-off work, and this we have already covered at paragraph 6.120.

6.211.   We see different considerations arising in the case of senior local government officers. It is part of their job to advise councillors, and to adjudicate on matters of propriety, and in doing so they must command the respect and trust of all political parties. There might well be some senior officers who are politically

---

[1] Membership of a parish or community council is permitted.

active but who are nevertheless totally able to detach themselves from such activity in carrying out their duties as neutral officers. Nevertheless we believe there will always be a very significant risk that they are viewed with suspicion by councillors of other parties, and that as a consequence the performance of their duties towards the council as a whole will be impaired. We propose therefore that senior officers should be dabarred from political activity.

6.212.   Here as before we define senior officers as those of principal officer grade and above, as it is such grades which are routinely involved in advice to elected members. About 70,000 officers in all would be affected—less than 3% of local authority employees. We are conscious that the civil service rules apply to staff at a much more junior level. Only manual and non-officer workers are 'politically free'. However, this very wide-ranging prohibition depends for its acceptability on the possibility of exemptions being granted on a case by case basis and on a reasonable consensus as to when such exemptions should be granted. The position is very different in local government where there are over 500 authorities, and we believe that the need is for a simple rule with no exemptions but applying to fewer staff.

6.213.   We propose that the definition of political activity should be as summarised at paragraph 6.207, with one modification. This concerns speaking and writing on matters of political controversy. It is common (and proper) practice for senior local government officers both to speak and write on behalf of their authority on such matters, and also to do so in a personal capacity at, for instance, conferences of their professional associations. The ban on speaking and writing should not apply where officers are acting in their official capacity, and it should only apply in their personal capacity if they are thereby seen to be engaging in party politics. The precise wording of this aspect of the prohibition would need careful attention.

6.214.   It remains to be considered how our recommendations should be implemented, and this question is related to the extent to which there is consensus on the subject. There has been a danger during our Inquiry of the issue becoming politically polarised, largely because of press speculation that the Government were contemplating a wide-ranging ban on local authority employees being councillors. This speculation has led to opponents of the Government saying they would resist such measures. This is unfortunate because the relatively narrow territory covered by our recommendation—that of the political activity of senior officers—has been the subject of wide consensus in the evidence. Those who have said that such activity is wrong include for example the Conservative and Labour parties; FUMPO and SOLACE, the Association of Metropolitan Authorities and the Association of District Councils.

6.215.   We hope that this consensus will be reflected in the reaction to our recomendation and accordingly that it would be practicable to implement it through agreed amendment to local authorities' terms and conditions of service. This is the best approach because political activity (with one exception—see below) is not a concept readily amenable to legislation and is not the subject of legislation in the civil service context. Flexibility moreover is required, in local as it is in central government, to deal with particular cases such as special advisers appointed on an overtly political basis. If however local authorities, through

162

LACSAB, do not take the necessary action or cannot reach agreement with the officers' unions then we believe legislation should be introduced.

6.216. There is one political activity on which legislation should be introduced in any case, because it is relatively straightforward: that of being a councillor. Section 80(1)(a) of the Local Government Act 1972 (section 31(1)(a) of the Scottish Act) already disqualifies an employee of a local authority from standing for election as a councillor in the **same** authority. Section 116 of the 1972 Act (section 67 of the Scottish Act) prevents a councillor, or someone who was a councillor in the last 12 months, being appointed as an officer of the **same** authority. These two provisions should be extended so that they apply, in the case of officers at principal officer grade and above, to being a councillor or officer in **another** authority.

Recommendations on political activity

6.217. We therefore recommend that:

(a)   the legislation should be amended so that persons who are councillors, or who are standing for election as councillors, or who have been councillors within the last year, may not be employed by another authority at the rank of principal officer or above;

(Pararaph 6.216)

(b)   the Local Authorities' Conditions of Service Advisory Board should take steps to include in the terms and conditions of officers at the rank of principal officer and above a prohibition on political activity, including:

(i)   standing for, and holding, public elected office;

(ii)   holding office in a political party;

(iii)   speaking or writing in public in a personal capacity in a way that might be regarded as engaging in party political debate;

(iv)   canvassing at elections;

(Paragraphs 6.211 to 6.215)

(c)   if the changes recommended at (b) are not made to officers' terms and conditions, legislation should be introduced to similar effect.

(Paragraph 6.215)

TRAINING FOR COUNCILLORS AND OFFICERS

6.218. It is clear from the discussion in this Chapter that there is a need for councillors and senior officers to develop a better understanding of each other's roles. Councillors need to understand and respect the delicate balance which senior officers must keep between serving the council as a whole and providing adequate advice to the majority party. Senior officers need to undersand and respect the political aspirations of councillors.

6.219. The scope for misunderstanding will always be greatest when a new council is elected. In those authorities where the whole council retires simultaneously, elections can result in 50% or more of councillors being new to their duties. There is a need for induction training of new councillors, and our research has shown that current arrangements are patchy[1]. There is also a need for senior officers to study the manifestos of the parties at election time so that they are ready to react positively to the policies of whoever wins a majority (or, in hung councils, to act creatively in developing policies which will command a majority). After election time there remains a continuing onus on councillors and officers to be sensitive to each other's position. In the case of chief officers this might involve a reduced stress on purely professional skills and increased development of wider managerial and political skills, and this has implications for patterns of career development and of training.

6.220.   These are issues to which individual local authorities will need to give careful attention in in-house training and officer postings. There is also however an important role at national level for the LGTB. The LGTB have recently been devoting an increasing proportion of their work to the development of political and managerial skills among senior officers, and have more recently begun to be involved also in the training of councillors. They have organised seminars and prepared papers on such matters as 'the management of hung authorities' and 'ethics in local government'. This is an aspect of their work which we commend and believe could profitably be expanded further.

6.221.   We therefore recommend that:

individual local authorities and the Local Government Training Board should place increased stress on training designed to ensure better understanding by councillors and officers of each other's roles, responsibilities and aspirations.

(Paragraphs 6.219 to 6.220)

---

[1] Leach et al, *Research Volume I*, Chapter Three.

CHAPTER 7

ELECTORAL ARRANGEMENTS AND COUNCIL SIZE

INTRODUCTION

7.1 We sought elaboration from the Department of the Environment as to what electoral matters fell within our terms of reference. We were told that the following matters were outside our terms of reference:

(a) the franchise—ie who may vote;

(b) the method of election—ie whether there should be a system of proportional representation and whether voting should be compulsory;

and that the following matters were within our terms of reference:

(a) the frequency of elections;

(b) the number of councillors in each ward;

(c) the number of councillors on each council.

7.2 In this Chapter we look at each of the three matters within our terms of reference. All three are linked, but the linkage is particularly strong between the frequency of elections and the number of councillors in each ward. We therefore look at these two matters first, and then go on to consider council size.

CURRENT ELECTORAL ARRANGEMENTS

England and Wales

(i) County councils

7.3 Each county is divided into electoral divisions with one member for each division. Elections are held every four years, with all members retiring simultaneously.

(ii) Metropolitan district councils

7.4 Each metropolitan district is divided into wards with three members per ward. The Local Government Act 1972 requires that the number of members must be divisible by three. Although in practice all wards have three members, six or nine member wards would be legally permissible. Elections are held in three years out of every four, with a third of members retiring at each election. Because a member retires in each ward at each election, the whole electorate have the opportunity to vote.

(iii) Shire district councils

7.5 Each shire district is divided into wards, most but not all of which are multi-member. About 40% of wards have one member, about 30% have two members, and about 30% have three members. A handful have four or more members. Wards are as far as possible based on indentifiable communities, but with a constant ratio of electors to councillors within the authority. Single member wards are therefore commonest in sparsely populated communities.

7.6 All members retire simultaneously unless the council decides instead to opt for a system of election by thirds. Where, however, they do so opt the number of

165

members per ward will still normally vary—unlike the position in metropolitan districts. The electorate in wards with only one or two members will not therefore have the opportunity to vote in every election year.

7.7   About 60% of district councils at present have whole council elections, and the remainder elections by thirds. Those councils with elections by thirds tend to be councils which were county or non-county boroughs prior to reorganisation (as these categories of council used to be required to have elections by thirds).

(iv) London borough councils

7.8   Each London borough is divided into wards of one, two or three members. About 55% of wards have three members, 43% two members and 2% one member. All members retire simultaneously with elections every four years.

Scotland
(i) Region and islands councils

7.9   Each region and islands area is divided into electoral divisions of one member each. All members retire simultaneously with elections every four years.

(ii) District councils

7.10   Each district is divided into wards of one member each. All members retire simultaneously with elections every four years.

Background

7.11   The background to this complex position can be found in the 19th century origins of elected local government. Under the Municipal Corporation Act of 1835 the newly created boroughs had three member wards with elections every year, and a third of members retiring each year. Under the Local Government Act of 1888 the new counties were divided into single member wards with all members retiring together every three years. The urban and rural district councils, which were created later by the Local Government Act 1894, were a hybrid with multi-member wards and whole council elections unless they opted for election by thirds.

7.12   The position was strongly criticised by the Maud Committee[1], the Redcliffe-Maud Commission[2] and the Wheatley Commission.[3] All three recommended that there should be a uniform system with single member wards and all members retiring simultaneously rather than by thirds. The Wheatley commission additionally recommended that whole council elections should be quadrennial rather than triennial, and the Redcliffe-Maud Commission also said this change should be considered.

7.13   The Wheatley Commission's electoral recommendations were followed in full in the Scottish reorganisation of 1975, as a result of which Scotland now

---

[1] Report of the Committee on the Management of Local Government, 1967, paragraphs 336 and 412.
[2] Report of the Royal Commission on Local Government in England, 1969, Cmnd 4040, paragraphs 463 to 474.
[3] Report of the Royal Commission on Local Government in Scotland, 1969, Cmnd 4150, paragraphs 902 to 911.

has the very simple arrangements set out in paragraphs 7.9 and 7.10. The recommendations of Maud and Redcliffe-Maud were not, however, followed in the re-organisation of 1974 in England and Wales except that whole council elections were made quadrennial rather than triennial.

PROPOSED REFORM OF ELECTORAL ARRANGEMENTS

7.14   We see just as great a need for reform in England and Wales as did the Maud Committee and Redcliffe-Maud Commission.

The need for a simple uniform system

7.15   As we have seen in Chapter Two, local electoral turn out is poor—about 40%. While we do not believe that the current electoral arrangements are a primary cause of this, a system which is as complex and inconsistent as the present one is hardly calculated to encourage electoral participation. Citizens have a reasonable expectation that the electoral arrangements should be simple, and that when they move from one area to another that the arrangements should be the same unless there is a clear case to the contrary. We cannot see such a case. The current differences seem to be almost entirely a matter of historical accident, relating to the electoral fashion at the time the antecedents of the current authorities were created. There should in future be a simple uniform system applying throughout Great Britain.

Single member wards

7.16   The main principle guiding this uniform system should be that every ward or division should be represented by only one member. Multi-member Parliamentary seats were abolished in the 19th century, and rightly so. Single member seats, whether at national or local level, provide a strong link between the member and his or her constituents. The electorate have a single person to whom they can go with any problems. There is no danger of members shuffling difficult problems onto each other or alternatively of seeking to compete with each other for kudos. Single member seats, because they are smaller, also increase the chance of independents and candidates from third parties being elected; and there is some evidence that they encourage higher turn-out. The critics of the first past the post electoral system concede that, whatever its weaknesses, it does have the advantage—unlike the single transferrable vote—of allowing single member seats to continue. It seems perverse for local government to have the first past the post electoral system, but at the same time to have multi-member wards. Multi-member wards should be abolished. We recognise that this would require reviews by the Local Government Boundary Commissions for England and Wales to divide up current multi-member wards, and that this process might require the change to be phased.

Abolition of elections by thirds

7.17   It remains to be considered whether councils should retire by thirds or simultaneously. Under the proposal for single member wards, elections by thirds would not be capable of being operated on the basis currently applying in metropolitan districts. Instead of the whole electorate voting in every election year, only those electors in wards where a member was retiring would be able to vote. This is, however, a workable system—and indeed is the system applying at present in those shire districts which have a combination of elections by thirds and some one member wards.

(i) Arguments for elections by thirds

7.18   The main arguments for a system of elections by thirds are as follows.

7.19   First, elections by thirds provide for political continuity. Earlier in this Report we have referred to the pace of political change, and the impact this can have on conventional relationships and ways of working. The pace of change will tend to be greatest where the whole council retires simultaneously, especially when the election takes place in a year that is untypical of the longer term political complexion of the area. This is illustrated by the experience of Greater Manchester Metropolitan County Council in the 1977 and 1981 elections. The swings experienced were as follows:

	Before 1977 election	1977 election	1981 election
Conservative	29	82	19
Labour	64	23	78
Liberal	12	–	9
Other	1	1	–
	106	106	106

There was a similar pattern in West Yorkshire and the West Midlands and also many of the shire counties. It can be seen that it is quite possible for the majority of those elected to be new to the council. This is particularly so following the abolition of aldermanic seats at the time of re-organisation. Elections by thirds slow the pace of change, and provide a greater opportunity for new councillors to learn from the experience of their colleagues.

7.20   Second, elections by thirds tend to produce councils that are more representative of the normal political complexion of the area. This is because elections by thirds avoid the possibility of the whole council being elected in an untypical electoral year, when one party is particularly popular or unpopular because of mid-term national factors. This argument is linked to that in the preceeding paragraph, and is illustrated by the election results quoted there.

7.21   Third, proponents of elections by thirds argue that they provide for sharper political accountability. Councillors are more immediately aware that they will have to defend their policies and actions at the hustings, and the political parties have to keep their local organisation in trim. There is less danger of politics becoming moribund in mid-term, and it is notable that politicians tend to be the strongest supporters of elections by thirds.

7.22   Fourth, elections by thirds provide an opportunity to resolve problems in hung councils. Where the parties on a hung council are not able to form a stable coalition with a working majority, four years is a long time to wait for a chance to elect a more viable council.

(ii) Arguments against elections by thirds

7.23　The main arguments against a system of elections by thirds are as follows.

7.24　First, elections by thirds discourage forward planning. They do not give councils the breathing space to plan ahead for their area, and can result in difficult decisions (for example, school closures) constantly being deferred because of the risk of an adverse reaction at the polls. This is not helped by the fact that local elections are held in May, very shortly after the setting of a rate. The Controller of Audit for England and Wales expressed the view in oral evidence that elections by thirds have a deleterious effect on the quality of decisions. Our research paper on Liverpool[1] suggests that preoccupation with annual elections was a factor in the period between 1974 and 1983, when rate levels were kept under tight control but important expenditure decisions were deferred. Elections by thirds can also lead to frequent changes of political control, with a resulting lack of consistency in policy.

7.25　Second, the continuity provided by elections by thirds might be viewed as a disadvantage. In paragraph 7.19 it was pointed out that whole council elections are much more likely than elections by thirds to provide major changes in council composition—both in terms of the individual councillors and in terms of political control. Some would argue that this has benefits. It reduces the number of authorities which will always be in the control of the same party. The constant possibility of a change in control is normally the most effective guarantee of minority rights. The rapid changes in personnel can also provide a refreshing change where councillors have become seemingly entrenched in their positions. Some of the cases of corruption in the late 1960s and early 1970s were in part attributed to councils remaining under the control of the same councillor for too long—a point made by the Report of the Salmon Commission.[2]

7.26　Third, elections by thirds can dilute public interest in elections. Public interest is likely to be heightened if the whole council is being elected and there is thereby a greater chance of changing the political control of the council. This point applies particularly to councils dominated by party politics, which now account for the great majority. Whole council elections might be considered to have a beneficial effect on turn-out, and the Wheatley Commission[3] argued that this was shown by its research results. It is interesting in this respect that the turn-out figures quoted in Chapter Two show a higher turn-out for the election of metropolitan county councils (whole council) than of metropolitan district councils (elections by thirds).

7.27　Fourth, because they are more frequent, elections by thirds tend to be more costly both for the political parties and for local authorities. The strength of this point is reduced under our proposal for single member seats, as only a third of wards would vote in any given year. Nevertheless, it should not be under-estimated. For local authorities there is not only the direct cost of the polling arrangements, but also the indirect cost arising from the annual disruption to

---

[1] Parkinson, *Research Volume IV*.
[2] Report of the Royal Commission on Standards of Conduct in Public Life, 1976, Cmnd 6524, paragraph 39.
[3] Report of the Royal Commission on Local Government in Scotland, 1969, Cmnd 4150, paragraph 904.

council business: for example, induction has to be arranged for new councillors and committee composition has to be reviewed.

(iii) Conclusion

7.28   The close balance of argument above is reflected in public opinion. In our attitude survey[1] 47% of electors said they would prefer whole council elections and 44% election by thirds. The figures were much the same in Scotland where all elections are on a whole council basis. While the arguments are much more balanced than those for and against single member wards, there is an equally great need to have a clear decision in favour of one system or the other so that the same arrangements apply throughout Great Britain. In our view the arguments for whole council elections carry the more weight. We are also influenced by the fact that Scotland has only recently adopted a uniform system of whole council elections, and that there has been no apparent difficulty with these arrangements. They could not reasonably be expected to switch to elections by thirds. While it would be feasible to have elections by thirds throughout England and Wales and whole council elections throughout Scotland, this would not be desirable. The simplest arrangement is to have whole council elections throughout Great Britain.

7.29   We consider that whole council elections should continue to be on a quadrennial basis. This provides a reasonable period for a council to plan ahead, and allows biennial spacing of elections in areas with two tiers of elected authorities. If, however, this was considered to be too infrequent a test of electoral opinion we see no over-riding argument against triennial elections - provided that the system was applied uniformly.

Recommendations
7.30   **In summary we recommend that:**

the legislation governing the election of councillors in England and Wales should be amended so that there are uniform arrangements throughout Great Britain based on:

    (i)   one councillor for every electoral ward or division;

    (ii)   the whole council being elected every four years. (Paragraphs 7.15, 7.16 and 7.28).

COUNCIL SIZE
Current arrangements
7.31   The number of councillors on each council is not the subject of primary legislation, but is determined by order for individual authorities on the basis of the recommendations of the Local Government Boundary Commissions for England, Wales and Scotland. The criterion to be followed by the Commissions is that they should:

---

[1] Young/NOP, *Research Volume III, Table 6.9.*

'make proposals to the Secretary of State for effecting changes appearing to the Commission desirable in the interests of effective and convenient local government'.[1]

7.32 The English Commission have established bands for council size to which they adhere, with very few exceptions, in dealing with reviews of individual authorities. There are no equivalent bands in Scotland and Wales.

7.33 The Table below shows the range of current council size, the English commission's bands, and the average ratio of councillors to population (in the national totals this ratio includes councillors of both tiers).

TABLE	Council Size			
	Commission's bands	Actual range	Actual average	Average ratio cllr: population
England				
Metropolitan districts	50–80	48–117	69	4,540
London boroughs[1]	50–70	48–70	60	4,530
Shire counties	60–100	43–106	77	9,280
Shire districts	30–60	20–68	45	2,140
Total/Ave.	**30–100**	**20–117**	**52**	**2,220**
Wales				
Counties	–	53–85	72	4,860
Districts	–	29–65	41	1,870
Total/Ave.	**–**	**29–85**	**48**	**1,350**
Scotland				
Regions	–	23–103	49	11,510
Islands	–	24–30	25	940
Districts	–	10–60	22	4,400
Total/Ave.	**–**	**10–103**	**27**	**3,080**
Great Britain	**–**	**10–117**	**48**	**2,200**

[1] Excludes the City of London, which has 161 members.

[1] This criterion is contained in sections 47 and 54 of the Local Government Act 1972 for the English and Welsh Commissions respectively, and in section 13 of the Local Government (Scotland) Act 1973 for the Scottish Commission.

7.34　The general pattern is for upper tier authorities and authorities with a large population to have a larger council, but fewer councillors per head of population. Nevertheless this is overlaid by marked national differences. Scotland has much smaller councils, and fewer councillors per head of population, than does England and Wales. Council size is similar between England and Wales, but this is deceptive. Most Welsh authorities have smaller populations than those in England. For any given population, Welsh authorities have more councillors than those in England and far more than those in Scotland.

The need for review

7.35　In Chapter Five (paragraph 5.8), we listed as one of the three weaknesses of the current local government model the fact that the corporate basis of decision taking by the whole council does not promote management efficiency. This problem can be exacerbated where there is a large number of councillors on the authority. It is moreover the councils responsible for the largest expenditure, and hence where management efficiency is most crucial, who generally have the most councillors. For example, Birmingham Metropolitan District Council, which covers a population of over 1 million and has an annual budget of over £500 million, has 117 councillors.

7.36　The Maud Committee[1], the Redcliffe-Maud Commission[2] and the Wheatley Commission[3] all drew attention to the management problems of over-large councils and recommended a maximum of 75 members. In their written evidence, the Audit Commission for England and Wales drew attention to the same considerations, suggesting a more radical reduction:

'from a management point of view, there would be much to be said for reducing the number of members on individual councils very considerably............These numbers do not seem necessary to secure effective local representation and invariably make for unwieldy administrative arrangements. Some of the substantial overhead cost within local government is devoted to servicing committees whose real purpose is often to find something for members to do. If membership of councils was much smaller economy, efficiency and effectiveness would be enhanced. Experience suggests that bodies with membership of more than 18–20 people are unwieldy and are too large to allow effective discussion and debate. It could also make it easier to recruit sufficient candidates of the appropriate calibre......... Finally it would reflect the current reality: in practice almost all authorities are run by a relatively small number of members who comprise "the leadership".'

Some would add the argument that some reduction in the number of councillors might be matched by a corresponding enhancement in their status.

7.37　The management of services is, however, only one aspect of a councillor's role. Another is the representation on the council of their area. A reduction in

---

[1] Report of the Committee on the Management of Local Government, 1976, paragraph 332.
[2] Report of the Royal Commission on Local Government in England, 1969, Cmnd 4040, paragraph 456.
[3] Report of the Royal Commission on Local Government in Scotland, 1969, Cmnd 4150, paragraph 917.

council size would mean that each councillor would need to cover a larger area and population (although this problem would be reduced by our recommendation that there should be single member wards). It would also reduce the opportunity for the citizen to participate in democratic institutions through being a councillor. Some argue that any reduction in the number of representatives tends in practice particularly to disadvantage women, ethnic minorities and other groups that are already under-represented. There would also be particular problems in the metropolitan areas, which have the biggest councils but which also have the smallest number of councillors per head of population. Birmingham, the largest district council in England with 117 councillors, might seem a much stronger candidate for reduction in council size than Rutland, the smallest with only 20. Each district councillor in Birmingham, however, already represents five times as many people as each district councillor in Rutland. Moreover the metropolitan areas at present have no county, parish or community councillors. It is interesting that Birmingham City Council has recently made a proposal to the Local Government Boundary Commission for the creation of 80 urban parishes with a total of 1,500 councillors.

7.38   It can be seen that the issue of council size is linked with structure. It is the existence of authorities covering large populations and areas following the 1974 and (in Scotland) 1975 reorganisations which creates the tension between the management and representative roles of councillors. In small authorities, whatever other disadvantage they may have, the two roles are more easily reconciled. It is noticeable that most local government systems abroad, whose councils tend to cover smaller areas, have fewer councillors on each council than in Great Britain but at the same time have more councillors per head of population. The average councillor abroad typically represents some 250–400 people, compared with 2,200 people in Great Britain.[1]

7.39   There is no simple solution to the question of council size. We consider that it should be reviewed in greater depth to see whether some reduction, to increase efficiency, would be compatible with maintaining the quality of democracy. It needs to be considered how far democracy is dependant on the number of councillors. As outlined in the paper prepared for us by John Gyford[2], local democracy is increasingly taking a direct participatory form which does not necessarily depend on the role of councillor as representative intermediary; community groups are making a direct impact on council business through lobbying and consultation and even through decentralised neighbourhood fora. Moreover, insofar as the representative role remains important we note that councillors' ability to carry out this role does not appear to be directly related to the number of electors they represent. Scottish district councillors represent on average twice as many people as their counterparts in England and Wales. Nevertheless our attitude survey[3] shows that their electors are more likely to be able to name them, and just as likely to have had contact with them. Even if council size was not to be reduced throughout Great Britain, there may be a case for reduction in England and Wales to a level nearer that in Scotland. The case for reduction in Wales is particularly strong. We note that South Glamorgan County Council, which we visited, had just had its membership reduced from 80 to 62

[1] Goldsmith and Newton, *Research Volume IV*.
[2] Gyford, *Research Volume IV*.
[3] Young/NOP, *Research Volume III,* Tables 2.10 and 2.12.

and that reviews were pending in other Welsh counties. The question of council size needs to be reviewed in the context of other avenues of representative democracy. When the Redcliffe-Maud[1] and Wheatley[2] Commissions recommended a reduction in the number of councils, and hence councillors, they saw at the same time a need for parish and community councils to provide an alternative means of local representation and expression. In considering whether further reductions in council size are warranted, it needs to be considered whether the role of parish and community councils should be enhanced and whether they should be extended to London and the metropolitan areas of England.

7.40   We therefore recommend that:

the Government should review council size, in the light of the current variations in the numbers of councillors per council and per head of population, with the aim of establishing the best balance between management efficiency and the quality of democracy. (Paragraph 7.39)

---

[1] Report of the Royal Commission on Local Government in England, 1969, Cmnd 4040, paragraph 271.
[2] Report of the Royal Commission on Local Government in Scotland, 1969, Cmnd 4150, paragraphs 847 to 849.

CHAPTER 8

DISCRETIONARY SPENDING

INTRODUCTION

8.1   Local authorities have power to incur expenditure only where they are expressly authorised to do so by statute. Nevertheless, the scope for them to exercise discretion in their spending decisions is wide. Many of their powers to spend on particular services allow wide discretion. In addition, they have general powers—in section 137 of the Local Government Act 1972 and section 83 of the Local Government (Scotland) Act 1973—to incur a limited amount of expenditure on activities which are in their opinion in the interests of their area.

8.2   Our terms of reference invited us to consider the need to clarify the limits and conditions governing discretionary spending, referring us in particular to the use of sections 137 and 142 of the 1972 Act and sections 83 and 88 of the Local Government (Scotland) Act 1973. We have chosen **not** to interpret discretionary spending in the widest possible sense as this would have taken us deep into consideration of individual services. We dealt with section 142 of the 1972 Act (section 88 of the Scottish Act) in our Interim Report. In our further considerations, we have for the most part concentrated on issues which arise from the use of sections 137 and 83. To some extent, however, the issues which arise in the context of those provisions are equally relevant in the context of discretionary spending under other statutory provisions. On such issues, our conclusions go beyond sections 137 and 83 and apply to discretionary spending generally.

8.3   This Chapter includes a brief description of the current law and practice under sections 137 and 83 and a summary of the views we have received in evidence about those powers. It goes on to discuss the case for a general discretionary power of the kind embodied in the two sections, the predominance of economic development initiatives as a use of the powers, the financial limit and the scope of the powers. Finally, we consider three subjects which are relevant to sections 137 and 83 but which also arise in the context of discretionary spending more generally namely:

(a)   unlawful discrimination and the use of local authority funds for political purposes;

(b)   the grant-aiding of voluntary bodies;

(c)   the creation of enterprise boards or other companies controlled by local authorities.

SECTIONS 137 AND 83: THE STATUTORY FRAMEWORK

8.4   Section 137 of the Local Government Act 1972 is the general discretionary power under which local authorities in England and Wales may incur expenditure which is in their opinion in the interest of their area, or of some or all of the inhabitants. Authorities' expenditure under the section is limited to the product of a 2p rate for their area (subsection (4)). The Secretary of State has power to vary the amount of 2p by order, but has not done so. Section 83 of the Local Government (Scotland) Act 1973 is the equivalent provision in Scotland, where

175

the limit set by a 2p rate product also remains unchanged. Copies of both sections, as amended by all legislation up to and including the Local Government Act 1986, are at Annex L.

8.5   Both sections contain the important proviso that local authorities shall not incur expenditure under the section "for a purpose for which they are, either unconditionally or subject to any limitation or to the satisfaction of any condition, authorised or required to make any payment by or by virtue of any other enactment" (sub-section (1)). We consider the implications of this proviso in paragraphs 8.30 to 8.34. Both sections contain express provision that local authorities may contribute towards the funds of any charity or non-profit making body in furtherance of its work in the United Kingdom or to any special appeal fund in the United Kingdom backed by another local authority (sub-section (3)). There is provision in both sections that a separate account should be kept of expenditure incurred under the sections (sub-section (7)), although this sub-section was not inserted in the Scottish legislation until 1984.[1]

8.6   There are two differences between the Scottish and English/Welsh legislation:

(a)   the Scottish legislation contains provision that section 83 may not be used by one local authority for a purpose for which another local authority has specific statutory responsibility unless invited to do so by that other authority (section 83(3A)). There is no comparable provision in section 137. We discuss this further in paragraph 8.89;

(b)   section 137 contains provision dictating how the 2p rate product limit must be computed (section 137(8)). There is no equivalent provision in Scotland. This difference is further referred to in paragraph 8.46.

8.7   Although these provisions first found their way onto the statute book in broadly their present form in 1972 and 1973[2], there were important precedents in earlier legislation. Section 2(5) of the Education and Local Taxation Account (Scotland) Act 1892 was their first precursor. This provided that county and town councils in Scotland might apply a specified sum 'under any scheme of public utility' framed by the council and approved by the Secretary of State. Under the Local Government (Scotland) Act 1947, county and town councils in Scotland gained powers to make payments "for any purpose which in the opinion of the council is in the interests of the area of the council or any part thereof"—subject to the approval of the Secretary of State and an expenditure limitation equivalent to the product of a 2d rate. Thus, by 1947, local authorities in Scotland had powers which looked very like the existing section 83, except that expenditure was subject to approval by the Secretary of State.

---

[1] Sub-section (7) of the Local Government (Scotland) Act 1973 was inserted by section 9 of the Rating and Valuation (Scotland) Act 1984
[2] Later amendments, designed largely to clarify the extent to which the powers might be used for economic and employment promotion measures, are discussed in paragraph 8.30. In addition, the sections have recently been amended by the Local Government Act 1986 to restrict their use for publicity.

8.8   There was no similar general discretionary provision in England and Wales until much later. However in 1963, section 6(1) of the Local Government (Financial Provisions) Act provided authorities in England and Wales with powers very similar to those subsequently enacted in section 137. Unlike in Scotland, there was no provision that expenditure must be approved by the Secretary of State. Expenditure was, however, limited to the product of a 1d rate (as opposed to the 2d rate then applying in Scotland).

SECTIONS 137 AND 83: USAGE

8.9   A thorough study of local authority usage of sections 137 and 83 over the period from local government reorganisation to 1981–82 was undertaken by Colin Crawford and Victor Moore of Reading University in 1982.[1] The same authors subsequently updated their analysis to cover 1982–83 (material included in the same publication) and Victor Moore undertook work in 1983–84 (unpublished). We commissioned the Institute of Public Finance Ltd (a trading company wholly owned by the Chartered Institute of Public Finance and Accountancy) to undertake a survey of the usage of sections 137 and 83 in 1984–85—the latest complete financial year at the time.[2] Drawn from these sources, a short summary of section 137/83 usage follows.

Amount of expenditure

8.10   No national data for expenditure under sections 137 and 83 was collected immediately in the years following reorganisation, so that figures subsequently collected for those years (by Crawford and Moore in 1982) must be treated with caution. Nevertheless, there appears to have been a substantial increase in the use of the powers over the years, with total expenditure by principal councils in Great Britain rising from an estimated £6 million in 1975–76 to some £136 million in 1984–85.

8.11   There has been a corresponding increase in the numbers of councils which make use of the power. In 1975–76, only some 35% of all councils appear to have done so. By 1984–85, 75% of all councils incurred some expenditure under the powers.

8.12   Notwithstanding these increases, aggregate national expenditure under the powers continues to be very much smaller than the amount which local authorities are entitled to spend under the 2p limit. In 1984–85, expenditure was only 32% of the amount available under the 2p ceiling. Aggregate expenditure under the powers is also small when set against local government activities as a whole, constituting only half a percent of total local authority rate and grant borne expenditure in 1984–85.

8.13   As shown in the table below, the aggregate Great Britain figures disguise important differences between classes of authority. The Greater London Council and the metropolitan county councils were as a group by far the most significant users of section 137 in 1984–85, both in cash terms and in the extent to

---

[1] Published by CIPFA under the title "The Free Two Pence" in October 1983. The publication also includes a full and useful commentary on the legal, statutory and financial background to the powers.

[2] IPF, *Research Volume IV*.

which they took advantage of the permissible 2p resource. Total expenditure by this group was £63 million and represented 83% of their permissible resources. By contrast, expenditure by the shire counties represented only 15% of their permissible resources.

TABLE   All authorities, Great Britain

Section 137/83 expenditure in 1984−85

	Actual expenditure £m	Expenditure in relation to value of 2p rate product %	Expenditure in relation to total rate and grant borne expenditure %
England and Wales			
Metropolitan counties and GLC	63.4	83	1.8
Shire counties	15.5	15	0.1
London boroughs	7.5	17	0.3
Metropolitan districts	13.6	36	0.3
Shire districts	23.7	22	1.2
Scotland			
Regions and Islands	9.1	38	0.3
Districts	2.9	13	0.4
All	**135.6**	**32**	**0.5**

8.14   In 1984−85, the 2p ceiling appears to have been a real constraint for a small minority of councils. Twenty one councils (including 14 outside the Greater London and metropolitan areas) spent within 20% of their ceilings. Since then, the abolition of the metropolitan counties and the GLC, and changes to the central government grant arrangements, have combined to make the 2p limit a constraint for a far more substantial number of authorities. We return to this issue in our discussion of the financial limit at paragraph 8.44.

Purpose of expenditure

8.15   Our research revealed that economic development and employment promotion measures were by far the largest single use of section 137/83 powers, accounting for some £90 million worth of expenditure in 1984−85, or 67% of the total. We return to the implications of this in paragraph 8.36.

8.16   Other significant categories of expenditure were legal and welfare advisory services, accounting for some £10 million worth of expenditure in 1984−85, and other welfare services, accounting for some £9 million.

THE EVIDENCE

8.17   In inviting written evidence on discretionary spending, we drew attention to our terms of reference and invited respondents in particular to comment on:

(a) whether a general discretionary power of the kind embodied in sections 137 and 83 was desirable;

(b) whether the current financial limit on the spending power was too high, too low or about right;

(c) whether there was a need to limit the discretion in any other way.

8.18   The great weight of evidence argued in favour of the retention of a general discretionary power. This view was almost unanimous among local authorities and those directly representing their interests. It was also supported by all the national political parties offering evidence on this subject and by the large majority of other organisations submitting evidence. The Law Society in Scotland argued that a general discretionary power to spend was inconsistent with an *ultra vires* regime (see paragraph 8.26 for further discussion of this point). The views of the members of the Audit Commission for England and Wales were divided, with the majority strongly favouring a retention of the section 137 powers but a minority fearing that arguably marginal activities under section 137 were proving an unhelpful distraction from the main business of local authorities. The majority of ratepayers' groups—including the National Union of Ratepayers' Associations—supported the retention of the 'free two pence'—although a substantial minority did not. Some 15 individuals wrote expressing concern about the grant-aiding of bodies or activities which they did not consider desirable. These individuals did not, however, draw conclusions about the case for a discretionary spending power in principle.

8.19   Some of those submitting evidence—including the Labour Party, the Association of Metropolitan Authorities and the Convention of Scottish Local Authorities—argued the case for a general competence power; ie a power similar to section 137/83 but **without** any financial ceiling (discussed at paragraph 8.23 and following). A much more commonly expressed view was that the real value of the financial ceiling should be restored to the level it had represented when it first came into force in 1974 (1975 in Scotland). Many—including the Association of District Councils—argued for some form of index linking.

8.20   We received some strong expressions of concern about some discretionary spending decisions on the grounds that they were either party political or socially undesirable in nature. Those concerned clearly felt that measures should be taken to stop such expenditure but were not specific about how this might be done.

8.21   A number of local authorities in the Greater London and metropolitan areas, and of the bodies representing their interests, drew our attention to the effects of the abolition of the Greater London and metropolitan county councils in halving the amount available for expenditure under section 137 in 1986–87 and thereafter. We consider this question in paragraphs 8.69 to 8.71.

8.22   Many bodies noted that a substantial proportion of section 137/83 expenditure was devoted to measures to promote the local economy and employment opportunities. Some of these bodies argued that there was a case for additional specific powers for such measures so that they should not fall to sections 137 and 83.

179

THE NEED FOR A GENERAL DISCRETIONARY POWER

A general competence power

8.23   Local authorities in this country operate within a framework laid down by statute.[1] This is true not only in the sense that their institutional and decision taking arrangements are dictated by statute, but also in the sense that they have no power to act except in so far as they are expressly authorised to do so by legislation. Under functional legislation, local authorities have a wide range of duties which they are statutorily required to perform, and an ·ven greater number of permissive powers enabling them to undertake certain defined activities if they so decide. Any activity which falls outside this code of duties and powers is *ultra vires*.

8.24   In the late 1960s the Maud Committee, and the Redcliffe-Maud and Wheatley Commissions all took the view that this *ultra vires* regime was in some respects unduly restrictive. It was argued that:

'The specific nature of legislation discourages enterprise, handicaps development, robs the community of services which the local authority might render, and encourages too rigorous an oversight by the central government';[2]

and that:

'a local authority should not be limited by its statutory range of functions'. Authorities should be able 'to act outside the cover of a specific enabling statute where the circumstances seem appropriate.'

8.25   These reports went on to argue that authorities should be granted a 'general competence' power under which they would have a general discretion to undertake activities which they considered to be in the interest of their areas. It was argued that such a power would generate 'an enterprising and forward looking attitude of mind.'[3] It was envisaged that the power would complement rather than replace the functional powers and duties expressly provided for in legislation. It was recognised that the power would need to be tempered by certain safeguards (providing, for example, against interference by one authority in the duties of another); but it was argued that the power should not be constrained by any financial limit, nor by a requirement to secure approval for its use by the Secretary of State.

8.26   We are not ourselves persuaded of the case for a general competence power which is unlimited by any financial ceiling. We see a fundamental difference between the principle that local authorities should be required to act within broad spheres of activity laid down centrally by Parliament (the *ultra vires* doctrine), and the principle that they should be in a position to react freely to local demands and pressures except in so far as they are expressly prohibited from doing so by statute (the general competence principle). Like the Maud, Redcliffe-Maud and Wheatley Reports, we see no case for over-turning the

---

[1] See Goldsmith and Newton, *Research Volume IV* for discussion of the different frameworks which apply abroad.
[2] Report of Committee on the Managerment of Local Government, 1967, paragraph 283.
[3] Report of Royal Commission on Local Government in Scotland, 1969. Cmnd 4150, paragraph 640.

traditional British arrangements under which the main spheres of local government activity are positively provided for in legislation. Unlike them, however, we have difficulty in seeing how these arrangements can logically be reconciled with a **quantitatively unlimited** power for individual authorities to engage in whatever activities they judge appropriate.

8.27   However, we agree with the arguments propounded by the Maud, Redcliffe-Maud and Wheatley Reports insofar as they make the case for a financially limited general discretion. Local authorities' prime responsibility must be to exercise those functions which are vested in them by statute. But we believe that it is important also that they should have adequate scope to respond to new local pressures in an innovative way which may not have been envisaged by Parliament. We therefore support the principle of a general discretionary power of the type incorporated in sections 137 and 83, giving local authorities wide discretion to incur expenditure which in their judgement is in the interests of their area, but subject to a fixed financial ceiling. We return in paragraph 8.62 to a discussion of the level at which the ceiling should be set.

Interface between sections 137 and 83 and functional powers

8.28   It follows from what we have said above that we see the powers in sections 137 and 83 as a limited element of 'general competence' superimposed upon an *ultra vires* regime. This combination inevitably leads to problems in establishing a dividing line between the scope of sections 137 and 83 and specific functional powers.

8.29   Much functional legislation is drafted to specify those respects in which local authorities **must** or **may** take action, rather than in terms of those in which they **may not** take action. This means that there is scope for ambiguity about activities which are not expressly provided for in legislation; they may be activities which Parliament has concluded that local authorities ought not to have power to pursue; or they may be activities which Parliament has simply not considered or concluded upon one way or the other. A financially limited general competence provision is valuable if it gives local authorities some flexibility to engage in the latter category of activities, ie those which are not foreseen in specific functional legislation. But—because of the way in which the legislation is drafted—there can be considerable difficulty in pinning down precisely what activities fall within this category.

8.30   As currently drafted, sections 137 and 83 attempt to tackle this difficulty by providing that the powers may not be used **for any purpose** for which there is authority in other legislation. This attempt to draw a line between the scope of section 137/83 and functional legislation has not proved entirely successful. The history of legislation on assistance to industry since the 1972 and 1973 Acts came into force exemplifies the difficulties which can arise. There are limited powers to make loans to industry for the purchase and development of land in section 3 of the Local Authorities (Land) Act 1963. The existence of these specific powers prompted legal debate about whether section 137 might be used for forms of assistance not expressly authorised in that legislation. In an attempt to clarify the position, the Local Government (Miscellaneous Provisions) Act 1982 inserted a declaratory provision in section 137 stating that the section might be used to authorise financial assistance to industry through loans, grants or guarantees.

This provision in turn gave rise to debate about whether or not the section might be used for assistance in forms other than loans, grants or guarantees. These doubts were resolved in turn with the passing of further legislation—the Local Authorities (Expenditure Powers) Act 1983—which says in terms that section 137 shall not be regarded as being restricted by the existence of section 3 of the 1963 Act nor by specific powers in local acts designated by order. The position on industrial assistance is therefore now clear. But it is arguable that the express clarification which has been found necessary in this context has if anything added to the ambiguity about the relationsip between section 137 and functional powers in other spheres.

8.31　A similar debate arose about the relationship between section 142 of the 1972 Act (section 88 of the Scottish Act) and sections 137 and 83.[1] There were two distinct schools of thought—both supported by legal opinion—about whether or not sections 137 and 83 might be used to authorise publicity which was not within the terms of sections 142 and 88. The Local Government Act 1986 has resolved this ambiguity by an amendment to sections 137 and 83 providing that the sections may **not** be used to authorise expenditure on publicity (except in very limited categories of circumstance defined in the statute).

8.32　There are many other areas of doubt. For example, there is scope for debate about whether the costs of advice centres should be attributed to sections 142 and 88 (which authorise the provision of public information at premises specially maintained for the purpose) or whether a distinction should be drawn between 'advice' and 'information' and the costs attributed to sections 137 and 83. There is also scope for debate about how far section 71 of the Race Relations Act 1976 may be construed as authority to incur expenditure on measures designed to promote good race relations. More generally, there is probably a tendency among local authorities (especially where they are in no danger of exceeding their 2p ceiling) to attribute to sections 137 and 83 a variety of grants to voluntary bodies where there are extensive powers for such purposes in functional legislation. Section 65 of the Health Services and Public Health Act 1968, section 19 of the Local Government (Miscellaneous Provisions) Act 1976 and section 13 of the Housing (Homeless Persons) Act 1977 are three of the main such powers, but there are many more. Section 12 of the Social Work (Scotland) Act 1968 is a particularly good example of a wide-ranging power, providing that:

> 'It shall be the duty of every local authority to promote social welfare by making advice, guidance and assistance on such a scale as may be appropriate to their area.'

8.33　We see no easy or final solution to this problem. Because of the way in which functional legislation is drafted, we do not think that there can be any watertight formula which might be written into sections 137 and 83 and which would provide for a clear and unambiguous boundary between those sections and functional powers. The principle that the sections should not be used for purposes for which there is provision elsewhere in legislation is in our view right. We do not therefore recommend any amendment to the existing terms of section 137 and 83 insofar as they attempt to define this boundary.

---

[1] Discussed in our Interim Report, Local Authority Publicity, HMSO 1985, paragraph 73.

8.34   However, we think that the problems and confusions which arise in this context might be ameliorated by the provision of some non-statutory guidance. It would be a massive and totally impractical task to attempt to codify all functional legislation in a way which comprehensively describes what local authorities may do, what they may not do and what is the proper territory of section 137/83. But non-statutory guidance might realistically aim to tackle those areas of activity for which sections 137 and 83 are currently most commonly used. We have been told that the Association of District Councils is contemplating the provision of such advice to its members. We know from our research[1] that such advice would be welcome among local authorities.

8.35   We therefore recommend that:

(a)   in addition to their specific statutory functions, local authorities should continue to have a financially limited discretionary power to spend in the interests of their area;

(Paragraph 8.27)

(b)   the Government should consult the local authority associations with a view to drawing up guidance for local authorities on the use to which sections 137 and 83 may properly be put. The guidance should in particular:

(i)   reaffirm the principle that these sections should not be used for purposes provided for elsewhere in legislation;

(ii)   give practical advice on the inter-relationship between the sections and functional powers in areas of particular concern.

(Paragraph 8.34)

ECONOMIC DEVELOPMENT POWERS

8.36   Measures designed to tackle unemployment, to assist industry or otherwise to promote the local economy are by far the largest single uses of sections 137 and 83, accounting for over two thirds of all expenditure under those sections in 1984−85. They are also the fastest growing. Section 137/83 expenditure on such measures has increased from £15 million in 1981−82 (45% of all section 137/83 expenditure in that year) to £90 million in 1984−85 (67% of all section 137/83 expenditure). This is in addition to expenditure on such measures under the Local Authorities (Land) Act 1963, the Inner Urban Areas Act 1978 and local act powers.

8.37   The range of activities pursued is wide. They include assistance by way of grants, loans, rent subsidies and guarantees to individual firms; the acquisition of equity in firms which have been unable to raise finance in the private market; support for co-operative ventures; capital investment in starter and other industrial units; and the provision of a variety of training schemes. The provision of advice—for the unemployed, for small or ailing businesses or for those thinking of starting up in business—is another important area of activity.

8.38   A number of those submitting evidence to the Committee have argued that there should be new specific powers authorising some or all of these activities.

---

[1] IPF, *Research Volume IV*.

This is an issue which was tackled—in part at least—by a joint official group set up in 1980 under the chairmanship of Sir Wilfred Burns. The Burns group was asked to look at local authorities' role in assisting industry and commerce and to report on 'the most appropriate fields of action for local authorities, and on any implications for legislation'.[1] The group concluded that local authority activities in this sphere 'should be kept complementary to rather than competitive with those of central government and the private sector', but beyond that reached few precise conclusions about what activities should be undertaken by local authorities. On the question of legislative change, the group concluded that it was possible either to proceed by way of a broadly drawn power subject to a financial limit, or by way of package of specific powers.

8.39   In a consultation paper issued in 1982, the Government sought views on a proposal to introduce a new power for local authorities to assist industry and commerce. This power was to be subject to an annual expenditure limit of the product of a half penny rate in the pound. The proposed financial limit was criticised on the grounds that it was too low, and the scope of the power was criticised as too limited. The proposal was never implemented.

8.40   We are not aware of any subsequent major statements which have taken significantly forward the debate about the proper role of local government in economic promotion. We have been impressed by some of the local authority initiatives which have been brought to our attention. And we have considerable sympathy with local authorities' concern to alleviate unemployment. But we are equally conscious that there are difficult underlying issues which have not yet been comprehensively addressed. These turn on complex questions about the role of the public sector as a whole in the promotion of the economy, the respective roles of different tiers of government and of government agencies, and about competition for available resources between different areas and different regions. These questions extend well beyond our remit.

8.41   It follows that we have reached no view about whether new specific powers for promotion of the economy are desirable. Nevertheless, we are uneasy that general discretionary powers which were intended to provide authority for innovatory or otherwise exceptional expenditure should have come to be so predominantly devoted to a single sphere of activity. The public expenditure involved is substantial. We believe that a full and thorough review of the proper role of local authorities in the economic development sphere should be undertaken, and that the case for new specific powers should be reconsidered on this basis.

8.42   We have noted the concern expressed by some local authorities that new specific powers might effectively reduce their scope for action by constraining the discretion currently afforded to them in sections 137 and 83. This is a concern which would need to be addressed in any review undertaken. However, we see no reason in principle why new powers should not be introduced expressly without prejudice to the continued use of sections 137 and 83 for activities which are not specifically authorised.

---

[1] Review of Local Authority Assistance to Industry and Commerce. Report of the Joint Group of officials of Local Authority Associations and Government Departments. Department of the Environment. July 1980.

8.43 **We therefore recommend that:**

the Government should initiate a review of the proper role of local author-ities in economic development, taking account of the role of other govern-ment agencies, with a view to identifying any areas in which additional local authority statutory powers should be introduced.

(Paragraph 8.41)

THE FINANCIAL LIMIT FOR SECTIONS 137 AND 83

8.44   We have said in paragraph 8.27 that we believe it to be right that a general discretionary power of the kind embodied in sections 137 and 83 should be sub-ject to an expenditure limit. Questions which follow are how that limit should be calculated and at what level it should be set.

8.45   The section 137/83 ceiling is currently set in a way which authorises indi-vidual authorities to spend up to the product of a 2p rate for their areas. The amount of 2p may be varied by the Secretary of State by order, but that power has never yet been used.

8.46   The situation is, however, less straightforward than appears from that short description of the statutory position. Section 137(8) provides that the pro-duct of a rate shall be computed in England and Wales by reference to the rules made under section 113 (1) (c) of the General Rate Act 1967.[1] The practical effect is that the ceiling does not represent simply the product of a 2p rate calculated by reference to rateable values in an area but rather the product of a 2p rate after taking account of any element of central government grant which is designed to equalise the product of a rate on a population basis. There is no provision com-parable to section 137(8) in the Scottish section 83. In the absence of such an express provision, we understand there to be no authoritative legal view as to whether the 2p rate product in Scotland should be calculated on a grant-inclusive or a grant-exclusive basis.

8.47   The current 2p rate product ceiling has been criticised on a number of grounds:

(a)   in England and Wales, rateable values have remained broadly constant in cash terms since reorganisation in 1974 and are now worth only about a quarter of their real value at that time. Revaluations of property for rating purposes have in practice been undertaken spasmodically. (Scottish revalu-ations were undertaken in 1978 and 1985. There has been no comprehensive revaluation exercise in England and Wales since 1974). A limit derived from a rateable value base is therefore inescapably unsatisfactory in that it will reflect the same somewhat arbitary and spasmodic pattern of change in terms of real values;

(b)   the linkage between the ceiling and central government grant arrange-ments can also give rise to arbitary and unpredictable changes in the level of the ceiling;

(c)   local government is differently organised in different areas so that there are two tiers of authority in most areas but only a single tier authority

---

[1] Currently the Rate Product (Amendment) Rules 1983. SI.268.

in the Scottish islands and, from 1 April 1986, in Greater London and the metropolitan counties. This means that the effective section 137/83 spending capacity of principal authorities is the product of a 4p rate in the pound in most areas of the country but the product of a 2p rate in the pound in the Scottish Islands, Greater London and the metropolitan areas.

8.48   These criticisms are, in our view, serious and substantial ones. They have been put to us particularly forcefully by those who are concerned about the level of the existing limit as it will apply in Greater London and the metropolitan areas from April 1986 onwards. Underlying the criticisms, however, are three separable issues of principle; viz, the basis on which the limit should be calculated, the level at which it should be pitched, and the special position in those areas of the country where there is only a single tier principal authority. We tackle each of these issues in turn.

The basis for calculating a limit

8.49   We start from the position that the section 137/83 expenditure limit should be easy to understand, predictable and equitable as between one area and another. Major fluctuations in the limit from year to year should be avoided. And some routine mechanism for maintaining the limit at a constant value in real terms is desirable.

8.50   In England at least, the present rate product base fails on almost all of these tests. This is largely as a result of two recent developments; namely, the abolition of the GLC and metroplitan counties, and changes in the methods of calculating Rate Support Grant. The effect of abolition is to halve the amount of permissable expenditure under section 137 in the relevant areas. This seems to us to be clearly inequitable. If parish councils are taken into account, the position is even less equitable. Parish councils also have power under section 137 to spend up to the product of a 2p rate. But they exist only in shire areas. Thus the amount theoretically available for expenditure under section 137 is (as from 1 April 1986) the product of a 6p rate in shire areas of the country and the product of a 2p rate in metropolitan areas and Greater London.

8.51   The effects of grant changes are less easily intelligible; but briefly the position is as follows. Some local authorities are much 'richer' than others in the sense that the rateable value of property in their areas is far higher. The resources element of Rate Support Grant, which was a featue of the grant arrangements in England and Wales from 1967 to 1980 and which continues to feature in Scotland, was designed to overcome this inequity in resources. A national standard rateable value per head of population was fixed at a level which reflected the rateable resources per head of population of authorities towards the top end of the resource scale. Resources element was paid by central government to make up the difference to those authorities who were below that point in the scale. Under the rate product rules, local authorities below that point were entitled to take account of the resources element in calculating the product of a 2p rate for section 137 purposes. Thus the effective 2p limit for most authorities was an amount per head of population which reflected the rateable resources of the richer authorities.

8.52   Under the Local Government, Planning and Land Act 1980, block grant replaced the resources and needs elements of the Rate Support Grant. There were no immediate repercussions for the section 137 ceiling. The block grant was calculated, *inter alia*, to compensate for differences in rateable resources in a way comparable to that adopted for the former resources element, and the rate product rules were amended to take appropriate account of the new arrangements. However, the Rate Support Grant settlement for English authorities in 1986–87—and to a lesser extent the settlement for the preceding year—had very significant implications for the section 137 ceiling for a number of authorities. The national standard rateable value implied in the block grant calculation was reduced from some £170 per head of population in 1984–85 to some £90 per head of population in 1986–87. Effectively, the element of block grant which is notionally attributable to resources is being used to equalise resources **down** to the level of those of the poorer authorities rather than to equalise **up** to the level of the richer ones. As a result, a large number of authorities have ceased to benefit from any grant which notionally supplements their rateable resources. Their grant inclusive rate product has thus dropped below their actual rate product.

8.53   For 64 authorities in England, the section 137 ceiling would have been reduced by more than 30% between 1985–86 and 1986–87 as a result of these changed grant calculations. However, shortly before the commencement of the financial year, it was announced that the Secretary of State would be consulting local government about proposals to ensure that the section 137 limits for 1986–87 were not reduced in this way.[1] We understand that it is proposed that this effect be achieved by further technical adjustment to the rate support grant calculations. We welcome the announcement as a short-term solution, but we do not think that the continuing uncertainty about the limits for future years, nor the potential for major yearly fluctuations, are satisfactory in the longer term.

8.54   There is a further serious longer term problem. As we have already said, some authorities are much richer in rateable resources than others. In the past, this potential inequity between areas has been ironed out of the section 137 ceiling calculation through its linkage with what was for many years a stable grant arrangement. The grant arrangements can no longer be relied upon to have an equalising effect. The rate product base has thus become a far less satisfactory basis for calculating the ceiling.

8.55   The problems caused in the section 137/83 context by abolition and by changes to the grant arrangements have so far arisen only in England (although there have been single tier authorities in the Islands of Scotland since reorganisation). But there are other weaknesses in a system which relies on rate products for calculating the ceiling which are common across Great Britain. First, on a year to year basis, the rate product does not change with price changes. Second, in so far as there are comprehensive rate revaluations, they are undertaken on a periodic basis. The result is substantial changes in the rate product and hence in the section 137 ceiling at arbitrary points in time. Third, the Government has published provisional proposals to phase out domestic rates over a period of years.[2] If these proposals are implemented, domestic rate valuation will also

---

[1] House of Commons Official Report, 20 March 1986, Col. 252.
[2] Paying for Local Government, January 1986. Cmnd 9414.

presumably be dispensed with, and a major part of the rate product will disappear.

8.56 In view of these cumulatively substantial difficulties with the present method of calculating the ceiling, we have considered alternatives. From our start-point that the arrangements should be staightforward and easy to understand, there are two basic options. First, the ceiling might be directly related to the population within each local authority area. Second, it might be related to the gross expenditure of individual authorities in the year in question. A variation on the second option would be to relate the ceiling to an authority's 'grant related expenditure assessment', the Government's assessment of what each authority needs to spend to provide a standard level of services. The practical effects of a switch to either of these two basic options for the major categories of authority is explored in the table below.

THE SECTION 137 CEILING
EFFECTS OF CHANGING THE BASIS OF THE CEILING BY CLASS OF AUTHORITY

	Percentage change in ceiling resulting from change to:		Actual section 137/83 expenditure in 1984−85 as percentage of:		
	Expenditure based ceiling %	Population based ceiling %	Expenditure based ceiling %	Population based ceiling %	2p rate product ceiling %
Eng. met counties	− 39	+ 12	114	62	70
Eng. shire counties*	+ 61	+ 11	8	12	70
Welsh counties*	+ 108	+ 25	17	28	35
Scot. regions*	+ 76	− 16	22	46	38
Scot. islands*	+ 30	− 75	26	136	33
Inner London boroughs	− 32	− 56	44	68	30
Outer London boroughs*	+ 41	− 11	6	10	9
Eng. met districts*	+ 4	+ 12	21	33	37
Eng. shire districts	− 75	+ 8	85	19	21
Welsh districts	− 54	+ 25	75	27	34
Scot. districts	− 57	− 18	29	15	13
England	− 3	+ 1	35	34	34
Scotland	+ 8	− 18	23	31	25
Wales	+ 35	+ 26	26	28	35
Great Britain	−	−	33	33	33

NOTES: (1) The ceilings implied in the first two columns have been fixed to secure a neutral position GB-wide. The expenditure based ceiling represents 1.4% of total rate and grant borne expenditure. The population based ceiling is the product of population and £3.73.

(2) Authorities marked with an asterisk are education authorities.

(i) An expenditure based ceiling

8.57 A switch to a ceiling representing a fixed proportion of each authority's total expenditure would have the advantage of providing for an automatic form of index linking. But it would also raise considerable difficulties. As the table illustrates, the major effect would be substantially to increase the value of the ceiling for those authorities with responsibility for education, and proportionally to decrease the ceiling for the rest. Assuming that the switch was made in such a way as to secure a neutral effect on the aggregate level of the ceiling across Great Britain, then our information for expenditure under sections 137 and 83 in 1984–1985 suggests that approximately a quarter of all district councils would need to spend less than in that year in order to accommodate the new ceiling. We do not think that a change of this magnitude would be justified. More fundamentally, the figures highlight the underlying weakness of this approach. There seems no good reason why some authorities' capacity to incur expenditure under a general discretionary power should be greater than that of other authorities simply because they have responsibility for services which involve greater expenditure. The anomalous effect would be most pronounced in Inner London where the education authority does not have the power to spend under section 137.

(ii) A population based ceiling

8.58 A switch to a ceiling fixed by reference to population numbers would result in far less dramatic changes for most individual authorities and for classes of authority. Again assuming a neutral effect across Great Britain, the section 137/83 ceiling would fall quite substantially for the Islands authorities in Scotland and for certain Inner London authorities where rateable values are high in relation to population. The ceilings for a few Welsh district authorities— where rateable values are low in relation to population—would increase by as much as 40–50%. Elsewhere, however, changes to the ceilings of individual authorities would be in the range of ±25%. Outside Inner London and the Scottish Islands, we estimate that only a handful of authorities would need to cut their section 137/83 expenditure from its level in 1984–85.

8.59. The major 'losers' under a population-based arrangement are the Inner London and Scottish Islands authorities, which are coincidentally also areas in which there is only a single tier authority. We further consider the position in those areas in paragraphs 8.69 to 8.71. Subject to some reservations about those areas, we believe that a population-based ceiling would produce a sensible and equitable result, and one which fairly closely reflects the relative position of individual authorities under the current arrangements. Given the effect of grant in equalising resources on a population basis, this fairly conservative result is not of course surprising. The population figures established for grant purposes might be used for this purpose also.

8.60 Like the rate product arrangements, a population-based rule would carry no in-built mechanism to reflect price movements over time. The limit initially determined is likely to be gradually eroded in real terms over time and would fall much more dramatically in the event of a further period of high inflation. We do not consider it satisfactory that the scope of this power should be eroded by default. It is therefore important that there should continue to be a power to amend the limit by order and that it should be regularly reviewed.

8.61   We therefore recommended that:

(a)   the current statutory arrangements under which the expenditure limit for sections 137 and 83 is calcuated by reference to the rate product in an area should be replaced by arrangements which relate to the population of an area;

(Paragraph 8.59)

(b)   the Government should regularly review the limit, and should have power to amend it by order.

(Paragraph 8.60)

The level of the limit

8.62   The level at which the section 137/83 ceiling should be pitched is inevitably something of a judgemental question rather than one which can be decided by reference to quantifiable criteria. We would, however, identify three relevant general principles which derive from our view of the role of these discretionary powers within the wider context of local government responsibilities.

8.63   First, we consider that the level of the limit should be a fixed and, in real terms, constant amount which is not variable between authorities according to any periodic external assessment of the needs of individual authorities, nor of the value of the activities which they chose to pursue under the powers. By definition, the powers are intended to provide scope for authorities to pursue activities which are **in their view** in the interests of their area, and which are not provided for in functional legislation. There is room for discussion about the scope of the discretion (see paragraph 8.73 and following). But, within the agreed scope of the sections, individual authorities should be the final arbiters in deciding how the money is spent.

8.64   Second, we consider that the ceiling should be not so high as to permit activities under the sections to assume a priority over local authorities' specific functional responsibilities. These responsibilities must be local authorities' primary concern. The ceiling should be pitched at a level which does not distort this balance.

8.65   Third, if the sections are to have any value, the level of the ceiling must be high enough to permit more than purely marginal activities.

8.66   In submitting evidence to us, those representing local authority interests have made much of the fall in the value of the current ceiling in real terms in England and Wales since it was first applied in 1974. 2p is now worth only about a quarter of its value then. While we would not dispute this fact, we do not draw the conclusion that the ceiling should be reinstated at its original 1974 (or, in Scotland, 1975) value. We see no reason to accept that the 1974–1975 level was the 'right' level in absolute terms. It represented a very substantial increase over the expenditure limits applying under previous discretionary powers[1]. No clear rationale for the level of the limit emerged from debate as the legislation proceeded through Parliament. And, in national aggregate terms at least, the ceiling has never been approached. Average expenditure under sections 137 and 83 was only 32% of the ceiling in 1984–85.

---

[1] The powers in section 6 of the Local Government (Financial Provisions) Act 1963 provided for a limit of the product of a 1d rate in England and Wales. In Scotland, the limit was 2d under the Local Government (Scotland) Act 1947. The 2p rate product rule thus represented an increase in the ceiling by a factor of 4.8 in England and Wales and of 2.4 in Scotland.

8.67   We do not consider that the position revealed by our research for 1984–85 was an unsatisfactory one. Few authorities appear to have been inhibited by the ceiling, with only 21 spending more than 80% of the permissable amount. In so far as there was pressure on the ceiling, it arose largely because of local authorities' concern to devote more resources to measures to promote the economy and alleviate unemployment. As we have explained in paragraphs 8.36 to 8.42, this is an area in which we think that the case for additional specific powers should be reviewed. We would not consider it appropriate to raise the section 137/83 ceiling in order to accommodate additional activity in what is already a substantial **functional** area.

8.68   It follows that we consider that the level of the ceiling applying in 1984–85 was a reasonable one. Translated into terms of expenditure per head of population, the aggregate 2p rate product limit across Great Britain in that year was equivalent to expenditure by all principal authorities of some £3.70 per head of population. This is equivalent to some £4.00 at current prices.

Areas with single tier local government
8.69   We have received a number of representations from those concerned about the effect of abolition on section 137 spending capacity in Greater London and the metropolitian areas. We have not undertaken a detailed study of actual expenditure levels under section 137 in those areas in 1985–86, nor of proposed expenditure plans in 1986–87. Without making any value judgements about the nature of the expenditure involved, we have however noted that there are boroughs in which there will cease to be scope in 1986–87 for the full volume of activity pursued under section 137 in 1985–86.

8.70   Regardless of the actual levels of expenditure in those areas, we take the view that it is wrong in principle that the discretionary spending capacity should be markedly different in different areas. We cannot see that there is a lesser case for expenditure under section 137 in London and the metropolitan areas than elsewhere. These powers are clearly not ones which could appropriately be conferred on single-purpose joint authorities, nor on the temporary and unelected residuary bodies. We therefore take the view that all single tier authorities (ie the Scottish Islands authorities, London boroughs and metropolitan districts) should have a section 137/83 expenditure limit set at double the level applying elsewhere.

8.71   In so far as problems will arise Greater London and the metropolitan areas as a result of the effective halving of the ceiling, they will already be emerging at the time of publication of this Report. Legislation to implement our recommendations would take time. We are aware that the Government has said that it is prepared to consider the circumstances of individual authorities with a view to overcoming any difficulties, but also that they have not been prepared to take action unless persuaded that the proposed expenditure in individual cases was in their view 'worthwhile'. We consider such central scrutiny of section 137 proposals to be at odds with the spirit of the legislation. In order to give immediate effect to the intention of our recommendation, we therefore recommend that the Secretary of State makes an order under section 137(4) and (5) of the 1972 Act to substitute in that section the amount of 4p for the amount of 2p in relation to London borough and metropolitan district councils.

191

Summary

8.72   In summary, we recommend that:

(a)   the section 137 and 83 limit should initially be set at a level equivalent to expenditure by individual authorities of £4.00 per head of population, but subject to (b) below;

(Paragraph 8.68)

(b)   the limit for single tier authorities should be double the level applying elsewhere;

(Paragraph 8.70)

(c)   as an interim measure, the Secretary of State should make an immediate order under section 137(4) and (5) to increase the current limit of 2p to 4p in relation to London borough and metropolitan district councils.

(Paragraph 8.71)

SCOPE OF SECTIONS 137 AND 83

8.73   We turn now from consideration of the amount that local authorities should be authorised to spend under sections 137 and 83 to consideration of the purposes for which they should be authorised to spend it. There has been a variety of recent criticisms of how some authorities have chosen to use these powers. These include concern about alleged use of the powers to secure party political advantage, to promote sectional interests, to engage in activities which have variously been described as 'controversial' or 'divisive', to promote campaigns on national or international issues, to subsidise the activities of personal acquaintances or political sympathisers and to finance arm's length companies which are said to be insufficiently accountable to the parent authority. These concerns may arise either from actions undertaken directly by the authority concerned or from the activities of bodies financed by the authority.

8.74   A number of the concerns arise in a context which goes wider than sections 137 and 83 and are dealt with elsewhere in this Report. In particular:

(a)   the scope for abuse of power when a member of a council has an interest in a grant-aided voluntary body is dealt within the context of conflicts of interest in Chapter Six;

(b)   the use of discretion for party political advantage is discussed in paragraphs 8.91 to 8.99;

(c)   mechanisms to secure greater open-ness about grants to voluntary bodies are considered in paragraphs 8.105 to 8.108;

(d)   a discussion of arm's length bodies is at paragraphs 8.110 to 8.116.

In this section, we attempt to deal with those concerns which raise questions specifically about the scope of sections 137 and 83.

8.75   We received evidence expressing concern about the use of discretionary spending powers for controversial purposes in a joint submission from the Department of the Environment, the Scottish Office and the Welsh Office[1] and also evidence expressing concern from members of the public, from ratepayers'

---

[1] Submission to the Committee of Inquiry into the Conduct of Local Authority Business: The use of local authorities' discretionary spending powers. September 1985.

groups and from individuals and groups more directly involved with the provision of local authority services.

8.76   We list below some examples of the types of activity which have caused concern:

— the funding and support of trade union information and resource centres for campaigning purposes;

— the funding of bodies whose concern is to campaign against privatisation proposals in the National Health Service;

— the funding of the Campaign for Nuclear Disarmament and of anti-nuclear issues generally;

— the funding of women's peace organisations;

— the establishment of inquiries in such areas as the use of firearms by the metropolitan police and the operation of the immigration and deportation regulations;

— the funding of national and international causes;

— the funding of groups whose members represent small or controversial minorities.

8.77   There are perhaps three strands underlying these concerns. There is the concern with campaigning. There is the concern that local authorities are using their discretionary spending powers to finance what some regard as sectional, divisive, socially unacceptable or even plain ridiculous activities; and there is the concern that the powers are being used to finance activities which are described as 'peripheral' or beyond local authorities' proper sphere of interest. We deal with each of these in turn.

Campaigning

8.78   A number of the activities described above involve 'campaigns'. This term can encompass a variety of activities—lobbying, co-ordination of views, the collation and dissemination of relevant information. It will often also encompass publicity. Local authority publicity was the subject of our Interim Report. New legislation on the subject has since been enacted in the Local Government Act 1986, the relevant parts of which came into effect on 1 April 1986. We do not propose to discuss the merits of this Act. Our views on publicity are already stated in our Interim Report, and the matter has been fully debated in both Houses of Parliament. It is important, however, to explain the effect of the Act in inhibiting campaigning. Our understanding of the current statutory position is that:

(a)   local authorities may in no circumstances publish material which appears to be designed to affect public support for a political party, nor finance another body or person to do so (section 2 of the 1986 Act);

(b)   they may themselves arrange for the publication of information only when it is:

(i)   incidental to the discharge of any of their functions (section 111 of the 1972 Act and section 69 of the 1973 Act); or

(ii)   expressly authorised or required under functional legislation (eg planning notices); or

(iii)   information about the services available in the area provided by them or by other local authorities or similar bodies (section 142 (1A) of the 1972 Act and section 88(1A) of the 1973 Act); or

(iv) information relating to their functions (section 142 (2)(a) of the 1972 Act and section 83 (2)(a) of the 1973 Act);

(c) they may provide finance for other bodies to issue publicity only where it is publicity which they themselves might issue under (b) above, or where it is incidental to a wider purpose for which financial support is given.

8.79 It will be seen that local authorities now have no powers themselves to publish material which does not relate to their functions or to the services of other local authorities in their area. Material on subjects such as the metropolitan police and foreign policy would, in our view, be most unlikely to be construed as falling within this definition. They may use sections 137(1) and 83(1) to grant-aid bodies which issue publicity on matters going wider than their functions; but, even here, the publicity must be no more than incidental to the main purpose for which the grant is given. These constraints are in our view considerable. They impose major limitations on local authorities' ability to engage in campaigning, whether directly or through other bodies, in so far as it involves the provision of public information. Concerns about campaigning must be seen against this perspective.

'Sectional' and 'socially divisive' activities

8.80 We are conscious that a few authorities have used their powers under sections 137 and 83 to undertake controversial activities which have been variously described in the evidence as sectional, divisive or socially unacceptable. The amounts of money involved are small in relation to section 137/83 expenditure as a whole, but the amount of debate generated has been considerable.

8.81 We do not consider practicable any attempt to proscribe support for what have been described as 'sectional' activities. In a paper prepared for the Committee[1], John Gyford has highlighted the growing importance of sectional interests in local politics and the limitations of any analysis which defines a local community as a unit of common interest rather than as a conglomerate of sectional interests. It would in our view be wrong if a local authority were to give disproportionate priority to a particular section of the population across the range of its services. Equally, however, it would be wrong to suggest that particular services should on no account be directed primarily towards particular sectional interests. A homelessness unit will by definition be concerned to supply services only to the homeless. The services of a business advice centre will be directed only to those engaged in, or wishing to start up in, business. On the same principle, a local authority might choose to devote a part of its section 137/83 resources to co-operate with a particular sectional group to provide services for its members. We see nothing in principle which is objectionable about this provided that the activities are not party political in nature, and that they are otherwise within the scope of sections 137 and 83.

8.82 Nor do we consider that it would be legislatively practicable to proscribe support for activities which are criticised as being 'divisive' or socially unacceptable. The problem in this context is that there is no consensus definition of the activities which ought to be proscribed. We are of course aware that there are certain activities for which sections of the population have no sympathy, and that such activities are on occasion supported by individual local authorities under sections 137 and 83. We are also, however, very conscious that those activities which may be considered unacceptable or of low priority by some people

---

[1] Gyford, *Research Volume IV*.

within the local community will be strongly supported by others. It is a matter of judgement to decide between these different viewpoints. It is right that elected local authorities should have responsibility for making such judgements.

'Peripheral' activities

8.83 We turn now to section 137 and 83 activities which have been criticised as falling outside the proper sphere of local government activities, for example activities concerned with a cause arising in another country, with defence policy, or with a service for which another public body has responsibility. We have seen some examples of such activities which would lead us to share these criticisms, but inevitably they are based on a subjective judgement as to what is proper to local government. The activities described extend beyond the statutory functions of local government, but it is the essence of a discretionary spending power that it should be used to promote activities extending beyond such functions. If the power were to be limited to functions there would be no purpose in having it. What needs to be considered is whether it would be possible to devise an objective criterion for what is the proper sphere of local government, which extends wider than the statutory functions of local government, but which improves on the criterion currently contained in sections 137(1) and 83(1): this is that the activity must in the opinion of the local authority be in the interests of their area or any part of it or all or some its inhabitants.

8.84 It would be possible to supplement this criterion by one or more of the following tests:

(i)   the activity must not concern the affairs of another country;

(ii) the activity must not overlap with the functions of central government;

(iii) the activity must not overlap with the functions of another public body.

We do not however consider that any of these criteria would be practicable. While we would certainly not wish to encourage the notion that local authorities should concern themselves with international affairs, there will be occasions when activities reasonably within their ambit do have overseas implications. Clearly Kent County Council has an interest in the international agreement with France to build a channel tunnel. It is moreover widely accepted that local authorities should 'twin' with authorities in other countries and promote an interest in their affairs, and sections 137 and 83 are normally relied on for related expenditure. The difficulty with the second possible criterion is that the sphere of central government is not limited by statute and covers almost everything, including indeed many matters which are also the statutory functions of local government. The criterion would *inter alia* rule out the promotion of economic development by local authorities. The third possible criterion is not quite so restrictive because the functions of other public bodies are limited by statute. Nevertheless we do not think it is workable. Local authorities have a legitimate over-lapping interest with other public bodies on a number of matters; for instance there is a close relationship between the environmental health responsibilities of local authorities and the functions of health authorities, water authorities and the Health and Safety Executive. While we would certainly not wish to encourage local authority interference in the work of other public bodies, it is not possible to draw a firm border line between them and the proper activities of local government.

8.85 We consider that the existing test of the 'interest of the area' is based on the right principle. It ties local authorities back territorially to issues which arise locally rather than those that arise exclusively in a national or international context and have no special local significance. It by no means gives local authorities a free hand especially when coupled with the limitation on campaigning which we have mentioned (paragraph 8.79). If it is considered necessary to clarify the scope of expenditure under sections 137 and 83, we believe this would best be achieved by maintaining the principle of 'benefit to the area', but defining more precisely the degree of benefit that must be achieved. There has been little caselaw as to this. The one English case dealing with the subject, *Lobenstein v Hackney LBC 16 July 1980 (unreported)* suggested that the benefit need not be great. On the other hand we are aware that the Secretary of State for Scotland, on legal advice, interpreted section 339 of the Local Government (Scotland) Act 1947—the predecessor of section 83—as requiring a 'direct and tangible' benefit for the inhabitants of the area[1]. There might be merit in including a similar qualification expressly in the statute. If this was done, then we suggest that the word 'direct' should be added, which is precedented elsewhere in legislation.

8.86 Ultimately, it must be accepted, as in our conclusions on sectional and socially divisive activities, that there may be occasions when local authorities will spend under sections 137 and 83 in a way which many would regard as unacceptable but which nevertheless is not illegal. That is the inevitable consequence of a discretion. Local authorities, however, must account to their electorates for such actions. More generally, if local authorities consistently use their discretionary powers in a way which is publicly criticised this may lead to pressures for their discretion to be withdrawn. In Chapter Three we made the point that the continued responsibility of local authorities for services depends on them delivering those services effectively and thereby contributing to good government. This point applies no less strongly in respect of their continued power to spend at their discretion. There is an onus on local authorities to use this power responsibly.

8.87 Two further questions arise. First, we are aware that the powers in sections 137(3) and 83(3) are usually interpreted as going rather wider than the powers in sub-section (1) in that they are not subject to the test that the expenditure must be in the interests of the area. But this interpretation is not free from doubt[2]. The powers provide that authorities may contribute to the funds of:

(a)   a charitable body in furtherance of its work in the UK;

(b)   any body which provides a public service in the UK other than for the purposes of gain;

(c)   any fund raised in connection with a particular event affecting persons in the UK on behalf of whom a public appeal has been made by another local authority.

8.88 It follows from what we have said above that we see no strong case for powers to contribute to continuing services—charitable or otherwise—when they have no direct bearing on the needs or circumstances of the local authority's own area. On the other hand we are conscious of the history behind this subsecton. It was originally introduced in Scotland in the Local Authorities (Expenditure on Special Purposes) (Scotland) Act 1961 following three mining disasters

---

[1] From 'The Free Two Pence' by Colin Crawford and Victor Moore, CIPFA, 1983. The information was supplied to Crawford and Moore by the Scottish Office.

[2] The powers in sub-section (3) are given 'subject as aforesaid' and it might as a result be argued that the 'interests of the area' test was intended to apply. On the other hand, if this test was intended to apply, it is difficult to see how sub-section (3) adds to sub-section (1) and hence what is its purpose.

in which it was widely perceived to be an anomaly that one local authority was not able to contribute to the disaster fund established by another because of the 'interests of the area' test. A more recent example of the use to which the sub-section might be put is provided by the fund set up following the Bradford football tragedy. We have no reason to believe that the sub-section has been much called upon by local authorities, nor that it has given rise to criticism. Nevertheless, it would be advantageous to clarify the relationship between sub-section (3) and (1) in the light of the current legal uncertainty.

8.89   Finally on scope, there is the question of whether or not local authorities should have power under section 137 to incur expenditure on activities for which a local authority of a different tier has express statutory responsibility. We have referred in paragraph 8.6 to the provision in the Scottish legislation under which an authority may not use section 83 for a purpose for which another local authority has statutory responsibility unless invited to do so by that other authority[1]. For reasons discussed in paragraph 8.84, we would not wish to see a total prohibition on the use of sections 137 and 83 for activities in areas where another public body has a statutory function. But we see no advantage in one locally elected body interfering without consent in an area for which another has responsibility. We note also the oddity that the authority without the functional responsibility might in theory use sections 137/83 to incur expenditure on activities from which the authority with functional responsibilty is expressly proscribed. Consideration would need to be given to the effect of such a provision on parish councils, most of whose expenditure under section 137 overlaps with the functions of other local authorities. Our recommendation does not apply to them.

8.90   We therefore recommend that:

Section 137 of the Local Government Act 1972 should be amended to incorporate a provision comparable to that in section 83(3A) of the Local Government (Scotland) Act 1973 under which a local authority may only use the power for a purpose for which another local authority has statutory responsibility with the consent of that authority.

(Paragraph 8.89)

UNLAWFUL DISCRIMINATION IN THE USE OF DISCRETION

8.91   There has been criticism that some local authorities have on occasion exercised discretion in a way which discriminates unacceptably between different organisations. For example, concern has been expressed in the evidence that some local authorities have placed advertising with selected newspapers while boycotting others and that some authorites have discriminated against certain organisations on irrelevant grounds in the letting of premises.

8.92   There are many circumstances in which it is proper for local authorities to discriminate between organisations. In deciding on applications for grant-aid from voluntary bodies, for example, an authority is bound to consider which bodies are likely to be most effective in meeting its objectives, and to discriminate between the bodies accordingly. There are, however, other circumstances in which discrimination is illegal. There are statutory prohibitions under the race relations and equal opportunities legislation. More generally there is the administrative law rule under which an authority acts illegally if it is activated by an

---

[1] Section 83(3A), inserted by section 6 of the Local Government and Planning (Scotland) Act 1982.

improper or irrelevant purpose in reaching a decision. Under this rule, a decision which discriminates between different organisations will not be illegal if the reasons for differentiating between the organisations are material to the decision. But a decision which discriminates between organisations on grounds which are irrelevant to the decision is illegal.

8.93   In general, we think that it can be left to the courts to define and deal with unlawful discrimination; our proposals for a new power of assistance in bringing legal proceedings should help to ensure that relevant cases come before the courts. However, we are conscious that particular concern has been expressed in this context about discretionary decisions which are said to have been motivated by **party political** considerations, and we believe there is a need for additional action in this context. While there is wide consensus on the principle that local authority discretion ought not to be exercised in a way which is intended to secure advantage for a particular political party, there are difficulties in formulating a clear-cut definition to describe and prohibit such activities. It is clearly wrong to grant-aid a body which is a proxy for a political party, to provide rent-free accommodation for one political party and not for others, to associate with one particular party in pursuing a project or providing a service, or to provide an indirect subsidy to a party by placing advertisements in their newspaper. It is equally wrong to use public money in a way which is unambiguously intended to buy votes for the controlling party on the authority, for example, by concentrating housing repair services in marginal wards regardless of their needs relative to other wards.

8.94   On the other hand, it is important to recognise that many local authorities operate in a party political environment under which a particular political party may be successful in obtaining a majority of seats on a local authority because of the policies it espouses. Though there is no exact science by which the effect may be measured, some policies are likely to be more successful than others in winning votes. The council house sales policy is a recent example of a policy which is generally held to have been successful in this respect. It would in our view be a total negation of the democratic process if local authorities were to be inhibited from pursuing certain policies simply because those policies were associated with the controlling party on the council and were likely to influence the electorate in favour of that party.

8.95   We have been following the recent Parliamentary debates on the Local Government Act 1986 with interest in this context. As introduced in the House of Lords, clause 2 rested on two tests in attempting to define party political material. It sought to proscribe the publication by local authorities of:

(a)   material which appears to be designed to affect public support for a political party; and

(b)   material which can reasonably be regarded as likely to affect public support for a political party.

The test described at (b) was lost as a result of an amendment carried at Committee Stage in the House of Lords against the advice of the Government, and the clause as enacted contains no reference to it. The Government has, however, said that it intends to introduce futher legislation in the next Parliamentary session to restore the effect of clause 2 as it stood before the Lords' amendment.

8.96   We do not propose to comment on the debate about the definition of party political in the specific publicity context, but we do not think that the recent legislation on it—in either its original or final form—provides a helpful precedent for a more general prohibition on party political activities at public expense. There are two reasons for this. First, we do not think that the test described at (a) above would be useful in a wider context than that of publicity in so far as it rests on **apparent** purpose. We argued in our Interim Report that the content of publicity material was likely to be the best test of its purpose[1]. But we do not think that this principle transfers well into a wider context where the motivation for a decision will often not be apparent from the decision itself. Second, for reasons we have explained in paragraph 8.94, we do not think that the test described at (b) above would begin to stand up to scrutiny on matters other than publicity.

8.97　In attempting to define unacceptable party political bias in the wider context, we do not think it is possible to improve on the principle already embodied in general administrative law and described in paragraph 8.92. This turns on the **purposes** for a decision or action and provides that an intention to secure electoral advantage for a particular political party must not be a primary motivating factor in the exercise of local authority discretion. Decisions must be defensible in terms of the powers under which they are taken (eg a section 137 decision must be capable of being argued to be in the interest of the area or of some or all of its inhabitants). While it is important to recognise that such decisions may have an influence on electoral behaviour, any such effect should be incidental rather than the main motivating factor.

8.98　We note that there is a precedent for a statutory definition of 'political' which rests on the test of 'main purpose' in section 3 of the Trade Union Act 1913 as amended by section 17 of the Trade Union Act 1984. Section 3(3)(f) refers to material:

> 'the main purpose of which is to persuade people to vote for a political party or candidate or to persuade them not to vote for a political party or candidate'.

If rigorously applied, we believe that this principle would outlaw the activities described in paragraph 8.93. It would for example be difficult to justify a decision to advertise exclusively in a paper with a particular party political bias other than in terms of a concern to promote the interests of that paper and/or that party.

8.99　Notwithstanding that this principle is already a feature of general administrative law, we argued in the context of local authority publicity in our Interim Report that there was advantage in having the position put beyond doubt in an express statutory provision[2]. We attach no less importance to this principle in the wider context of local authority discretion.

8.100　We therefore recommend that:

> **there should be a declaratory provision in statute embodying the existing common law prohibition on local authorities using their discretion for the main purpose of securing electoral advantage for a particular candidate or political party.**

(Paragraph 8.89)

---

[1] Local Authority Publicity, HMSO 1985, paragraph 133.
[2] Local Authority Publicity, HMSO 1985, paragraph 227.

GRANTS TO VOLUNTARY BODIES

8.101   Local authorities gave some £350 million in grants to voluntary bodies in 1983–84, the latest year for which we have information. The majority of this funding was granted under specific service powers—such as social services or education powers—not under sections 137 or 83. Such grants fall into two general categories: arm's length and programme. Arm's length grants are designed to assist a voluntary organisation in achieving its general objectives. Programme grants are given under a contractual arrangement for a specific project or services. About 60% of grants are in the former category, and about 40% in the latter.

8.102   We welcome the use made by local authorities of voluntary organisations, who in many cases are able to provide services more effectively than through direct provision. We are aware, however, of some concern in the evidence that local authorities are abusing their powers to grant-aid bodies which are party political in nature or which aim to promote peripheral, divisive or unnecessary causes. We have not been able fully to explore the extent to which the criticisms are justified. But we recognise that this is an area of concern that needs to be addressed.

8.103   In so far as the issues are ones of campaigning, overt party political bias or the abuse of patronage, they are dealt with respectively in paragraphs 8.78 and 8.79, 8.91 to 8.99 and Chapter Six respectively. We have recommended new safeguards in these areas where the existing ones are inadequate. In so far as the issues relate to 'sectional, divisive and socially unacceptable' or 'peripheral' activities our discussion in paragraphs 8.80 to 8.86 is relevant. We concluded there that it is not practicable to define such activities in a way which would provide a consensus basis of acceptablility. This is best decided by elected members.

8.104   We are aware that criticisms of such activities have sometimes related to grants to voluntary bodies. We have considered whether some limitation on grants should be introduced by reference to the status of the body, but see no merit in this. Certainly a limitation to registered charities would be much too restrictive. The requirements of the Charity Commissioners exclude, for example, self-help groups. There are also significant delays in registration. Nor do we consider that it would be productive or practicable to devise a wider criterion for the objectives of bodies receiving grant. We are aware that such a criterion exists in section 40(5)(b) of the General Rate Act 1967 for the purpose of rate relief. This provision limits rate relief to 'organisations which are not established or conducted for profit and whose main objects are charitable or are otherwise philanthropic or religious or concerned with education, social welfare, science, literature or the fine arts'. This definition has not proved easy to apply in practice and has been the subject of much litigation in the courts. Moreover, whatever its merits in the context of rate relief, it would not be suitable for our purposes. It needs to be considered that local authorities widely give grants to, or enter into contracts with, profit making companies. For example grants are given to companies under sections 137 and 83 for economic development purposes. Services are increasingly contracted out to companies rather than performed direct by local authorities. It would be quite anomalous to place a greater limitation on voluntary organisations, which are by definition non-profit making, than applied more widely. Provided that the activity to which the grant relates is within a local authority's powers then it would be wrong to introduce any further restriction by reference to the status of the body receiving it.

8.105   In so far as grants to voluntary bodies have caused concern we believe that the best way of tackling them is to provide for greater open-ness about the nature of the bodies that benefit from grant and about the purpose for which grant is given, and to provide that there is careful monitoring to ensure that grant is actually used for the purposes for which it is given. Local authorities should not in our view be prohibited for making grants to certain bodies simply because the bodies in question are controversial or unpopular with a section of the population; but they should be prepared to stand by and account for unpopular decisions. The public have a right to know what purpose public funds are being put, and to be informed of the nature of bodies who are benefitting from public subsidy. Greater open-ness will provoke more informed public debate and will reduce the scope for misinformation and mistrust.

8.106   We have been impressed by the proposals put to us in written evidence by the National Council for Voluntary Organisations in this respect. They suggest that local authorities might be required to publish an annual statement listing all grants to voluntary bodies in excess of £1,000, and that this list should be available to the public on demand together with the authority's annual report. The list would state the name of the body involved, the amount of the grant and the purpose for which the grant is given. In addition, they propose a requirement that local authorities make available for public inspection copies of the annual reports of all organisations listed. Given that much controversy can arise when even relatively small amounts of money are involved, we do not share their view that new requirements for open-ness should be limited to grants in excess of £1,000. Otherwise, we endorse their proposals.

8.107   We recognise that some of the smallest voluntary organisations may not produce annual reports as such. We would not wish to see such bodies burdened with over-bureaucratic requirements. Nevertheless, we consider that any body receiving a public grant should be required to produce at least an annual public statement of their accounts and of the use to which any grant has been put. This statement should be made available for inspection, together with a copy of the body's constitution and membership, in place of an annual report as such.

8.108   There is limited advantage in a requirement that the purpose of any grant must be clearly and publicly stated if there are inadequte arrangements for monitoring and no mechanisms to ensure that the funds made available are actually used for the activities for which they are granted. Local authorities clearly need to monitor the activities of bodies which are grant-aided. In order to ensure continuing **public** accountability, we suggest that there should be a requirement that the annual report (or public annual statement) of all grant-aided bodies include a brief statement of the use to which the grant has been put.

8.109   In summary, we recommend that:

(a)   local authorities should be statutorily required to maintain a list of all grants to voluntary bodies, and to publish it annually as part of or together with the authority's annual report;

(Paragraph 8.106)

201

(b)   the list should state the name of the body involved and the amount of the grant and should indicate the purpose for which the grant was given;

(Paragraph 8.106)

(c)   the use to which such grants are put should be monitored and to this end:

(i)   each voluntary body receiving grant should be required to publish an annual report or annual statement which should state the use to which the grant has been put;

(ii)   local authorities should be required to make such annual reports or annual statements available for public inspection.

(Paragraphs 8.107 and 8.108)

ENTERPRISE BOARDS AND 'ARM'S LENGTH' COMPANIES

8.110   A number of local authorities have set up under their control Companies Act companies to undertake certain activities. It is normal for such companies to be wholly-owned by the local authorities. The best known examples are perhaps the Greater London Enterprise Board and the West Midlands Enterprise Board, but we estimate there to be in the order of some 30–50 such companies nationally (excluding transport companies for which see below). Most of them are concerned with economic development. Their activities include the promotion of co-operatives, the provision of industrial premises, the acquisition of equity in particular types of company and the provision of advice, loans, grants or guarantees to particular businesses. Other than in the contexts mentioned below, there are no express powers for local authorities to set up such companies, and there is scope for argument about their legal basis.

8.111   In specific contexts, the Government has promoted the setting up of arm's length companies. The Transport Act 1985 provides that bus undertakings held by passenger transport executives (in metropolitan areas) and by certain district councils (outside metropolitan areas) shall be transferred to a limited company set up by, and initially wholly-owned by, the relevant parent authority. The Airports Bill currently before Parliament proposes that local authorities controlling airports should be required to set up companies to operate them.

8.112   The arguments in favour of setting up an arm's length company to pursue certain activities have been put to us as follows:

(a)   the traditional local authority organisational structure is not capable of adaptation for effective operation in a business enviornment. Decisions need to be taken quickly and material treated in strict confidence. The committee system cannot operate on this basis;

(b)   a company is likely to generate more confidence in the private sector and to attract private investment;

(c)   a company may be more flexible in its recruitment policy and conditions of service and hence in a better position to attract suitably qualified staff.

8.113   The concerns expressed about arm's length companies are very much the mirror image of the arguments in favour of them. They are held to be insufficiently accountable to the parent authority and hence to the electorate at large. In an adjournment debate on 26 July 1985, Mr Christopher Chope MP argued that one such company was:

> 'devoid of public accountability. Its members and directors are appointed by the city council, but need not be elected members of that council. Once appointed, they are accountable to the company and not to the public.
>
> The public and press are denied access to agendas, supporting papers and minutes, thereby being denied all the public safeguards in the Local Government (Access to Information) Act 1985.
>
> The Company board meets in private and, most sinister of all, councillors who are not on the board are denied access to information. Board members may be paid fees and the board may be so constituted that minority parties on the city council are not represented on it.
>
> Although directors are governed by the company legislation and the company must keep accounts and make and file an annual return, the controls on members of the board are a far cry from open accountability to the electorate and the public. Yet the company is wholly dependent on public funds or the guarantee of such funds'[1].

8.114 These concerns are ones which should not be lightly dismissed. They are consistent with themes which we have been pursuing throughout this Report: namely, more open-ness, better accountability and the conduct of business within the spirit of the law. We have no doubt that some of the activities which are being pursued by arm's length companies are valuable and should be continued. But we should on balance prefer to see them pursued through machinery which operates **within** the organisation of a local authority.

8.115 In so far as there is a case for such companies, we consider that it can only properly be assessed in the context of a detailed appraisal of the requirements of the service in question. Such detailed appraisal is outside our remit. We have proposed that the Government should initiate a review of the proper role of local authorities in the economic development sphere (paragraph 8.43) and we would consider it appropriate that the case for enterprise boards should be addressed in that context.

8.116 Where arm's length companies are set up, there should in our view be specific enabling legislation and certain statutory safeguards. In particular, we would suggest that:

(a) the purpose, functions and powers of local authority created companies should be clearly spelt out in their Articles of Association. In principle, such companies should not have powers to apply funds from public sector sources on activities which are beyond the powers of the parent authority;

(b) on the precedent of the Transport Act 1985, there should be provision for audit by persons who are not only qualified under the Companies Act but who are also approved by the Audit Commission (Accounts Commission in Scotland);

---

[1] House of Commons Official Report, 26 June 1985, Column 1463.

(c) there should be a requirement for a full report and statement of accounts to the parent authority at at least quarterly intervals;

(d) members of the boards of such companies should be subject to rules governing declarations of interest which are similar to those applying to members of local authorities;

(e) councillors should constitute a majority of members.

8.117 In summary we recommend that:

(a) the case for enterprise boards should be considered in the context of the review proposed in paragraph 8.43 of the role of local authorities in economic development;

(Paragraph 8.115)

(b) the law in relation to local authority controlled companies should be amended:

(i) to make clear that they may be set up only where there is specific enabling legislation;

(ii) to incorporate safeguards concerning their articles of association, their membership and their audit and reporting arrangements.

(Paragraph 8.116)

CHAPTER 9

PUBLIC CHALLENGE

INTRODUCTION

9.1   We have said that local authorities are creatures of statute. The actions they take, and the way in which decisions may lawfully be reached, are governed by a set of statutory rules. We have made a number of recommendations in this Report for clarifying and amending those rules.

9.2   But rules are of little value if they are ignored. It has been argued that the existing arrangements for enforcement are inadequate to secure compliance with the rules; and that members of the public are, for practical purposes, in no position effectively to challenge actions which are outside the rules. In this Chapter, we explore those arguments and we consider what, if anything, needs to be done to strengthen public rights of challenge.

9.3   The Chapter is concerned exclusively with the mechanisms to challenge breaches of the law, procedural abuse and maladministration. It is not concerned with mechanisms to challenge the **merits** of decisions. On the merits of general policy questions, local authorities are directly accountable to the electorate. On the merits of specific case decisions, there is a variety of mechanisms through which individuals may pursue a challenge (eg through planning appeals); but we have not been concerned to look at these in this Report.

9.4   The Chapter outlines the existing mechanisms for challenge through the audit service, the ombudsmen and the courts; it identifies certain weaknesses and suggests a number of ways in which the procedures might be modified to overcome them. It goes on to identify certain residual weaknesses which arise from the gaps between the mechanisms and to consider how these might be tackled. In a final section, we consider the question of penalties (as opposed to procedures for challenge), commenting in particular on the provisions for disqualification and surcharge.

9.5   A number of those submitting evidence have made the point that the mechanisms for challenge of local authority decisions are already more rigorous than those applying in certain other contexts. We would not disagree that the mechanisms are in certain respects different both as between the public and private sectors and as between local authorities and other public sector bodies. Nor would we wish to imply that there is a need for reform in the context of local authority challenge which is necessarily greater than that in other contexts. Given our terms of reference, we have, however, concentrated our attention exclusively on the issues as they affect local authorities. We leave it to others to conclude to what extent our recommendations are equally relevant in other contexts.

EXISTING ARRANGEMENTS FOR CHALLENGE

9.6   Local authority decisions and actions may be challenged by the auditors, the ombudsmen and various courts and tribunals. We briefly describe the role and procedures of each of these below.

9.7 A system of compulsory local authority audit has existed since the Poor Law Reform Act of 1834. The function of the district auditor has traditionally been to identify monies not duly accounted for, losses caused by negligence or misconduct and illegal payments. The functions of the service were, however, significantly broadened in England and Wales with the passing of the Local Government Finance Act 1982, which imposed on auditors an additional duty to promote economy, efficiency and effectiveness.

9.8 The procedures for local government audit in England and Wales are governed by Part III of the 1982 Act. This Act provided for the establishment of the Audit Commission, an independent body of persons appointed by the Secretary of State in consultation with the local authority associations and other interested partes. Among its other functions, it is the job of the Audit Commission to appoint auditors to each local authority. Audit may be undertaken either by a member of the district audit service employed by the Commission or by a private accountancy firm. The district audit service conducts about 75% of all audits.

9.9 Auditors' responsibilities include:

(a) a duty to satisfy themselves that the local authority's accounts comply with relevant statutory requirements and that proper procedures have been observed in their compilation (section 15(1)(a) and (b) of the 1982 Act);

(b) a duty to satisfy themselves that the local authority has made proper arrangments for securing economy, efficiency and effectiveness in the use of its resources (section 15(1)(c) of the 1982 Act);

(c) a discretion to apply to the courts for a declaration where it appears to them that a particular item of account is contrary to law (section 19(1) of the 1982 Act);

(d) a duty to certify amounts due from those responsible where it appears to them that a relevant sum has not been included in the accounts or a loss has been incurred as a result of wilful misconduct (section 20(1) of the 1982 Act).

9.10 The responsibilities at (c) and (d) are the important ones in the areas with which we have been concerned. Under section 19, where the auditor is successful in obtaining a court declaration that a particular item of account is unlawful, then the persons responsible may be ordered by the court to repay the amount involved either in whole or in part (the so-called surcharge). If they are members of the authority and the amount involved exceeds £2,000, the court may also order them to be disqualified from being a member of an authority for a specified period. The court may not, however, order surchage or disqualification in cases where those concerned have acted reasonably or in the belief that the expenditure involved was authorised by law and must in any event take account of the circumstances and the ability of those involved to pay.

9.11 The penalties flowing from an auditor's certificate under section 20 are even more severe. Persons responsible for a failure to bring a relevant sum into account or for loss caused by wilful misconduct are liable to repay the amount involved regardless of their circumstances (a second form of surcharge). If they are members and the amount involved exceeds £2,000, they are automatically disqualified from membership of a local authority for five years. Those named in a certificate may appeal against it to the courts, who have power to confirm or quash the certificate.

9.12   In addition to the declaration and certificate provisions, auditors have at their disposal two other ways of drawing attention to problems across the range of their responsibilites. First, under section 15(3) of the 1982 Act, they may make a 'report in the public interest' on any matter arising from the audit either immediately or at the conclusion of the audit. Second, under the 1983 Code of Audit Practice for Local Authorities in England and Wales, they may issue a qualified opinion on the accounts if they feel that they cannot confirm that the accounts 'fairly present' the affairs of the authority. However, we understand that such qualified opinions are normally the result of a failure to comply with particular accounting conventions rather than with the sort of issues with which we are concerned.

9.13   All these responsibilities stand on their own in the sense that auditors must form their own views on whether action needs to be taken regardless of whether or not the matters involved are ones which have given rise to complaints or controversy. But auditors also have certain duties to consider and pursue objections raised by the public. Any local government elector for the area in question has a right to question the auditor about the accounts and to attend before the auditor to make objections on any of the matters which the auditor is in a position to pursue. If the auditor decides against pursuing the objection, whether by seeking a court declaration under section 19 or issuing a certificate under section 20, then the elector has a right to demand from the auditor a written statement of reasons. If the elector is dissatisfied with the auditor's decision, he or she may go on to appeal direct to the court.

9.14   Auditors considered a total of some 730 questions and objections from members of the public in 1984–85.

The audit service: Scotland

9.15   Audit arrangements are somewhat different in Scotland. In particular, there is no provision for disqualification; there is a different allocation of responsibilities between the Accounts Commission and the auditor; there is a lesser role for the courts and a major role for the Secretary of State; public rights are weaker; and the audit service has no general responsibility for promoting 'economy, efficiency and effectiveness'. The Scottish arrangements, which are governed by the Local Government (Scotland) Act 1973, are set out below.

9.16   Members of the Commission for Local Authority Accounts are appointed by the Secretary of State for Scotland in consultation with the local authority associations and other interests. The position of Controller of Audit, the head of the professional audit staff of the Commission, is statutory. Audits must be undertaken either by auditors who are officers of the Commission or by professional accountants appointed by the Commission.

9.17   As in England and Wales, the auditors have general duties to satisfy themselves that the relevant statutory requirements have been complied with and that proper practices have been observed in the compilation of the accounts. There the similarities cease. The Controller of Audit (rather than the local auditor) may make a report to the Commission if there is any matter arising out of the accounts which he or she considers should be brought to the attention of the authority concerned, or to the public (section 102(2) of the 1973 Act). In addition, the Controller of Audit must make a **special report** to the Commission if he or she considers:

(a) that any item of account is contrary to law;

(b) that there has been a failure to account for any sum which ought to have been brought into account;

(c) that loss has been caused by negligence or misconduct of any person, or by failure to comply with any statutory duty (section 102(3) of 1973 Act).

9.18 The Commission must consider the special report and any observations on it made by the authority concerned and any affected persons. It may hold a hearing on the report, and must do so if requested by one of the parties. It may also state a case on any matter of law arising from the report for the opinion of the Court of Session.

9.19 If the Commission agrees with the special report in any of the three respects listed in paragraph 9.17, then it must forward the report to the Secretary of State and may recommend that the Secretary of State makes an order requiring the persons responsible to repay to the authority an amount not exceeding the relevant loss. The Secretary of State in turn may make an order to that effect but shall not do so if he is satisfied that the persons involved acted reasonably or in the belief that their action was authorised by law. In making an order, the Secretary of State must have regard to all the circumstances of the case, including the ability of the persons involved to pay. There is no provision for appeal to the courts against the Secretary of State's decision.

9.20 In Scotland, any 'interested party' may object to the accounts of a local authority and they have a right to a hearing with the auditor. (The term 'interested party' is not defined in the legislation). There is, however, no statutory requirement for the auditor to inform the objector of the decision, nor the reasons for it. Nor does the objector have any right of appeal to the Commission or any other superior body. Twenty two formal objections were made over the five years to 1985, and a further 353 complaints were dealt with informally.

The local ombudsmen

9.21 Section 23 of the Local Government Act 1974 provided for the establishment of a Commission for Local Administration in England and a Commission for Local Administration in Wales. Section 21 of the Local Government (Scotland) Act 1975 provided for the appointment of a Commission for Local Administration in Scotland. There are three Commissioners covering different parts of England and one in each of Wales and Scotland. They are commonly known as local ombudsmen.

9.22 The local ombudsmen's task is to consider complaints from the public that they have suffered an injustice as a result of maladministration by a local authority. Maladministration is not defined in the legislation but includes such

208

factors as neglect, bias, unfairness, incompetence and excessive delay. In most cases maladministration amounts to a failure to follow the proper procedures.

9.23 Ombudsmen can only act on receipt of a complaint, not on their own initiative, and the complaint must normally be submitted via a councillor, not direct. Other than in exceptional circumstances, complaints cannot be accepted if there is some other remedy available (eg through the courts or a planning appeal) nor if the action in question affects most or all of the inhabitants of the area. Nor can the merits of a local authority's decision be questioned if it is within their lawful discretion and no maladministration has arisen.

9.24 Where the ombudsman decides to investigate a complaint, he or she must afford to the authority concerned, and to any individual named in the complaint, an opportunity to comment. The ombudsmen's investigations must be conducted in private. Ombudsmen have power to require that relevant information be supplied to them and have the same powers as the High Court in respect of the attendance and examination of witnesses.

9.25 On completing an investigation the ombudsman must send a report of the findings to all parties concerned, and make it available for public inspection. If the conclusion is that there has been maladministration leading to injustice, then the authority concerned is bound to consider the report and to notify the ombudsman of any action it proposes to take in consequence. If the ombudsman is dissatisfied, he or she may issue a further report. But if the local authority ultimately concludes that it should not take action following a report, there is nothing further that either the ombudsman or the complainant can do.

9.26 The legislation in England and Wales provides that there shall be a Representative Body for each country on which the authorities subject to the local ombudsmen are represented. These bodies act as a focal point for local authority views on ombudsmen issues and as a channel of communication between the ombudsmen and local authorities.

9.27 In 1984–85, the local ombudsmen in England received 3,389 complaints. Two hundred and ninety-two complaints were the subject of full formal reports during that year and maladministration causing injustice was found in 193 cases. In the same year, the Welsh ombudsman received 249 complaints, 37 of which became the subject of formal reports and maladministration causing injustice was found in 13 cases. The ombudsman in Scotland received about 600 complaints in 1984–85. Sixty-four were made the subject of formal reports and maladministration causing injustice was found in 20 cases.

9.28 A considerable number of ombudsman cases (483 in England in 1984–85) are settled locally in advance of a formal report. The Commissions for Local Administration have sought to promote complaints procedures within individual authorities so that grievances may be settled without reference to any outside agency. In September 1978, a code of practice on complaints procedures was sent to local authorities by the English Commission and the Representative

Body. Various research work is currently underway[1] which should provide a fuller picture of the prevalence and nature of internal grievance mechanisms.

The courts: England and Wales

9.29   Members of the public may challenge a local authority decision or action through the courts in a number of different ways categorised, for our purposes, as follows:

(i)   ordinary actions

(ii)   statutory appeals and remedies

(iii)   relator actions

(iv)   judicial review.

It is judicial review with which we are primarily concerned.

(i) Ordinary actions

9.30   In the same way that members of the public may bring an action against a private body or individual, they may also bring an ordinary civil action against a local authority where there is cause of action arising from interference with private rights. This may arise, for example, if the local authority breaches a contract with him or her, or commits negligence or a nuisance affecting him or her personally. Such actions may be brought in either the County or High Courts following normal court procedures. This kind of action does not raise issues peculiar to local authorities, and is not further pursued in this Report.

(ii) Statutory appeals and remedies

9.31   Many statutes provide a special appeal procedure for a person aggrieved by a local authority's decision in a particular sphere of its functional activities. Some of these procedures provide for a review of the merits of decisions and others for an appeal against their legality. Examples are the provisions for appeal on rating valuation matters to the Local Valuation Court and the Lands Tribunal, the provisions for appeal to the county courts on various housing matters and the provisions for appeal to the Secretary of State on the merits of planning decisions. These mechanisms arise in specific functional areas and, again, are not pursued further.

(iii) Relator actions

9.32   Where a member of the public wishes to challenge a local authority's decisions by ordinary action but has insufficient interest to do so he or she may ask the Attorney-General to lend his or her name to a relator action in order that the matter may come before the courts. A relator action is conducted by the individual who is responsible for all the costs, but each step has to be approved by the Attorney-General. The Attorney-General has an absolute discretion whether or not to lend his or her name to an action and a decision in this respect

---

[1] The University of Sheffield is undertaking a study on complaints mechanisms in local government for the English and Welsh Commissions for Local Administration, the Department of the Environment and the Economic and Social Research Council. Work for the Local Government Legal Society and the Society of Town Clerks' Education and Research Trust has been undertaken by Patrick Birkenshaw.

cannot be challenged. Although in theory relevant to the issues with which we are concerned, relator actions are in practice rarely brought.

(iv) Judicial review

9.33   A member of the public may apply for judicial review of any decision or action by a public sector body under rules laid down by the courts. These are known as the judicial review procedures and are set out in Order 53 of the Rules of the Supreme Court. These rules were first introduced in 1977; but their effect was largely to simplify and expedite pre-existing arrangements. They were subsequently given statutory force by section 31 of the Supreme Court Act 1981. The judicial review procedures overlap the procedures for ordinary actions and for statutory remedies in that they may apply even where another remedy is available. But they also go wider in that review may be sought of **any** decision or action by a public sector body on the grounds that it is illegal. The procedures are, however, discretionary; the court has discretion to decide not to consider a case and may so decide, for example, if there is an alternative statutory remedy. It also has discretion as to the grant of remedies.

9.34   The grounds for challenge under the judicial review procedures will normally be one of the following:

(a)   the authority has taken an action which is outside its statutory powers;

(b)   the authority has acted illegally in the *Wednesbury*[1] sense; that is, they have taken into account irrelevant matters, or have failed to take into account relevant matters; or have come to a decision so unreasonable that no reasonable authority would ever have come to it; or have acted in bad faith or been influenced by malice or improper purposes;

(c)   there has been procedural impropriety;

(d)   the authority has failed to comply with a statutory duty.

9.35   The courts have been clear that judicical review is **not** appropriate to question the merits as opposed to the legal propriety of a local authority action. For example, in the case of *Luby v Newcastle-under-Lyme Corporation (1964) 2 QB 64*, Lord Justice Diplock said:

'The court's control over the exercise by a local authority of a discretion conferred upon it by Parliament is limited to ensuring that the local authority has acted within the powers conferred. It is not for the court to substitute its own view of what is a desirable policy in relation to the subject-matter of the discretion so conferred. It is only if it is exercised in a manner which no reasonable man could consider justifiable that the court is entitled to interfere.'

9.36   The procedures for judicial review are in two stages. The applicant must first obtain leave to bring the application from a High Court judge. This must

---

[1] *Associated Provincial Picture Houses Ltd v Wednesbury Corporation (1948) 1KB 223.*

normally be sought within three months of the act complained of. Leave will only be granted if:

(a) the applicant can show a prima facie case;

(b) he or she is considered to have 'sufficient interest' in the matter to which the application relates.

The applicant may proceed with the case only if he or she obtains leave.

9.37 What constitutes a 'sufficient interest' is not laid down in the legislation or Order 53. It is clear from certain cases[1] that a ratepayer will normally be considered to have sufficient interest to challenge the expenditure decisions of local authorities, but the position of an elector in cases involving expenditure is less clear. Nor is it clear that either an elector or a ratepayer would necessarily be considered to have sufficient interest to bring a case over a matter which did not involve expenditure.

9.38 Costs in judicial review actions are within the discretion of the court but normally follow the event, so that unsuccessful applicants may have to bear not only their own but also the local authority's costs. Even a short High Court action can cost more than £50,000. Legal aid is available only to applicants of very limited means and even in such cases, though technically available, is unlikely to be granted.

9.39 In 1985, 217 cases for judicial review were brought in which local authorities were the respondents. This was a marked increase on 1980 when only 34 cases were brought. The actions were brought by private individuals in about 80% of cases in 1985. Nine cases were brought by other local authorities.[2]

The courts: Scotland

9.40 Although the Scottish legal system is different from that in England and Wales, its effect is similar in the context with which we are concerned. Ordinary actions and statutory appeals and remedies are available to the citizen in similar fashion. In addition, an individual may challenge the decisions of a local authority through an action of declarator, reduction or interdict or under statute law for failure to carry out a statutory duty.[3] These actions cover ground similar to the scope of English/Welsh judicial review arrangements described at paragraph 9.34. Such actions must be brought in the Court of Session, the supreme court in Scotland. English case law is available to the Scottish courts, and the Wednesbury principles are applied in the some way as they are south of the border.

9.41 New procedures were introduced in the Court of Session in May 1985 under the title of 'Judicial Review'.[4] These were intended to speed up procedures

---

[1] *R v GLC ex parte Blackburn (1976) 1 WLR 5590.* The decision of the Court of Appeal in *IRC v National Federation of Self Employed and Small Businesses Ltd (1980) QB 407* (House of Lords decision reported at (1982) AC 617).
[2] These figures were obtained with special permission by inspection of the records held by the Crown Office.
[3] Secton 91 of the Court of Session Act 1868.
[4] Governed by the Act of Sederunt (Rules of Court Amendment No 2) (Judicial Review), 1985 (SI 1985 No 500).

rather than to institute change of legal substance, and are based largely on the English/Welsh model.

9.42   Under the procedures there is no requirement that an applicant obtain the leave of the court to bring a case. However, the application may be dismissed by the court if the applicant cannot show title and interest. Our understanding is that what constitutes title and interest in Scotland is more restrictive than what would be regarded in England and Wales as constituting sufficient interest under the 'leave' arrangements.

MODIFICATIONS TO THE EXISTING ARRANGEMENTS

9.43   Each of the three mechanisms we have described above has weaknesses. The audit service is sometimes accused of being insufficiently active in dealing with complaints of unlawful expenditure and of providing for too slow a remedy. The ombudsmen arrangements are criticised because the public has no access to the service other than through a councillor, because their remit is too limited and because their decisions are not enforceable. The judicial review procedures are criticised for being insufficiently accessible to members of the public because of the requirement to obtain leave, the need to establish 'sufficient interest' and, even more significantly, because of the costs involved. Against the background of these criticisms, we examine the case for change in each of these services in this section and make recommendations.

The audit service: England and Wales

9.44   In carrying out its tasks of acting against unlawful expenditure and wilful misconduct leading to financial loss, the audit service in England and Wales has been the subject of two main criticisms. First, it is argued that the service tends to be too slow in taking action where problems are identified given its focus on end-year accounts. Second, it is argued that auditors tend to be insufficiently active in pursuing illegality by local authorities, especially now that they are devoting increasing attention to issues relating to value for money.

9.45   We think that both criticisms can be overstated. In particular, notwithstanding the requirement for end of year audited accounts, there is no reason in principle why the audit service should not take action as soon as a problem is identified, rather than waiting for the end of the year. The actions of the auditor in Liverpool over the rate setting for 1985–86 illustrate the point; not only did he issue a certificate of wilful misconduct leading to financial loss in September, six months before the end of the relevant financial year; he also gave all councillors written warning of his intention to do so on 21 May 1985.[1] The instances in which the auditor gets to the point of issuing a certificate of wilful misconduct or seeking a declaration of unlawful expenditure are rare—as explained in paragraph 9.113; but behind these lie a far larger number of cases in which authorities hold back from, or reconsider, action in the light of views expressed by the auditor.

(i) Greater publicity for reports

9.46   Nevertheless, we believe that there are certain reforms which could usefully be introduced to make the service more effective. First, we believe that

---

[1] Parkinson, *Research Volume IV*.

reports in the public interest should be more rapidly and better publicised, thereby strengthening the sources of information through which authorities may be held directly accountable to the electorate. Such reports may be issued in the course of an audit and may be used to draw attention to problems which the auditor has been unable to resolve in discussion with officers. The present requirement is that a report in the public interest must be taken into consideration by the authority as soon as practicable. This effectively means that the contents of a report may not be publicly available until some months after its issue, and that it is even then only 'published' in the sense that it comprises part of the papers for a council or committee meeting. Accordingly we propose that the requirements for publicity be improved. In particular, in addition to the requirement that such reports be considered by the authority as soon as practicable, we propose that the chief executive of an authority should be placed under a duty immediately to notify all members of the authority of receipt of a report in the public interest, to provide a copy of any such report to members on request and to make copies available to the public for inspection.

(ii) Immediate action to prevent losses

9.47 Second, we note that the auditors' powers to seek from the courts a declaration of unlawful expenditure is not accompanied by a power to seek an interim injunction. Nor have they express powers to approach the court for an expedited hearing for an order of mandamus if they have reason to believe that an authority is failing to undertake a duty and that failure will result in financial loss. This effectively means that auditors are able to apply legal remedies less quickly than other interested parties if, for example, they take the view that certain phased payments are illegal and ought immediately to stop, or that an authority is failing in a statutory duty and in danger of incurring a consequent loss. We therefore propose that there should be new powers to seek an interim injunction restraining unlawful expenditure and to seek an expedited hearing for an order of mandamus.

(iii) Conflicts of roles

9.48 Third, we believe that there would be advantage in creating greater distance between the job of the auditor on the ground and the job of the audit service as adjudicator under section 20 of the 1982 Act and as quasi-prosecutor under section 19 of the Act (see paragraphs 9.9 and 9.10). In saying this, we are **not** endorsing the occasionally expressed view that there is or may be unhealthy collusion between the auditor and the administration within individual local authorities. We are impressed rather by the argument—endorsed by the Audit Commission itself—that the job of the auditor is in some respects a particularly difficult one. Auditors need to develop a close and positive working relationship with the authorities they audit, particularly if they are to be effective in their role of helping the authority to secure 'economy, efficiency and effectiveness in its use of resources'. On the other hand, any action they may take to seek a section 19 declaration against the authority, or to issue a section 20 certificate on a matter with general policy import (such as delays in rate-setting), will inevitably cause tension and is likely to lead to some breakdown in the spirit of trust between the auditor and the authority.

9.49 We are impressed by the Scottish arrangements in this respect. In Scotland, it is the Controller of Audit—the professional head of the Audit

Service—who has the responsibility to make a special report to the Commission for Local Authority Accounts where it is considered that there has been illegal expenditure or a loss caused by negligence or misconduct. It is the Commission which has the responsibility of reaching an initial view as to whether surcharge or any other action is appropriate, and accordingly to make recommendations to the Secretary of State. We would not wish to bring the Secretary of State into the process in England and Wales, but we do think that the precedent is helpful in so far as it distances the individual auditor from decisions as to illegality and surcharge. We therefore propose that the auditor's responsibilities under sections 19 and 20 of the 1982 Act be transferred to the Audit Commission. Such a change should also have the incidental advantage of promoting a more integrated and specialist source of expertise on difficult and contentious legal issues within the audit service.

9.50 A line would need to be drawn dividing the responsibilities of auditors from those of the Audit Commission, particularly insofar as the rights of the public are concerned. Our view is that it should continue to be for the local auditors to hear objections from the public, and to notify the objector of their decisions, and their reasons, where they decide not to pursue an objection. There might be a new requirement that the local auditor notify the objector where an issue is referred to the Commission for further consideration, and the Commission might in turn be placed under an obligation to inform the objector of its decision, and the reasons for it. These are, however, matters which we would hope that the Secretary of State would explore in more detail with the Commission and the audit service before instituting change.

The audit service: Scotland

9.51 The English/Welsh and Scottish audit arrangements are based on different traditions, and we see little advantage in any attempt to bring them into line for uniformity's sake alone. As we have already said, however, there are some respects in which we feel that Scottish arrangements offer useful lessons for those south of the border, and there are some respects in which the converse is true. We consider the case for some possible changes to the Scottish arrangements below.

(i) Role of the courts

9.52 A major difference between the English/Welsh and the Scottish audit arrangements is that the courts in Scotland have a much smaller statutory role. It is the Commission that must form a view as to whether there has been unlawful expenditure or misconduct leading to financial loss and the Secretary of State who has the responsibility to decide whether to impose surcharge. There is no provision for appeal to the courts against the Secretary of State's decision.

9.53 None of the evidence from Scotland has queried the role of the Secretary of State in the audit process. Nor does there appear to be any pressure to introduce the courts into the process. However, for reasons discussed in the final section of this Chapter, we have concluded that the penalty of disqualification is appropriate in certain circumstances under the audit provisions and that it ought to be extended to Scotland, but that it is not a penalty which it would be right to expect the Secretary of State to impose. It follows that we take the view that the courts should be given a new role in Scotland in deciding upon disqualification.

9.54 Difficult questions follow about how, and to what extent, the courts should be brought into the audit process in Scotland. If the courts are to reach decisions on disqualification, should they not also have responsibility for reaching decisions on surcharge? On the model of the English/Welsh section 19, should it be for the Accounts Commission to approach the Court of Session for a declaration of unlawful expenditure? Or should it be for the Commission to reach a decision against which an authority might appeal to the courts? These are complex and important questions. We propose that they should be further explored by the Secretary of State for Scotland in consultation with interested parties.

(ii) Conflicts of roles

9.55 In England and Wales we have said that the auditor faces something of a conflict of roles. This problem does not appear to arise in Scotland. As discussed in paragraph 9.49, auditors on the ground are already distanced from the process of pursuing allegations for illegality and of misconduct. Moreover they do not have the potentially conflicting statutory duty to satisfy themselves that authorities make proper arrangements for securing economy, efficiency and effectiveness in the use of resources.

(iii) Immediate action to prevent losses

9.56 The Scottish arrangements are in principle equally open to the criticism made of those in England and Wales that they fail to provide for immediate redress where an authority is considered to be incurring expenditure illegally or where there is misconduct leading to financial loss. In England and Wales, we have concluded that the Audit Commission should have new powers to seek an interim injunction to restrain allegedly unlawful expenditure or to apply for an order of mandamus to compel an authority to carry out a duty. The applicability of these arrangements to Scotland depends not only on the differing basis of judical review but also on the extent to which the courts are to be involved at all in the audit process. We have proposed that they should have such a role in relation to disqualification, but that the full extent of their involvement should be further examined by the Secretary of State. This examination should also cover the possible introduction in Scotland of procedures equivalent to those for immediate injunctions and an order of mandamus which we have proposed for England and Wales.

(iv) Greater publicity for reports

9.57 In England and Wales, we have proposed a new duty for chief executives immediately to notify all members of an authority on receipt of a report in the public interest, and for such reports to be made publicly available. There is no direct equivalent to a report in the public interest in Scotland. There are, however, requirements for the Controller of Audit to notify the authority concerned where he submits any report concerning them to the Commission, and for the Commission to notify the authority concerned if and when it forwards a special report to the Secretary of State. In the interests of open-ness and full and immediate debate, it would seem appropriate that requirements similar to those we have proposed in England and Wales should be applied to such reports.

216

(v) Rights of the public

9.58   Finally, we have been struck by the fact that the Scottish arrangements provide for lesser formal rights to individuals than their English/Welsh conterparts, although the part played by informal arrangements is clearly very important. In particular:

(a)   public rights are limited to 'interested persons', as opposed to 'electors' in England and Wales;

(b)   an 'interested person' may lodge an objection to the accounts with the auditor but has no right to question the auditor before doing so;

(c)   he or she has no right to receive notice of the decision of the Controller of Audit with respect to any formal objection lodged, nor of the reasons for the decision;

(d)   he or she has no right of appeal against the Controller of Audit's decision.

9.59   We see no justification for these lesser formal rights and recommend that the Scottish legislation is brought into line with the English/Welsh legislation in these repects. In both Scotland and England/Wales, we consider that all public rights under the audit legislation should extend to **all local electors and rate-payers** and that the references in both the 1973 Scottish Act and the 1982 Act should be amended accordingly. The precise nature of objectors' right of appeal in Scotland will need to reflect decisions reached about the role of the courts.

Recommendations on the audit service

9.60   In summary, we recommend that:

(a)   to improve publicity for auditors' reports in the public interest in England and Wales, and reports by the Controller of Audit and the Accounts Commission in Scotland, the chief executive of an authority should be placed under a statutory duty:

(i)   immediately to notify all councillors of the receipt of a report;

(ii)   to provide a copy to councillors on request;

(iii)   to make copies available for public inspection;

(Paragraphs 9.46 and 9.57)

(b)   the responsibilities of auditors in England and Wales under section 19 of the Local Government Finance Act 1982 (unlawful expenditure) and section 20 of the 1982 Act (wilful misconduct leading to financial loss or failure to bring an item to account) should be transferred to the Audit Commission;

(Paragraphs 9.48 to 9.50)

(c)   the Audit Commision for England and Wales should be given new statutory powers to seek:

(i)   an interim injunction to restrain a local authority from incurring unlawful expenditure;

(ii)   an expedited hearing for an order of mandamus to compel an authority to take action where failure to do so would be unlawful and would result in financial loss.

(Paragraph 9.47)

(d) the courts in Scotland should be given new responsibilities for deciding on audit matters. The precise character and extent of these responsibilities should be reviewed by the Secretary of State for Scotland in consultation with interested parties, and this review should include consideration of the case for procedures similar to those proposed for England and Wales at (c) above;

(Paragraphs 9.52 to 9.56)

(e) the existing statutory rights of the public to object to the accounts, both in England and Wales and in Scotland, should be extended to all electors and ratepayers;

(Paragraph 9.59)

(f) in addition, ratepayers and electors in Scotland should be given new statutory rights similar to those currently existing in England and Wales to:

(i) question the auditor on any matters arising from the accounts;

(ii) receive notice of the decision of the Controller of Audit with respect to the objection, and of the reasons for the decision;

(iii) appeal against a decision not to pursue the objection.

(Paragraph 9.59)

The local ombudsmen

9.61   The three Commissions for Local Administration have over the years made a number of recommendations for the reform of their procedure and the widening of their remit. Those made by the English Commission are detailed in full in an Appendix to their annual report for 1985. Some of the recommendations have been accepted by the Government but still await implementation by way of amendment to the legislation. Many of the more substantial proposals have not been accepted. We consider some of these below. We are conscious, also, that the House of Commons Select Committee on the Parliamentary Commissioner for Administration has been considering the implications of the failure of some local authorities to remedy injustice found by the local ombudsmen. Their conclusions are expected to be published in May or June 1986.

9.62   Two of the ombudsmen's proposals were the subject of wide comment, most of it in their support, in the evidence. These are proposals for direct public access to the ombudsmen and for a mechanism for the enforcement of their decisions.

(i) Direct access

9.63   Under section 26 of the Local Government Act 1974 and section 24 of the Local Government (Scotland) Act 1975, the ombudsmen may not entertain a complaint against a local authority unless it is referred to them by a member of the authority concerned. They may dispense with this requirement, but only if satisfied that a member of the authority has been asked to refer the complaint and has failed to do so.

9.64   There is in our view a number of strong arguments against this requirement for referral through a councillor, and we recommend that it is repealed. First, we believe it is wrong in principle that complainants should be expected to direct their complaints against a council through a member of the executive decision making body for that council. In this respect, the councillor's position is not analogous to that of a Member of Parliament (who has a role in referring complaints against central government actions to the Parliamentary ombudsman) as most MPs are not a part of the executive. Second, any general filter of this kind undertaken other than by the ombudsman seems to us to be unnecessary and undesirable. Third, our research has shown that there is a strong body of opinion even among councillors themselves that direct access is desirable.[1] Fourth, we note that the principle of direct access has already been broached in a limited context in Scotland, where complaints about the Scottish Special Housing Association and about new town development corporations may be made direct by the complainant to the local ombudsman.[2]

9.65   We note that informal arrangements have been agreed between the Representative Body and the ombudsmen in England for dealing with complaints received direct by the ombudsmen. Under these arrangements, such complaints are forwarded to the civic head of authority for internal settlement or formal reference back to the ombudsman. These arrangements seem a sensible half-way house. But they are not in our view a satisfactory alternative to a right of direct access.

9.66   It is important that local authorities should have an early opportunity internally to settle any complaints before they are investigated in detail by the ombudsman. Referral through a councillor is, however, neither a necessary nor a very direct way of achieving this. There is a separate requirement in the legislation that the ombudsman should not proceed to investigate a complaint without first satisfying himself that the authority concerned has had an opportunity to investigate, and reply to, the complaint.

(ii) Enforcement

9.67   We have said in paragraph 9.25 that there is at present nothing that either the ombudsman or the complainant can do if the local authority decide not to take any action following an ombudsman's report that the individual has suffered maladministration leading to injustice. This happens relatively rarely. In England, the number of cases which had not been settled to the ombudsman's satisfaction were 92 by March 1985, 6% of those in which maladministration and injustice had been found. A further 85 were awaiting settlement. The comparable figure in Wales was nine cases (4·4% of reports finding maladministration) and 11 cases (5% of reports finding maladministration) in Scotland.

9.68   Notwithstanding this relatively modest 'failure' rate, we accept the view put to us forcefully by all of the three Commissions that there should be some mechanism for enforcement. As the Welsh Commissioner put it in written evidence, 'it is intolerable that any injustice caused by maladministration identified

---

[1] SCPR, *Research Volume II*, Table 7.21.
[2] The Law Reform (Miscellaneous Provisions) (Scotland) Act 1985 brought these bodies within the remit of the ombudsman and disapplied the requirements for referral in that context.

in the course of an objective and impartial investigation should be allowed to go unremedied'. Although the cases where no action is taken are proportionately few, they are in our view bound to affect the public perception of the value of the service, and in the longer term to discourage complainants from approaching the ombudsman.

9.69. The Northern Ireland legislation provides a useful precedent for an enforcement mechanism. Under section 7 of the Northern Ireland Commissioner for Complaints Act 1969, complainants may apply to the county court if the Commissioner has found maladministration resulting in injustice and if they are dissatisfied with remedies offered to them. The court has power to order that appropriate compensation be made or that the authority concerned take appropriate remedial action. In order that the investigation already undertaken by the Commissioner should not unnecessarily be duplicated, the court is required to accept the report as evidence of the facts unless the contrary is proved. We recommend that consideration be given to the application of similar rules in the context of local ombudsmen's decisions in Great Britain.

9.70 Other major proposals for the reform of the ombudsman arrangements are as follows:

(a)   certain of the current exclusions to the ombudsmen's jurisdiction—in connection with commercial and contractual matters, certain personnel matters and internal school and college matters—should be removed;

(b)   the ombudsmen should have power themselves to initiate investigations rather than be limited to acting in response to complaints received;

(c)   the scope of the ombudsmen's jurisdiction should be extended to include cases which result from action affecting most or all of the inhabitants of an area;

(d)   the role of the Representative Bodies in England and Wales should be reviewed.

We consider each of these proposals in turn.

(iii) Exclusions from jurisdiction

9.71   Under Schedule 5 to the 1974 Act and Schedule 5 to the 1975 Act, the ombudsmen are currently precluded from looking into personnel matters; into actions taken by an authority relating to contractual matters or commercial transactions; into complaints concerning conduct, curriculum, internal organisation, management and discipline in schools and colleges; and into action in connection with the investigation or prevention of crime or of civil or criminal proceedings in court. The ombudsmen have pressed for the repeal or modification of all these exclusions. The Secretary of State for the Environment has accepted the case for some changes to the Schedule, but has not yet taken steps to implement change. The Schedules may be amended by order without resort to primary legislation.

9.72   We have a particular interest in paragraph 4 of the Schedule which excludes all personnel matters from the ombudsmen's remit. Successive Secretaries of State have taken the view that it would not be defensible to give to local

220

authority employees (past or present) a right which is not available to employees outside. We have some sympathy with this viewpoint; the primary function of the ombudsmen is in our view to provide support for the consumers of local government services rather than for those who are employed to provide them. However, we do not believe that the issues arise in quite the same form in the context of potential staff. We have recommended the adoption of a statutorily prescribed code of practice governing officer **appointment** procedures (paragraph 6.196 and following); and we have proposed that it should be made statutorily explicit that breach of the code should constitute prima facie maladministration about which an unsuccessful applicant should be in a position to complain to the ombudsmen. Paragraph 4 of Schedule 5 will accordingly need to be amended at least insofar as it prohibits the ombudsmen from considering complaints that proper selection procedures have not been followed.

9.73 Going beyond this particular concern about the implications of paragraph 4 to the Schedule, we believe that there is a case for a wider review of the Schedule 5 exclusions. The Secretaries of State have already agreed that there is a case for repeal or modification of some of the exclusions. In respect of others of them, it is arguable that they add little to the general statutory prohibition on the pursuit of cases where the complainant has an alternative remedy. In respect of others again, it is arguable that there is simply no case for their retention. We have, for excample, not been convinced that cases involving commercial and contractual transactions with members of the public are different in kind from cases involving other local authority dealings with the public and that they should therefore as a matter of general principle be excluded from the ombudsman's remit.

9.74 Subject to the provisos that the ombudsmen should not normally have jurisdiction in cases where the complainant has an alternative remedy, we take the general view that externally imposed filters on cases which the ombudsmen may pursue should be reduced to the minimum. To this end, we propose that the Secretaries of State review and modify the exclusions in Schedule 5 to the two Acts.

(iv) Power to initiate investigations

9.75 The ombudsmen at present only have power to pursue an investigation where a complaint from the individual concerned is referred to them in writing. The English ombudsmen have argued that they should have a power to investigate on their own initiative. 'The ombudsman service exists to investigate possible injustice caused by maladministration (and) it should not be hindered by the fact that a complainant is not readily forthcoming, perhaps because he or she is dead. After a decade's experience it is clear that a number of cases brought to notice in the media seem more significant and serious than some complaints properly referred to the ombudsman by individuals'.[1]

9.76 Again, we see advantage in removing this limitation on the ombudsman's remit. Research undertaken by JUSTICE in 1976–77 showed a very strong middle class bias among complainants, with over 70% of complaints being made

---

[1] The Local Ombudsmen. Report for the year ended 31 March 1985. Appendix 4, paragraph 20.

by non-manual households.[1] A power to take the initiative in an investigation could help towards redressing this imbalance. The ombudsman should not pursue a case except where there was good ground for concern, nor conduct an investigation into the general procedures of an authority rather than an individual case where there was reason to suppose that injustice has occurred. Subject to those provisos, we consider that a power to initiate investigations would be a useful addition to the ombudsman's powers.

(v) Cases affecting most or all inhabitants of an area

9.77   Under section 26(7) of the 1974 Act (section 24(7) of the 1975 Act), the ombudsman may not conduct an investigation in respect of any action which in his opinion affects most or all of the inhabitants of the area of the authority concerned. The Scottish ombudsman has argued that this is an indefensible anomaly on the grounds that 'the wider the maladministration is spread, the less it is possible for the ombudsman to intervene.'

9.78   While we have some sympathy with this viewpoint, we consider that any relaxation of this rule could be seen as a step towards a fundamental change in the role of the ombudsman. The local ombudsman's current primary concern is to secure redress for particular individuals who have suffered injustice as a result of a local authority action. They have no more general remit to take positive steps to ensure that the services of a local authority are well-administered. It can be argued that the general standards of fairness in service delivery are matters which the local authority alone should be in a position to determine, and for which it should be accountable direct to the electorate. And, as we have said at paragraph 9.9, the general effectiveness of service delivery is—in England and Wales at least—a matter with which the auditor has a concern. A role for the ombudsman in considering actions which affect all or most inhabitants of an area could take him into overlapping territory.

9.79   In the next section, we look more generally at the roles of the various agencies concerned with the challenge of local authority decisions, at how they relate to each other and at the gaps between them. This suggestion is relevant in that context.

(vi) The role of the Representative Body

9.80   Under section 24(1) of the 1974 Act, the Secretary of State is required by order to designate a Representative Body for each of England and Wales. The bodies must be representative of those authorities which the ombudsmen have power to investigate. There is no comparable provision in the Scottish legislation.

9.81   The main tasks of the Representative Bodies are to receive and publish the reports of the Commissioners, to consider, comment on and pass on to the local authorities any general conclusions reached by the ombudsmen about the operation of their powers, and to consider and comment on the Commissioners' annual estimates of expenditure. The Commissioners are bound to take account of any comment received from the Representative Bodies on their estimates, and

---

[1] See 'The Local Ombudsmen. A review of the first five years'. JUSTICE 1980, page 60.

to refer to the Secretary of State for decision any questions on which they cannot reach agreement.

9.82   We note that the Representative Body in England has tended to take a negative view of proposals from the Commission for modifications to their procedures. We also consider it anomalous in principle that a body which represents those who are the subject of investigation should play a major part in dictating the budget of the investigators. There is no parallel here with the position of the Parliamentary ombudsman who is accountable not to the Government but to the Commons Select Committee. We note that JUSTICE has recommended the abolition of the Representative Bodies and that the cost of the ombudsmen's services should be a charge against central government funds.[1] We believe that the Government should review the case for such a change.

Recommendations on the local ombudsmen

9.83   In summary, we recommend that:

(a)   the legislation should be amended to enable the local ombudsmen to consider complaints received direct from members of the public;

(Paragraph 9.64)

(b)   there should be a new statutory right for complainants to apply to the county or sheriff court for a remedy in cases where the local ombudsman has found maladministration leading to injustice and the complainant is dissatisfied with the remedy offered by the local authority;

(Paragraphs 9.68 and 9.69)

(c)   the Government should review and modify the exclusions from the ombudsmen's jurisdiction in Schedule 5 to the Local Government Act 1974 and Schedule 5 to the Local Government (Scotland) Act 1975;

(Paragraphs 9.73 and 9.74)

(d)   the local ombudsmen should be given new powers to investigate individual cases on their own initiative;

(Paragraph 9.76)

(e)   the Government should reconsider the case for charging the costs of the local ombudsmen's service direct to central government funds and the need for the Representative Bodies.

(Paragraph 9.82)

Judicial review

9.84   The special judicial review procedures in England and Wales have in our view proved their worth in providing a more straightforward and speedy mechanism for the judicial review of administrative action, and we have no reason to suppose that the new procedures will not also prove their worth in

---

[1] 'The Local Ombudsmen. A review of the first five years'. JUSTICE 1980, paragraphs 76 and 80.

Scotland. Several important cases have been settled through these procedures over the past year while we have been sitting. There are, however, two major reasons why judicial review remains beyond the reach of many who might wish to challenge the legality of local authority decisions. The first and most important of these is costs, to which we return in the next section. The second potential problem is in establishing sufficient interest. We are also aware that the requirement to obtain leave under the English/Welsh procedures has been criticised, but this is not a question on which we have formed a view.

9.85   As we have explained in paragraph 9.36, complainants in England and Wales will be granted leave to apply for judicial review only if the court considers they have 'sufficient interest' in the matter which is the subject of the complaint. In Scotland, the case may be dismissed if the complainant cannot show title and interest. Although the precedents are not entirely clear, it appears that both electors and ratepayers might have difficulty in establishing that they have such an interest in cases where they have not personally suffered injustice or financial loss. Thus, for example, an elector or ratepayer who was concerned that the local authority was illegally discriminating in favour of members of a particular political party in their recruitment policy might have difficulty in establishing sufficient interest to bring an action in the courts. We do not consider that this hurdle is a necessary or a desirable one.

9.86   We therefore recommend that:

> **the legislation should be amended so that any elector or ratepayer is deemed to have sufficient interest to seek judicial review of an action taken by his or her local authority.**

(Paragraph 9.85)

A NEW POWER OF ASSISTANCE

9.87   In the previous sections, we have looked at the audit service, the ombudsmen and the judicial review arrangements as self-standing mechanisms for the challenge of local authority decisions, and we have made a number of recommendations for their reform. In this section, we attempt to look at mechanisms for public challenge as a whole, and to address ourselves to problems arising at the interface of the various mechanisms and from the gaps between them.

9.88   For the purpose of discussion, we draw two distinctions. First, we distinguish between forums for challenge in which an individual is expected to take on an adversarial role against an authority and those forums which provide something of an 'uncle' figure to probe and pursue a complaint on an individual's behalf. Second, we distinguish between what we have termed respectively 'private interest' grievances and 'public interest' grievances. Private interest grievances arise when an individual feels that his or her personal rights have been infringed. Public interest grievances arise when an individual feels that a local authority has acted in a way which is prejudicial not specifically to the individual but to the community at large.

9.89   On this model, both the ombudsman and the auditor are 'uncle' figures (although the auditor does not of course act solely in response to complaints). Within their respective remits, both are in a position to take forward complaints and objections made by members of the public at no cost to the individual. The auditor deals with 'public interest' grievances and the ombudsman with 'private interest' grievances. The courts are an adversarial forum for arbitration in both public interest and private interest cases, but with the burden of pursuit of cases left to the individual.

9.90   As an 'uncle' figure in the context of private interest cases, the remit of the ombudsman is clearly severely limited. Other than in very special circumstances, the ombudsman is precluded from taking up any case in which the complainant has an alternative remedy including, most significantly, those cases in which the complainant has an action in law. Thus the ombudsman is, for example, precluded from helping an individual who wishes to challenge a possession order served on him or her by the local authority or a failure to provide schooling for his or her child. Given these limitations to the ombudsman's remit, the income limits on the legal aid scheme and the complexities of the law, we do not think there is room for complacency about public rights of challenge in the 'private interest' context. The questions arising are, however, not ones which are central to our terms of reference and we have not pursued them.

9.91   'Public interest' cases are more closely aligned with our wider terms of reference, bearing as they do on general questions about the propriety of local authority actions in the pursuit of their business. Auditors clearly have a very important role in this context, given their responsibilities to identify expenditure which is contrary of law and misconduct leading to financial loss. But there is a significant area in the 'public interest' category which does not fall within the auditors' remit; namely, those decisions and actions which do not involve expenditure or financial loss but which nevertheless may be illegal. There is also the category of 'procedural' disputes which, although in many cases arguably within the auditors' formal remit (because expenditure decisions taken in other than a properly constituted forum are not legally valid), do not sit well with the auditors' other responsibilities and their professional expertise.

9.92   These two categories of case are not in our view insignificant, although cases arising in the former category are likely to be relatively few in number. In the 'non-expenditure' category, we have in mind local authority actions such as a decision to impose a contract condition which illegally discriminates between different contractors, a general failure to comply with a statutory duty (such as the provision of information) or a decision **not** to take action where the decision stems from improper motives. In the procedural category, we have in mind disputes about whether or not standing orders have been complied with and whether due notice has been given of council meetings.

9.93   Regardless of whether or not the auditor has a remit, all these matters are in theory ones which an individual may bring before the courts for judicial review. We have already tackled the problem that an individual may face in establishing sufficient interest (paragraph 9.85).But that leaves the major and very real disincentive of cost. Individuals seeking judicial review of a local authority decision must bear in mind that they carry the risk not only of having to carry their own costs but also of having the authority's costs awarded against them.

9.94   In considering how the cost disincentive might be tackled, we have been impressed by a precedent set by the 'power of assistance' in the sex discrimination, race relations and housing legislation. The Equal Opportunities Commission and the Commission for Racial Equality both have powers to assist individuals with advice and in bringing a case to court where:

(a)   the case raises an important issue of principle; or

(b)   having regard to the complexity of the case or the circumstances of the individual, it would be unreasonable to expect the individuals concerned to take the case forward on their own; or

(c)   some other special considerations apply.[1]

The Secretary of State has similar powers under the housing legislation in respect of right-to-buy cases.[2] In all three contexts, cases are pursued in the name of the individual complainant but under the direction of, and at the expense of, the relevant Commission or the Secretary of State.

9.95   We believe that such a power might usefully be introduced in the context of 'public interest' complaints against local authorities. In order to keep costs and the bureaucracy involved to a minimum, it should be operated in a selective way concentrating on cases where:

(a)   there are implications for an authority's services at large or, on procedural issues, for its conduct of business generally; or

(b)   there are important issues of principle where clarification of the law is desirable; or

(c)   there is evidence of persistent breaches of the law.

The existence of such a power could also in itself be expected to reduce the incidence of deliberate illegality and hence the number of potential cases.

9.96   There remains the question of to whom this power should be entrusted. We had evidence from JUSTICE in favour of a new institution for enforcement purposes. However, we do not think that the task is one of sufficient scale to justify the creation of a new tailor-made body. The task might be seen as a logical extension of the Attorney-General's role in 'relator' actions, but on balance we feel that this office is not sufficiently remote from the political process (and there are in any case no equivalent arrangements in Scotland). Nor has the Attorney-General any special expertise in the area. The Secretaries of State might undertake the task but, again, we consider that they are too close to the political process and that there are likely to be cases in which they are perceived as being other than strictly neutral assessors of the issues in dispute. We feel that the task would be better entrusted to a body which was seen to be independent of both central and local government influence.

---

[1] Section 75 of the Sex Discrimination Act 1975. Section 66 of the Race Relations Act 1976.
[2] Section 170 of the Housing Act 1985.

226

9.97 The auditor, the ombudsmen and the courts themselves all fall within this definition. Although the task we envisage is in some respects not dissimilar from the existing discretion of the English/Welsh audit service to seek declarations of unlawful expenditure in the courts, we do not think that a wider remit on questions of legality would sit happily with their primary concerns with financial propriety and value for money. Furthermore, we believe the service would be very reluctant to take on this new task. For the ombudsmen too, a role in this context would be a major departure from their current sphere of interest in that:

(a)   it would involve them in consideration of questions of law as opposed to questions of maladministration;

(b)   it would take them outside their current exclusive concern with 'private interest' cases into the territory of 'public interest' concerns.

On the other hand, the task is closer in nature to the main thrust of their business, which is to help individuals with complaints.

9.98   An alternative approach would be to amend the rules governing judicial review so that the High Court itself has a role in tackling this problem. What we envisage would not be a power of assistance as such but a power for the High Court judge to guarantee that costs would be met from the public purse in advance of a case being brought. On considering an application for leave, the judge might also consider whether the case conformed with the tests suggested in paragraph 9.95. In cases where the judge considered that it did so conform, the judge might order that all costs incurred by the applicant in pursuit of the case and any costs ultimately awarded against the applicant, should be met from public sources. This option has attractions in that it builds on existing procedures and places responsibility for the decisions with an authoritative and independent body. On the other hand, it must be borne in mind that a potential complainant may well be daunted by the complexity and cost of the application procedures themselves. The courts are hardly an 'uncle' figure to most people, and the judges might well feel reluctant to use the power, especially in cases involving political controversy. The power might in practice be used too restrictively to meet the need.

9.99   We take the view that the best answer would be to entrust the task to the ombudsman service. Application would not involve cost and the ombudsman service is close to local government. Each Commission for Local Administration would need to establish a unit to administer the service, with a remit explicitly different from that of the ombudsman service generally. Specifically, it would need new powers to consider applications for assistance from individuals wishing to bring a legal action against their local authority against the tests outlined in paragraph 9.95, and to assist in such cases as it judged appropriate. Exclusions to the type of case in which it was empowered to assist would need detailed consideration, but they would be unlikely to flow from the current exclusions from the ombudsman's remit. In particular, it would be clearly inappropriate to provide that cases which affected most or all of the inhabitants of an area should be debarred from consideration, and it would be important to provide that cases referred by officers and members of an authority—as well as by ordinary members of the public—could be considered. Arrangements for liaison between the three Commissions for Local Administration and with the Audit and Accounts Commissions would need careful consideration.

9.100 Under the arrangements for judicial review in England and Wales, an application for leave must normally be made within three months of the act complained of. In view of the time necessary to consider applications for assistance, there may be a need to waive this rule in cases where assistance is granted.

9.101 We therefore recommend that:

(a) there should be a new statutory power of assistance for individuals wishing to challenge a decision by their local authority in the courts in cases where:

(i) there are implications for an authority's services at large or, on procedural issues, for its conduct of business generally; or

(ii) there are important issues of principle where clarification of the law is desirable; or

(iii) there is evidence of persistent breaches of the law;

(Paragraph 9.95)

(b) the new power should be vested in the three Commissions for Local Administration.

(Paragraph 9.99)

DISQUALIFICATION AND SURCHARGE

9.102 The sanctions which may be applied against those in local government who are responsible for breaches of the law remain to be considered. There are many contexts in which a breach of the law will not result in a legal sanction against any individual. Councillors who take wrong decisions in good faith may reasonably be required to account for themselves to the electorate and officers through internal procedures; but they should not be penalised in law. There are other contexts in which there is statutory provision for criminal proceedings to be brought, and fines to be imposed, on individuals who break the law. The provisions governing failure to disclose a pecuniary interest are one example of this. It is, however, the audit provisions for disqualification and surcharge which have given rise to particular controversy, and it is in relation to these penalties that we wish to comment.

Disqualification

9.103 We believe that disqualification is correct in principle in appropriate circumstances. We do not consider that an individual in public office who wilfully abuses the trust imposed on him or her should continue to serve in that capacity. Wilful misconduct leading to financial loss and the authorisation of activities which are known to be unlawful in our view constitute such a breach of trust.

9.104 Under the present audit provisions for England and Wales, there are two sets of circumstances in which councillors may be disqualified from holding office:

228

(a)   under section 19 of the 1982 Act, the **court** may order that a person be disqualified for a period at its discretion if the court concludes that there has been unlawful expenditure in excess of £2,000; if the person concerned is responsible for incurring or authorising that expenditure; and if the court concludes that he or she did not act reasonably nor in the belief that the expenditure was lawful;

(b)   under section 20 of the 1982 Act, a member of a local authority is automatically disqualified for a period of five years if the **auditor** certifies that a loss of over £2,000 has been incurred by wilful misconduct on his or her part. The member concerned may appeal to the court to vary or quash the auditor's certificate. But the court has no discretion to vary the penalty if the certificate stands.

9.105   It follows from what we have said above that we do not think these provisions are wrong in essence in so far as they lead to disqualification. However, we consider that the differences in approach between sections 19 and 20 are difficult to justify and, in particular, that it is wrong that the auditor should under section 20 have to act as judge in a matter leading automatically to disqualification. The differences between the sections 19 and 20 approaches are even more marked on surcharge, and we return to this question in that context.

9.106   Having endorsed the principles of disqualification as a penalty for wilful misconduct or deliberate illegality, we believe that there are three additional circumstances in which is should apply.

(i) Disqualification of officers

9.107   We have recommended in Chapter Six that the office of chief executive should be a statutory appointment and that all functions involving the propriety of council business should be vested in the chief executive, including certain new statutory functions which we propose. Some of these are of a largely formal nature (eg to act as registrar for the upkeep of the register of interests) but others are more substantial (eg settling disagreements as to the party composition of committees). We believe that an individual should be disqualified from holding the office of chief executive if he or she is found **knowingly and wilfully** to have abused his or her statutory responsibilities. It is, for example, conceivable (although hopefully not likely) that a chief executive might knowingly favour a particular party in determining committee places or provide misleading advice to the council as to the legality of a proposal before it. In such circumstances, we believe that the courts should have powers to order that the individual is disqualified from holding the office of chief executive for a period of time.

(ii) Disqualification of councillors in non-expenditure cases

9.108   The possibility of disqualification for illegal actions at present arises only under the audit provisions and, as a result, is a penalty only in cases which involve illegal expenditure or financial loss. As we have said earlier in this Chapter (paragraph 9.91), there is an important category of cases where the legality of an action or decision may be at issue but no expenditure or financial loss is directly involved. In Chapter Six (paragraph 6.14), we have stated the importance that we attach to the principle that individuals should not hold elected office as councillors unless they are prepared to abide by the law. We therefore consider that it would be appropriate to provide that the penalty of disqualification should apply in any case where a member of a council has authorised a decision or action which he or she knows to be unlawful. The councillor's possible defences should be the same as those available under section 19 of the 1982 Act. We believe that the courts should have discretion to order disqualification for a period of time in such cases.

(iii) Scotland

9.109 The penalty of disqualification does not at present arise in Scotland under the audit provisions. Following a recommendation from the Commission for Local Authority Accounts, the Secretary of State may in certain circumstances order surcharge (see paragraph 9.19). The Secretary of State, however, has no powers to order disqualification and this will only arise in consequence of an order for surcharge when this leads to the bankruptcy of any councillor involved. The logic of our position is that there should be new provision in Scotland for disqualification both in surcharge cases involving losses in excess of £2,000 and in the two additional contexts to which reference is made in paragraphs 9.107 and 9.108. We propose accordingly.

9.110 In their written evidence to us, the Commission for Local Authority Accounts suggested that the Secretary of State's role as final arbiter in audit cases could cause difficulty if the sanction of disqualification was to be introduced. There is in our view considerable force to this argument. The task of the Secretary of State in combining a political with a quasi judicial role is a delicate one even in the most straightforward of circumstances. Cases involving the possibility of disqualification and surcharge will rarely be straightforward and often arise from circumstances of acute party political controversy. It may be difficult for the Secretary of State to be **seen to be** acting in a non-partisan manner in a matter over which there is such party political controversy. In these circumstances, it seems to us to be particularly invidious that the Secretary of State should have responsibility to decide whether or not particular individuals should be allowed to serve in elected office. As we have said in paragraph 9.53, we are thus led to the conclusion that there is a need to involve the courts rather than the Secretary of State in at least this aspect of the Scottish audit process.

Surcharge

9.111 Provision for surcharge was first introduced in the Poor Law Reform Act of 1834, which gave auditors the power to recover illegal losses incurred by poor law guardians. Reflecting these origins it is based on the principle of councillors (and officers) acting as trustees for ratepayers' money. In the 19th century illegal payments by councillors were not uncommon. Councillors were moreover property owners and hence men of means. The budgets of their councils were much smaller relative to their means than is the case now. Surcharge therefore was a realistic means of restoring losses incurred by councillors, and was widely used. The use of surcharge was still widespread in the middle of this century but was in decline by the time of re-organisation. Between 1945–46 and 1949–50 there were 159 cases in England and Wales, but only 41 between 1965–66 and 1969–70. Over the whole period between 1945 and 1974 there were 549 cases, 34 of which involved more than £1,000.

9.112 During this period surcharge did not apply to all authorities. From their creation in 1835 to 1933, county boroughs and non-county boroughs had their

230

own audit arrangements with no provision for surcharge. The Local Government Act 1933 enabled them to opt into district audit, and hence surcharge, but did not require them to do so. There was still a dual system in 1967 when the Maud Report[1] recommended the abolition of surcharge. This recommendation was not accepted. Instead the Local Government Act 1972 extended district audit, and with it surcharge, to all local authorities in England and Wales at the same time limiting its application from 'negligence and misconduct' to 'wilful misconduct'. Surcharge already existed throughout Scotland at the time of the Local Government (Scotland) Act 1973. The Scottish legislation continues to apply in any case where there has been negligence or misconduct leading to financial loss, but the penalty of surcharge is at the discretion of the Secretary of State, and not automatic.

9.113   The incidence of cases has continued to decline. In 1973 11 councillors on Clay Cross Urban District Council were surcharged a total of £6,935 for failing to increase council rents, but this case was brought under the pre-reorganisation legislation. Under the post-reorganisation legislation there have been 24 cases of surcharge in England and Wales—over 12 years—all under what is now section 20 of the Local Government Finance Act 1982. Of these, principal as opposed to parish councils were involved in only 12, and councillors as opposed to officers in only five. The total amount of money involved was £314,533. The cases involving the largest sums were the certificates issued in September 1985 against 49 Liverpool councillors (£106,103) and 32 Lambeth councillors (£126,947). There have been no instances of surcharge in Scotland following reorganisation. The Accounts Commission has recommended surcharge on two occasions. In the first case the Secretary of State did not accept the recommendation. The second is with the Secretary of State for decision at the time of the submission of our Report.

9.114   This account of the background is informative. It shows that, despite the major cases in the last year, surcharge has become very rare—especially in relation to councillors. While the recent cases have been untypical they have, however, served to stimulate debate about the extent to which surcharge remains an appropriate sanction. There has been a private member's Bill[2] to abolish disqualification and surcharge, and widespread discussion in the press.

9.115   Those that argue against surcharge do so on four main grounds. First it is argued that surcharge is so substantial a penalty as to inhibit auditors from taking action where they might otherwise have done so.[3] Second it is argued to be so significant—if remote—a threat as to discourage people from standing as councillors. Third it is argued that it is no longer appropriate in the 20th century given that local authority budgets—and hence the scale of possible losses—are so huge in relation to the means of councillors and officers. Fourth, and most significantly, it is criticised as being inequitable to local government in that there is no provision for individuals elsewhere in the public sector personally to repay

---

[1] Report of the Committee on the Management of Local Government, 1967, paragraph 290.
[2] The Surcharge and Disqualification of Councillors (Abolition) Bill was introduced by Mr Eddie Loyden MP and debated on 14 February 1986. It did not receive a Second Reading.
[3] The Controller of Audit for England and Wales has said that 'seeing people, often with very limited means bankrupted; their houses sold from under them and so on to pay surcharge is something that fills me and the auditors who have to carry out the duty with nothing other than horror'.

losses incurred in analogous circumstances. There is in particular no such sanction in the case of Ministers and civil servants.

9.116 Those that argue for the retention of surcharge do so primarily on the grounds that it is an effective deterrent: that it results in councillors holding back from breaches of the law which they might otherwise have contemplated. On this argument the absence of surcharge cases is a mark of its success. It is also argued that surcharge emphasises the duty of stewardship of public funds involved in taking on the office of councillor. It clearly places councillors in a different position from that of non-councillors, and thereby provides a safeguard against their merely acting as a delegate of their party or of some other outside interest. Moreover, it is also pointed out that surcharge does not arise where individuals have authorised an unlawful action in good faith—only where they have deliberately breached the trust involved in being a councillor or officer.

9.117 These two sets of arguments are not contradictory, but rather give weight to different considerations. We can see the strength of both, and recognise that they are the subject of strongly and sincerely held views.

9.118 In making our own assessment of the position we believe that surcharge should not be seen in isolation, but as one of several provisions that are designed to ensure that the law is observed. The observance of the law has been a recurring theme not only of this Chapter but of our whole Report. We attach major importance to the prevention of its breach, and have made a number of recommendations which should assist in this respect. We have recommended a new reference to the law in the National Code of Local Government Conduct, together with a strengthening of the Code's status; a new duty for the chief executive to advise the council where a proposed action or inaction might be unlawful; and the extension of the sanction of disqualification to non-expenditure cases, to chief executives, and to Scotland. These measures should increase respect for the law, and deter its breach. Where it is breached we have recommended a new 'stop' procedure for an immediate injunction to be brought so as to forestall the consequences of its breach. This should prevent unlawful expenditure being incurred on any significant scale, and hence is particularly relevent to the debate about surcharge.

9.119 If surcharge did not already exist we doubt whether it would occur to anyone today to recommend its introduction. Its usage is already very limited, and we would expect and hope it to become even more so under our proposed procedure to put a 'stop' on unlawful expenditure before it takes place. It may well fall into disuse. Reflecting wider differences within society at large, there are differences of view within the Committee on the case for abolishing surcharge. But we are conscious that it does act as a deterrent. And we are agreed that, ahead of the proposed 'stop' procedure having the chance to prove itself, it would be imprudent to abolish surcharge.

9.120 There are, however, certain respects in which we consider that its application should be modified. At present, there are three different provisions for the application of surcharge, two under the English/Welsh legislation and one in Scotland. Under section 19 of the 1982 Act (England and Wales), the auditor may apply to the court for a declaration that expenditure is contrary to law and the **court** may order that any person responsible for incurring unlawful expenditure should repay it **in whole or in part.** As well as considering whether the individual acted reasonably or in good faith, the court must take account of the individual's ability to pay.

9.121 The provisions in section 20 of the 1982 Act are different. The **auditor** must certify that there has been loss due to wilful misconduct or a failure to bring a relevant item to account, to specify the sum involved and to identify those responsible. On the issue of such a certificate, the individuals involved are **automatically** liable to repay the amount **in full.** Although there is provision to appeal to the courts, the courts have no discretion to take account of the individuals circumstances, nor to provide that the amount involved be repaid only in part.

9.122 In Scotland, under section 104 of the 1973 Act, it is the Secretary of State who has the final decision to order surcharge. But he has discretion as to whether or not to make an order at all, he has discretion in determining the precise amount which individuals should be required to pay and he is in any event bound to take account of their ability to pay.

9.123 We consider that the provisions in section 20 of the 1982 Act are wrong in that they allow for no discretion to be exercised in deciding whether the amounts involved should be repaid in part or in full having regard to the circumstances and the means of the individual to pay.

9.124 As regards procedure, we had evidence from the district auditors employed by the Audit Commission that the procedure under section 20 whereby the auditor makes a report which results automatically in surcharge might be better replaced by the procedure under section 19 whereby he or she makes an application to the court. The district auditors argued that difficult questions of law can arise in wilful misconduct cases under section 20 and that it is appropriate for the courts rather than the auditor to be the arbiter on such matters. There is also a feeling that a decision resulting in surcharge is an excessive responsibility for an appointed auditor.

9.125 We think that district auditors may have under-estimated certain problems involved in the section 19 procedures. Although the auditor does not have to make a report, he or she does have to take the decision to apply to the court, and to act as quasi-prosecutor in the court proceedings. In *Pickwell (Metropolitan District Auditor) v London Borough of Camden and others (1983) 1 QB 978,* Lord Justice Ormrod referred to the auditor's 'embarrassing role as a litigant with the burden of proof'. It may perhaps be significant that there have been only two applications under section 19 since 1974. While on balance we consider it would be better for the courts to be the arbiters on surcharge cases, we think that any such change in the procedure should be coupled with a duty on the audit service to make the necessary application to the court. This duty should apply to both section 19 and section 20 cases. Under our recommendation at paragraph 9.60(b), it will be the Audit Commission rather than the local auditor who has the responsibility to apply to the court. The duty should remove some of the embarrassment from the role of quasi-prosecutor, and counter any reluctance to use the procedure.

9.126   In Scotland, we have recommended a review of the extent to which it is desirable to involve the courts in the audit process. One possible outcome is that responsibility for ordering surcharge would pass from the Secretary of State to the courts. Without prejudging this outcome, we emphasise that we would not wish to see lost the current ability to exercise discretion in ordering surcharge, whether it is exercised by the Secretary of State or a court.

Recommendations

9.127   In summary we recommend that:

(a)   the legislation should be amended to give the courts discretion to order that a person is disqualified from holding the office of chief executive for a period of time in cases where he or she has acted unlawfully and the court is not satisfied that he or she acted reasonably or in the belief that the action was authorised by law;

(Paragraph 9.107)

(b)   the legislation should also be amended to give the courts discretion to order the disqualification of councillors for a period of time in any case, involving expenditure or otherwise, where they have authorised an illegal decision or action and the court is not satisfied that the councillor acted reasonably or in the belief that the action was authorised by law;

(Paragraph 9.108)

(c)   the Scottish audit legislation should be amended so as to provide for the additional penalty of disqualification in cases where surcharge of over £2,000 is currently applicable;

(Paragraph 9.109)

(d)   the procedures leading to surcharge and disqualification in section 20 of the Local Government Finance Act 1982 (wilful misconduct leading to financial loss) should be brought into line with those in section 19 of that Act (illegal expenditure) except that in both cases there should be a duty rather than a discretion to apply to the court.

(Paragraphs 9.124 and 9.125)

CHAPTER 10

RECOMMENDATIONS

Chapter Five: The Decision Taking Process

Decision taking models

1   The system of decision taking in local government should continue to be one in which:

(i)   the council is a corporate body;

(ii)   decisions are taken openly by, or on behalf of, the whole council, without any separate source of executive authority;

(iii)   officers serve the council as a whole.

(Paragraphs 5.30 to 5.35)

Membership of committees

2   Local authorities should be statutorily required to include provisions in their standing orders governing the composition of committees and sub-committees with delegated powers to take decisions on behalf of the council. These provisions should provide:

(i)   for the composition of such committees and sub-committees to reflect, as far as practicable, the composition of the council as a whole, except in so far as individual parties or councillors might waive their rights;

(ii)   for the chief executive to be responsible for the detailed application of this rule.

(Paragraphs 5.46 to 5.53)

Access to committee meetings and documents

3   The legislation should be amended so that the rights of members of the public and the press to attend meetings and inspect documents do not apply to meetings of committees and sub-committees which are purely deliberative with no powers to take decisions on behalf of the council.

(Paragraph 5.63)

4   The law in respect of councillors' rights to inspect documents and attend meetings should be amended so that:

(i)   these rights are all contained in statute, with no reliance on common law;

(ii)   these rights do not apply to committees and sub-committees which are purely deliberative with no powers to take decisions on behalf of the council;

(iii)   the chief executive is responsible for deciding whether councillors have a need to inspect a document or attend a meeting in order to carry out their duties;

(iv)   councillors do not have a right to inspect documents in which they have a pecuniary interest if those documents are not open to public inspection.

(Paragraphs 5.68 to 5.70)

Delegation of chairmen of committees

5   The legislation should be amended to allow committees and sub-committees to delegate urgent decisions between meetings to their chairmen, subject to:

(i)   the chief executive's agreement in each case that the matter is urgent;

(ii)   the decision being reported to the next meeting of the committee or sub-committee;

(iii)   the relevant documents being subject to the provisions introduced by the Local Government (Access to Information) Act 1985;

(iv)   the chairmen not having a pecuniary interest in the matter.

(Paragraph 5.77)

Co-option

6   The legislation should be amended so that:

(i)   decision taking committees and sub-committees may consist only of councillors, and in particular only councillors may vote on such committees;

(ii)   local authorities may invite advisers to attend meetings of decision taking committees on such terms as they may determine but without the right to vote;

(iii)   the names of advisers should be made publicly known, together with the terms of their attendance at meetings;

(iv)   anyone else attending meetings of committees should sit in an area separately set aside for the press and public, unless specifically asked to address the committee on a particular agenda item;

(v)   advisers attending meetings may not be persons disqualified from council membership (subject to recommendation 7(ii)).

(Paragraphs 5.92 to 5.102)

7   In view of the current statutory position of magistrates in relation to police committees and of the churches and teachers in relation to education committees, the Government should review whether these groups should continue to have some special rights in relation to the police and education services. This review should be on the basis that:

(i)   any continued role should be purely deliberative or consultative, and should not involve voting rights on decision taking committees, nor should it conflict in any other way with the rules at recommendation 6(i) to (iv);

(ii)   in principle the rule at 6(v) should also apply; however in view of the special circumstances of teachers the review should consider whether they

236

should be able to attend meetings as advisers even though they would be disqualified from council membership by virtue of being employees of the council.

(Paragraphs 5.103 to 5.107)

Standing orders and local conventions

8   Local authorities should be statutorily required to include in their standing orders provisions:

(i)   to ensure that the composition of decision taking committees reflects the membership of the whole council;

(ii)   to include the procedures recommended at 5(i) to (iv) for the taking of decisions by chairmen of committees between meetings;

(iii)   to set aside a period at council meetings for question time;

(iv)   to set aside a period at council meetings for business chosen by the minority parties;

(v)   to require clearance of the public gallery in the event of disturbances;

(vi)   to set out responsibility for the appointment of staff;

(vii)   to safeguard against summary suspension of standing orders.

(Paragraphs 5.112 to 5.126)

9   Individual local authorities should draw up, and make publicly available, conventions setting out the working relationships between the political parties and between councillors and officers insofar as such issues are not covered by standing orders.

(Paragraphs 5.129 and 5.130)

Chapter Six: Councillors and Officers: Roles and Relationships
Councillors and the National Code of Local Government Conduct

10   The National Code of Local Government Conduct should be amended to make clear that:

(i)   councillors hold office by virtue of the law and must act within the law;

(ii)   sectional loyalties as well as private gain may create conflicts with councillors' public duty.

(Paragraphs 6.15 and 6.16)

11   The Code should be statutorily prescribed by the Secretary of State following consultation with the local authority associations.

(Paragraph 6.19)

12   It should be made statutorily explicit that breach of the Code constitutes prima facie maladministration.

(Paragraph 6.19)

13 All local authorities and councillors should statutorily be required to have regard to the Code.

(Paragraph 6.19)

14 Individual councillors should also undertake to have regard to the Code as part of their statutory declaration on accepting office.

(Paragraph 6.22)

15 The statutory declaration on accepting office should:

(i) be extended to Scotland;

(ii) be made in solemn form.

(Paragraph 6.21)

The disqualification rules for council membership

16 Employees of local authorities should continue to be able to become councillors in other authorities, provided that they are not employed at the rank of principal officer or above, on which see recommendation 50.

(Paragraphs 6.30 to 6.34)

17 The legislation should be amended to allow employees of joint boards and joint authorities to become councillors on the authorities nominating the members of such boards and authorities provided that they are not themselves nominated to membership.

(Paragraph 6.38)

The pecuniary and non-pecuniary interests of councillors

18 Local authorities should be statutorily required to keep a public register of the pecuniary and non-pecuniary interests of councillors on the following basis:

(i) the register should include any interest which could reasonably be regarded as likely to affect councillors' conduct or influence their actions, speeches or vote;

(ii) the register should specifically require entry of land and property owned by councillors in the authority's area, paid employments, and interests in companies above a specified minimum; but otherwise it should be for individual councillors to decide what interests fall within the criteria at (i) above;

(iii) councillors with no relevant interests should be required to state this;

(iv) the chief executive should be the registrar, with a statutory duty to maintain the register;

(v) completion of the register should not alter the requirement to declare interests orally at meetings as and when they arise.

(Paragrahs 6.46 to 6.49)

19   Failure to complete the proposed statutory register should be an offence, but local authorities should be statutorily prohibited from imposing other disabilities for non-completion of registers.

(Paragraph 6.48)

20   The statutory definition of pecuniary interests should be widened to include those who are involved, by employment or contract, in the promotion of the pecuniary interests of others on matters coming before the council.

(Paragraph 6.50)

21   Where councillors declare a pecuniary interest at a meeting they should be statutorily required to withdraw from the room.

(Paragraph 6.51)

22   The National Code of Local Government Conduct should be amended so that it distinguishes between the declaration by councillors of their non-pecuniary interests and abstention from voting and speaking where such interests arise: non-pecuniary interests should always be declared, but disabilities on voting and speaking should apply only where the interest is clear and substantial.

(Paragraph 6.52)

23   The National Code of Local Government Conduct should be amended to draw attention to the problems of councillors becoming leaders of their council where they have a substantial recurring interest, whether pecuniary or non-pecuniary, in the affairs of the area.

(Paragraph 6.55)

Party groups
24   The national political parties should take steps:

(i)   to ensure that party groups keep a publicly available list of those attending their meetings;

(ii)   to ensure observance of their model standing orders insofar as they limit the numbers of non-councillors attending meetings of party groups, preclude non-councillors from voting at such meetings, and prevent non-councillors from determining the policy to be followed by the party group on matters before the council for decision;

(iii)   to debar from attendance at party group meetings persons disqualified from council membership following surcharge proceedings by the auditor;

(iv)   to ensure that the National Code of Local Government Conduct is implemented in respect of conflicts of interests arising at meetings of party groups, and to amend their model standing orders accordingly.

(Paragraphs 6.65, 6.73, 6.74 and 6.78)

Councillors' remuneration
25   Attendance allowance and financial loss allowance should be replaced by a basic flat rate allowance payable to all councillors as an annual sum.

(Paragraph 6.108)

26   The levels of basic flat rate allowance should be banded according to the type of council and its population.

(Paragraph 6.113)

27   The initial rates of basic flat rate allowance should be £4,000 per annum in the largest authority, and £1,500 in the smallest; and should be regularly reviewed.

(Paragraph 6.113)

28   The special responsibility allowance arrangements should continue, but each local authority should be statutorily required to draw up a scheme for disbursing the allowance on the following basis:

(i)   the scheme should specify amounts payable for particular posts in such a way that the total payable equates to the maximum prescribed for the authority by the Secretary of State;

(ii)   all councillors in posts specified by the scheme should be entitled to the amount specified.

(Paragraph 6.109)

29   No councillor should be entitled to more than one special responsibility allowance.

(Paragraph 6.110)

30   The special responsibility allowance maxima currently prescribed for classes of authority and for individual councillors within each class should be doubled and subsequently kept under regular review.

(Paragraph 6.115)

Time-off work for council duties

31   Private sector employers should take a positive and flexible attitude to granting paid and unpaid leave to employees for council duties.

(Paragraph 6.119)

32   There should be a statutory upper limit of 26 days per year on the paid leave which public sector employers may grant to employees for council duties.

(Paragraphs 6.120 and 6.121)

33   Where public sector employers grant paid leave to employees for council duties they should, as far as is practicable, recover from those employees any allowance received by them for the period concerned.

(Paragraph 6.122)

34   Employers should ensure that employees' pension rights are not adversely affected as a result of leave required for council duties.

(Paragraph 6.123)

The chief executive

35　Local authorities should be statutorily required to appoint a chief executive, who should be the head of the authority's paid staff with overall managerial responsibility for the discharge of functions by officers.

(Paragraph 6.151)

36　All statutory functions relating to the propriety of council business, whether currently existing or recommended in this Report, should be vested in the chief executive rather than any other officer.

(Paragraph 6.151)

The officer as arbiter

37　Chief executives should be given the following new statutory functions in relation to the propriety of council business:

(i)　to decide on the detailed application of the rules for party balance on committees;

(ii)　to decide whether a councillor has a need to inspect a document or attend a meeting;

(iii)　to agree that a matter is urgent before the chairman of a committee may take a decision on it;

(iv)　to act as the registrar responsible for the upkeep of the register of councillors' interests;

(v)　without prejudice to their general duty to advise the council, to provide advice at the request of any councillor as to the legality of any proposed action or inaction by the council.

(Paragraphs 6.154 and 6.155)

The officer as professional manager

38　The chief executive should be statutorily responsible for the appointment, discipline and dismissal of staff below the rank of principal officer, except where staff are appointed to serve the political groups or their leaders.

(Paragraphs 6.163 to 6.165)

39　The chief executive should be statutorily responsible for initiating action for the discipline or dismissal of staff at or above the rank of principal officer.

(Paragraph 6.165)

40　The Local Authorities' Conditions of Service Advisory Board should take steps to amend the terms and conditions of service of officers so that they reflect the statutory arrangements for discipline and dismissal proposed above.

(paragraph 6.165)

The officer as adviser

41　Local authorities should be able, if they wish, to attach officers to the party groups or their leaders.

(Paragraph 6.172)

42 Such arrangements should be subject to the following safeguards:

(i) the officers should be clearly differentiated from officers serving the council as a whole: they should not carry out or be involved in executive functions and should report direct to councillors, not through the chief executive;

(ii) they should be strictly limited in number and seniority;

(iii) the facility should be made available to minority parties;

(iv) it should be made clear whether or not the appointment is being made on political criteria.

(Paragraph 6.172)

43 The Local Authorities' Conditions of Service Advisory Board should take steps to amend officers' terms and conditions of service so that no special inhibition is placed on attendance at party groups.

(Pargraph 6.175)

44 The attendance of officers at party groups should be subject to the following safeguards:

(i) all requests for attendance should be addressed to the chief executive, who should decide which officers should attend;

(ii) the chief executive should notify the other parties, and offer a similar facility.

(Paragraph 6.176)

45 The safeguards listed in recommendations 42 and 44 should be included in the conventions which we have recommended that all local authorities should prepare (recommendation 9), as should such other rules governing officer advice as might be locally appropriate.

(Paragraph 6.178)

Appointments and dismissals

46 A Code of Practice should be introduced setting out procedures designed to ensure that appointments made by local authorities are based on merit and fair and open competition.

(Paragraphs 6.196 to 6.198)

47 In the case of chief executives, these procedures should include provision for an independent assessor on selection committees.

(Paragraph 6.198)

48 The Code should be statutorily prescribed by the Secretary of State following consultation with the local authority associations: local authorities should be required to have regard to it, with breach of its provisions constituting prima facie maladministration and subject to the local ombudsman.

(Paragraphs 6.197 to 6.199)

49   The legislation should be amended to prevent a local authority dismissing a chief executive except on the vote of two thirds of the membership of the council.

(Paragraph 6.203)

Political activity

50   The legislation should be amended so that persons who are councillors, or who are standing for election as councillors, or who have been a councillor within the last year, may not be employed by another authority at the rank of principal officer or above.

(Paragraph 6.216)

51   The Local Authorities' Conditions of Service Advisory Board should take steps to include in the terms and conditions of officers at the rank of principal officer and above a prohibition on political activity, including:

(i)   standing for, and holding, public elected office;

(ii)   holding office in a political party;

(iii)   speaking or writing in public in a personal capacity in a way that might be regarded as engaging in party political debate;

(iv)   canvassing at elections.

(Paragraphs 6.211 to 6.215)

52   If the changes recommended at 51 are not made to officers' terms and conditions, legislation should be introduced to similar effect.

(Paragraph 6.215)

Training

53   Individual local authorities and the Local Government Training Board should place increased stress on training designed to ensure better understanding by councillors and officers of each others' roles, responsibilities and aspirations.

(Paragraphs 6.219 to 6.220)

Chapter Seven: Electoral Arrangements and Council Size

54   The legislation governing the election of councillors in England and Wales should be amended so that there are uniform arrangements throughout Great Britain based on

(i)   one councillor for every electoral ward or division;

(ii)   the whole council being elected every four years.

(Paragraphs 7.15, 7.16 and 7.28)

55   The Government should review council size, in the light of the current variations in the numbers of councillors per council and per head of population, with the aim of establishing the best balance between management efficiency and the quality of democracy.

(Paragraph 7.39)

The need for a general discretionary power

56   In addition to their specific statutory functions, local authorities should continue to have a financially limited discretionary power to spend in the interests of their area.

(Paragraph 8.27)

57   The Government should consult the local authority associations with a view to drawing up guidance for local authorities on the use to which sections 137 and 83 may properly be put. The guidance should in particular:

(i)   reaffirm the principle that these sections should not be used for purposes provided for elsewhere in legislation;

(ii)   give practical advice on the inter-relationship between the sections and functional powers in areas of particular concern.

(Paragraph 8.34)

Economic development powers

58   The Government should initiate a review of the proper role of local authorities in economic development, taking account of the role of other governmental agencies, with a view to identifying any areas in which additional local authority statutory powers should be introduced.

(Paragraph 8.41)

The financial limit for sections 137 and 83

59   The current statutory arrangements under which the expenditure limit for section 137 and 83 is calculated by reference to the rate product in an area should be replaced by arrangements which relate to the population of an area.

(Paragraph 8.59)

60   The Government should regularly review the limit, and should have the power to amend it by order.

(Paragraph 8.60)

61   The limit should initially be set at a level equivalent to expenditure by individual authorities of £4.00 per head of population, but subject to recommendation 62.

(Paragraph 8.60)

62   The limit for single tier authorities should be double the level applying elsewhere.

(Paragraph 8.70)

63 As an interim measure, the Secretary of State should make an immediate order under section 137(4) and (5) of the Local Government Act 1972 to increase the current limit of 2p to 4p in relation to London borough and metropolitan district councils.

(Paragraph 8.71)

The scope of sections 137 and 83

64 Section 137 of the Local Government Act 1972 should be amended to incorporate a provision comparable to that in section 83(3A) of the Local Government (Scotland) Act 1973 under which a local authority may only use the power for a purpose for which another local authority has statutory responsibility with the consent of that authority.

(Paragraph 8.89)

Discrimination in the use of discretion

65 There should be a declaratory provision in statute enbodying the existing common law prohibition on local authorities using their discretion for the main purpose of securing electoral advantage for a particular candidate or political party.

(Paragraph 8.99)

Grants to voluntary bodies

66 Local authorities should be statutorily required to maintain a list of all grants to voluntary bodies, and to publish it annually as part of or together with the authority's annual report.

(Paragraph 8.106)

67 The list should state the name of the body involved and the amount of the grant, and should indicate the purpose for which the grant was given.

(Paragraph 8.106)

68 The use to which such grants to voluntary bodies are put should be monitored, and to this end:

(i) each voluntary body receiving grant should be required to publish an annual report or annual statement which should state the use to which the grant has been put;

(ii) local authorities should be required to make such annual reports and statements available for public inspection.

(Paragraphs 8.107 and 8.108)

Enterprise boards and arm's length companies

69 The case for enterprise boards should be considered in the context of the review proposed at recommendation 58 of the role of local authorities in economic development.

(Paragraph 8.114)

70   The law in relation to local authority controlled companies should be amended:

(i)   to make clear that they may be set up only where there is specific enabling legislation;

(ii)   to incorporate safeguards concerning their articles of association, their membership and their audit and reporting arrangements.

(Paragraph 8.116)

Chapter Nine: Public Challenge
The audit service

71   To improve publicity for auditors' reports in the public interest in England and Wales, and reports by the Controller of Audit and the Accounts Commission in Scotland, the chief executive of an authority should be placed under a statutory duty:

(i)   immediately to notify all councillors of the receipt of a report;

(ii)   to provide a copy to councillors on request;

(iii)   to make copies available for public inspection.

(Paragraphs 9.46 and 9.57)

72   The responsibilities of auditors in England and Wales under section 19 of the Local Government Finance Act 1982 (unlawful expenditure) and section 20 of that Act (wilful misconduct leading to financial loss or failure to bring an item to account) should be transferred to the Audit Commission.

(Paragraph 9.49)

73   The Audit Commission for England and Wales should be given new statutory powers to seek:

(i)   an interim injunction to restrain a local authority from incurring unlawful expenditure;

(ii)   an expedited hearing for an order of mandamus to compel an authority to take action where failure to do so would be unlawful and would result in financial loss.

(Paragraph 9.47)

74   The courts in Scotland should be given new responsibilities for deciding on audit matters. The precise character and extent of these responsibilities should be reviewed by the Secretary of State for Scotland in consultation with interested parties, and this' review should include consideration of the case for procedures similar to those proposed for England and Wales at recommendation 73.

(Paragraphs 9.53, 9.54 and 9.56)

75   The existing statutory rights of the public to object to the accounts, both in England and Wales and in Scotland, should be extended to all electors and ratepayers.

(Paragraph 9.59)

76   In addition, ratepayers and electors in Scotland should be given new statutory rights similar to those currently existing in England and Wales to:

(i)   question the auditor on any matters arising from the accounts;

(ii)   receive notice of the decision of the Controller of Audit with respect to the objection, and of the reasons for the decision;

(iii)   appeal against a decision not to pursue the objection.

(Paragraph 9.59)

The local ombudsmen

77   The legislation should be amended to enable the local ombudsmen to consider complaints received direct from members of the public.

(Paragraph 9.64)

78   There should be a new statutory right for complainants to apply to the county or sheriff court for a remedy in cases where the local ombudsman has found maladministration leading to injustice and the complainant is dissatisfied with the remedy offered by the local authority.

(Paragraphs 9.68 and 9.69)

79   The Government should review and modify the exclusions from the local ombudsmen's jurisdiction in Schedule 5 to the Local Government Act 1974 and Schedule 5 to the Local Government (Scotland) Act 1975.

(Paragraphs 9.73 and 9.74)

80   The local ombudsmen should be given new powers to investigate individual cases on their own initiative.

(Paragraph 9.76)

81   The Government should reconsider the case for charging the costs of the local ombudsmen's service direct to central government funds and the need for the Representative Bodies.

(Paragraph 9.82)

Judicial review

82   The legislation should be amended so that any elector or ratepayer should be deemed to have sufficient interest to seek judicial review of an action taken by his or her local authority.

(Paragraph 9.85)

A new power of assistance

83   There should be a new statutory power of assistance for individuals wishing to challenge a decision by their local authority in the courts in cases where:

(i)   there are implications for an authority's services at large or, on procedural issues, for its conduct of business generally; or

247

(ii)   there are important issues of principle where clarification of the law is desirable; or

(iii)   there is evidence of persistent breaches of the law.

(Paragraph 9.95)

84   The new power should be vested in the three Commissions for Local Adminstration.

(Paragraph 9.99)

Disqualification and surcharge

85   The legislation should be amended to give the courts discretion to order that a person is disqualified from holding the office of chief executive for a period of time in cases where he or she has acted unlawfully and the court is not satisfied that he or she acted reasonably or in the belief that the action was authorised by law.

(Paragraph 9.107)

86   The legislation should also be amended to give the courts discretion to order the disqualification of councillors for a period of time in any case, involving expenditure or otherwise, where they have authorised an illegal decision or action and the court is not satisfied that the councillor acted reasonably or in the belief that the action was authorised by law.

(Paragraph 9.108)

87   The Scottish audit legislation should be amended so as to provide for the additional penalty of disqualification in cases where surcharge of over £2,000 is currently applicable.

(Paragraph 9.109)

88   The procedures leading to surcharge and disqualification in section 20 of the Local Government Finance Act 1982 (wilful misconduct leading to financial loss) should be brought into line with those in section 19 of that Act (illegal expenditure) except that in both cases there should be a duty rather than a discretion to apply to the court.

(Paragraphs 9.123 and 9.124)

LIST OF ANNEXES

ANNEX A	Letter inviting evidence
ANNEX B	List of those who submitted written evidence
ANNEX C	List of those who gave oral evidence
ANNEX D	Brief account of research projects
ANNEX E	Visits undertaken by Committee members
ANNEX F	Local authority areas and populations
ANNEX G	List of local authority associations
ANNEX H	Conventions on relations between political parties represented on Cheshire County Council
ANNEX I	National Code of Local Government Conduct 1975
ANNEX J	Basic flat rate allowance — Tables
ANNEX K	Proposed statutory functions of chief executives
ANNEX L	Section 137 of the Local Government Act 1972 and section 83 of the Local Government (Scotland) Act 1973

LETTER INVITING EVIDENCE   21 March 1985.

Dear Sir or Madam,

1.   I have been appointed to chair a Committee to look at the way local authorities conduct their business.

2.   The Committee's terms of reference are

'To inquire into practices and procedures governing the conduct of local authority business in Great Britain with particular reference to

(a)   the rights and responsibilities of elected members;

(b)   the respective roles of elected members and officers;

and

(c)   the need to clarify the limits and conditions governing discretionary spending by local authorities

and to make any necessary recommendations for strengthening the democratic process.'

3.   I am aware that some current practices and procedures within the ambit of these terms of reference have been perceived in some quarters as 'abuses'. I should emphasise however that the Committee has not prejudged this. We propose to examine the facts and only then to form a judgement of the issues.

4.   I am writing to invite you to submit written evidence. The notes attached list some of the main topics on which the Committees would particularly welcome information and views. They are not, however, intended to be exclusive.

5.   The Committee has been asked to submit an early Interim Report on the particular topic of local authority spending on advertising and information out of public funds. I am particularly anxious to have the early views and suggestions of all those interested in this subject, in advance of evidence on the wider subject matter covered in the note attached. Local authorities have statutory powers to provide information about services in their area. Recently there have been examples of authorities using advertising campaigns to oppose the Government's policies on 'rate-capping' and absolution of the GLC and the Metropolitan County Councils. I should welcome your views on the discretion which should properly be given to local authorities to provide information and advertise out of public funds. If you consider that there should be some limits on this discretion, for instance that some types of advertising should not be allowed, please say what kind of limit.

6.   If anyone wishes part or all of their evidence to be given in confidence please say so; the Committee will then observe strict confidentiality and not directly refer to such evidence in its proceedings or its Report. Where confidence is not requested, the Committee will be free to quote from it in its Report if it wishes to do so.

7.   In order to meet the timescales which the Committee has been set, I must ask for your evidence on information and advertising to be received by 27 April

1985. Evidence on other topics should be submitted by 21 June 1985. All evidence should be sent to the Secretariat at the above address.

DAVID WIDDICOMBE QC

TOPICS FOR EVIDENCE

The Committee would particularly welcome information and views on the topics listed below. In identifying these topics, the Committee has attempted to highlight certain practices and procedures which have attracted attention and which are viewed at least in some quarters as a cause for concern. The Committee wishes to emphasise, however, that it has in no sense pre-judged whether these practices and procedures are desirable or otherwise. Nor indeed, at this stage, has it had an opportunity to form a view as to their prevalence.

The first item headed 'The Role of the Party Caucus' seeks views on ways in which the institutions and procedures of local government may be brought more closely into line with the political decision taking processes. This heading may be used more generally for any suggestions for the strengthening of effective decision taking, and of democracy, in local government. Respondents are, however, asked to note that questions of the financing of local government, the electoral system, the structure of local government and functional responsibilities for particular services are expressly outside the Committee's remit.

1. The Role of the Party Caucus

It has been suggested that local government procedures do not sufficiently recognise the realities of the decision taking process, in particular that in authorities with a high degree of political organisation decisions are often taken in party political caucuses and not by the Council or its committees. It is argued that local authority institutions and procedures should be re-assessed and brought more into line with political reality by the adoption, for example, of the 'Westminster System', with a 'cabinet' of the ruling political party responsible to the Council as a whole. The Committee would welcome your views on this question generally, and the adoption of the Westminster system in particular, recognising that different arrangements may be appropriate in different authorities.

2. Role of Minority Group Members

There is a suggestion that the rights of members of minority groups are being eroded. It is sometimes claimed that their participation in the decision taking process has been undermined by the exercise of majority group control over such matters as committee agendas, papers and timetables, and by the exclusion of minority groups from membership of committees. The Committee is concerned to establish whether this is the case and, if so, what steps if any should be taken to protect the rights of minority group members.

3. Mechanism for Public Challenge of Local Authority Decisions

At present, there are narrow limits within which the public may challenge local authority actions and decisions through means other than the electoral process. The Committee would be interested to know whether respondents feel that public rights of challenge should be strengthened and, if so, what mechanisms they would propose to this end—such as a strengthening of the audit service and/or the Local Government Ombudsman's powers and procedures, or facilitating public access to the courts.

4. Freedom of Information

The Local Government (Access to Informaton) Bill currently progressing through Parliament could lead to significant changes in the law in this area over the period during which the Committee will be considering its remit. The Committee would welcome views, in the light of progress on the Bill, on whether more should be done to increase public access to local authority proceedings and papers and, if so, what.

5. Members' Conflicts of Interest

Notwithstanding the National Code of Conduct agreed following the recommendations of the Redcliffe-Maud Report on Conduct in Local Government (1974)[1], it is possible that more should be done to safeguard the public interest where a member's allegiance to a particular sectional group may conflict with his responsibilities towards his electorate at large. Particular concern has been expressed where a member of one authority serves as an officer of another, or as a paid employee of an organisation funded by local government. The Committee would welcome information and views and suggestions in this area generally.

6. Influence of Interest Groups

It has been suggested that groups representing particular interests have sometimes exerted disproportionate influence on Council proceedings, for instance through co-option onto Committees, and that this has weakened the role of elected members. The Council would welcome information and views on this, and in particular on whether local authorities should have greater or less discretion to co-opt people onto committees and sub-committees.

7. Members' Allowances

The Committee will be seeking to update some of the factual information assembled by the Robinson Committeee on the Remuneration of Councillors (1977), and to assemble a fuller picture than is currently available on the use of allowances across the country as a whole. It would welcome views on the current system of allowances and on any changes which respondents might consider desirable.

On a related theme, it would welcome views on whether the alleged trend towards members who work full-time (or virtually so) on council business should be encouraged, and on whether any consequent changes to the allowance rules and procedures should be adopted.

8. The Role of Officers

The traditional concept of 'political neutrality' of officers may be changing. It is, for example, sometimes said that the recruitment and dismissal of chief officers is, on occasion, decided on a party political basis and that officers have

---

[1] Published in Department of the Environment Circular 94/75 (Scottish Development Department Circular 95/75 and Welsh Office Circular 166/75).

been encouraged (through the granting of paid leave etc) to participate in activities of a party political nature.

There may also be a need for clarification of the proper relationship between officers and individual members, groups of members and the Council as a whole. There appears to be a divergence of view, for example, on whether there is a need to strengthen the accountability of officers to the majority group, or whether there is a need to take steps to safeguard the professional independence of an officer in advising the Council as a whole.

The Committee would welcome views on the proper role of officers, and on what changes, if any, might be desirable in this area.

9. Discretionary Spending

The Committee has been asked to consider the need to clarify the limits and conditions governing discretionary spending by local authorities. It would welcome information on the use of s 137 of the Local Government Act 1972 (s 83 of the Local Government (Scotland) Act 1973). It would also welcome views on whether a general discretionary power of this kind is desirable; on whether the current limit on the spending power of the product of a 2p rate is too low, too high or reasonable; and so whether there is a need to limit the discretion in any way.

LIST OF THOSE WHO SUBMITTED WRITTEN EVIDENCE

LOCAL AUTHORITIES

Adur District Council
Avon, County of
Aylesbury Vale District Council
Basingstoke and Deane Borough Council
Beverley, Borough of
Birmingham, City of
Blaenau Gwent, Borough of
Blyth Valley, Borough of
Bolsover District Council
Bolton Metropolitan Borough
Boothferry Borough Council
Braintree District Council
Bromley, London Borough of
Bury, Metropolitan Borough of
Calderdale, Metropolitan Borough of
Cambridge City Council
Camden, London Borough of
Carlisle, City of
Cheshire County Council
Christchurch, Borough of
Cotswold District Council
Coventry, City of
Croydon, London Borough of
Cumbria County Council
Derbyshire County Council
Durham County Council
Ealing, London Borough of
East Carlton Parish Council
East Devon District Council
East Lothian District Council
Eastleigh, Borough of
Edinburgh, City of, District Council
Enfield, London Borough of
Epping Forest District Council
Epsom and Ewell, Borough of
Essex County Council
Fareham Borough Council
Felpham Parish Council
Fife Regional Council
Forest of Dean District Council
Fraserburgh Community Council
Glanford Borough Council
Glasgow, City of
Gloucestershire County Council

Grampian Regional Council
Gravesham Borough Council
Greater London Council
Greater Manchester Council
Greenwich, London Borough of
Gwent County Council
Hammersmith and Fulham, London Borough of
Haringey, London Borough of
Hart District Council
Hartlepool, Borough of
Havering, London Borough of
Hertfordshire County Council
Hillingdon, London Borough of
Holcombe, Parish Council of
Hollingbourne Parish Council
Hook Parish Council
Inner London Education Authority
Inverclyde, District of
Islington, London Borough of
Kensington and Chelsea, Royal Borough of
Kent County Council
Kerrier District Council
Kilmarnock and Loudoun District Council
Kingston-upon-Hull, City of
Kingston-upon-Thames, Royal Borough of
Leicester City Council
Lewes District Council
Lewisham, London Borough of
Lincolnshire County Council
London, City of
Lothian Regional Council
Maldon, The District Council
Manchester, City of
Moray District Council
Newark and Sherwood District Council
Newcastle-upon-Tyne, City of
Newham, London Borough of
North Shropshire District Council
North West Leicestershire District Council
North Yorkshire County Council
Norwich, City of
Nottingham, City of
Old Basing Parish Council
Oldham Metropolitan Borough Council
Orkney Islands Council
Oxford City Council
Pembury Parish Council
Portsmouth, City of
Purbeck District Council
Rochdale, Metropolitan Borough of
Ross and Cromarty District Council

255

Roxburgh District Council
Rushmoor, Borough of
Sandwell, Metropolitan Borough of
Scarborough Borough Council
Sefton, Metropolitan Borough of
Sevenoaks District Council
Sheffield, City of
Shropshire County Council
Slough Corporation
Solihull, Metropolitan Borough of
Somerset County Council
South Bucks District Council
South Glamorgan, County of
South Norfolk District Council
South Staffordshire District Council
South Wight Borough Council
South Yorkshire County Council
Southwark, London Borough of
Staffordshire Moorlands District Council
Stirling District Council
Strathclyde Regional Council
Stratton-on-the-Fosse Parish Council
Stroud District Council
Sutton, London Borough of
Tayside Regional Council
Tendring District Council
Trafford Metropolitan Borough Council
Tyne and Wear County Council
Wandsbeck District Council
Wandsworth Borough Council
Warwickshire County Council
Watford, Borough of
West Devon, Borough of
West Lothian District Council
West Yorkshire County Council
Winchester, City of
Windsor and Maidenhead, Royal Borough of
Wolverhampton, Metropolitan Borough of
Wrexham Maelor Borough Council
Wychavon District Council
Wycombe District Council
Yateley Town Council

ORGANISATIONS

Advertising Standards Authority
Advice Services Alliance
Advice Services Alliance—London
Aims of Industry
Association of British Chambers of Commerce
Association of Chief Architects of Scottish Local Authorities
Association of Chief Police Officers of England, Wales and Northern Ireland

Association of Chief Technical Officers
Association of Councillors
Association of County Councils
Association of Directors of Education in Scotland
Association of Directors of Social Services
Association of Directors of Social Work (Scotland)
Association of District Councils
Association of District Councils—Somerset Branch
Association of District Secretaries
Association of Liberal Councillors
Association of Local Authority Valuers and Estate Surveyors
Association of London Authorities
Association of London Borough Planning Officers
Association of Metropolitan Authorities
Association of Polytechnic Teachers
Association of Scottish Chambers of Commerce
Audit Commission—District Auditors
Audit Commission for Local Authorities in England and Wales
Birmingham Conservative Association
Blyth Valley Council for Voluntary Service
British Association of Social Workers
Cabinet Office
Campaign for Homosexual Equality
Catholic Education Council
Central Council of Physical Recreation
Central Office of Information
Centre for Policy Studies
Chartered Institute of Public Finance and Accountancy
Chartered Institute of Public Finance and Accountancy—Scottish Branch
Chief Leisure Officers Association
Commission for Local Administration in England
Commission for Local Administration in Wales
Commission for Local Authority Accounts in Scotland
Commission for Racial Equality—North and Scotland Regional Office
Commissioner for Local Administration in Scotland
Community Projects Foundation
Community Rights Project
Confederation of British Industry
Conservative Group for Homosexual Equality
Conservative National Local Government Advisory Committee
Conservative Party
Consultative Group of Greater London Chambers of Commerce and Trade
Convention of Scottish Local Authorities
Councils for Voluntary Service—National Association
County Surveyors Society
County Surveyors Society—Scottish Branch
Croydon Area Watchdog Group
Crypt Association
Department of Education and Science
Department of the Environment
District Planning Officers' Society

Dundee West Conservative Association
Educational Institute of Scotland
Efficiency in Local Government
Federated Union of Managerial and Professional Officers
Federation of Industrial Development Authorities
Federation of Scottish Ratepayers
Federation of Sussex Amenity Societies
Free Church Federal Council
General Municipal, Boilermakers and Allied Trades Union
General Synod of the Church of England Board of Education
Glasgow Chamber of Commerce
Greenock and Port Glasgow Conservative Association
Guild of Senior Officers of the Greater London Council and the Inner London
    Education Authority
Hackney Ethnic Minorities Alliance
Havant and Emsworth Chamber of Commerce
Home Office
Incorporated Society of British Advertisers Limited
Independent Broadcasting Authority
Institute of Chartered Secretaries and Administrators
Institute of Housing
Institute of Legal Executives
Institute of Leisure and Amenity Management
Institute of Personnel Management
Institute of Public Relations—Local Government Group
Institute of Wastes Management
Institution of Building Control Officers
Institution of Civil Engineers
Institution of Environmental Health Officers
Islington Chamber of Commerce and Trade
Justice
Kensington Square Residents' Association
Kilmarnock and Loudoun Conservative Association
Labour Party
Labour Party—Harrow East Constituency
Labour Party—Scottish Council
Labour Party—Spalding Branch
Landscape Institute
Law Society—Local Government Group
Law Society of Scotland—Public Service and Commerce Group
Leicester Council for Voluntary Service
Lewisham Ratepayers Association
Library Association
Llantrisant Green Group
Local Authorities' Conditions of Service Advisory Board
Local Government Information Unit
Local Government Reform Society
Local Government Training Board
London Association of Community Relations Councils
London Government Public Relations Association
London Voluntary Service Council
Magistrates' Association

258

Manchester Chamber of Commerce and Industry
Matthew Trust
Metropolitan Planning Officers' Society
National and Local Government Officers Association
National Association of Citizens Advice Bureaux
National Association of Community Relations Councils
National Association of Funeral Directors
National Association of Head Teachers
National Association of Local Councils
National Association of Ratepayers—North West Region
National Association of Schoolmasters/Union of Women Teachers
National Association of Schoolmasters/Union of Women Teachers—Scotland
National Association of Teachers in Further and Higher Education
National Chamber of Trade
National Chamber of Trade—Essex Council
National Confederation of Parent-Teacher Associations
National Council for Voluntary Organisations
National Council for Voluntary Organisations—Standing Conference of
    Rural Community Councils
National Federation of Self Employed and Small Businesses
National Federation of Self Employed and Small Businesses—The Merseyside
    Region and Liverpool Branch Office
National Federation of Self-Help Organisations
National Pharmaceutical Association
National Union of Conservative and Unionist Associations—North Western
    Area
National Union of Ratepayers' Association
National Union of Teachers
Newcastle-upon-Tyne Council for Voluntary Service
Newham North West Conservative Association
Newspaper Society
Northavon Alliance
Organisation of Private Tenants
Peace Through NATO
Pembroke and District Citizens Advice Bureau
Plaid Cymru
Private Tenants' Rights Project—Kensington and Chelsea
Ramblers' Association
Ratepayers' Action Group Executive for Lothian Region
River Thames Society
Royal Institution of Chartered Surveyors
Royal Town Planning Institute
Rushmoor Council of Community Service
Runnymede Trust
Sandwell Council for Community Relations
Scottish Association of Directors of Water and Sewerage Services
Scottish Development Department
Scottish National Party
Scottish Office
Scottish Police Federation
Scottish Society of Directors of Planning

Scottish Trades Union Congress
Social Democratic Party
Social Democratic Party—Greenwich Area
Socialist Educational Association
Society of Chief Personnel Officers in Local Government
Society of County and Regional Public Relations Officers
Society of County Librarians
Society of County Secretaries
Society of County Treasurers
Society of Directors of Administration in Scotland
Society of Directors of Environmental Health
Society of Directors of Trading Standards in Scotland
Society of District Councils Public Relations Officers
Society of Education Officers
Society of Local Authority Chief Executives
Society of Local Authority Chief Executives—Scottish Branch
South Hams Association of Ratepayers
South Yorkshire Charity Information Service Trust
Southampton Chamber of Commerce
Southwark Council for Voluntary Service
Spastics Society
Steatham Area Gay Group
Surbiton Constituency Labour Party
Surrey Chief Housing Officers' Association
Sussex Rural Community Council
Teignmouth and Shaldon Environment Society
Town and Country Planning Association
Trades Union Congress
United Grand Lodge of England
Wales Council for Voluntary Action
War Widows Association of Great Britain
Welsh Counties Committee
Welsh Office
West Leicester Liberal Association
Westbury Constituency Labour Party
Wimborne and Colehill District Ratepayers Association
Wrekin Conservative Association

INDIVIDUAL COUNCILLORS OR COUNCILLORS ON BEHALF OF GROUPS OF COUNCILLORS

Adams D R, Wrekin District Council
Alston J A, Norfolk County Council
Andrew G E, North Devon District Council
Avery K R, Caradon District Council
Ball Mrs J, City of Edinburgh District Council
Banks S, London Borough of Waltham Forest
Bateman P T, Metropolitan Borough of Wolverhampton
Bell J S, Tameside Metropolitan Borough
Benn H, London Borough of Ealing
Best N A, Southampton City Council
Blackaby Miss B, London Borough of Greenwich

Bond E, Oxfordshire County Council
Bond M, County of Dorset
Bonney N, Aberdeen City Council
Bore A, City of Birmingham
Bosworth N, City of Birmingham
Bower R J, Arun District Council
Bradbury W J, Nottingham City Council
Brown J F W, Carrick District Council
Brown P, London Borough of Bromley (jointly with C Gaster)
Bryan M, Braintree District Council
Buckingham K, Tyne and Wear County Council
Byford Mrs M, Charnwood District Council
Calvert N, Royal Borough of Kingston-upon-Thames
Carter A, Leeds City Council
Chadwick D, Sheffield City Council
Chadwick E S M, Havant Borough Council
Cheetham G, Sheffield City Council
Clein E, London Borough of Merton
Clough Mrs C M, London Borough of Southwark
Connarty M, Stirling District Council
Cooney F, Hereford and Worcester County Council
Cordle S, Sheffield City Council
Cordwell Dr J, Gloucestershire County Council
Cowd H, London Borough of Merton
Crabbe W, Thamesdown Borough Council
Craven District Council (Group of individual councillors)
Cunninghame District Council (Conservative and Independent Minority
    Group)
Curtis C, Hampshire County Council
Curtis D, Hertsmere Borough Council
Davidson Dr P S, Fife Regional Council
Dismore A, City of Westminster
Dodd Mrs I J, Harborough District Council
Dolphin P W, Newbury District Council
Dore Dr J, Hertfordshire County Council
Dunstan Mrs R, Carrick District Council
Eckersley T, London Borough of Southwark
Edge G, West Midlands County Council
Edwards B, Islwyn Borough Council
Edwards T A, Bath City Council
Elwes H W G, Gloucestershire County Council
Epping Forest District Council (Loughton Residents Association Group and
    Labour Group)
Epson E, Crawley Borough Council
Evans G, Chelmsford Borough Council
Evans G, Cynon Valley Borough Council
Falmouth Councillors on Carrick District Council
Farrer T, Cumbria County Council
Fielder Lt. Col. J A, Hertfordshire County Council
Fisher P, Metropolitan Borough of Knowsley
Foote-Wood C, Durham County Council

261

Freeman G H, Stratford-on-Avon District Council
Frost H, District Council of Maldon
Goldrein N C, Merseyside County Council
Gorton J V, Kent County Council and Sevenoaks District Council
Graham Miss B, North Yorkshire County Council
Grant J P, Rustington Parish Council
Hallows C, City of Liverpool
Hamilton W, East Yorkshire Borough of Beverley
Hammersmith and Fulham, London Borough of (Conservative Group)
Handford M A, Hinckley and Bosworth Borough Council
Hart A H, Kent County Council
Heslop D I, Sheffield City Council
Hill D, Worthing Borough Council
Hill G, Wear Valley District Council
Hodge Mrs M, London Borough of Islington
Hutton Mrs M D, Essex County Council
Ingle, Group Captain A, Arun District Council
Jameson J, Dumfries and Galloway Regional Council
Janes M H T, Borough of Broxbourne
Jarman Mrs P, Cynon Valley Borough Council
Jenkyns Patricia M, London Borough of Lambeth
Jones Cllr Mrs J, Llanarthney Community Council
Jones R H, Ribble Valley Borough Council
Jordon M R, Preston District Council
Kearney N J, Royal Borough of Kensington and Chelsea
Kershaw J, City of Manchester
Kettle K, London Borough of Ealing
King J A, London Borough of Waltham Forest
King-Hele Mrs M, Waverley Borough Council
Kingston-upon-Thames, Royal Borough of (Liberal Group)
Knight R, Essex County Council
Lacey B, London Borough of Brent
Lager M C M, Braintree District Council
Laxon C, Canterbury City Council
Leigh Mary, London Borough of Lambeth
Lemkin J (on behalf of GLC Conservative Group)
Lewis I D, Surrey Country Council
Little Mrs C M, Wombourne Parish Council
Lunn W, Sandwell Metropolitan Borough
MacDonald A H, London Borough of Bromley
Maden R, Hereford and Worcester County Council
Marshall W S, Derbyshire County Council
Marshfield S, Avon County Council
Maynard K, Cheshire County Council
McArthur J L, Western Isles Islands Council
Meikle J, Taunton Deane Borough Council
Miles A G, London Borough of Greenwich
Minckley Mrs C, Nottinghamshire County Council
Moore B, City of Newcastle-upon-Tyne
Moore J R, West Yorkshire County Council
Morgan C T, Lliw Valley Borough Council

Morgan I, Medina Borough Council
Morton M, London Borough of Camden
Motherwell District Council (Labour Majority Group)
Murray A M, Central Regional Council
Murrell A S, Blyth Valley District Council
Parsons Mrs D C, Purbeck District Council
Patnick I, South Yorkshire County Council
Payne M, Sedgemoor District Council
Pearson A, County of Cleveland
Pearson Mrs H, Middlesbrough Borough Council
Peterborough City Council (submissions from Labour, Conservative and
    Liberal Groups)
Pettit Mrs P V, West Yorkshire County Council
Platt Baroness of Writtle, Essex County Council
Porter Lady Shirley, City of Westminister
Powell-Jones Sylvia, Borough of Christchurch
Pym L J, London Borough of Barnet
Ramage J, Fife Regional Council
Rapson S, City of Portsmouth
Rees F L, London Borough of Harrow
Riddell F, Stirling District Council
Roberts J, London Borough of Hackney
Robertson I B, Grampian Regional Council
Rose J, Hertfordshire County Council
Roy Dr H, Sandwell Metropolitan Borough Council
Rutherford W A, Annandale and Eskdale District Council
Salinger B, London Borough of Haringey
Schofield C, Salford Metropolitan District Council
Shepherd P, West Sussex County Council
Simper J, King's Lynn and West Norfolk Borough Council
Sivell T O S, Caradon District Council
Smith Professor D, Inner London Education Authority
Smith G, Tyne and Wear County Council
Smith I, Fife Regional Council
Smith M, Sandwell Metropolitan Borough Council
Smith R H, Welwyn Hatfield District Council
Smith T, North East Derbyshire District Council
Sofer Anne, Greater London Council
Sonley C C, Borough of Beverley
Southampton, City of (Labour Group)
Stead B, Inner London Education Authority
Stevenson S J S, Kyle and Carrick District Council
Stranz W, Hereford and Worcester County Council
Swanwick J A, Ruchcliffe Borough Council
Swindin Mrs J E C, Ipswich Borough Council
Taylor A, Coventry District Council
Taylor A W, South Bucks District Council
Taylor P, South Oxfordshire District Council
Taylor R, Metropolitan Borough of Rochdale
Tetlow B H, Greater Manchester County Council
Thomson J, Motherwell District Council

Timmis R, London Borough of Lambeth
Tomlins T H, Cheshire County Council
Tranchard D, Borough of Bournemouth
Tremlett G, Greater London Council
Trent A, Borough of Poole
Tyler T G M, South Holland District Council
Veitch A, Clydebank District Council
Walsh J, Bolton Metropolitan Council
Waltham Forest, London Borough of (Labour Group)
Ward M, Greater London Council
Watkins R F, Cardiff City Council
Watson R M, Metropolitan Borough of Sefton
Watts C J, Hertsmere Borough Council
Weston A, East Hampshire District Council
Whitfield J F, Surrey County Council
Williams C A, London Borough of Lambeth
Williams H G, Lliw Valley Borough Council
Williams P, Mid Glamorgan County Council
Willis E, Taff-Ely Borough Council
Wilson J T, West Yorkshire Metropolitan County Council
Wilton F B, Gloucestershire County Council
Woolger G J, Borough of Rushmoor

INDIVIDUALS
Abbey R
Alexander M B
Allchin M V
Allen D E J
Alton David, MP
Amess David, MP
Anderson Mrs L G
Aram J D
Archard Lt Cdr R V
Arram J M
Atkins L J
Attwood A S
Baker E T
Baker Nicholas, MP
Barnes W
Barry Dr D H
Blackmore D
Blunt S W
Bols D R S
Booth W
Bottomely Peter, MP
Boynton Sir John
Braddon R H
Brain Rvd P
Briggs R C H
Britto D K
Broadbent A

264

Brooks P R B
Brown A J G
Brown M
Bulger Dr G
Burslam D S
Carey J F
Chapman A
Chope Christopher, MP
Churchill Winston S, MP
Clarke D J
Clephan D P
Clifford-Hindley J
Collins B T
Cowper Miss A S
Cox Miss D M
Croft P
Crole G M
Cunningham Dr Jack, MP
Daley D S
Davis H J
Deane G F
Delima D
Dexter H
Dickins Geoffrey, MP
Digman E G (on behalf of Royal Borough of Kingston-upon-Thames
    Corporate Management Team)
Dougherty D P
Driscoll T
Dwyer D B
Elliott C
Endon G
England C P
Farley B
Finsberg Sir Geoffrey, MP
Fleming J A C
Forward B I
Foulkes Professor D L
Fraser G W
Frost R S
Gardner C E
Goldsmith M
Gorman Mrs T E
Gorst A
Haigh Mrs M
Harris, Lord of Greenwich
Hayes J W
Hender J D
Henny A
Hewitt H M
Holt Richard, MP
Hoyle D

Hughes J
Hull A H S
Jack Mrs S B
Jasper S
Kennedy Mrs M
Killingworth M A
Kirby E
Kirkman Mrs M J
Knowles Michael, MP
Knowles R S B
Laws G
Leslie M
Line G G
Lock, Sir Duncan
Longman A V
Lyons M T
Marlow Tony, MP
Marsh E A
May P
McDougall K
McFarlane Mrs F D
McLean J
Mellor Miss D
Miller T W
Milligan Mrs J E
Mills C M
Molson, The Rt. Hon. Lord
Moore G C
Moore V
Morgan D G
Morris-Thomas J
Morton O B
Mumby Mrs M
Mustow S N
Necker G L
O'Brian F
Ollerhead A
Oppenheim Phillip, MP
Osborn Sir John, MP
Owen Dr J S
Page A
Pailing J
Paterson G B
Paterson Professor J
Preston C
Puig P G
Pycock G
Rayner J D
Readman V
Rees R C
Rennison Mrs A

Rhodes J
Rose B
Ross G
Samuels A
Saunders T
Scialom M C E
Sharpe B
Shaw E
Shields R M C
Skinner Miss J B
Smith J J K
Snare R T
Somerville G S
Speight Mrs C
Spencer Derek, MP
Stephen D
Stevens A G
Straw Jack, MP
Stroud J H
Taylor D
Taylor Mrs M
Tombs D A
Upex D
Urquhart Mrs B
Warwick G
Watkins G L
Watson Mrs J M
Webber Miss E
Webster K B
Webster Mrs L
Welsh S H D
Wheatcroft C C
Wilcox Mrs I
Wilkinson W
Wilks Mrs A
Wilks Mrs S J
Williamson H M
Wright S J
Wynn-Jones G

LIST OF THOSE WHO GAVE ORAL EVIDENCE

Conservative Party[1]
Labour Party[1]

Association of County Councils[3]
Association of District Councils[3]
Association of London Authorities[3]
Association of Metropolitan Authorities[3]
Convention of Scottish Local Authorities[3]
Greater London Council[1]
London Boroughs Association[3]

Department of the Environment[3])
Scottish Office[3]) Jointly
Welsh Office[3])

Cabinet Office[1])
Central Office of Information[1]) Jointly

Audit Commission for Local Authorities in England and Wales[3]
Commission for Local Authority Accounts in Scotland[3]

Commission for Local Administration in England[2])
Commission for Local Administration in Scotland[2]) Jointly
Commission for Local Administration in Wales[2])

Federated Union of Managerial and Professional Officers[2]

National Council for Voluntary Organisations[2]

National and Local Government Officers' Association[2]

Society of Local Authority Chief Executives[3]

Institute of Public Relations[1])
Society of County and Regional Public Relations Officers[1]) Jointly
Society of District Councils' Public Relations Officers[1])

Advertising Standards Authority[1]
Efficiency in Local Government[1]
Independent Broadcasting Authority[1]

[1] Publicity only
[2] Other issues only
[3] Publicity and other issues

ANNEX D
RESEARCH

The following research reports and papers which were commissioned by the Committee appear in the Research Volumes associated with this Report as indicated.

The Political Organisation of Local Authorities
(Research Volume I)

A report jointly by Steve Leach and Chris Game, Institute of Local Government Studies, University of Birmingham; John Gyford, University College London; and Dr Arthur Midwinter, University of Strathclyde.

This research project was based on two surveys carried out in 1985: a questionnaire addressed to all local authorities and an interview survey in 103 authorities. The project reports on all aspects of the political organisation of local authorities, including the extent to which authorities are politically controlled, the workings of party groups, committee composition, co-option, officer-member roles and relations, and the appointment of officers.

The Local Government Councillor
(Research Volume II)

(i) The Characteristics and Attitudes of Councillors, by Jude England, Social and Community Planning Research.

This report is based on a questionnaire which was sent to 10% of councillors in 1985. It reviews the characteristics of elected members and their time devoted to, and attitudes towards, council work.

(ii) Members' Allowances, by Phillip Ramsdale and Stuart Capon, the Institute of Public Finance Ltd.

This reports on allowances claimed by elected members. It is based on a questionnaire which was sent in 1985 to directors of finance in all local authorities.

The Local Government Elector
(Research Volume III)

(i) Attitudes to Local Government, by Dr Ken Young.

This reports on a questionnaire survey carried out by National Opinion Polls Market Research Ltd on public attitudes to local government.

(ii) Local Electoral Behaviour, by Professor W L Miller, University of Glasgow.

This reviews the extent to which people vote at local elections and the influences on their electoral choice. It makes use of the NOP survey mentioned above.

269

(iii)   Appendices—NOP Market Research Ltd.

This is the supporting documentation to the reports at (i) and (ii) above. It comprises the survey methodology used by NOP Market Research Ltd and the questionnaire.

Aspects of Local Democracy
(Research Volume IV)

(i) An Analysis of Local Authority Discretionary Expenditure in 1984–85, by Phillip Ramsdale and Stuart Capon, the Institute of Public Finance Ltd.

This reports on spending by local authorities under section 137 of the Local Government Act 1972 and section 83 of the Local Government (Scotland) Act 1973. It is based on the same questionnaire survey as was carried out for allowances (see Research Volume II(ii) above).

(ii) Decision Making by Liverpool City Council: Setting the Rate 1985–86, by Michael Parkinson, Centre for Urban Studies, University of Liverpool.

This reviews the decision making process leading up to the setting of a rate, identifying the roles of councillors, the local party, officers and the auditor.

(iii)   Party Politics in Local Government: an historical perspective, by Dr Ken Young.

This reviews the development of party politics in local government from the early 19th century.

(iv)   Diversity, Sectionalism and Local Democracy, by John Gyford, University College, London.

This reviews trends towards a more participatory form of local government, primarily in metropolitan areas.

(v)   Local Government Abroad, by Professor Michael Goldsmith, University of Salford, and Professor Ken Newton, University of Dundee.

This reviews the political and decision taking process in local authorities in other Western countries.

ANNEX E

LOCAL AUTHORITIES VISITED BY MEMBERS OF THE COMMITTEE

City of Bradford

London Borough of Brent

City of Glasgow

Greater London Council

Kent County Council

City of Newcastle-upon-Tyne

City of Portsmouth

City of Sheffield

County of South Glamorgan

South Yorkshire County Council

Strathclyde Regional Council

West Midlands County Council

West Yorkshire County Council

ANNEX F

LOCAL AUTHORITY AREAS AND POPULATIONS

Counties in England and Wales

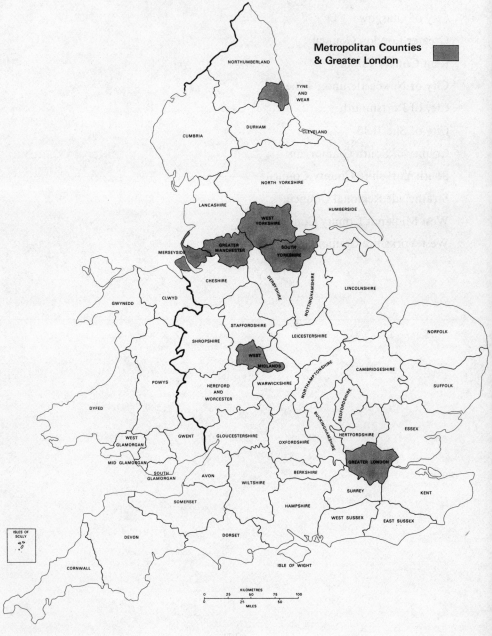

Metropolitan Counties
& Greater London

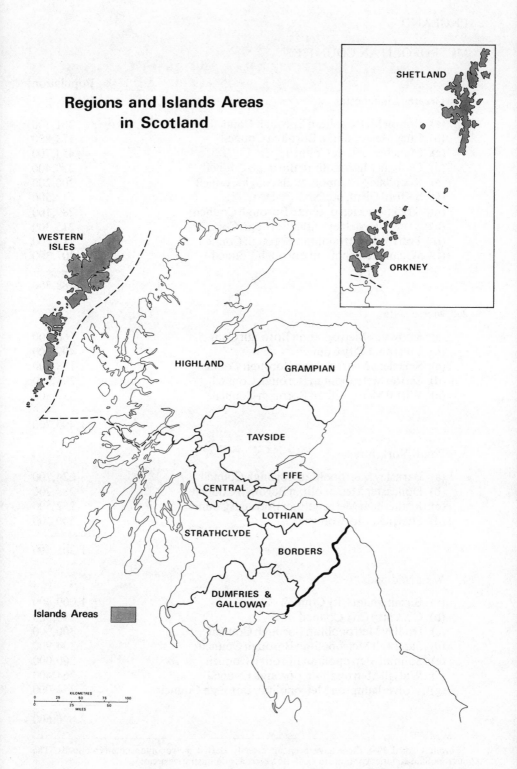

Regions and Islands Areas in Scotland

SHETLAND

WESTERN ISLES

ORKNEY

HIGHLAND

GRAMPIAN

TAYSIDE

FIFE

CENTRAL

LOTHIAN

STRATHCLYDE

BORDERS

DUMFRIES & GALLOWAY

Islands Areas

KILOMETRES
0   25   50   75   100
MILES
0   25   50

ENGLAND

METROPOLITAN COUNTIES[1]

	Population
1. Greater Manchester	
(a) Bolton Metropolitan Borough Council	261,300
(b) Bury Metropolitan Borough Council	173,800
(c) Manchester City Council	454,700
(d) Oldham Metropolitan Borough Council	220,400
(e) Rochdale Metropolitan Borough Council	206,200
(f) Salford City Council	242,500
(g) Stockport Metropolitan Borough Council	289,100
(h) Tameside Metropolitan Borough Council	215,300
(i) Trafford Metropolitan Borough Council	217,700
(j) Wigan Metropolitan Borough Council	307,300
	2,588,300
2. Merseyside	
(a) Knowsley Metropolitan Borough Council	168,500
(b) Liverpool City Council	497,200
(c) St Helens Metropolitan Borough Council	188,800
(d) Sefton Metropolitan Borough Council	298,700
(e) Wirral Metropolitan Borough Council	337,500
	1,490,700
3. South Yorkshire	
(a) Barnsley Metropolitan Borough Council	224,200
(b) Doncaster Metropolitan Borough Council	288,200
(c) Rotherham Metropolitan Borough Council	252,500
(d) Sheffield City Council	540,500
	1,305,400
4. West Midlands	
(a) Birmingham City Council	1,009,400
(b) Coventry City Council	313,300
(c) Dudley Metropolitan Borough Council	300,600
(d) Sandwell Metropolitan Borough Council	304,900
(e) Solihull Metropolitan Borough Council	200,000
(f) Walsall Metropolitan Borough Council	264,400
(g) Wolverhampton Metropolitan Borough Council	254,000
	2,646,600

[1]From 1 April 1986 there have been no directly elected metropolitan county councils. The metropolitan counties continue to exist, however, as administrative areas.

274

5. West Yorkshire

    (a) Bradford City Council   464,400
    (b) Calderdale Metropolitan Borough Council   191,200
    (c) Kirklees Metropolitan Borough Council   377,700
    (d) Leeds City Council   712,200
    (e) Wakefield City Council   310,700

    2,056,200

6. Tyne and Wear

    (a) Gateshead Metropolitan Borough Council   209,600
    (b) Newcastle-upon-Tyne City Council   281,100
    (c) North Tyneside Metropolitan Borough Council   194,000
    (d) South Tyneside Metropolitan Borough Council   158,000
    (e) Sunderland Metropolitan Borough Council   299,400

    1,142,100

ENGLISH NON-METROPOLITAN COUNTIES

1. Avon

    (a) Bath City Council   84,700
    (b) Bristol City Council   396,600
    (c) Kingswood District Council   86,800
    (d) Northavon District Council   123,100
    (e) Wansdyke District Council   78,000
    (f) Woodspring District Council   170,600

    939,800

2. Bedfordshire

    (a) Luton Borough Council   165,400
    (b) Mid Bedfordshire District Council   107,800
    (c) North Bedfordshire Borough Council   133,500
    (d) South Bedfordshire District Council   109,000

    515,700

3. Berkshire

    (a) Bracknell District Council   89,300
    (b) Newbury District Council   127,600
    (c) Reading Borough Council   136,400
    (d) Slough Borough Council   98,500
    (e) Royal Borough of Windsor and Maidenhead   133,800
    (f) Wokingham District Council   129,700

    715,300

4. Buckinghamshire

(a)	Aylesbury Vale District Council	138,300
(b)	Chiltern District Council	91,800
(c)	Milton Keynes Borough Council	145,800
(d)	South Bucks District Council	61,400
(e)	Wycombe District Council	157,300
		594,600

5. Cambridgeshire

(a)	Cambridge City Council	99,600
(b)	East Cambridgeshire District Council	55,200
(c)	Fenland District Council	68,500
(d)	Huntingdonshire District Council	131,100
(e)	Peterborough City Council	141,200
(f)	South Cambridgeshire District Council	113,600
		609,200

6. Cheshire

(a)	Chester City Council	116,400
(b)	Congleton Borough Council	82,600
(c)	Crewe and Nantwich Borough Council	96,300
(d)	Ellesmere Port and Neston Borough Council	80,800
(e)	Halton Borough Council	122,700
(f)	Macclesfield Borough Council	150,200
(g)	Vale Royal District Council	112,500
(h)	Warrington Borough Council	175,900
		937,400

7. Cleveland

(a)	Hartlepool Borough Council	92,400
(b)	Langbaugh Borough Council	148,900
(c)	Middlesbrough Borough Council	146,900
(d)	Stockton-on-Tees Borough Council	174,500
		562,700

8. Cornwall

(a)	Caradon District Council	71,400
(b)	Carrick District Council	77,500
(c)	Kerrier District Council	86,000
(d)	North Cornwall District Council	67,400
(e)	Penwith District Council	54,700
(f)	Restormel Borough Council	80,100
		437,100

9. Cumbria

    (a) Allerdale District Council   95,500
    (b) Barrow-in-Furness Borough Council   74,000
    (c) Carlisle City Council   101,400
    (d) Copeland Borough Council   71,800
    (e) Eden District Council   44,100
    (f) South Lakeland District Council   96,800

    483,600

10. Derbyshire

    (a) Amber Valley District Council   109,400
    (b) Bolsover District Council   70,900
    (c) Chesterfield Borough Council   97,200
    (d) Derby City Council   214,700
    (e) Erewash Borough Council   104,200
    (f) High Peak Borough Council   82,200
    (g) North East Derbyshire District Council   96,300
    (h) South Derbyshire District Council   69,300
    (i) West Derbyshire District Council   67,500

    911,700

11. Devon

    (a) East Devon District Council   109,600
    (b) Exeter City Council   100,800
    (c) Mid Devon District Council   59,700
    (d) North Devon District Council   79,500
    (e) Plymouth City Council   255,300
    (f) South Hams District Council   68,100
    (g) Teignbridge District Council   97,900
    (h) Torbay Borough Council   115,100
    (i) Torridge District Council   48,800
    (j) West Devon Borough Council   43,500

    978,300

12. Dorset

    (a) Bournemouth Borough Council   147,200
    (b) Christchurch Borough Council   40,800
    (c) North Dorset District Council   49,700
    (d) Poole Borough Council   122,700
    (e) Purbeck District Council   42,600
    (f) West Dorset District Council   81,200
    (g) Weymouth and Portland Borough Council   59,700
    (h) Wimbourne District Council   73,900

    617,800

13. Durham

    (a) Chester-le-Street District Council   52,500
    (b) Darlington Borough Council   100,300
    (c) Derwentside District Council   86,800
    (d) Durham City Council   87,500
    (e) Easington District Council   97,600
    (f) Sedgefield District Council   89,900
    (g) Teesdale District Council   24,600
    (h) Wear Valley District Council   64,500

                                        603,700

14. East Sussex

    (a) Brighton Borough Council   145,600
    (b) Eastbourne Borough Council   80,000
    (c) Hastings Borough Council   78,700
    (d) Hove Borough Council   89,600
    (e) Lewes District Council   82,700
    (f) Rother District Council   79,000
    (g) Wealden District Council   123,300

                                        678,900

15. Essex

    (a) Basildon District Council   156,600
    (b) Braintree District Council   114,700
    (c) Brentwood District Council   71,100
    (d) Castle Point District Council   86,300
    (e) Chelmsford Borough Council   146,100
    (f) Colchester Borough Council   140,700
    (g) Epping Forest District Council   114,800
    (h) Harlow District Council   76,800
    (i) Maldon District Council   50,000
    (j) Rochford District Council   74,500
    (k) Southend-on-Sea Borough Council   157,400
    (l) Tendring District Council   118,900
    (m) Thurrock Borough Council   124,400
    (n) Uttlesford District Council   64,400

                                   1,496,700

16. Gloucestershire

    (a) Cheltenham Borough Council   86,300
    (b) Cotswold District Council   70,900
    (c) Forest of Dean District Council   73,500
    (d) Gloucester City Council   91,600
    (e) Stroud District Council   103,600
    (f) Tewkesbury Borough Council   83,300

                                        509,200

17. Hampshire

(a)	Basingstoke and Deane Borough Council	136,300
(b)	East Hampshire District Council	95,000
(c)	Eastleigh Borough Council	97,600
(d)	Fareham Borough Council	92,600
(e)	Gosport Borough Council	77,200
(f)	Hart District Council	79,000
(g)	Havant Borough Council	117,400
(h)	New Forest District Council	151,800
(i)	Portsmouth City Council	188,600
(j)	Rushmoor Borough Council	80,600
(k)	Southampton City Council	203,900
(l)	Test Valley Borough Council	97,100
(m)	Winchester City Council	92,400

                                                              1,509,500

18. Hereford and Worcester

(a)	Bromsgrove District Council	88,700
(b)	Hereford City Council	47,900
(c)	Leominster District Council	37,800
(d)	Malvern Hills District Council	85,800
(e)	Redditch District Council	70,800
(f)	South Herefordshire District Council	47,900
(g)	Worcester City Council	76,200
(h)	Wychavon District Council	97,200
(i)	Wyre Forest District Council	93,000

                                                                645,300

19. Hertfordshire

(a)	Broxbourne Borough Council	81,000
(b)	Dacorum Borough Council	132,400
(c)	East Hertfordshire District Council	114,900
(d)	Hertsmere Borough Council	88,500
(e)	North Hertfordshire District Council	110,600
(f)	St Albans City Council	127,700
(g)	Stevenage Borough Council	75,400
(h)	Three Rivers District Council	79,800
(i)	Watford Borough Council	76,000
(j)	Welwyn Hatfield District Council	94,000

                                                                980,300

20. Humberside

    (a) East Yorkshire Borough of Beverley   108,000
    (b) Boothferry Borough Council   61,100
    (c) Cleethorpes Borough Council   68,500
    (d) East Yorkshire Borough Council   77,200
    (e) Glanford Borough Council   67,800
    (f) Great Grimsby Borough Council   91,700
    (g) Holderness Borough Council   47,500
    (h) Kingston upon Hull City Council   265,600
    (i) Scunthorpe City Council   64,200

    851,600

21. Isle of Wight

    (a) Medina Borough Council   68,700
    (b) South Wight Borough Council   52,200

    120,900

22. Kent

    (a) Ashford Borough Council   89,600
    (b) Canterbury City Council   126,600
    (c) Dartford Borough Council   76,900
    (d) Dover District Council   103,200
    (e) Gillingham Borough Council   94,500
    (f) Gravesham Borough Council   95,300
    (g) Maidstone Borough Council   132,100
    (h) Rochester upon Medway City Council   145,400
    (i) Sevenoaks District Council   111,100
    (j) Shepway District Council   87,800
    (k) Swale Borough Council   110,600
    (l) Thanet District Council   120,100
    (m) Tonbridge and Malling Borough Council   99,800
    (n) Tunbridge Wells Borough Council   98,700

    1,491,700

23. Lancashire

(a)	Blackburn Borough Council	142,300
(b)	Blackpool Borough Council	146,000
(c)	Burnley Borough Council	90,600
(d)	Chorley Borough Council	92,300
(e)	Fylde Borough Council	70,900
(f)	Hyndburn Borough Council	79,300
(g)	Lancaster City Council	127,600
(h)	Pendle Borough Council	85,000
(i)	Preston Borough Council	124,800
(j)	Ribble Valley Borough Council	51,500
(k)	Rossendale Borough Council	64,000
(l)	South Ribble Borough Council	98,800
(m)	West Lancashire District Council	107,300
(n)	Wyre Borough Council	98,700
		1,379,100

24. Leicestershire

(a)	Blaby District Council	79,000
(b)	Charnwood Borough Council	142,100
(c)	Harborough District Council	62,600
(d)	Hinkley and Bosworth Borough Council	91,800
(e)	Leicester City Council	281,700
(f)	Melton Borough Council	43,100
(g)	North West Leicestershire District Council	78,900
(h)	Oadby and Wigston Borough Council	52,800
(i)	Rutland District Council	34,100
		866,100

25. Lincolnshire

(a)	Boston Borough Council	52,000
(b)	East Lindsey District Council	107,600
(c)	Lincoln City Council	77,200
(d)	North Kesteven District Council	81,100
(e)	South Holland District Council	63,200
(f)	South Kesteven District Council	99,400
(g)	West Lindsey District Council	76,100
		556,600

26. Norfolk

(a)	Breckland District Council	99,600
(b)	Broadland District Council	99,400
(c)	Great Yarmouth Borough Council	82,900
(d)	King's Lynn and West Norfolk Borough Council	124,500
(e)	North Norfolk District Council	86,100
(f)	Norwich City Council	123,700
(g)	South Norfolk District Council	98,300
		714,500

27. Northamptonshire

    (a) Corby District Council   51,100
    (b) Daventry District Council   58,900
    (c) East Northamptonshire District Council   62,200
    (d) Kettering Borough Council   71,600
    (e) Northampton Borough Council   165,800
    (f) South Northamptonshire District Council   66,200
    (g) Wellingborough Borough Council   64,000

                                539,800

28. Northumberland

    (a) Alnwick District Council   29,400
    (b) Berwick-upon-Tweed Borough Council   26,400
    (c) Blyth Valley Borough Council   78,200
    (d) Castle Morpeth Borough Council   50,300
    (e) Tynedale District Council   54,800
    (f) Wansbeck District Council   61,600

                                300,700

29. North Yorkshire

    (a) Craven District Council   48,200
    (b) Hambleton District Council   76,400
    (c) Harrogate Borough Council   142,300
    (d) Richmondshire District Council   47,200
    (e) Ryedale District Council   88,000
    (f) Scarborough Borough Council   102,900
    (g) Selby District Council   83,500
    (h) York City Council   102,600

                                691,100

30. Nottinghamshire

    (a) Ashfield District Council   106,300
    (b) Bassetlaw District Council   103,700
    (c) Broxtowe Borough Council   104,400
    (d) Gedling Borough Council   106,300
    (e) Mansfield District Council   100,000
    (f) Newark and Sherwood District Council   105,400
    (g) Nottingham City Council   279,700
    (h) Rushcliffe Borough Council   94,300

                             1,000,100

31. Oxfordshire

(a)	Cherwell District Council	115,900
(b)	Oxford City Council	114,200
(c)	South Oxfordshire District Council	133,100
(d)	Vale of White Horse District Council	106,500
(e)	West Oxfordshire District Council	86,000
		555,700

32. Shropshire

(a)	Bridgnorth District Council	51,100
(b)	North Shropshire District Council	51,500
(c)	Oswestry Borough Council	31,500
(d)	Shrewsbury and Atcham Borough Council	89,300
(e)	South Shropshire District Council	34,600
(f)	The Wrekin District Council	128,600
		386,600

33. Somerset

(a)	Mendip District Council	92,700
(b)	Sedgemoor District Council	91,600
(c)	South Somerset District Council	137,200
(d)	Taunton Deane Borough Council	89,300
(e)	West Somerset District Council	30,100
		440,900

34. Staffordshire

(a)	Cannock Chase District Council	85,300
(b)	East Staffordshire District Council	94,700
(c)	Lichfield District Council	89,900
(d)	Newcastle-under-Lyme Borough Council	118,500
(e)	South Staffordshire District Council	101,600
(f)	Stafford Borough Council	117,200
(g)	Staffordshire Moorlands District Council	96,000
(h)	Stoke-on-Trent City Council	249,400
(i)	Tamworth Borough Council	66,800
		1,019,400

35. Suffolk

(a)	Babergh District Council	75,800
(b)	Forest Heath District Council	55,000
(c)	Ipswich Borough Council	118,800
(d)	Mid Suffolk District Council	73,000
(e)	St Edmundsbury Borough Council	89,500
(f)	Suffolk Coastal District Council	101,500
(g)	Waveney District Council	102,300
		615,900

36. Surrey

    (a) Elmbridge Borough Council   111,600
    (b) Epsom and Ewell Borough Council   67,000
    (c) Guildford Borough Council   125,800
    (d) Mole Valley District Council   77,300
    (e) Reigate and Banstead Borough Council   117,000
    (f) Runnymede Borough Council   71,800
    (g) Spelthorne Borough Council   90,900
    (h) Surrey Heath Borough Council   78,400
    (i) Tanbridge Borough Council   76,600
    (j) Waverley Borough Council   112,800
    (k) Woking Borough Council   85,200

                                      1,014,400

37. Warwickshire

    (a) North Warwickshire Borough Council   60,200
    (b) Nuneaton and Bedworth Borough Council 112,700
    (c) Rugby Borough Council   86,300
    (d) Stratford-on-Avon District Council   102,800
    (e) Warwick District Council   115,700

                                        477,700

38. West Sussex

    (a) Adur District Council   57,800
    (b) Arun District Council   124,900
    (c) Chichester District Council   99,900
    (d) Crawley Borough Council   83,600
    (e) Horsham District Council   103,600
    (f) Mid Sussex District Council   118,700
    (g) Worthing Borough Council   94,200

                                        682,700

39. Wiltshire

    (a) Kennet District Council   67,200
    (b) North Wiltshire District Council   107,700
    (c) Salisbury District Council   102,000
    (d) Thamesdown Borough Council   156,700
    (e) West Wiltshire District Council   102,600

                                        536,200

Population

LONDON BOROUGHS

		Population
1.	Barking and Dagenham	149,400
2.	Barnet	298,200
3.	Bexley	218,400
4.	Brent	254,900
5.	Bromley	298,400
6.	Camden	177,300
7.	Croydon	318,900
8.	Ealing	288,700
9.	Enfield	263,300
10.	Greenwich	216,000
11.	Hackney	187,900
12.	Hammersmith and Fulham	150,700
13.	Haringey	200,100
14.	Harrow	201,400
15.	Havering	239,700
16.	Hillingdon	232,200
17.	Hounslow	197,800
18.	Islington	165,200
19.	Kensington and Chelsea	136,000
20.	Kingston-upon-Thames	134,100
21.	Lambeth	244,200
22.	Lewisham	232,100
23.	Merton	164,000
24.	Newham	209,400
25.	Redbridge	226,500
26.	Richmond-upon-Thames	160,600
27.	Southwark	215,600
28.	Sutton	169,600
29.	Tower Hamlets	144,600
30.	Waltham Forest	215,100
31.	Wandsworth	258,300
32.	Westminster	182,000
	Corporation of the City of London	5,400
		6,756,000

---

[1]From 1 April 1986 there has been no directly elected council for London. London, however, continues to exist as an administrative area.

WALES

COUNTIES

1. Clwyd

    (a) Alyn and Deeside District Council   73,300
    (b) Colwyn Borough Council   50,300
    (c) Delyn Borough Council   64,700
    (d) Glyndwr District Council   40,300
    (e) Rhuddlan Borough Council   53,300
    (f) Wrexham Maelor Borough Council   114,400

      396,300

2. Dyfed

    (a) Carmarthen District Council   53,100
    (b) Ceredigion District Council   61,700
    (c) Dinefwr Borough Council   37,000
    (d) Llanelli Borough Council   74,500
    (e) Preseli District Council   70,100
    (f) South Pembrokshire District Council   38,600

      335,000

3. Gwent

    (a) Blaenau Gwent Borough Council   78,500
    (b) Islwyn Borough Council   66,100
    (c) Monmouth District Council   75,400
    (d) Newport Borough Council   138,900
    (e) Torfaen Borough Council   90,800

      439,700

4. Gwynedd

    (a) Aberconwy Borough Council   51,900
    (b) Arfon Borough Council   54,400
    (c) Dwyfor District Council   26,200
    (d) Meirionydd District Council   31,500
    (e) Ynys Môn—Isle of Anglesey Borough Council   68,700

      232,700

5. Mid Glamorgan

(a)	Cynon Valley Borough Council	66,100
(b)	Merthyr Tydfil Borough Council	59,000
(c)	Ogwr Borough Council	131,500
(d)	Rhondda Borough Council	80,000
(e)	Rhymney Valley District Council	103,900
(f)	Taff-Ely Borough Council	93,400
		533,900

6. Powys

(a)	Brecknock Borough Council	40,800
(b)	Montgomery District Council	48,300
(c)	Radnor District Council	21,500
		110,600

7. South Glamorgan

(a)	Cardiff City Council	281,200
(b)	Vale of Glamorgan Borough Council	113,200
		394,400

8. West Glamorgan

(a)	Afan Borough Council	51,900
(b)	Lliw Valley Borough Council	60,200
(c)	Neath Borough Council	65,100
(d)	Swansea City Council	187,400
		364,600

SCOTLAND

	Population
REGIONS	
1. Borders	
(a) Berwickshire District Council	18,300
(b) Ettrick and Lauderdale District Council	33,300
(c) Roxburgh District Council	35,200
(d) Tweeddale District Council	14,300
	101,100
2. Central	
(a) Clackmannon District Council	47,800
(b) Falkirk District Council	143,700
(c) Stirling District Council	81,100
	272,600
3. Dumfries and Galloway	
(a) Annandale and Eskdale District Council	35,800
(b) Nithsdale District Council	57,000
(c) Stewartry District Council	23,000
(d) Wigtown District Council	30,100
	145,900
4. Fife	
(a) Dunfermline District Council	128,800
(b) Kirkcaldy District Council	149,400
(c) North East Fife District Council	65,900
	344,100
5. Grampian	
(a) Aberdeen City Council	214,000
(b) Banff and Buchan District Council	83,200
(c) Gordon District Council	68,700
(d) Kincardine and Deeside District Council	45,600
(e) Moray District Council	85,500
	497,000

6. Highland

(a)	Badenoch and Strathspey District Council	10,100
(b)	Caithness District Council	27,400
(c)	Inverness District Council	58,300
(d)	Lochaber District Council	19,500
(e)	Nairn District Council	10,100
(f)	Ross and Cromarty District Council	47,400
(g)	Skye and Lochalsh District Council	11,000
(h)	Sutherland District Council	13,200
		197,000

7. Lothian

(a)	East Lothian District Council	80,800
(b)	Edinburgh City Council	439,700
(c)	Midlothian District Council	81,900
(d)	West Lothian District Council	141,000
		743,400

8. Strathclyde

(a)	Argyll and Bute District Council	65,700
(b)	Bearsden and Milngavie District Council	39,600
(c)	Clydebank District Council	50,800
(d)	Clydesdale District Council	57,900
(e)	Cumbernauld and Kilsyth District Council	63,000
(f)	Cumnock and Doon Valley District Council	44,300
(g)	Cunninghame District Council	137,600
(h)	Dumbarton District Council	78,700
(i)	East Kilbride District Council	82,400
(j)	Eastwood District Council	55,000
(k)	Glasgow City Council	744,000
(l)	Hamilton District Council	108,400
(m)	Inverclyde District Council	99,100
(n)	Kilmarnock and Loudoun District Council	81,100
(o)	Kyle and Carnick	113,300
(p)	Monklands District Council	109,300
(q)	Motherwell District Council	149,700
(r)	Renfrew District Council	206,900
(s)	Strathkelvin District Council	89,600
		2,376,400

9. Tayside

   (a) Angus District Council   93,900
   (b) Dundee City Council   178,800
   (c) Perth and Kinross District Council   121,700

                                 394,400

ISLANDS

1. Orkney   31,500

2. Shetland   23,400

3. Western Isles   19,300

ANNEX G

LOCAL AUTHORITY ASSOCIATIONS

The following is a list of the six local authority associations to which reference is made in the Report together with a note of the type of authority they represent:

Association of County Councils

Membership of the Association is open to the 47 county councils in England and Wales and the ILEA. At present 45 county councils are members, with no single political party holding on overall majority.

Association of District Councils

Membership of the Association is open to the 296 non-metropolitan district councils in England, the Isles of Scilly and the 37 district councils in Wales. At present 332 district councils and the Isles of Scilly are members, with majority control held by the Conservative Party.

Association of London Authorities

Membership of the Association is open to the 32 London boroughs and the ILEA. At present there are 13 members (including the ILEA) and majority control is held by the Labour Party.

Association of Metropolitan Authorities

Membership of the Association is open to the 32 London boroughs, the Corporation of the City of London, the ILEA, the 36 metropolitan district councils and the joint authorities established under the Local Government Act 1985. At present all 36 metropolitan district councils, the Corporation of the City of London, the ILEA and 31 London boroughs are members. Majority control is held by the Labour Party.

Convention of Scottish Local Authorities

All the regional (8), island (3), and district (53) councils in Scotland are members of the Convention. Majority control is held by the Labour Party.

London Boroughs Association

Membership of the Association is open to the 32 London boroughs and the Corporation of the City of London. At present 22 of the boroughs and the Corporation are members, with majority control held by the Conservative Party.

CHESHIRE COUNTY COUNCIL

CONVENTIONS ON RELATIONS BETWEEN THE POLITICAL PARTIES
REPRESENTED ON THE COUNCIL

1. *Introduction*

1.1   The formal business of the Council is regulated by Standing Orders and
other chapters of the 'Red Book'. Other important aspects of business are less
easily regulated by formal rules drafted in legal or semi-legal language. These are
set out for the guidance of members of the Council and chief officers in this
statement of conventions.

1.2   The conventions are to be read alongside and as subordinate to the Standing Orders and other Red Book provisions.

2. *Definitions*

2.1   For purposes of this statement a 'Committee' refers also to a sub-
committee.

2.2   'Committee Chairmen and Vice-Chairmen' are the members appointed
to those offices by the Council.

2.3   'Party Spokesmen' are any members nominated by a party group not
holding the chair or vice-chair of a committee to be its spokesman on that committee.

3. *Titles*

3.1   The Chairman of the Policy and Resources Committee will be known as the
Leader of the Council and the Vice-Chairman of that Committee as the Deputy
Leader of the Council.

3.2   The Leader of the largest party group not holding committee chairs will be
known as the Leader of the Opposition.

4. *Entitlement to information*

4.1   Any member of the Council may ask the appropriate chief officer for written factual information about a department or service. Such requests will be met
subject to any legal requirements and to 4.2 below. A copy of the chief officer's
response will be given to the chairman and party spokesmen of the appropriate
committee, unless the member's letter is marked 'personal' or the information
provided is of a routine or minor nature. This arrangement is additional to the
provisions for briefing (see sections 5 and 6).

4.2   If a chief officer considers that information requested under 4.1 could only
be provided at unreasonable cost he shall seek direction from the chairman of the
committee as to whether it should be provided.

4.3   A chief officer may on his own initiative provide information as in 4.1 to a committee chairman. Such information will be supplied to the spokesmen of other parties, unless it is of a routine or minor nature.

4.4   Chief officers should keep local members informed of significant issues affecting their divisions.

5. *Briefings on committee business*

5.1   Formal briefings will be arranged for the chairman and vice-chairman (jointly) of committees to consider the business to be transacted at each meeting as set out on the agenda. The chairman may at his or her discretion invite spokesmen of other parties or other appropriate chairmen or vice-chairmen, to attend such briefings. Such an arrangement is without prejudice to 5.2.

5.2   Any party not holding the chair or vice-chair of a committee may request a briefing on the business to be transacted at a committee meeting. Such a request shall be made by the leader or relevant spokesman to the Chief Executive who will make the appropriate arrangements with the chief officer(s) concerned.

6. *Briefing of party groups*

6.1   In addition to the formal arrangements described above, all party groups may request a private and confidential briefing, including, but where appropriate going beyond, the provision of written information, on matters of policy which are or may become the subject of discussion by the Council or any committee.

6.2   Such a request shall be made by the leader or relevant spokesman of the party group concerned to the Chief Executive who will make the appropriate arrangements with the chief officer(s) concerned. A chief officer may nominate a member of his staff to provide such a briefing.

7. *Filling of Casual Vacancies*

7.1   Selection Sub-Committee is responsible for making appointments to committees under Standing Order 21 in accordance with principles agreed from time to time.

7.2   When a casual vacancy in the office of county councillor (whether consequent upon death, resignation or any other reason) arises, the appointment of members, co-opted members and other persons to committees and subcommittees, education service appointments and outside organisations to fill vacancies shall be dealt with as follows: —

(1)   No such vacancy shall be filled until such time as the consequential by-election has taken place and the new member has presented his declaration of acceptance of office.

(2)   If the filling of a vacancy in representation on an outside organisation arising from the death or resignation of a member is considered to be urgent,

the Chairman of the Selection Sub-Committee in accordance with SO.26 may approve the filling of that vacancy.

(3) Subject to the above, such vacancies may be filled either:—

(a) at the next ordinary meeting of the Selection Sub-Committee after the by-election has taken place and the new members has presented his or her declaration of acceptance of office;

(b) through the Chairman of the Selection Sub-Committee under SO.26 approving such proposals as may be notified to the County Secretary and Solicitor.

(4) Any proposal to request the approval of the Chairman of the Selection Sub-Comittee under SO.26 to the filling of any vacancy or under SO.21.4 to the mutual exchange of Committee places shall be submitted to the County Secretary and Solicitor by the appropriate party group officer. Any such notice should indicate the date from which the filling/change is to take effect. Not less than three clear working days notice should be allowed for the appropriate approvals to be obtained.

8. *Panels established by committees*

8.1 Subject to Standing Orders 21–23 a committee may establish on an ad hoc or standing basis a panel of members of the committee, excluding co-opted members, to consider an issue in more detail.

8.2 Places on panels should normally be allocated to party groups in accordance with the formulas agreed by the Selection Sub-Comitee (at present 2:2:1, 3:3:1, 4:4:2 and 5:5:2) or appropriate multiples.

8.3 The chairman of such panels shall be the chairman of the parent committee and the membership shall where appropriate include the Vice-Chairman and party spokesmen.

8.4 A party group may, on notification to the County Secretary and Solicitor, substitute another member in the place of any member who is unable to attend a panel meeting, having regard to the desirability of maintaining continuity of attendances. Any substituted member should be a member of the parent committee or sub-committee.

8.5 Panels will have delegated powers only where a specific decision must clearly be taken by the panel, eg staff appointments and disciplinary appeals or where the parent committee agrees that there are grounds of urgency. SO.31 Notices do not apply in relation to panel meetings.

8.6 For the purpose of his duty as a member, but not otherwise, a member may, on application to the County Secretary and Solicitor, be supplied with a copy of the agenda and reports for any panel meeting.

8.7 The chairman (or in the case of dispute the panel itself) may invite to panel meetings members who are not panel members or substitutes. Where a panel is to

294

discuss a local issue, the local member or members have the right to be advised and to attend.

8.8   The minutes of all meetings of panels established by committes and sub-commitees shall be submitted to the next ordinary meeting of the parent committee or sub-committee.

8.9   Subject to the above the Standing Orders of the Council shall apply to panel meetings as they apply to meetings of committees.

9. *Dates of committee and panel meetings*

Subject to the duty of Selection Sub-Committee to prepare the calendar of meetings of committees, proposals for the date of additional committee meetings and to cancel or vary the date of a meeting shall be dealt with under Standing Order 26. Arrangements for panel meetings shall be determined by the chairman in informal consultation with the party spokesmen.

10. *Appointment of representatives*

10.1   The appointment of representatives to any outside body of a permanent nature or involving regular attendance will be made by the Selection Sub-Committee, confirmed when time permits by the Parliamentary and Organisation Committee. That Sub-Committee will also determine questions relating to approved duty.

10.2   Where an invitation to the Council to be represented at a conference or other occasion is confined to one member, the committee in question should normally be recommended to appoint the chairman or his or her nominee.

10.3   Where the invitation is to appoint more than one representative, and the occasion in the opinion of the committee so justifies, consideration should be given to appointing in addition the spokesmen of other parties or their nominees as necessary in order to achieve an appropriate political balance.

10.4   Where more than one representative is appointed to attend a conference, the chairman of the appointing committee, or in the absence of the chairman, the vice-chairman or other representative appointed in the place of the chairman, will be regarded as the leader of the delegation. Where the delegation is entitled to cast only one vote on behalf of the County Council, that vote shall be cast by the leader in accordance with the procedure set out below. In the absence of the leader any other member of the delegation may cast the vote in accordance with the procedure.

(1)   Before the conference takes place any member of the delegation may request the County Secretary & Solicitor to convene a meeting of the appointed representatives. Such a meeting shall be competent to settle:

(a)   the procedure to determine the policy of the Council on any issue to be raised where that is not apparent from existing Council or committee decisions,

(b)   how the vote on any issue shall be cast;

(c)   any other procedural matter germane to the conference in question.

(2) In any case where the delegation may vote and the above procedure has not been followed the leader of the delegation shall first determine the wishes of each member of the delegation and shall cast the vote or abstain, as the case may be, in accordance with the wishes of a majority of the delegation.

(3) In the case of an equality of votes within the delegation in respect of any matter under consideration the leader shall have a second or casting vote.

11. *Services for members and party groups*

11.1 Accommodation will be provided for members on a basis to be determined by the Parliamentary and Organisation Committee, after consultation with the party leaders.

11.2 Secretarial and administrative services will be made available to the Chairman and Leader of the Council and to the leaders of other party groups and, if resources allow, to other members.

11.3 Any request for the development of services for members will be referred to the Parliamentary and Organisation Committees after consultation with the party leaders.

11.4 Reprographic services will be provided for the use of party groups by the County Secretariat subject to the availability of resources, at a cost to be determined from time to time by the Parliamentary and Organisation Committee.

12. *Press statements and relations with the media*

12.1 Official press statements arising out of Council business will be made with the agreement of the chairman of the Council or committee in consultation with other party leaders or spokesman as appropriate. They will indicate whether any party group did not support the decision concerned.

12.2 The relevant party spokesmen will be sent a copy of press statements immediately they are published, and will have the right to issue a separate statement under 12.4 below.

12.3 Where a committee decision is carried against the chairman's party group, the spokesmen of the party group or groups representing the majority on that occasion will have the right to involvement in the preparation of any official press statement issued in relation to that decision.

12.4 Press statements arising out of Council business issued in a party capacity by the leader or spokesman of any party may at his or her request be processed by the Public Relations and Information Officer; such press releases are published personally by the members concerned. Any costs incurred will be charged as in 11.4 to the party issuing the statement. Chief officers may be requested to provide factual information to assist in the preparation of such statements.

12.5 Chief officers may deal with any request for information or questions asked by the press, television or radio, and may accept invitations to broadcast or appear on television in order to give the facts of a situation or explain the

Council's policies. Where possible the appropriate chairman and party spokesmen should be informed as soon as practicable.

13. *Review*

13.1   These conventions will be reviewed annually.

13.2   The Chief Executive will initiate a special review at any time if required by a change in the political balance on the Council or in the appointments of committee chairmen, or on the request of any of the parties.

John Colin   Leader of Labour Group

                                  Leader of Conservative Group

R A Stidwell   Spokesman of Alliance Group

13.6/RR/MT/DIS
1.1.86

NATIONAL CODE OF LOCAL GOVERNMENT CONDUCT[1]

This Code is a guide for all councillors elected or co-opted to local authorities in England, Wales and Scotland. It supplements both the law enacted by Parliament and the Standing Orders made by individual councils. It has been agreed by the Associations representing local authorities in all three countries and by the Government.

CONTENTS

1. Law, Standing Orders and National Code

2. Public duty and private interest

3. Disclosure of pecuniary and other interetsts

4. Membership and chairmanship of council committees and sub-committees

5. Councillors and officers

6. Use of confidential and private information

7. Gifts and hospitality

8. Expenses and allowances

9. Use of council facilities

1. Law, Standing Orders and National Code

Make sure that you fully understand the rules of conduct which the law, Standings Orders and the national code require you to follow. It is your personal responsibility to apply their requirements on every relevant occasion. Seek any advice about them that you need from your council's appropriate senior officer or from your own legal adviser.

2. Public Duty and Private Interest

(i)   Your over-riding duty as a councillor is to the whole local community.

(ii)   You have a special duty to your own constituents, including those who did not vote for you.

(iii)   Whenever you have a private or personal interest in any question which councillors have to decide, you must not do anything to let that interest influence the decision.

(iv)   Do nothing as a councillor which you could not justify to the public.

(v)   The reputation of your council, and of your party if you belong to one, depends on your conduct and what the public believes about your conduct.

(vi)   It is not enough to avoid actual impropriety; you should at all times avoid any occasion for suspicion or the appearance of improper conduct.

---

[1] Circulated in Joint Circular 94/75 (Department of the Environment), 95/75 (Scottish Development Department), and 166/75 (Welsh Office). October 1975.

3. Disclosure of Pecuniary and Other Interests

(i)   The law makes specific provision requiring you to disclose pecuniary interests, direct and indirect. But interests which are not pecuniary can be just as important. Kinship, friendship, membership of an association, society, or trade union, trusteeship and many other kinds of relationship can sometimes influence your judgement and give the impression that you might be acting for personal motives. A good test is to ask yourself whether others would think that the interest is of a kind to make this possible. If you think they would, or if you are in doubt, disclose the interest and withdraw from the meeting unless under Standing Orders you are specifically invited to stay.

(ii)   The principles about disclosure of interest should be borne in mind in your unofficial relations with other councillors—at party group meetings, or other informal occasions no less scrupulously than at formal meetings of the council, its committees and sub-committees.

4. Membership and Chairmanship of Council Committees and Sub-Committees

(i)   You, or some firm or body with which you are personally connected, may have professional business or personal interests within the area for which the council is responsible; such interests may be substantial and closely related to the work of one or more of the council's committees or sub-committees, concerned with (say) planning or developing land, council housing, personnel matters or the letting of contracts for supplies, services or works. Before seeking or accepting membership of any such committee or sub-committee, you should seriously consider whether your membership would involve you (a) in disclosing an interest so often that you could be of little value to the committee or sub-committee, or (b) in weakening public confidence in the impartiality of the committee or sub-committee.

(ii)   You should not seek or accept the chairmanship of a committee or sub-committee whose business is closely related to a substantial interest or range of interests of yourself or of any body with which you are associated.

5. Councillors and Officers

(i)   Both councillors and officers are servants of the public, and they are indispensable to one another. But their responsibilities are distinct. Councillors are responsible to the electorate and serve only so long as their term of office lasts. Officers are responsible to the council and are permanently appointed. An officer's job is to give advice to councillors and the council, and to carry out the council's work under the direction and control of the council and its committees.

(ii)   Mutual respect between councillors and officers is essential to good local government. Close personal familiarity between individual councillor and officer can damage this relationship and prove embarrassing to other councillors and officers.

(iii)   If you are called upon to take part in appointing an officer, the only question you should consider is which candidate would best serve the whole council.

You should not let your personal or political preferences influence your judgement. You should not canvass the support of colleagues for any candidate and you should resist any attempt by others to canvass yours.

6. Use of Confidential and Private Information

As a councillor you necessarily acquire much information that has not yet been made public and is still confidential. It is a grave betrayal of trust to use confidential information for the personal advantage of yourself or of anyone known to you.

7. Gifts and Hospitality

Treat with extreme caution any offer or gift, favour or hospitality that is made to you personally. The person or organisation making the offer may be doing or seeking to do business with the council, or may be applying to the council for planning permission or some other kind of decision. Working lunches and other social occasions arranged or authorised by the council or by one of its committees or sub-committees may be a proper way of doing business, provided that no extravagance is involved. Nor can there be any hard and fast rule about acceptance or refusal of tokens of goodwill on special occasions. But you are personally responsible for all such decisions and for avoiding the risk of damage to public confidence in local government. The receipt or offer of gifts should be reported to the chief executive.

8. Expenses and Allowances

There are rules entitling you to claim expenses and allowances in connection with your duties as a councillor. These rules should be scrupulously observed.

9. Use of Council Facilities

Make sure that any facilities—such as transport, stationery, or secretarial services—provided by the council for your use in your duties as a councillor are used strictly for those duties and for no other purpose.

ANNEX J

TABLE 1

Basic flat rate allowance: proposed rates compared with current allowances

	1	2	3	England and Wales		6	7	8
				4	5			
	Councils	Councillors	Take-up	Current Average (AA/FLA)	Proposed Rate (BFRA)	Number of councils with losers	Number of councillors losing	Percentage of councillors losing
			%	£	£			%
Met Districts								
Over 1 million	1	117	92	2,250	3,250			
500,000–1 million	2	186	93	1,112	3,000			
250,000–500,000	19	1,334	93	1,406	2,900			
Under 250,000	14	848	95	1,232	2,800			
Total	36	2,485	94	1,324	2,889	23	200	8
London Boroughs								
Inner	13	828	87	594	2,600			
Outer	20	1,226	81	611	2,800			
Total	33	2,054	83	605	2,716	7	20	1

302

Shire Counties								
Over 2 million	–	–	–	–	3,500			
1 million–2 million	6	536	90	1,008	3,250			
500,000–1 million	27	2,138	88	1,080	3,000			
250,000–500,000	11	787	89	1,157	2,900			
Under 250,000	3	162	85	607	2,800			
Total	47	3,623	88	1,073	3,007	20	190	5
Shire Districts								
Over 400,000	1	68	?	?	2,750			
200,000–400,000	8	445	91	1,080	2,600			
150,000–200,000	13	675	91	950	2,500			
100,000–150,000	101	5,305	88	522	2,250			
50,000–100,000	180	7,542	86	558	2,000			
Under 50,000[1]	31	1,006	75	338	1,500			
Total	334	15,041	87	570	2,103	50	200	1
Total England and Wales	450	23,203	87	741	2,390	100	610	3
(Total Scotland)	65	1,610	98	2,213	2,865	32	440	27
Total Great Britain	515	24,813	88	845	2,423	132	1,050	4

[1] includes Isles of Scilly.

TABLE 2

Basic flat rate allowance: proposed rates compared with current allowances

				Scotland			
1	**2**	**3**	**4**	**5**	**6**	**7**	**8**
Councils	Councillors	Take-up	Current Average (AA/FLA) £	Proposed Rate (BFRA) £	Number of councils with losers	Number of councillors losing	Percentage of councillors losing
		%					%
Regions							
Over 2 million	1	103	99	3,444	4,000			
1 million – 2 million	–	–	–	–	3,750			
500,000 – 1 million	1	49	?	?	3,500			
250,000 – 500,000	4	179	98	2,229	3,400			
Under 250,000	3	110	99	1,170	3,300			
Total	**9**	**441**	**99**	**1,951**	**3,530**	**4**	**80**	**18**

Islands	3	55	94	1,682	2,500	2	10	18
Districts								
Over 400,000	2	128	99	3,613	3,250			
200,000–400,000	2	111	100	3,246	3,100			
150,000–200,000	1	44	100	2,852	3,000			
100,000–150,000	10	283	98	2,735	2,750			
50,000–100,000	20	344	98	1,581	2,500			
Under 50,000	18	204	94	955	2,000			
Total	53	1,114	98	2,225	2,645	26	350	31
Total Scotland	65	1,610	98	2,213	2,865	32	440	27
(Total England and Wales)	450	23,203	87	741	2,390	100	610	3
Total Great Britain	515	24,813	88	845	2,423	132	1,050	4

Notes

Columns 1 and 2

These columns show, respectively, the number of councils and councillors in each population band. Where there are no such councils, this has been shown by a dash.

Columns 3 and 4

These columns show, respectively, the percentage of councillors in each population band currently receiving allowance, and the average sum received. In both cases they refer to attendance allowance and financial loss allowance, but not special responsibility allowance. The information has been derived from the survey of allowances in 1984–85 conducted by IPF Ltd for the Committee (see *Research Volume II*), but the average receipt of allowance has been adjusted to 1985–86 rates. Where IPF Ltd did not receive returns for any council within a population band, this has been shown by a question mark.

Column 5

This shows the rate of basic flat rate allowance which we propose should apply for each population band.

Columns 6, 7 and 8

These columns show the extent to which councillors would receive less in basic flat rate allowance, applying at the rate in column 5, than they currently receive in attendance allowance or financial loss allowance. Column 6 shows the number of councils where at least one councillor would be worse off. Column 7 shows the number of councillors who would be worse off, and column 8 expresses this figure as a percentage of all councillors.

General

The data in columns 2–4 and 6–8 should not be taken as precise. It is derived from the IPF survey responses, and account must be taken of possible inaccuracies arising from grossing and from the need, in some cases, to make inferences based on the questionnaire responses. This caveat applies in particular to columns 6–8. Because of the reduced certainty applying to these columns, the data is given only at summary level not for individual population bands.

ANNEX K

PROPOSED STATUTORY FUNCTIONS OF CHIEF EXECUTIVES

In paragraph 6.151 of this Report it is proposed that all statutory functions relating to the propriety of council business should be vested in the chief executive rather than any other officer.

Part 1 of this Annex lists **existing** statutory functions in the Local Government Act 1972 and the Local Government (Scotland) Act 1973 which are currently vested in officers, but which leave individual authorities the discretion to designate the officer concerned. Under our proposals all these functions would be vested specifically in the chief executive. The list is not necessarily exhaustive, and no examination has been made of other legislation.

Part 2 of this Annex lists **new** statutory functions which we recommend in this Report. Again all would be vested in the chief executive.

Most chief executives' duties would be non-statutory, and this Annex does not therefore purport to be a job description.

Part 1: existing statutory functions

Function	Section of Local Government Act 1972	Section of Local Government (Scotland) Act 1973
Declaration of acceptance of office can be in presence of proper officer	83(4)	—
Resignation of councillors to be delivered to proper officer	84	34
Proper officer may convene meeting of council for purposes of election of chairman	88(2)	—
General notice of pecuniary interest can be given to proper officer	96(2)	40(1)
Proper officer shall record any disclosures or general notices of pecuniary interests	96(2)	40(2)
Proper officer can exclude confidential parts of reports before giving them to the public	100B(2)	50B(2)
Proper officer shall make summary of proceedings, etc	100C(2)	50C(2)
Proper officer to compile list of documents	100D(1)	50D(1)

Part 1: existing statutory functions (continued)

Function	Section of Local Government Act 1972	Section of Local Government (Scotland) Act 1973
Proper officer permitted not to open to inspection documents containing exempt information	100F(2)	50F(2)
Criminal offence for officer having custody etc of documents to obstruct/refuse to supply copies, etc	100H(4)	50H(4)
Officers receiving council money to pay it to proper officer	115(2)	—
Officer to be responsible for proper administration of financial affairs	151	95
Proper officer to receive and retain, etc documents deposited pursuant to standing orders of Parliament or enactments, etc	225(1)	197(2)
Accounts of authority and of any proper officer shall be open to inspection of members	228(3)	—
Proper officer can certify photocopies of documents	229(5)	—
Authorisation of documents. Proper officer may sign notices, documents, etc on behalf of the authority	234	193
Legal proceedings deemed duly served if served on proper officer	—	190
Proper officer can sign claim on behalf of authority for liquidation, etc	—	191
Proper officer to sign summons to attend meeting	Schedule 12 Paragraph 4(2)(b)	Shedule 7 Paragraph 2(1)(b)

Part 2: proposed new statutory functions

Function	Recommendation number in Chapter Ten
Decide on detailed application of rules for party balance on committees	2(ii) and 37
Decide whether a councillor has a need to inspect a document or attend a meeting	4(iii) and 37

Part 2: proposed new statutory functions (continued)

Function	Recommendation number in Chapter Ten
Decide that a matter is urgent before the chairman of a committee may take a decision on it	5(i) and 37
Act as registrar responsible for upkeep of the register of councillors' interests	18(iv) and 37
At the request of a councillor provide advice as to the legality of any proposed action or inaction by the council (without prejudice to their general duty to advise the council)	37
Appointment, discipline and dismissal of staff below the rank of principal officer	38
Initiation of action for the discipline or dismissal of staff at or above the rank of principal officer	39
Notify councillors of auditors' reports and provide copies to councillors and public	71

ANNEX L

SECTION 137 LOCAL GOVERNMENT ACT 1972 (AS AMENDED)

Power of local authorities to incur expenditure for certain purposes not otherwise authorised

137.—(1) A local authority may, subject to the provisions of this section, incur expenditure which in their opinion is in the interests of their area or any part of it or all or some of its inhabitants, but a local authority shall not, by virtue of this subsection, incur any expenditure for a purpose for which they are, either unconditionally or subject to any limitation or to the satisfaction of any condition, authorised or required to make any payment by or by virtue of any other enactment.

(2) It is hereby declared that the power of a local authority to incur expenditure under subsection (1) above includes power to do so by contributing towards the defraying of expenditure by another local authority in or in connection with the exercise of that other authority's functions.

(2A) Without prejudice to the generality of subsection (1) above, the power of a local authority to incur expenditure under that subsection includes power to incur expenditure in giving financial assistance to persons carrying on commercial or industrial undertakings.

(2B) Financial assistance under subsection (2A) above may be given by lending or guarantee, or by making grants.

(2C) A local authority may incur expenditure under subsection (1) above on publicity only:

(a) for the purpose of promoting the economic development of the authority's area where the publicity is incidental to other activities undertaken or to be undertaken by the authority for that purpose, or

(b) by way of assistance to a public body or voluntary organisation where the publicity is incidental to the main purpose for which the assistance is given;

but the following provisions of this section apply to expenditure incurred by a local authority under section 142 below on information as to the services provided by them under this section, or otherwise relating to their functions under this section, as they apply to expenditure incurred under this section.

(2D) In subsection (2C) above—

"publicity" means any communication, in whatever form, addressed to the public at large or to a section of the public; and

"voluntary organisation" means a body which is not a public body but whose activities are carried on otherwise than for profit".

(3)   A local authority may, subject as aforesaid, incur expenditure on contributions to any of the following funds, that is to say—

(a)   the funds of any charitable body in furtherance of its work in the United Kingdom; or

(b)   the funds of any body which provides any public service in the United Kingdom otherwise than for the purposes of gain; or

(c)   any fund which is raised in connection with a particular event directly affecting persons resident in the United Kingdom on behalf of whom a public appeal for contributions has been made by the Lord Mayor of London or the chairman of a principal council or by a committee of which the Lord Mayor of London or the chairman of a principal council is a member.

(4)   The expenditure of a local authority under this section in any financial year shall not exceed the product of a rate of 2p in the pound for their area for that year or if some other amount, whether higher or lower, is fixed by an order made by the Secretary of State shall not exceed the product of a rate of that amount in the pound for their area for that year.

(4A)   For the purpose of determining whether a local authority have exceeded the limit set out in subsection (4) above, their expenditure in any financial year under this section shall be taken to be the difference between their gross expenditure under this section for that year and the aggregate of the amounts specified in subsection (4B) below.

(4B)   The amounts mentioned in subsection (4A) above are—

(a)   any grant paid to the local authority for that year under the Local Government Grants (Social Need) Act 1969, in so far as the grant is in respect of an activity in relation to which the authority have incurred expenditure in that year under this section;

(b)   the amount of any repayment in that year of the principal of a loan for the purpose of financing expenditure under this section in any year;

(c)   so much of any amount raised by public subscription as is spent in that year for a purpose for which the authority are authorised by this section to incur expenditure;

(d)   any grant received by the authority for that year out of the European Regional Development Fund or the Social Fund of the European Economic Community, in so far as the grant is in respect of an activity in relation to which the authority incurred expenditure in that year under this section;

(e)   the amount of any repayment in that year of a loan under this section made by the authority in any year; and

(f)   the amount of any expenditure—

(i)   which is incurred by the authority in that year in circumstances specified in an order made by the Secretary of State; or

(ii)   which is incurred by the authority in that year and is of a description so specified; or

(iii)   which is defrayed by any grant or other payment to the authority which is made in or in respect of that year and is of a description so specified.

(5)   A statutory instrument containing an order under this section may apply to all local authorities or may make different provision in relation to local authorities of different descriptions.

(6)   Any such instrument shall be subject to annulment in pursuance of a resolution of either House of Parliament.

(7)   The accounts of a local authority by whom expenditure is incurred under this section shall include a separate account of that expenditure, and section 24 of the Local Government Finance Act 1982 (rights of inspection) shall apply in relation to any such separate account of a local authority as it applies in relation to any statement of accounts prepared by them pursuant to regulations under section 23 of that Act.

(8)   The product of a rate of 2p or any other amount in the pound for any area shall be computed for the purposes of this section by reference to the product of a rate of 1p in the pound for that area as determined for those purposes in accordance with rules made under section 113(1)(c) of the General Rate Act 1967.

(9)   In this section "local authority" includes the Common Council.

SECTION 83 OF THE LOCAL GOVERNMENT (SCOTLAND) ACT 1973 (AS AMENDED)

Power of local authorities to incur expenditure for certain purposes not otherwise authorised

83.—(1)   A local authority may, subject to the provisions of this section, incur expenditure which in their opinion is in the interests of their area or any part of it or all or some of its inhabitants, but a local authority shall not, by virtue of this subsection, incur any expenditure for a purpose for which they are, either unconditionally or subject to any limitation or to the satisfaction of any condition, authorised or required to make any payment by or by virtue of any other enactment.

(2)   It is hereby declared that subject to subsection (3A) below, the power of a local authority to incur expenditure under subsection (1) above includes power to do so by contributing towards the defraying of expenditure by another local authority in or in connection with the exercise of that other authority's functions.

(2A)   Without prejudice to the generality of subsection (1) above, the power of a local authority to incur expenditure under that subsection includes power to incur expenditure in giving financial assistance to persons carrying on commercial or industrial undertakings.

(2B)   Financial assistance under subsection (2A) above may be given by lending or guarantee, or by making grants.

(2C)   A local authority may incur expenditure under subsection (1) above on publicity only by way of assistance to a public body or voluntary organisation where the publicity is incidental to the main purpose for which the assistance is given; but the following provisions of this section apply to expenditure incurred by a local authority under section 88 below on information as to the services provided by them under this section, or otherwise relating to their functions under this section, as they apply to expenditure incurred under this section.

(2D)   In subsection (2C) above—

"publicity" means any communication, in whatever form, addressed to the public at large or to a section of the public; and

"voluntary organisation" means a body which is not a public body but whose activities are carried on otherwise than for profit.

(3)   A local authority may, subject as aforesaid, incur expenditure on contributions to any of the following funds, that is to say—

(a)   the funds of any charitable body in furtherance of its work in the United Kingdom; or

(b)   the funds of any body which provides any public service in the United Kingdom otherwise than for the purposes of gain; or

(c)   any fund which is raised in connection with a particular event directly affecting persons resident in the United Kingdom on behalf of whom a public appeal for contributions has been made by a chairman of a regional, islands or district council, a chairman of a community council, a lord-lieutenant or by a body of which any of these persons is a member.

(3A)   Where one of any two local authorities is a regional council and the other a district council, neither authority shall under the foregoing provisions of this section—

(a)   incur; or

(b)   unless invited to do so by the other authority, contribute towards defraying,

expenditure which the other authority are, either unconditionally or subject to any limitation or to the satisfaction of any condition, expressly authorised (or required) to incur by or by virtue of any enactment other than this section.

(4)   The expenditure of a local authority under this section in any financial year shall not exceed the product of a rate of 2p in the pound for their area for that year or, if some other amount, whether higher or lower, is fixed by an order

made by the Secretary of State, shall not exceed the product of a rate of that amount in the pound for their area for that year.

(4A)   For the purpose of determining whether a local authority have exceeded the limit set out in subsection (4) above, their expenditure in any financial year under this section shall be taken to be the difference between their gross expenditure under this section for that year and the aggregate of the amounts specified in subsection (4B) below.

(4B)   The amounts mentioned in subsection (4A) above are—

(a)   any grant paid to the local authority for that year under the Local Government Grants (Social Need) Act 1969, in so far as the grant is in respect of an activity in relation to which the authority have incurred expenditure in that year under this section;

(b)   the amount of any repayment in that year of the principal of a loan for the purpose of financial expenditure under this section in any year;

(c)   so much of any amount raised by public subscription as is spent in that year for a purpose for which the authority are authorised by this section to incur expenditure;

(d)   any grant received by the authority for that year out of the European Regional Development Fund or the Social Fund of the European Economic Community, in so far as the grant is in respect of an activity in relation to which the authority incurred expenditure in that year under this section;

(e)   the amount of any repayment in that year of a loan under this section made by the authority in any year; and

(f)   the amount of any expenditure—

(i)   which is incurred by the authority in that year in circumstances specified in an order made by the Secretary of State; or

(ii)   which is incurred by the authority in that year and is of a description so specified; or

(iii)   which is defrayed by any grant or other payment to the authority which is made in or in respect of that year and is of a description so specified.

(5)   A statutory instrument containing an order under this section may apply to all local authorities or may make different provision in relation to local authorities of different descriptions.

(6)   Any such instrument shall be subject to annulment in pursuance of a resolution of either House of Parliament.

(7)   The accounts kept under section 96 of this Act by a local authority shall include a separate account of any expenditure incurred by the authority under this section.

Printed for Her Majesty's Stationery Office by Commercial Colour Press, London E7. 6/86, C53, Dd.601797.